CAMPING with the CORPS OF ENGINEERS

NOW WITH GPS COORDINATES

BY MICAH WRIGHT

8TH EDITION

(Front cover lifestyle pictures courtesy of the US Army Corps of Engineers)

P.O. Box 2832
Elkhart, IN 46515-2832
1.800.272.5518 (not for reservations)
website: www.cottagepub.com
e-mail: info@cottagepub.com

CAMPING with the CORPS OF ENGINEERS

BY MICAH WRIGHT

8TH EDITION

Printed in the United States of America

Camping with the Corps of Engineers 8th Edition

ISBN 0-937877-51-4

Cottage Publications, Inc.
P.O. Box 2832
Elkhart, IN 46515-2832
1.800.272.5518 (not for reservations)
website: www.cottagepub.com
e-mail: info@cottagepub.com

CONTENTS

INTRODUCTION

The information in this book is derived from many sources, including information provided by district and project office input. Some information came from personal visits, camping and people who have used the facilities. We wish to thank those U. S. Army Corps of Engineers personnel and other individuals who have contributed to making this book a success. Included herein are listings on hundreds of projects and campgrounds.

The Corps of Engineers is a Corps of the United States Army under the Department of Defense. As such, it operates much the same as any other government agency – in constant change. This is due to many factors, including but not limited to the following: size of the Corps, direction from congress and higher U. S. army commands, leeway granted the project officers by their district officers, size of the area utilized, budget concerns, safety, weather and other uses in the area. Since the 2001 terrorist attack and the continuing threats, many changes have been instituted by the government to protect the dams and facilities, and as a result, you may expect to be checked for identity and/or searched prior to participating in dam tours or other related facilities.

When using this book, please be remember that facilities are subject to change at anytime. Campgrounds may be closed due to flooding, low flow augmentation releases, excessive soil erosion, insufficient funding, usage or personnel to supervise usage and other reasons. New campgrounds may be opened without notice. Additionally, free areas which require a fee part of the year may not have some amenities such as water or electric available during the free or reduced fee season. Therefore, particularly when you are going to be traveling some distance, it is imperative that you call the campground or project office prior to departure for information necessary to meet your needs. Prices change, free parks may be closed or converted to fee parks, or parks may be consigned to other agencies (state, county, city, etc.) or leased to concessionaires.

In addition to the project addresses provided at the start of each project, a listing of districts are in the book for your use. Known fees are listed and subject to change without notice. Fees may be collected by roving patrol, ranger, gate attendant or self deposit (honor system). Also note that the symbols for some amenities, such as electric and water hookups, do not mean all sites have those amenities, but rather at least some are available. Other symbols for amenities such as golf courses, laundry facilities, marinas, etc., may be there as an indication that they are located nearby.

Your interest and assistance in providing us with updated information will be appreciated. Thanks to those who have provided information in the past. Please forward to Cottage Publications, P. O. Box 2832, Elkhart, IN 46515-2832. 1-800-272-5518. We have always found that the majority of Corps of Engineers Campgrounds are well maintained and administered. Hoping you will find them the same and get lots of use from this publication. Happy Camping.

GENERAL INFORMATION

The U. S. Army Corps of Engineers is the nation's leading federal provider of high quality outdoor recreation opportunities for the public. The Corps operates more than 2,500 recreation areas and leases an additional 1,800 sites. The Corps hosts 360 million visits a year at its lakes, beaches and other areas with estimates that 25 million americans visit a Corps project at least once a year.

General regulations for the Corps of Engineers recreational facilities are contained in Title 36, U. S. Code. You may procure a copy at most Corps facilities.

Unless otherwise noted, for information on group camping areas and pavilion rentals, contact the project office.

Most projects will accept payment by personal check requiring such information as phone number, driver's license number and address. Many, including the National Recreation Reservation Service, accept Master/Visa cards, American Express and Discover cards.

Many campgrounds and projects have much to offer that is not listed under the camping information. The listed information is taken from that received from the districts and projects, some more detailed than others. Common amenities not listed are fire rings, lampposts, tables, grills and public telephones. Contact the project you plant to visit to obtain a complete listing. You may want to visit the district websites listed on the address page.

Golden Age and Golden Access Passports are no longer issued, but they are still honored by the Corps of Engineers.

America the Beautiful - The National Parks and Federal Recreational Lands Senior Pass. You must be a citizen or permanent resident of the United States of the age 62 or older. This pass provides for access to and use of federal recreation sites that charge entrance standard amenity fees. It also provides a 50% discount on some expanded amenity fees such as camping, boat launching, etc. These passes must be obtained in person at National Parks Service, National Forest Service, U.S. Fish and Wildlife, Bureau of Land Management and Bureau of Reclamation recreation sites that charge fees. Identification is required to verify proof of age and residency. A $10 fee is charged for this pass, and it is good for your lifetime.

America the Beautiful - The National Parks and Federal Recreation Lands Access Pass. This pass must be acquired from the same entities listed under the senior pass information above. You will be required to provide proof of residency and have documentation issued by a federal agency such as the Veteran's Administration, Social Security Disability Income or Supplemental Income, or document issued by a atate agency such as a vocational rehabilitation agency, or a statement issued by a licensed physician. This pass provides the same discounts listed under the senior pass. There is no fee and the pass is good for your lifetime.

America the Beautiful - The National Parks and Federal Recreational Lands Annual Pass. This pass is not honored by the Corps of Engineers.

Corps of Engineers Day Pass - Anyone may purchase this pass from any Corps of Engineers site charging day use fees. You may also purchase it through the mail from Corps projects or district offices. Addresses for project offices are under each Lake heading in this book. District office addresses are contained in the address section of this publication. The fee for 2011 is $30 and is good for one year.

These discounts for entry and camping apply to the card-holder and those accompanying them in a private noncommercial vehicle, which includes recreational vehicles.

Concessionaires normally do not offer the discount, but some honor them. Ask! A few state parks systems honor the passes; most don't.

Pets are permitted at most Corps campgrounds. They must be in the camper, vehicle, pen or on a leash no longer than 6'. Owners are requested to clean up after their pets. Pets are not allowed on beach areas where swimming is designated nor in rest rooms/showers, etc. Additional pet requirements and restrictions may apply at individual campgrounds and parks.

For the National Recreation Reservation Service (NRRS), call toll free, 1-877-444-6777, TDD 877-833-6777, or use the website, www.recreation.gov. Have the following information available when you call to place the reservation: Name of campground and project (lake, river, etc.), camp site number if possible or the type of site desired, arrival and departure dates, name, address and phone number, vehicles, trailers, tents and other equipment you will be bringing, license numbers of all vehicles you will be bringing, Golden Age/ Access Passport Number or America the Beautiful Senior or Access Pass(if you have one), and your credit card number(Master, Visa, American Express or Discover) to pay for the reservation stay. Many campground reservations required a 2 or 3-day minimum stay on weekends. Additionally, most projects require a cancellation fee when making the reservation.

Some campers may desire to contract as a gate attendant. Contact the district in the area you desire. Additionally, the Corps of Engineers has a volunteer program available for those who wish to help in many different areas. Call 1-800-865-8337, or visit the website, www.orn.usace.army.mil/volunteer/

Due to circumstances surrounding the World Trade Center building terrorist attack and continued terrorist threats, security at Corps projects has been enhanced. Some amenities and tours (such as dams and power plants) may not be available. Contact the project for further information.

REMEMBER TO WEAR YOUR LIFE JACKETS WHEN ON THE WATER.

SYMBOLS

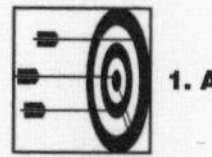
1. Archery Range

2. Ball Field

3. Bath House/ Showers

4. Basketball Court

5. Bike Trails

6. Boat Launch

7. Campfire Area

8. Campfire Programs

9. Canoeing

10. Comfort Stations

11. Drinking Water

12. Dump Station

13. Electric Hookups

14. Equestrian Trail

15. Golf Nearby

16. Handicap Site

17. Handicap Facilities

18. Handicap Fishing Pier

19. Hiking/Nature Trail

20. Laundry in Camp or Nearby

21. LP Gas Nearby

22. Marina

23. Visa/MC Accepted

24. Motorbike Trail

25. Multi-Use Court

26. Off-Road/ATV Area

27. Pets On Leash

28. Picnic/Public Use Area

29. Pier/Dock

30. Playground

31. Skiing Trail

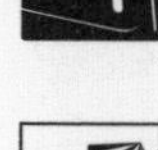

32. Swimming Beach

33. Tennis Court

34. Tent Camping Only. No RVs

35. Tenting

36. Water Hookups

Huntsville
Tennessee
River
65
59
20
Birmingham
Black Warrior
River
Coosa
River
4
Tuscaloosa
Lake
Martin
8
59
7
20
3
85
5
10
Tombigee
River
Montgomery
9
2
Alabama
River
6
65
231
1
ALABAMA
Mobile
10

ALABAMA

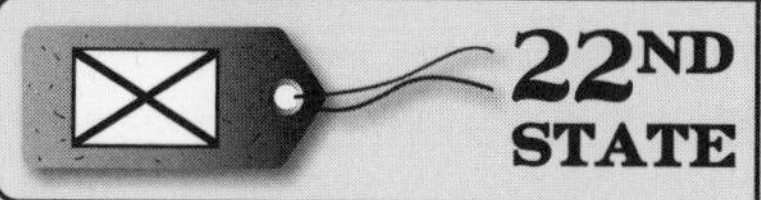

State Capital: **Montgomery**
Nickname: **Yellowhammer State**
Statehood Year: **1819**

CLAIBORNE LAKE (MB) 1
GPS: 31.62, -87.55

This 5,900-acre lake with over 60 miles of shoreline is 3 miles NW of Claiborne off US 84 on the Alabama River, NE of Mobile in southwestern Alabama. Alcohol prohibited. Site Manager, Alabama River Lakes, 1226 Powerhouse Road, Camden, AL 36726. (334) 682-4244.

BELLS LANDING RECREATION AREA

From Hybart, 3 mi S on SR 41. All year; 14-day limit. 14 free primitive sites. RV limit 20'. **GPS: 33.0407, -81.804**

DAMSITE WEST BANK RECREATION AREA

From Claiborne, NW on SR 48. All year; 14-day limit. 2 free primitive sites.

HAINES ISLAND RECREATION AREA

From Monroeville, 8 mi N on SR 41; 10 mi W on CR 17. All year; 14-day limit. 12 free primitive sites. Picnic shelter. RV limit 40'. **GPS: 31.72577, -87.46929**

ISACC CREEK CAMPGROUND

From Monroeville, 8 mi N on SR 41 to CR 17 W; follow signs. All year; 14-day limit. 66 sites with 50-amp service; 17 handicap sites; 4 pull-through sites. $16 base, premium waterfront sites $18 ($8 & $9 with federal senior pass). Extra vehicle fee may be charged. Fish cleaning station, picnic shelter, multi-use court. RV limit in excess of 65'. (251) 282-4254. NRRS. **GPS: 31.62222, -87.55028**

SILVER CREEK RECREATION AREA

From Claiborne, 8 mi NW on US 84. All year; 14-day limit. 8 free primitive sites. RV limit 20'. **GPS: 31.6696, -87.5**

COFFEEVILLE LAKE (MB) 2
BLACK WATER & TOMBIGBEE WATERWAY
GPS: 31.745, -88.1431

An 8,800-acre lake, Coffeeville is 97 miles in length, located 3 miles SW of Coffeeville off US 84 and N of Mobile in west-central Alabama near the Mississippi state line. Demopolis Site Office, Black Warrior-Tombigbee River Lakes, 384 Resource Management Drive, Demopolis, AL 37632. (334) 289-3540.

LENOIR LANDING PARK

Off Hwy 69 between Jackson and Coffeeville. All year; 14-day limit. Free primitive sites. Picnic shelter. ORV prohibited. **GPS: 31.86, -88.16**

OLD LOCK 1 PARK

Off Hwy 69 between Jackson and Coffeeville. All year; 14-day limit. Free primitive sites. Picnic shelter. ORV prohibited. **GPS: 31.57, -88.04.**

SERVICE PARK CAMPGROUND

From Coffeeville, 4 mi W on US 84, following signs. All year; 14-day limit. 32 sites with 50-amp elec/wtr; 2 tent only sites. Tent sites with elec/wtr, $14 ($7 with federal senior pass). Elec/wtr sites $16 base, $18 at premium locations ($8 & $9 with federal senior pass). RV limit in excess of 65'; 10 pull-through; 1 handicap. ORV prohibited. At reserved sites, 2-night minimum stay required on weekends, 3 nights on holiday weekends. (251) 754-9338. NRRS. Note: Park was being renovated late in 2010 & was closed; February 2011 re-opening scheduled, but check current status before arriving. **GPS: 31.745, -88.14306**

DEMOPOLIS LAKE (MB) 3
BLACK WARRIOR & TOMBIGBEE WATERWAY
GPS: 32.54, -87.87

A 10,000-acre lake just N of Demopolis at the confluence of the Black Warrior & Tombigbee Rivers, it extends 48 miles upriver on the Black Warrior and 53 miles up the Tombigbee. It is W of US 43 and S of Tuscaloosa in west-central Alabama. Campground checkout time 3 p.m. Demopolis Site Office, Demopolis Lake, 384 Resource Management Drive, Demopolis, AL 36732. (334) 289-3540.

BELMONT PARK

From Belmont at jct with CR 23, E on CR 22, then NE on Belmont Park access rd. All year; 14-day limit. Free primitive sites. Picnic shelter ($25), pit toilets, tbls, fire ring, lantern pole, drinking water. ORV prohibited. Non-campers pay $3 day use fee at boat ramp. **GPS: 32.55, -87.87**

LOCK 5 PARK

From Cedarville, 2 mi W on CR 16 to split with Owl Rd; continue SW to park; on Big German arm of lake. All year; primitive sites. Picnic shelter, toilets, lantern poles, fire rings, tables. ORV prohibited. **GPS: 32.59, -87.74**

RUNAWAY BRANCH II PARK

From Birdeye at jct with CR 25, S on US 43 (Demopolis Hwy) toward Demopolis; 1 mi W on CR 11; S on Runaway II Park access rd. All year; primitive sites. Picnic shelter, tables, lantern posts, fire rings, drinking water, pit toilets. ORV prohibited. **GPS: 32.56, -87.84**

FORKLAND CAMPGROUND

From Demopolis, 9 mi N on US 43; at Forkland, 1 mi SW (left) on CR, following signs. All year; 14-day limit. 42 sites with elec/wtr. Sites with 30-amp elec/wtr, $16 ($8 with federal senior pass); sites with 50-amp elec/wtr, $18 ($9 with federal senior pass). RV limit in excess of 65 ft; 13 pull-through. At reserved sites, 2-night minimum stay required/ weekends, 3 nights/ holiday weekends. Picnic shelter with elec for up to 50 people & 2 vehicles, $25. ORV prohibited. (334) 289-5530. NRRS. **32.62222, -87.88056**

FOSCUE CREEK CAMPGROUND

From Demopolis, 3 mi W on US 80 (signs); 2 mi N (right) on Maria Ave. S of confluence of Black Warrior Tombigbee Rivers. 54 sites with 50-amp elec/water $16 base, $18 at premium locations, $20 full hookups ($8, $9 & $10 with federal senior pass). RV limit in excess of 65'; 2 pull-through, 9 handicap, full hookups. 3 group shelters, $25-$35. $3 visitor fee. Non-campers pay $5 for dump station, $3 for boat ramp. At reserved sites, 2-night minimum stay required/weekends, 3 nights/holiday weekends. Group camping, amphitheater. (334) 289-5535. NRRS. **GPS: 32.5156, -87.86944**

HOLT LAKE (MB) 4
BLACK WARRIOR & TOMBIGBEE WATERWAY
GPS: 33.31, -87.40

This 3,200-acre lake is 6 mi NE of Tuscaloosa and NW of Peterson. It is 18 miles long on Black Warrior River. ORV prohibited. Resource Manager, Holt Lake, P. O. Box 295, Peterson, AL 35478. (205) 553-9373/554-1684.

BLUE CREEK PARK

From Tuscaloosa, 13 mi N on SR 69; 10 mi E on CR 38; 2.5 mi on Blue Creek Rd. All year; 14-day limit. 18 free sites. Lantern poles, fire rings, no drkg wtr. **GPS: 33.43688, -87.37980**

BURCHFIELD CREEK CAMPGROUND

From Tuscaloosa, I-20/59 exit 86, CR 59 to Brookwood; 0.8 mi E on SR 216; 16.6 mi NW on CR 59; veer left 0.1 mi on Ground Hog Rd; 1.2 mi left at stop sign on Lock 17 Rd; 3.9 mi left at grocery store to park. All year; 14-day limit. 36 sites with 50-amp elec/wtr & 1 tent site with elec. Tent site $12 ($6 with federal senior pass). $16 base at RV/tent sites, $18 for premium locations ($8 & $9 with federal senior pass). RV limit in excess of 65 ft; 2 pull-through sites, 24 handicap sites. At reserved sites, 2-day minimum stay required on weekends, 3 days on holiday weekends. Picnic shelter for up to 100 people, $30. Non-campers pay $4 day use fee, $5 for dump station, $3 for boat ramp. (205) 497-9828. NRRS. **GPS: 33.44778, -87.36583**

DEERLICK CREEK CAMPGROUND

From Tuscaloosa at I-20/59 exit 73, 4.2 mi W on US 82 (McFarland Blvd); 14 mi NE on Rice Mine Rd (CR 30); 3.6 mi on CR 87 (New Watermelon Rd); 3.5 mi on CR 42 (Lake Nicol Rd); 3.2 mi left on CR 89 (Deerlick Rd). Open March 1 through November 19. 40 sites with 50-amp elec/wtr, $16 base, $18 at premium locations ($8 & $9 with federal senior pass). 6 primitive tent sites, $12 ($6 with federal senior pass). RV limit 40 ft; 90 pull-through sites, 1 handicap site with elec/wtr. Picnic shelter with elec, $30. Horseshoe pits, paved bicycle trail, amphitheater. At reserved sites, 2-night minimum stay required on weekends, 3 nights on holiday weekends. Non-campers pay $4 day use fee, $5 for dump station, $3 for boat ramp. (205) 759-1591. NRRS. **GPS: 33.25944, -87.43028**

TENNESSEE-TOMBIGBEE WATERWAY (MB) 5

GPS: 33.56, -88.51

The Tennessee-Tombigbee Waterway is a navigable link between the lower Tennessee Valley and the Gulf of Mexico. Stretching 234 mi from

Demopolis, AL to Pickwick Lake in the NE corner of MS, this man-made channel has a series of ten locks and dams forming ten pools. Off-road vehicles prohibited. The Tom Bevill Visitor Center, Carrollton, AL, 35447. (205) 373-8705 (open daily except on some federal holidays) is an 1830-1850 era antebellum style center with a restored 1926 sternwheeler "U.S. Snagboat," interpretive exhibits, artifacts, group tours. Campground checkout time 3 p.m.; visitors fee is $3, and fee of $3 for a third and fourth vehicle is charged. Resource Manager, Waterway Management Center, 3606 W Plymouth Road, Columbus, MS 39701. (662) 327-2142.

COCHRANE CAMPGROUND

From Aliceville, 10 mi S on SR 17 (signs); 2 mi W of Huyck Bridge (signs); turn right, then 2 mi on access rd. All year; 14-day limit. 60 sites with elec/wtr, $12 base, $14 at premium locations ($6 & $7 with federal senior pass). RV limit in excess of 65 ft; 3 handicap sites. At reserved sites, 2 night minimum stay required on weekends, 3 nights on holiday weekends. Picnic shelter, emergency night exit, handicap fishing area. (205) 373-8806. NRRS 3/1-10/31. **GPS: 33.08111, -88.26444**

PICKENSVILLE CAMPGROUND

From Pickensville at jct with SR 14, from caution light, 2.6 mi W on SR 86 across waterway bridge, on right. All year; 14-day limit. 176 sites with elec/wtr (29 full hookups). $16 base, $20 at premium sites ($8 & $10 with federal senior pass). RV limit in excess of 65 ft; 4 handicap sites with elec/wtr, 1 handicap site with full hookups. At reserved sites, 2 night minimum stay required on weekends, 3 nights on holiday weekends. Fish cleaning station, picnic shelters, handicap accessible fishing area. (205) 373-6328. NRRS 3/1-10/31. **GPS: 33.22639, -88.27667**

WALTER F. GEORGE LAKE (MB) 6
GPS: 31.6267, -85.0633

This 45,000-acre lake is on the Chattahoochee River at the Alabama-Georgia state line, adjacent to Ft. Gaines, Georgia, W of Albany, Georgia and N of Dothan, Alabama. Campground checkout time 3 p.m. Visitor vehicles to 9:30 p.m.; visitor fee charged. Off-road vehicles prohibited. Picnic shelters available (for reservations call 334-585-6537). Resource Manager, Walter F. George Lake, Rt. 1, Box 176, Ft. Gaines, GA 31751-9722. (229) 768-2516/(334) 585-6537. See Georgia listings.

BLUFF CREEK CAMPGROUND

From Phenix City, 3 mi S on US 431; 18 mi S (left) on SR 165; E (left) at signs, across railroad; on right. All year; 14-day limit. 88 sites with elec/wtr, $20 ($10 with federal senior pass). RV limit 40 ft; 6 pull-through sites. At reserved sites, 2-night minimum stay required on weekends, 3 nights on holiday weekends. Picnic shelter, fish cleaning station. (256) 855-2746. NRRS 2/25-10/2. **GPS: 32.1797, -85.0133**

HARDRIDGE CREEK CAMPGROUND

From Ft. Gaines, Georgia, 3 mi W across river; 1 mi W on SR 46; 3 mi N on SR 97, E at sign. All year; 14-day limit. 77 sites. 57 sites with elec/wtr, $20 ($10 with federal senior pass); 20 sites with full hookups, $22 ($11 with federal senior pass. Double sites $44. RV limit 30 ft. At reserved sites, 2-night minimum stay required on weekends, 3 nights on holiday weekends. Picnic shelter. (334) 585-5945. NRRS during 1/1-10/2. **GPS: 31.64056, -85.10222**

WHITE OAK CREEK RECREATION AREA

From Eufaula, 8 mi S on US 431; 2 mi SE (left) on SR 95; E (left) at sign prior to the White Oak Creek bridge. All year; 14-day limit. 130 sites with elec/wtr, $20 ($10 with federal senior pass). RV limit 40 ft; 5

pull-through sites. At reserved sites, 2-night minimum stay required on weekends, 3 nights on holiday weekends. Picnic shelter, fish cleaning station. (334) 687-3101. NRRS. **GPS: 31.76805, -85.125**

WARRIOR LAKE (MB) 7
BLACK WARRIOR & TOMBIGBEE WATERWAY
GPS: 32.52, -87.88

This 7,800-acre lake is 6 miles SE of Eutaw off SR 14 and SW of Tuscaloosa. Public use areas. Demopolis Site Office, Demopolis Lake, 384 Resource Management Drive, Demopolis, AL 36732. (334) 289-3540.

JENNINGS FERRY CAMPGROUND

From Eutaw, 5.7 mi E on SR 14, across Warrior River Bridge. All year; 52 sites with elec/wtr, $18 ($9 with federal senior pass). RV limit 65 ft; 8 pull-through sites. At reserved sites, 2 night minimum stay required on weekends, 3 nights on holiday weekends. Non-campers pay $5 for dump station, $3 for boat ramp (205) 372-1217. **GPS: 32.84944, -87.72194**

WEST POINT LAKE (MB) 8
GPS: 32.9183, -85.1883

This 25,900-acre lake is 35 miles along the Chattahoochee River, located SW of Atlanta and I-85 on the Alabama/Georgia state line near West Point, Georgia. Resource Manager, W Point Lake, 500 Resource Manager Drive, W Point, GA 31833-9517. (706) 645-2937. See Georgia listings.

AMITY RECREATION AREA

From Lanett, 7 mi N on CR 212, 0.5 mi E on CR 393 (signs). All year; 14-day limit. 96 sites. 3 tent sites, $16 ($8 with federal senior pass). 93 sites with elec/wtr, $22 ($11 with federal senior pass). At reserved sites, 2-night minimum stay required on weekends, 3 nights on holiday weekends. Amphitheater. (334) 499-2404. NRRS. **GPS: 32.97083, -85.22222**

WILLIAM 'BILL' DANNELLY LAKE (MB) 9
GPS: 32.11, -87.39

This 24 square mile lake encompasses 105 miles of the Alabama river starting NW of Camden. Resource Manager, William B. Dannelly Lake, 1226 Powerhouse Road, Camden, AL 36726-9109. (334) 682-4244.

CHILATCHEE CREEK CAMPGROUND

From Alberta, 11 mi SE on CR 29 (signs); left on Chilatchee Road. 3/1-11/12; 14-day limit (only primitive camping available 11/13-3/1). 53 sites. $12 at 6 primitive sites without hookups ($6 with federal senior pass); $16 at 25 elec/wtr sites ($8 with federal senior pass); $18 at 22 waterfront sites ($9 with federal senior pass). RV limit 65 ft; 3 pull-through sites, 5 handicap sites with 50-amp elec/wtr. Picnic shelter, fish cleaning station. (334) 573-2562. NRRS. **GPS: 32.14139, -87.27417**

ELM BLUFF

From Camden, 15.5 mi NE on SR 41. Free. All year; 14-day limit. 10 primitive sites. **GPS: 32.16460, -87.11318**

MILLERS FERRY CAMPGROUND

From Camden, 11 mi NW on SR 28; right before Lee Long Bridge (signs). All year; 14-day limit. 66 sites with elec/wtr, $16 base, $18 at 29 waterfront sites with elec ($8 & $9 with federal senior pass). RV limit in excess of 65 ft; 6 pull-through sites, 12 handicap sites. Picnic shelter, multi-use courts. NRRS. **GPS: 32.11583, -87.38972**

SIX MILE CREEK PARK

From Selma at jct with US 80, 9 mi S on SR 41; 1.6 mi W (right) on CR 139 (signs); 0.7 mi N on CR 77. All year; 14-day limit. 31 sites with elec/wtr, $16 base, $18 at prime sites ($8 & $9 with federal senior pass. RV limit in excess of 65 ft; 3 handicap sites. 2 picnic shelters. (334) 875-6228. NRRS. **GPS: 32.32417, -87.01583**

R.E. (BOB) WOODRUFF LAKE (MB) 10
GPS: 32,3233, -86.7833

This 20 square mile lake is SE of Selma off US 80, 5 miles N of Benton, 8 miles W of Montgomery. A fee may be charge for visitors. Site Manager, Alabama River Lakes, 8493 US 80 W, Hayneville, AL 36040. (334) 872-9554/8210.

GUNTER HILL CAMPGROUND

From Montgomery at I-65 exit 167, 9 mi W on SR 80; 4 mi N (right) on CR 7 (signs). All year; 14-day limit. 146 sites with elec/wtr, $18 ($9 with federal senior pass). RV limit in excess of 65 ft. 10 handicap, primitive sites available. 2 group shelters, 4 playgrounds. (334) 269-1053. NRRS.
GPS: 32.36667, -86.46667

PRAIRIE CREEK RECREATION AREA

From Montgomery, 25 mi W on SR 80, 5 mi N on CR 23 (signs), 3 mi W on CR 40. All year; 55 sites elec/wtr, 7 tent only sites. Tent sites $12 base, $14 at premium locations ($6 & $7 with federal senior pass). Sites with elec, $16 base, $18 at premium waterfront locations ($8 & $9 with federal senior pass). RV limit 35 ft; 2 pull-through, 2 handicap. Picnic shelter, fish cleaning station. (334) 418-4916. NRRS.
GPS: 32.3375, -86.76944

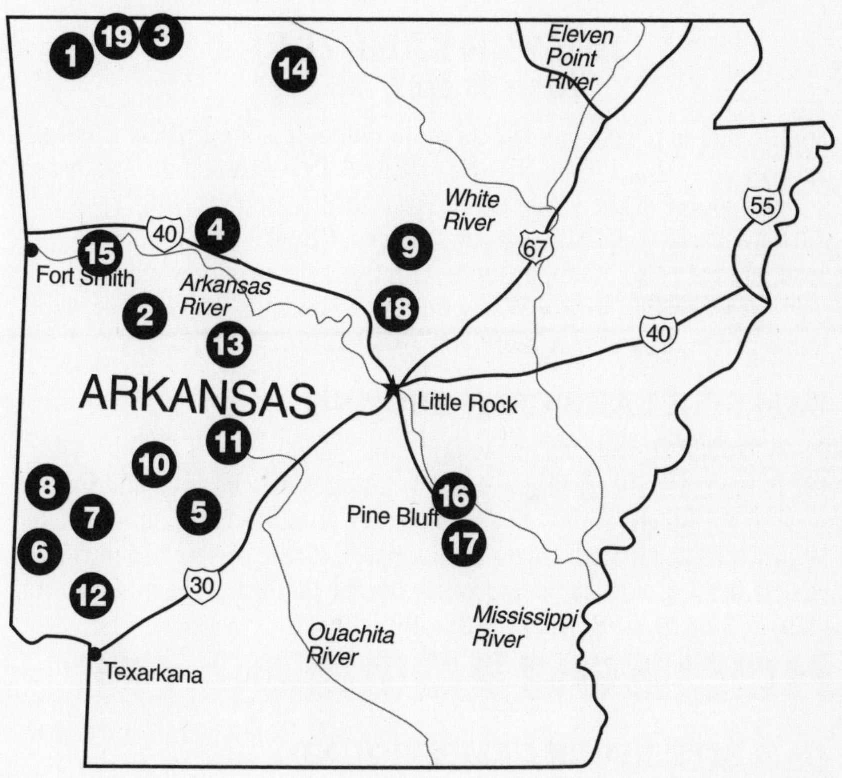
Eleven
Point
River
1
19
3
14
White
River
40
4
9
67
55
15
Fort Smith
Arkansas
River
18
2
40
13
ARKANSAS
Little Rock
11
10
8
5
16
7
Pine Bluff
6
17
12
30
Mississippi
River
Ouachita
River
Texarkana

ARKANSAS

State Capital: **Little Rock**
Nickname: **The Natural State**
Statehood Year: **1836**

25TH STATE

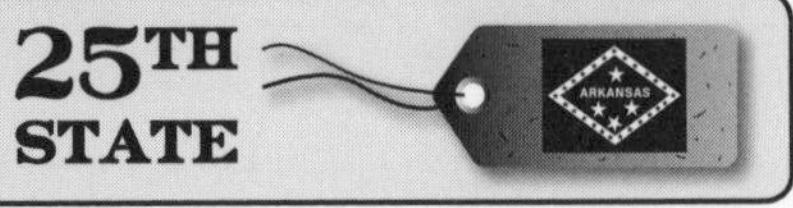

Little Rock District - A fee may be charged for use of the dump station by non-campers. An extra fee may be charged for sites with water hookups.

BEAVER LAKE (LR) 1
GPS: 36.4167, -93.8483

This 28,000-acre lake has 487 mi of shoreline. It is 9 mi NW of Eureka Springs on US 62, 186 mi NW of Little Rock in northwestern Arkansas. It is the source of the White River. Trout fishing, scuba diving, river rafting, nature trails. Campground checkout time 3 p.m. Alcohol prohibited at parks. Campgrounds with free sites in winter may have reduced amenities. Visitor center Resource Manager, Beaver Lake, 2260 N 2nd Street, Rogers, AR 72756. (479)636-1210/253-5866.

DAM SITE LAKE CAMPGROUND

From Eureka Springs, 4.5 mi W on US 62 (signs); 3 mi S (left) on SR 187 (signs). 4/1-10/31; 14-day limit. Some sites may be open and free off-season, but no amenities. 48 sites with wtr/elec: $18 for 30-amp, $20 for 50-amp ($9 & $10 with federal senior pass). Picnic shelter $75 plus $4 vehicle use fee. Non-campers pay day use fee for dump, beach, boat ramp. (479) 253-5828. **GPS: 36.430908, -93.859619**

DAM SITE RIVER CAMPGROUND

From Eureka Springs, 4.3 mi W on US 62 (signs); 2.5 mi S (left) on SR 187 across & below dam (signs). 4/1-10/31; 14-day limit. 59 elec sites: 30-amp elec, $18; 50-amp elec, $20 ($9 & $10 with federal senior pass). RV limit in excess of 65'. At reserved sites, 2-night minimum stay required on weekends, 3 nights on holiday weekends. River rafting trips available nearby. Non-campers pay day use fee for boat ramp, picnicking, dump station, beach. (479) 253-9865. NRRS. **GPS: 36.42194, -93.84583**

HICKORY CREEK PARK

From Springdale at jct with US 412, 1 mi N on US 71; 4.5 mi E on SR 264; 1 mi N (right) on Cow Face Rd (CR 6602, signs); E (left) on Hickory Creek Rd. 4/1-10/31; 14-day limit. 61 sites with elec: 30-amp elec, $19; 50-amp elec $22 ($9.50 & $11 with federal senior pass). During 11/1-3/31, some sites may be open at lower fees with reduced amenities. RV limit 50'. Two picnic shelters, $75 (plus $4 vehicle day use fee) all year. At reserved sites, 2-night minimum stay required on weekends, 3 nights on holiday weekends. Non-campers pay $4 day use fee for dump station, picnicking, beach, boat ramp. (479) 750-2943. NRRS. **GPS: 36.24278, -94.0375**

HORSESHOE BEND EAST CAMPGROUND

From Rogers at jct with US 71, 5 mi E on SR 94 (signs). 4/1-10/31; 14-day limit. 3 tent sites, $14 ($7 with federal senior pass); 188 sites with 30-amp elec, $16 ($8 with federal senior pass); double sites $32. RV limit in excess of 65'. Picnic shelters, $75 plus $4 vehicle day use fee. At reserved sites, 2-night stay required on weekends, 3 nights on holiday weekends. Non-campers pay day use fee for boat ramp, beach, dump station. (479) 925-7195. NRRS. **GPS: 36.28667, -94.01944**

INDIAN CREEK CAMPGROUND

From Gateway, 5 mi E & 4 mi S (right) on Indian Creek Rd (signs, CR 89). 5/1-9/8; 14-day limit. Some may be open & free off-season, but no amenities. 33 sites with elec, $16 ($8 with federal senior pass). Picnic shelter. Non-campers pay day use fee for boat ramp, dump station, beach, picnicking. **GPS: 36.4236, -93.8914**

LOST BRIDGE NORTH CAMPGROUND

From Garfield at jct with SR 62, 6 mi SW on SR 127 (signs); turn on 127 Spur, then left on Marina Rd. 4/1-9/30; 14-day limit. 48 sites with 30-amp elec, $18 ($9 with federal senior pass). RV limit 60'; 9 pull-through sites. At reserved sites, 2-night minimum stay required on weekends, 3 nights on holiday weekends. Non-campers pay day use fee for boat ramp, picnicking, beach, dump station. (479) 359-3312. NRRS. **GPS: 36.41083, -93.89333**

LOST BRIDGE SOUTH CAMPGROUND

From Garfield at jct with SR 62, 5 mi SE (right) on SR 127 (signs); left on Marina Rd. 5/1-9/30; 14-day limit. 36 sites with 50-amp elec: $17 with elec, $20 with elec/wtr ($8.50 & $10 with federal senior pass). RV limit 55'. Picnic shelter. At reserved sites, 2-night minimum stay required on weekends, 3 nights on holiday weekends. Non-campers pay day use fee for boat ramp, beach, picnicking, dump station. (479) 359-3755. NRRS. **GPS: 36.41083, -93.89333**

PRAIRIE CREEK CAMPGROUND

From Rogers at jct with US 71 (signs), 4 mi E on SR 12; 1 mi N on N Park Rd. 4/1-10/31; 14-day limit. 112 sites with elec: $16 for 30-amp; $17 for 50-amp; $19 for 50-amp elec/wtr ($8, $8.50 & $9.50 with federal senior pass). Double sites $36. During 11/1-3/31, some sites may be open at reduced fees & reduced amenities. RV limit in excess of 65'; 3 pull-through sites. 6 picnic shelters, $25-$75 (one for 300 people with full kitchen, serving station, restrooms, PA system). At reserved sites, 2-night minimum stay required on weekends, 3 nights on holiday weekends. Showers renovated late in 2010. Non-campers pay $4 day use fee for boat ramp, picnicking, beach, dump station. (479) 925-3957. NRRS (4/1-10/31) **GPS: 36.35472, -94.05056**

ROCKY BRANCH CAMPGROUND

From Rogers at jct with US 71 (signs), 11 mi E on SR 12 (signs); 4.5 mi NE on SR 303 (signs); on left. All year; 14-day limit. During 4/1-10/31, 44 sites with elec: $16 for 30-amp, $17 for 50-amp ($8 & $8.50 with federal senior pass). During 11/1-3/31, some sites with elec are $12. Two picnic shelters, $75 plus $4 vehicle day use fee; call office for reservations. Non-campers pay day use fee for picnicking, boat ramp, beach, dump station. (479) 925-2526. **GPS: 36.3343, -93.9334**

STARKEY CAMPGROUND

From Eureka Springs, 4 mi W on US 62 (signs); 4 mi SW on SR 187; 4.3 mi W (right) on CR 2176 (Mundell Rd, signs). 5/1-9/8; 14-day limit. 23 sites with 30-amp elec, $16 ($8 with federal senior pass). Picnic shelter, $75 plus $4 vehicle day use fee; call office for reservations. Change shelter at beach. Non-campers pay $4 day use fee for dump station, boat ramp, beach, picnicking.(479) 253-5866. **GPS: 36.3903, -93.877**

WAR EAGLE CAMPGROUND

From Springdale at jct with US 71, 10 mi E on SR 412 (signs); 3 mi NW on CR 95. All year; 14-day limit. During 5/1-9/8, 26 sites with 30-amp elec, $16 ($8 with federal senior pass); rest of year, some sites open for $12 ($6 with federal senior pass). Picnic shelter, $75 plus $4 vehicle day use fee; for reservations call office. Day use fees for boat ramp, beach, dump station, picnicking. (479) 750-4722. **GPS: 36.21853, -94.01606**

BLUE MOUNTAIN LAKE (LR) 2
GPS: 35.1017, -93.6433

This 2,910-acre lake is 1.5 mi SW of Waveland on SR 309 off SR 10, 5 mi E of Blue Mountain and 101 mi NW of Little Rock. A day use fee may be charged in free camping areas. Some campground amenities are reduced, along with fees, during the November through February off-season. Formerly free camping areas are now available only for day use. Both of the lake's current campgrounds provide boat launching ramps

& fish cleaning stations. Visitor center, interpretive programs. Park Manager, Rt. 1, Box 173AA, Blue Mountain Lake, Waveland, AR 72842-9600. (479) 947-2372. GPS: 35.1017, -93.6433.

OUTLET AREA CAMPGROUND

From Waveland at jct with SR 10, 1.8 mi S (right) on SR 309 across & below dam on Petit Jean River (signs). All year; 14-day limit. 38 sites, most with hookups. During 3/1-10/31, 30-amp elec/wtr, $16; 50-amp elec/wtr, $18 ($8 & $9 with federal senior pass). During 11/1-2/28, 30-amp elec/wtr, $14; 50-amp elec/wtr, $16 ($7 & $8 with federal senior pass. 3 multi-family sites at fees twice the per-site rate. RV limit in excess of 65 ft. At reserved sites, 2-night minimum stay required on weekends, 3 nights on holiday weekends. (479) 947-2101. NRRS (3/1-10/31). **GPS: 35.10056, -93.6525**

WAVELAND CAMPGROUND

From Waveland, 0.9 mi S (signs), then 0.9 mi W; just upstream from dam. All year; 14-day limit. 51 sites with elec/wtr. During 3/1-10/31, 30-amp elec/wtr $16; 50-amp elec/wtr $18 ($8 & $9 with federal senior pass). During 11/1-2/28, 30-amp elec/wtr $14; 50-amp elec/wtr $16 ($7 & $8 with federal senior pass). RV limit 40 ft. Picnic shelter ($25), fish cleaning station, amphitheater, change shelter at beach. At reserved sites, 2-night minimum stay required on weekends, 3 nights on holiday weekends. (479) 947-2102. NRRS (5/15-9/15). **GPS: 35.1075, -93.65806**

BULL SHOALS LAKE (LR) 3
GPS: 36.3633, -925733

This 45,440-acre lake is 15 mi W of Mountain Home on SR 178 in N-central Arkansas, SE of Branson, Missouri. Off-road vehicles prohibited. Campground checkout time 3 p.m. Visitor center. (870) 425-2700. Resource Manager, Bull Shoals Lake, P. O. Box 2070, Mountain Home, AR 72654-2070. See Missouri listings.

BUCK CREEK CAMPGROUND

From Protem (sign), MO., 5.5 mi SE on SR 125 (signs). 4/1-9/30; 14-day limit. 2 sites without hookups, $14 ($7 with federal senior pass); 36 sites with elec, $18 ($9 with federal senior pass); double sites $36. RV limit 40 ft. Picnic shelter for up to 50 people & 10 vehicles, $42. Marine dump station, change shelter. At reserved sites, 2-night minimum stay required on weekends, 3 nights on holiday weekends. (417) 785-4313. NRRS (5/16-9/13). **GPS: 36.48667, -92.7944**

DAM SITE PARK CAMPGROUND

From Bull Shoals, 1 mi SW on SR 178 (signs); on bluff overlooking lake. 4/1-9/30; 14-day limit. 35 sites with elec, $18 ($9 with federal senior pass). RV limit 40 ft. Picnic shelter. At reserved sites, 2-night minimum stay required on weekends, 3 nights on holiday weekends. (870) 445-7166. NRRS (5/1-9/30). **GPS: 36.37389, -92.57417**

HIGHWAY 125 PARK

From Peel, 5.1 mi N on SR 125. 4/1-10/31; 14-day limit. 38 sites with elec, $18 ($9 with federal senior pass). RV limit 45 ft. Picnic shelter for up to 50 people & 20 vehicles, $42.. Marine dump station. At reserved sites, 2-night minimum stay required on weekends, 3 nights on holiday weekends. (870) 436-5711. NRRS (5/16-9/13; closed to reservations in 2010 due to renovations; call for current status). **GPS: 36.48972, -92.77278**

LAKEVIEW PARK

From Mountain Home at jct with US 62, 6 mi NW to Midway on SR 5; 7.1 mi SW on SR 178 (signs); N on Boat Dock Rd; on bluff overlooking lake. 4/1-10/31; 14-day limit. 88 sites, 17 with wtr/elec, 71 with elec; base fee $18 ($9 with federal senior pass). RV limit 40 ft. Group camping area available. 2 picnic shelters: GS1 for up to 50 people & 10 vehicles, $52; GS2 for up to 25 people & 10 vehicles, $40. At reserved sites, 2-night minimum stay required on weekends, 3 nights on holiday weekends. (870) 431-8116. NRRS (5/17-9/13). Note: Renovations scheduled in 2010; check current status. **GPS: 36.37667, -92.54694**

LEAD HILL CAMPGROUND

From Lead Hill at jct with SR 14, 3.5 mi N through Diamond City on SR 7 (signs). 4/1-10/31; 14-day limit. 75 sites with elec, $18 ($9 with federal senior pass). RV limit 40 ft; 4 pull-through sites. Picnic shelters: GS2 for up to 50 people & 15 vehicles, $42; GS11 for up to 100 people & 20 vehicles, $52. Marine dump station, change shelter. No reservations in 2010 due to construction. When reservations resume, reserved sites will require 2-night minimum stay on weekends, 3 nights on holiday weekends. NRRS during 5/17-9/13. **GPS: 36.47472, -92.92194**

OAKLAND PARK

From Oakland, 4 mi W on SR 202. 4/1-10/31; 14-day limit. 32 sites with elec, $18 ($9 with federal senior pass). RV limit 40 ft. Picnic shelter for up to 36 people & 10 vehicles, $42. Change shelter at beach. At reserved sites, 2-night minimum stay required on weekends. 3 nights on holiday weekends. (870) 431-5744. NRRS (5/17-9/13). **GPS: 36.44389, -92.62028**

TUCKER HOLLOW PARK

From Lead Hill at jct with SR 7, 7 mi NW on SR 14 (sign); 3 mi N on SR 281, then E; on bluff overlooking lake. 4/1-10/31; 14-day limit. 30 sites with elec, $18 ($9 with federal senior pass); double sites $34. RV limit 40 ft. Two picnic shelters: GPR1 for up to 25 people & 10 vehicles & GRP2 for up to 50 people & 25 vehicles, $52. Change shelter at beach. Due to renovations, no reservations taken in 2010; check current status. When reservations resume, reserved sites will require 2-night minimum stays on weekends, 3 nights on holiday weekends. (870) 436-5622. NRRS (5/17-9/13). **GPS: 36.47611, -93.00694**

DARDANELLE LAKE (LR) 4

GPS: 35.25, -93.1667

This 34,300-acre lake has 315 mi of shoreline and is adjacent to SW side of Russellville, E of Fort Smith and N of Dardanelle on SR 22. Visitor center. Resource Manager, Dardanelle Lake, 1598 Lock and Dam Road, Russellville, AR 72802-1087. (479) 968-5008.

CANE CREEK PARK

From Scranton, 3.5 mi NE on SR 197; 2 mi N on paved rd. 5/1-10/31; 14-day limit. 16 free primitive sites on 48 acres. Boat ramp open all year. Pit toilets.

DELAWARE PARK

From Subiaco at jct with SR 22, 3 mi N on SR 197; 2.5 mi NE on SR 393. 5/1-LD; 14-day limit. 13 tent sites, $10 ($5 with federal senior pass). Picnic shelter, $50. No day use fees. Pit toilets. **GPS: 35.397363, -93.274658**

OLD POST R0AD CAMPGROUND

From Russellville at jct with US 64, 2.2 mi S on SR 7; 1 mi W on Lock & Dam Rd (signs); overlooks N bank of Arkansas River. All year; 14-day limit. 40 sites with elec, $18 ($9 with federal senior pass). RV limit in excess of 65 ft. Eight picnic shelters, $50. Soccer field, tennis court, softball (fees). At reserved sites, 2-night minimum stay required on weekends, 3 nights on holiday weekends. Day use fee for boat ramp, picnicking, dump station. (479) 968-7962. NRRS (3/1-10/31). **GPS: 36.24722, -93.1625**

PINEY BAY PARK

From London, 4 mi E on US 64; 3 mi N on SR 359 (signs). All year; 14-day limit. 91 sites, 85 with elec. Sites without hookups, $10 ($5 with federal senior pass); elec sites $18 base, $20 with elec/wtr ($9 & $10 with federal senior pass). RV limit in excess of 65 ft. Picnic shelter,

$50.. Amphitheater. At reserved sites, 2-night minimum stay required on weekends, 3 nights on holiday weekends. Day use fees for boat ramp, dump station, picnicking, beach. (479) 885-3029. NRRS (3/1-10/31). **GPS: 35.39944, -93.31414**

RIVERVIEW PARK

From Russellville at jct with US 64, 4.5 mi S on SR 7 across outlet, then NW; immediately below dam & powerhouse. 3/1-10/31; 14-day limit. 18 sites. 10 sites without hookups, $10 ($5 with federal senior pass); 8 sites with elec, $18 ($9 with federal senior pass). Pit toilets, drkg wtr. Dump at Old Post Road Park. Picnic shelter, $50. **GPS: 35.247559, -93.174316**

SHOAL BAY PARK

From New Blaine at jct with SR 22, 1.6 mi NW on SR 197 (signs); on Shoal Bay arm of lake. All year; 14-day limit. 82 sites with elec, $16 base, $18 with elec/wtr ($8 & $9 with federal senior pass). RV limit 50 ft; 2 pull-through sites. 2 picnic shelters, $50. Amphitheater. At reserved sites, 2-night minimum stay required on weekends, 3 nights on holiday weekends. Day use fees for boat ramp, dump station, beach, picnicking. (479) 938-7335. NRRS (3/1-10/31)). **GPS: 35.31, -93.43056**

SPADRA PARK

From Clarksville at jct with US 64, 2 mi S through Jamestown on SR 103; on bluff overlooking Arkansas River. All year; 14-day limit. 29 sites. 5 tent sites, $10 ($5 with federal senior pass); 24 RV/tent sites with elec, $14 base, $18 with wtr/elec ($7 & $9 with federal senior pass. Picnic shelter, $50. (479) 754-6438. No reservations. Day use for boat ramp, dump station, picnicking, beach. **GPS: 35.525537, -93.473877**

SWEEDEN ISLAND CAMPGROUND

From Atkins at jct with SR 324, 15 mi SW through Wilson on SR 105 to Lock & Dam #9; on bluff overlooking Arkansas River. 3/1-10/31; 14-day limit. 28 sites. 6 tent sites, $10 ($5 with federal senior pass); 22 sites with elec, $16 ($8 with federal senior pass). Picnic shelters (fee). No day use fees. (479)641-7500. **GPS: 35.168945, -93.011475**

DEGRAY LAKE (VK) 5
GPS: 34.22, -93.11

This 13,500-acre lake with 207 mi of shoreline is 8 mi NW of Arkadelphia and W of I-30 exit 78 off SR 7. It is 67 mi SW of Little Rock. Visitor center, interpretive programs. DeGray has 20 recreation areas, 724 campsites, 18 boat ramps and 12 swimming beaches. Resource Manager, DeGray Lake, 729 Channel Avenue, Arkadelphia, AR 71923. (870) 246-5501.

ALPINE RIDGE CAMPGROUND

From Alpine at jct with SR 8, 10 mi E through Fendley on SR 346. All year; 14-day limit. 49 sites with elec, all $12 during 10/1-4/30; premium sites $18 during 5/1-9/30 ($6 & $9 with federal senior pass). RV limit 40 ft. At reserved sites, 2-night minimum stay required on weekends, 3 nights on holiday weekends. NRRS during 5/1-9/30. **GPS: 34.25861, -993.22833**

ARLIE MOORE CAMPGROUND

From Bismarck, 2.2 mi SE on SR 7; 2 mi W on Arlie Moore Rd. All year; 14-day limit. 19 tent sites, $10 & $12 ($5 & $6 with federal senior pass). 38 sites with elec, $16 during 10/1-4/30 ($8 with federal senior pass), $18 during 5/1-9/30 ($9 with federal senior pass). RV limit 30 ft. Picnic shelter, amphitheater. At reserved sites, 2-night minimum stay required on weekends, 3 nights on holiday weekends. NRRS during 5/1-9/30. **GPS: 34.27167, -93.20**

CADDO DRIVE CAMPGROUND

From Bismarck, 3.5 mi SE on SR 7; 2.7 mi W on gravel Edgewood Rd. All year; 14-day limit. 27 tent sites, $10 & $12 ($5 & $6 with federal senior pass). 45 sites with elec, $12 during 10/1-4/30 & $18 during 5/1-9/30 ($6 & $9 with federal senior pass). RV limit 40 ft; 2 pull-through sites. Picnic shelter for up to 100 people and 15 vehicles. At reserved sites, 2-night minimum stay required on weekends, 3 nights on holiday weekends. NRRS during 5/1-9/30. **GPS: 34.26111, -93.1875**

EDGEWOOD CAMPGROUND

From Bismarck, 4.8 mi SW; 3 mi W on Edgewood Rd (S of Caddo Drive Park). All year; 14-day limit. 4 tent sites with elec, $12 ($6 with federal senior pass). 45 sites with elec, $12 during 10/1-4/30; premium sites $18 during 5/1-9/30 ($6 & $9 with federal senior pass); double sites $24 & $34. RV limit 30 ft; 9 pull-through sites. Boat rentals nearby. At reserved sites, 2-night minimum stay required on weekends, 3 nights on holiday weekends. NRRS during 5/1-9/30. **GPS: 34.25556, -93.185**

IRON MOUNTAIN CAMPGROUND

From I-30 exit 78, 2.5 mi N on SR 7; 2.5 mi W across dam on Skyline Dr; N on Iron Mountain Rd. All year; 14-day limit. 69 sites with elec, $12; premium sites $18 during 5/1-9/30 ($6 & $9 with federal senior pass). RV limit 30 ft.' At reserved sites, 2-night minimum stay required on weekends, 3 nights on holiday weekends. NRRS during 5/1-9/30. **GPS: 34.22, -127.7**

LENOX MARCUS

From Lambert at jct with SR 84, 0.8 mi SW; 2.2 mi S on gravel road. 200 acres of remote camping, free. All year; 14-day limit. Pit toilets, drkg wtr. 30 picnic sites. **GPS: 34.26700, -93.21710**

OZAN POINT CAMPGROUND

From Alpine, 6.8 mi NE through Fendley on SR 346, then 1.5 mi E on gravel road. 3/1-10/31; 14-day limit. $6. 50 small primitive sites; 15-ft RV limit for pickup campers & vans. **GPS: 34.23900, -93.20600**

POINT CEDAR CAMPGROUND

From Point Cedar at jct with SR 84, 3.5 mi SW. 3/10-11/30; 14-day limit. 62 sites, $6. RV limit 40'. **GPS: 34.29320, -93.26510**

SHOUSE FORD CAMPGROUND

From Point Cedar at jct with SR 84, 3.5 mi SE on Shouse Ford Rd. All year; 14-day limit. 99 sites with elec, $12; premium sites $18 during 5/1-9/30 ($6 & $9 with federal senior pass). RV limit 40 ft. At reserved sites, 2-night minimum stay required on weekends, 3 nights on holiday weekends. NRRS 5/1-9/30. **GPS: 34.28944, -9326778**

DEQUEEN LAKE (LR) 6
GPS: 34.0983, -94.3817

This 1,680-acre lake is 4 mi NW of DeQueen off US 71 and 96 mi SW of Hot Springs (N of Texarkana) near the Oklahoma state line. Non-campers pay day use fees for use of dump stations. Resource Manager, DeQueen Lake, 706 DeQueen Lake Road, DeQueen, AR 71832. (870) 584-4161.

BELLAH MINE CAMPGROUND

From DeQueen, 7 mi N on US 71; 5.3 mi W on Bellah Mine Road (signs). All year; 14-day limit. 24 sites with elec/wtr, $13 base, $15 for premium sites during 3/1-11/30 ($6.50 & $7.50 with federal senior pass); $10 rest of year ($5 with federal senior pass). RV limit n excess of 65'. At reserved sites, 2-night minimum stay required on weekends, 3 nights on holiday

weekends. Picnic shelter $25. (870) 386-7511. NRRS (515-9/15).
GPS: 34.1444, -94.39639

OAK GROVE CAMPGROUND

From DeQueen, 3 mi N on US 71; 5.5 mi W on DeQueen Lake Rd; 0.3 mi N (signs). All year; 14-day limit. 36 sites with elec/wtr, $13 base, $15 for premium sites during 3/1-10/31 ($6.50 & $7.50 with federal senior pass); $10 rest of year ($5 with federal senior pass). RV limit in excess of 65 ft; 7 pull-through sites. Picnic shelter with wtr & elec for up to 150 people & 50 vehicles, $25. Amphitheater. At reserved sites, 2-night minimum stay required on weekends, 3 nights on holiday weekends. (870) 642-6111. NRRS (3/15-9/15). **GPS: 34.09667, -94.39444**

PINE RIDGE CAMPGROUND

From DeQueen, 3 mi N on US 71; 5.5 mi W on DeQueen Creek Rd; 1.5 mi W on county rd (signs), then N. All year; 14-day limit. 38 sites without hookups, $9 during 3/1-10/31 ($4.50 with federal senior pass); $6 rest of year ($3 with federal senior pass). 17 sites with wtr/elec, $13 base, $15 at premium sites during 3/1-10/31 ($6.50 & $7.50 with federal senior pass); $10 rest of year ($5 with federal senior pass). RV limit in excess of 65 ft; 4 pull-through sites. Group primitive camping for up to 120 people and 1 vehicle, $25. Fish cleaning station. At reserved sites, 2-night minimum stay required on weekends, 3 nights on holiday weekends. NRRS during 5/15-9/15. **GPS: 34.08111, -94.38111**

DIERKS LAKE (LR) 7
GPS: 34.145, -94.10

This 1,360-acre lake is 72 mi SW of Hot Springs and N of Texarkana, E of DeQueen and 5 mi NW of Dierks in southwestern Arkansas. Visitor center. Resource Manager, Dierks Lake, P. O. Box 8, Dierks, AR 71833. (870) 286-3214/2346.

BLUE RIDGE CAMPGROUND

From Dierks, 3 mi NE on US 70; 4 mi NW on SR 4; 2.6 mi W on County RD (signs). All year; 14-day limit. 22 sites with elec/wtr (5 reservable), $13 during 3/1-10/31 & $8 rest of year ($6.50 & $4 with federal senior pass). Fish cleaning station. **GPS: 34.1946, -94.0896**

HORSESHOE BEND CAMPGROUND

From Dierks, 3 mi W on US 70; 3.5 mi NW on Lake Rd (signs); below dam. All year; 14-day limit. 11 sites with wtr/elec, $11 ($5.50 with federal senior pass). Picnic shelter for up to 100 people & 1 vehicle, 1/2 day $25, 1 day $40. Change shelter at beach. (870) 286-3214). **GPS: 34.152255, -94.115273**

JEFFERSON RIDGE CAMPGROUND

From Dierks, 5 mi W on US 70; 5 mi NW on Green Chapel Rd (signs); access E on W side of dam. All year; 14-day limit. 85 sites with wtr/elec (52 reservable), $13 base, $15 at premium locations during 3/1-10/31 ($6.50 & $7.50 with federal senior pass); $7.50 rest of year ($3.75 with federal senior pass). RV limit in excess of 65 ft; 41 pull-through sites. Amphitheater, fish cleaning station. Picnic shelter, 1/2 day $25, 1 day $40. At reserved sites, 2-night minimum stay required on weekends, 3 nights on holiday weekends. NRRS during 5/15-9/15. **GPS: 34.10722, -94.05056**

GILLHAM LAKE (LR) 8

GPS: 34.15, -94.10

This 1,370-acre lake is 6 mi BW of Gillham, 15 mi N of DeQueen, E of US Route 71 and SW of Little Rock near the Oklahoma state line. Non-campers pay day use fees for use of dump stations. Resource Manager, Gillham Lake, 706 DeQueen Lake Road, DeQueen, AR 71852. (870) 584-4162.

BIG COON CREEK CAMPGROUND

From project office, 0.5 mi NE on county rd to dam; 1 mi NW, access NE. All year; 14-day limit. 31 sites with elec/wtr, $13 base, $15 at premium sites during 3/1-10/31 ($6.50 & $7.50 with federal senior pass); $11 rest of year ($5.50 with federal senior pass). RV limit in excess of 65 ft; 2 pull-through sites. Fish cleaning station, amphitheater, nature trails, canoeing. At reserved sites, 2-night stay required on weekends, 3 nights on holiday weekends. (870) 385-7126. NRRS (5/15-9/15). **GPS: 34.1733, -94.32**

COSSATOT REEFS CAMPGROUND

From Gillham, 6 mi NE past project office near dam on Cossatot River. All year; 14-day limit. 30 sites with elec/wtr, $13 base, $15 at premium sites during 3/1-10/31 ($6.50 & $7.50 with federal senior pass); $10 rest of year ($5 with federal senior pass). 2 walk-to tent sites, $9 base, $13 premium locations ($4.50 & $6.50 with federal senior pass). RV limit in excess of 65 ft. Picnic shelter for up to 100 people & 1 vehicle, $25. Amphitheater, fish cleaning station, nature trails, canoeing, hiking trail. 3-night minimum stay required on holidays. (870) 386-7261. NRRS (5/15-9/15). **GPS: 34.17333, -94.32**

LITTLE COON CREEK CAMPGROUND

From Gillham, 6 mi NE past project office; 1 mi NW past Coon Creek Park on county road. All year; 14-day limit. 10 sites with wtr/elec, $13 during 3/1-10/31 ($6.50 with federal senior pass); $10 rest of year ($5 with federal senior pass). **GPS: 34.2271, -94.2681**

GREERS FERRY LAKE (LR) 9

GPS: 35.525, -92.01

This 31,500-acre lake is N of Heber Springs on SR 25, 65 mi N of Little Rock. Campground checkout time 4 p.m. Visitor center with interpretive programs. Fish hatchery. Project Office, Greers Ferry Lake, P. O. Box 1088, Heber Springs, AR 72543-9022. (501) 362-2416.

CHEROKEE CAMPGROUND

From Drasco, 7.5 mi W to Brownsville on SR 92 (signs); 4.5 mi S; on N side of lower lake just W of Silver Ridge Peninsula. 5/15-9/15; 14-day limit. 17 sites without hookups, $12 ($6 with federal senior pass). 16 sites with elec, $14 base, $16 at prime locations ($7 & $8 with federal senior pass). Pit toilets. No reservations. **GPS: 35.13916, -92.740479**

CHOCTAW CAMPGROUND

From Clinton, 5 mi S to Choctaw (sign) on US 65; 3.8 mi E on SR 330 (signs); on W end of upper lake. 4/1-10/31; 14-day limit. 55 sites without hookups, $14 ($7 with federal senior pass). 91 sites with elec, $17 base, $19 prime locations ($8.50 & $9.50 with federal senior pass). RV limit in excess of 65 ft. Picnic shelter, marina. NRRS (5/15-9/5). **GPS: 35.53556, -92.38111**

COVE CREEK CAMPGROUND

From Heber Springs, 6.3 mi SW on SR 25; 3 mi NW on SR 16; 1.2 mi NE (signs); on S end of lower lake. 4/1-10/31; 14-day limit. 34 sites without hookups, $14 ($7 with federal senior pass). 31 sites with elec, $17 base, $19 prime locations ($8.50 & $9.50 with federal senior pass). RV limit in excess of 65'. Picnic shelter. **GPS: 35.461234, -92.15328**

DAM SITE CAMPGROUND

From Heber Springs, 3.4 mi N on SR 25B (signs); on W side of dam. All year; 14-day limit. 104 sites without hookups, $14 ($7 with federal senior pass). 158 sites with elec, $17 base; $19 at prime locations; $20 with elec/wtr ($8.50, $9.50 & $10 with federal senior pass). RV limit in excess of 65'. Picnic shelters (fees), marine dump station. Golf carts & ATV or ORV prohibited. Visitor center, marina. NRRS (5/15-9/6).
GPS: 35.52194, -91.9975

DEVILS FORK CAMPGROUND

From Greers Ferry at jct with SR 92, 0.5 mi N on SR 16, W side following signs. All year; 14-day limit. 55 sites with elec, $17 base, $19 at premium locations ($8.50 & $9.50 with federal senior pass). RV limit in excess of 65'. Picnic shelter. NRRS (5/15-9/5). **GPS: 35.58806, -92.18528**

HEBER SPRINGS CAMPGROUND

From Heber Springs, 2 mi W on SR 110, 0.5 mi N, following signs. 4/1-10/31; 14-day limit. 36 sites without hookups, $14 ($7 with federal senior pass). 106 sites with elec, $17 base, $19 at premium locations ($8.50 & $9.50 with federal senior pass). RV limit in excess of 65 ft. Picnic shelter (fee), marina, store, phone. NRRS (5/15-9/5). **GPS: 35.50389, -92.06639**

HILL CREEK CAMPGROUND

From Drasco, 12 mi W past Brownsville (sign) on SR 92; 3 mi NW on SR 225 (signs); 2 mi S; on shore of upper lake. 4/1-9/5; 14-day limit. 16 sites without hookups, $14 ($7 with federal senior pass); 30 sites with elec, $17 ($8.50 with federal senior pass). RV limit in excess of 65 ft. Picnic shelter, marina. NRRS (5/15-9/5). **GPS: 35.61083, -92.14917**

JOHN F. KENNEDY CAMPGROUND

From Heber Springs, 4.4 mi N on SR 25; 1 mi E across dam; S side (signs), below dam on Little Red River (trout stream). All year; 14-day limit. 74 sites with elec, $17 base, $20 at 13 sites with elec/wtr ($8.50 & $10 with federal senior pass). RV limit in excess of 65 ft. Picnic shelter. NRRS during 4/15-9/5. **GPS: 35.2083, -91.99306**

MILL CREEK CAMPGROUND

From Bee Branch, 13.2 mi NE on SR 92 (signs); 3 mi N; on shore of upper lake. 5/15-9/15; 14-day limit. 39 sites without hookups, $12 ($6 with federal senior pass); formerly free. Picnic shelter. No reservations. **GPS: 35.65, -92.22**

NARROWS CAMPGROUND

From Greers Ferry, 2.5 mi NW on SR 16; across bridge, N side (signs); near center of lake. 4/1-10/31; 14-day limit. 60 sites with elec, $17 base, $19 at prime locations ($8.50 & $9.50 with federal senior pass). RV limit in excess of 65 ft. Overflow area. Picnic shelters. NRRS (5/15-9/5). **GPS: 35.56389, -92.19806**

OLD HIGHWAY 25 CAMPGROUND

From Heber Springs, 6.2 mi N on SR 25; 2.8 mi W on old SR 25 , following signs; on lakeshore 1 mi from dam. 4/1-10/31; 14-day limit. 36 sites without hookups, $14 ($7 with federal senior pass). 89 sites with elec, $17 base, $19 at prime locations ($8.50 & $9.50 with federal senior pass). RV limit in excess of 65 ft. Picnic shelters, group camping area (no elec) with 16 sites for up to 128 people & 48 vehicles, $150. NRRS (5/15-9/5). **GPS: 35.53417, -92.02194**

SHILOH CAMPGROUND

From Greers Ferry at jct with SR 92, 3.5 mi SE on SR 110 (signs); on mid-lake shore. 4/1-10/31; 14-day limit. 56 sites without hookups, $14 ($7 with federal senior pass). 60 sites with elec, $17 base, $19 at prime locations ($8.50 & $9.50 with federal senior pass). RV limit in excess of 65'. Picnic shelter, marina. Group camping area (no elec) with 17 sites for up to 204 people & 12 vehicles, $150. NRRS (5/15-9/5). **GPS: 35.5375, -92.14583**

SUGAR LOAF CAMPGROUND

From Bee Branch, 12 mi NE on SR 92, following signs; 1.5 mi W on SR 337; on upper lake. 4/1-10/31; 14-day limit. 39 sites without hookups, $14 ($7 with federal senior pass). 57 sites with elec, $17 base, $19 at prime locations ($8.50 & $9.50 with federal senior pass. RV limit in excess of 65'. Picnic shelter, marina. NRRS (5/15-9/5).
GPS: 35.54583, -92.27222

LAKE GREESON (VK) 10
GPS: 34.1483, -93.715

This 7,260-acre lake is 12 mi long. It is 6 mi N of Murfreesboro on SR 19, 69 mi NE of Texarkana. Visitors to 10 p.m. Visitor center. 31-mi cycle trail. ORVs permitted. Campsites that are free sites or open with lower fees in winter may have reduced amenities. Resource Manager, Lake Greeson Field Office, 155 Dynamite Hill Road, Murfreesboro, AR 71958. (870) 285-2151.

ARROWHEAD POINT CAMPGROUND

From E of Newhope at jct with SR 369, 0.5 mi E on US 70, then SE to campground. All year; 14-day limit. 23 sites without hookups (12 for tents), $6 during 3/1-10/31 ($3 with federal senior pass); free off-season but reduced facilities. RV limit 35 ft. Pit toilets. No reservations.
GPS: 34.244665, -93.803983

BEAR CREEK CAMPGROUND

From Kirby at jct with US 70, 0.5 mi S on SR 27; 1.4 mi W. All year; 14-day limit. 19 sites (5 tent sites) without hookups, $5 during 3/1-10/31 ($2.50 with federal senior pass); free off-season but reduced facilities. RV limit 30 ft. Pit toilets. **GPS: 34.239173, -93.667184**

BUCKHORN CAMPGROUND

From Murfreesboro at jct with SR 27, 6 mi N on SR 19; 3 mi NW of dam; 2 mi E on gravel road following signs. All year; 14-day limit. 9 sites without hookups, $5 ($2.50 with federal senior pass); free off-season but reduced facilities. RV limit 30 ft. Pit toilets. **GPS: 34.1786, -93.7307**

COWHIDE COVE CAMPGROUND

From Kirby at jct with US 70, 5.9 mi S on SR 27; 2.7 mi W. All year; 14-day limit. 2 tent sites, $10 during 3/1-10/31 ($5 with federal senior pass); $6 rest of year ($3 with federal senior pass). 47 sites with elec, $13 base, $16 at premium sites during 3/1-10/31 ($6.50 & $8 with federal senior pass); $11 & $14 off-season ($5.50 & $7 with federal senior pass). RV limit 40 ft; 2 pull-through sites. ORVs prohibited. At reserved sites, 2-night minimum stay required on weekends, 3 nights on holiday weekends. Interpretive trail. NRRS (5/1-9/30). **GPS: 34.17444, -93.66861**

DAM AREA CAMPGROUND

From Murphreesboro, 6 mi N on Hwy 69; at the dam on E side. All year; 14-day limit. 24 sites with elec, $18 during 3/1-10/31 ($9 with federal senior pass); $14 rest of year ($7 with federal senior pass). RV limit 60 ft. Picnic shelter. **GPS: 34.1499, -93.7136**

KIRBY LANDING CAMPGROUND

From Kirby at jct with SR 27, 2.2 mi SW on US 70, then 1.2 mi S on access rd. All year; 14-day limit. 104 sites with elec, $13 base, $16 at premium sites during 3/1-10/31 ($6.50 & $8 with federal senior pass); $11 & $14 during off-season ($5.50 with federal senior pass). RV limit 45 ft; 6 pull-through sites. At reserved sites, 2-night minimum stay required on weekends, 3 nights on holiday weekends. Interpretive trail, ORVs prohibited. NRRS (5/1-9/30). **GPS: 34.23168, -93.69361**

LAUREL CREEK CAMPGROUND

From Kirby at jct with US 70, 2.4 mi S on SR 27; 3.4 mi SW on gravel rd. All year; 14-day limit. 24 sites, $5 during 3/1-10/31 ($2.50 with federal senior pass); free rest of year but reduced amenities. RV limit 20 ft. Pit toilets, no drkg wtr. **GPS: 34.1879, -93.7049**

PARKER CREEK CAMPGROUND

From the dam, 1.7 mi NW on gravel rd. All year; 14-day limit. 3 tent sites & 8 RV/tent sites without hookups, $10 ($5 with federal senior pass) during 3/1-10/31; $6 rest of year ($3 with federal senior pass). 49 sites with elec, $13 base, $16 at premium sites during 3/1-10/31 ($6.50 & $8 with federal senior pass); $11 & $14 rest of year ($6.50 & $7 with federal senior pass). RV limit 35 ft. ORVs prohibited. At reserved sites, 2-night minimum stay required on weekends, 3 nights on holiday weekends. NRRS (5/1-9/30). **GPS: 34.14167, -93,74583**

PIKEVILLE CAMPGROUND

From dam, 1.7 mi NW on gravel rd to Parker Creek Campground, then 1.5 mi NW. All year; 14-day limit. 12 sites (1 for tents), $5 during 3/1-10/31 ($2.50 with federal senior pass); free rest of year but reduced amenities. RV limit 30 ft. Pit toilets, no drkg wtr. **GPS: 34.1669, -93.7365**

ROCK CREEK

From dam, 6.7 mi NW around W side of dam on gravel roads, following signs. All year; 14-day limit. 14 free primitive sites. Pit toilets, no drkg wtr. **GPS: 34.2078, -93.7669**

SELF CREEK/JIM WYLIE CAMPGROUND

From Daisy at jct with US 70, 1 mi W across bridge on US 70. All year; 14-day limit. 76 sites. Tent sites & RV/tent sites without hookups, $10 during

3/1-10/31 ($5 with federal senior pass); $6 rest of year ($3 with federal senior pass). Sites with elec, $13 base, $16 at premium locations during 3/1-10/31 ($7 & $8 with federal senior pass); $11 & $14 off-season ($5.50 & $7 with federal senior pass). RV limit 45 ft; 23 pull-through sites. Picnic shelter for up to 60 people & 41 vehicles. **GPS: 34.2387, -93.7636**

STAR OF THE WEST CAMPGROUND

Near Newhope, from jct with SR 369, 4 mi W on US 70, then SW. All year; 14-day limit. 21 sites (8 for tents), $5 during 3/1-10/31 ($2.50 with federal senior pass); free rest of year but reduced amenities. Pit toilets. RV limit 50 ft; some pull-through sites. **GPS: 34.2403, -93.8332**

LAKE OUACHITA (VK) 11
GPS: 34.56939, -93.19464

This 40,060-acre lake is 13 mi NW of Hot Springs on US 270 and SR 277. It is 67 mi SW of Little Rock. It features 690 mi of shoreline, more than 200 islands -- many available for primitive camping. All reservable campsites are available on a first-come basis between 10/1 and 4/30. The Corps manages 17 campgrounds, with sites ranging from primitive to paved pull-throughs and modern amenities. Visitors to 10 p.m. ORV prohibited. Visitor center. Resource Manager, Lake Ouachita Field Office, 1201 Blakely Dam Road, Royal, AR 71968-9493. (501) 767-2108/2101.

AVANT CAMPGROUND

From Blue Springs at jct with SR 7, 16 mi W on SR 298; S to Avant; W on Camp Story Rd, continuing on Avant Campground access rd. All year; 14-day limit. Free primitive camping at undesignated sites; no facilities, no drkg wtr. **GPS: 34.6404, -93.3793**

BIG FIR CAMPGROUND

From Mt. Ida at jct with US 270, 5.1 mi NE on SR 27; 6.5 mi E on SR 188, then 4.5 mi E on gravel rd; on W end of lake. All year; 14-day limit.

29 sites without hookups, $10 & $14 during 3/1-10/31 ($5 with federal senior pass); free rest of year but limited services. RV limit 20'. Pit toilets, drkg wtr. **GPS: 34.313, -93.24483**

BRADY MOUNTAIN CAMPGROUND

From Royal at jct with US 270, 4 mi N through Bear in Brady Mountain Rd. All year; 14-day limit. 17 tent sites, $10 & $12 during 3/1-10/31 ($5 with federal senior pass); $8 rest of year ($4 with federal senior pass). 57 sites with elec, $14 base, $16 at premium locations (some 50-amp elec) during 3/1-10/31; $8 rest of year but reduced services. RV limit 55 ft. Picnic shelter, fish cleaning station, interpretive trail, marina, bridle trail. 3-night minimum stay required on holidays. (501) 760-1146. NRRS (5/1-9/30). **GPS: 34.58806, -93.26472**

BUCKVILLE CAMPGROUND

From Blue Springs at jct with SR 7, 16 mi W on SR 298, then S through Avant & 3.6 mi on gravel Buckville Rd, following signs; on N end of lake. All year; 14-day limit. 5 free primitive sites. RV limit 20 ft. Pit toilets, no drkg wtr. **GPS: 34.612, -93.3485**

CEDAR FOURCHE CAMPGROUND

From Lena at jct with SR 298, 1.1 mi S on gravel Rock Springs Rd; at split with Lena Landing access rd, continue W on Rock Springs Rd; right, then W on Cedar Fourche Rd. All year; 14-day limit. Free primitive camping. No facilities except showers, toilets. **GPS: 34.6649, -93.2826**

CRYSTAL SPRINGS CAMPGROUND

From Crystal Springs at jct with US 270, 2.9 mi N on Crystal Springs Rd. All year; 14-day limit. 11 tent sites, $10 base, $12 at premium locations during 5/1-9/30 ($5 & $6 with federal senior pass); $8 rest of year but reduced services ($4 with federal senior pass). 63 sites with elec, $16 base, $18 at premium locations during 5/1-9/30 ($8 & $9 with federal senior pass); $8 & $12 rest of year but reduced services ($4 & $6 with federal senior pass). RV limit 55 ft; 6 pull-through sites. Picnic shelter for up to 125 people & 21 vehicles, fish cleaning station, change shelter. At reserved sites, 2-night minimum stay required on weekends, 3 nights on holiday weekends. Overflow camping offered on major holidays. (501) 991-3390. NRRS (5/1-9/30). **GPS: 34.54694, -93.36111**

DENBY POINT CAMPGROUND

From Silver, 0.7 mi E on US 270; 0.8 mi N on Denby Rd. All year; 14-day limit. 9 tent sites, $10 base, $12 at premium locations during 5/1-9/30 ($5 & $6 with federal senior pass); $8 rest of year but reduced services ($4 with federal senior pass). 58 sites with elec, $14 base, $16 at premium locations during 5/1-9/30 ($7 & $8 with federal senior pass); $8 & $10 rest of year but reduced services ($4 & $5 with federal senior pass). RV limit 55 ft. Two group camping areas with elec for up to 125 people & 12 vehicles: Loop A $60, Loop B $65. Fish cleaning station, interpretive trail, amphitheater. Boat rentals nearby. At reserved sites, 2-night minimum stay required on weekends, 3 nights on holiday weekends. (501) 867-4475. NRRS (5/1-9/30). **GPS: 34.55194, -93.49333**

IRONS FORK

From Story at jct with SR 27, 8.3 mi E on SR 298; 1.3 mi SE on gravel rd; at N side of lake. All year; 14-day limit. 45 free primitive sites. Pit toilets, concrete tbls, ground grills, lantern posts. **GPS: 34.6903, -93.3725**

JOPLIN CAMPGROUND

From Joplin at jct with US 270, 2.4 mi N on Mountain Harbor Rd, turning left at campground sign. All year; 14-day limit. 50 RV/tent sites without hookups, $10 base, $12 at premium locations during 5/1-10/31 ($5 & $6 with federal senior pass); $8 rest of year but reduced amenities. 36 sites with elec, $14 base, $16 at premium locations during 5/1-10/31 ($7 & $8 with federal senior pass); $10 & $12 rest of year but reduced amenities ($5 & $6 with federal senior pass). 30-ft RV limit, but recommended for small RVs such as fold-outs, truck & van campers without slide-outs. Bridle trail, fish cleaning station. Boat rentals, marina nearby. At reserved sites, 2-night minimum stay required on weekends, 3 nights on holiday weekends. NRRS (5/1-9/30). **GPS: 34.57528, -93.44028**

LENA LANDING CAMPGROUND

From Lena at jct with SR 298, 1.1 mi S on gravel Rock Springs Rd; SE on Lena Landing access rd. All year; 14-day limit. 10 sites without hookups, $12 base, premium sites $14 during 3/1-10/31 ($6 & $7 with federal senior pass); free off-season but no amenities. RV limit 35'. **GPS: 34.6698, -93.2762**

LITTLE FIR CAMPGROUND

From SR 27 at Rubie, 3 mi E on SR 188; 2.2 mi N; turn right at campground sign. All year; 14-day limit. 29 sites without hookups, $12 base, $14 at premium locations during 3/1-10/31 ($6 & $7 with federal senior pass); free camping off-season, but no amenities (off-season fees charged previously). RV limit 55 ft. Group camping, $30. Flush toilets in-season, fish cleaning station, pedestal grill, lantern post, concrete tbls. **GPS: 34.699, -93.4726**

RABBIT TAIL CAMPGROUND

From Blue Springs at jct with SR 7, 16 mi W on SR 298; S through Avant on Bucksville Rd; E on access rd to Rabbit Tail Campground. All year; 14-day limit. Free primitive camping at undesignated sites. No facilities, no drkg wtr. **GPS: 34.6193, -93.338**

STEPHENS PARK

From Mountain Pine, 1 mi W on Blakely Dam Rd past school, below dam. All year; 14-da limit. 9 sites without hookups, $12 base, $14 at premium locations during 3/1-10/31 ($6 & $7 with federal senior pass); free camping off-season, but no amenities (off-season fees charged previously). RV limit 35 ft. Flush showers in-season, concrete tbls, pedestal grills, lantern posts, picnic shelter. Boat ramp at Avery Park. **GPS: 34.5708, -93.1903**

SPILLWAY PARK

Below dam. Group camping area with 6 sites, $30. Call project office for information. **GPS: 34.5667, -93.2186**

TOMPKINS BEND CAMPGROUND

From Joplin, 1 mi W on US 270; 2.4 mi N on Shangri-La Rd. All year; 14-day limit. 13 tent sites, $10 base, $12 at premium locations during 5/1-9/30 ($5 & $6 with federal senior pass); $8 rest of year but reduced amenities. 61 sites with elec, $14 base, $18 at prime locations (some 50-amp elec) during 5/1-9/30; rest of year, $8 & $12 but reduced amenities ($4 & $6 with federal senior pass). RV limit 55 ft. Amphitheater, fish cleaning station. At reserved sites, 2-night minimum stay required on weekends, 3 nights on holiday weekends. (501) 867-4476. NRRS (5/1-9/30). **GPS: 34.57306, -93.46889**

TWIN CREEK CAMPGROUND

From Silver, 1 mi NW on gravel road. All year; 14-day limit. 15 sites without hookups, $10 base, $14 at premium locations during 3/1-10/31 ($5 & $7 with federal senior pass); free rest of year, but no amenities. RV limit 20 ft. Overflow camping offered on major holidays. Boat rentals nearby. Flush toilets in-season, pit toilets off-season, pedestal grills, lantern posts, concrete tbls. **GPS: 34.5478, -93.5119**

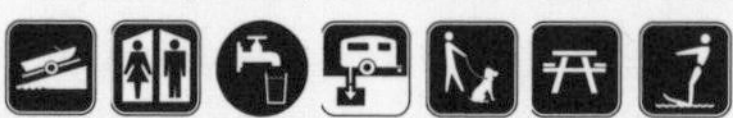

WASHITA CAMPGROUND

From Story at jct with SR 298, S on US 27 to Washita Campground; on

Muddy Creek arm of lake at confluence with Ouachita River. All year; 14-day limit. Free primitive camping at undesignated sites. No facilities, no drkg wtr. **GPS: 34.6578, -93.5321**

MILLWOOD LAKE (LR) 12
GPS: 33.695, -93.9617

This 29,000-acre lake is 9 mi E of Ashdown on SR 32 and 28 mi N of Texarkana. For lake level information, call (870) 898-4533/1-888-687-9830. Visitor center, interpretive programs. For 2011, none of the Millwood campgrounds is utilizing recreation.gov (the National Recreation Reservation Service) for reservations. Project Manager, Millwood Tri Lakes Office, 1528 Highway 32 E, Ashdown, AR 71822. (870) 898-3343, extension 3.

BEARD'S BLUFF CAMPGROUND

From Ashdown, 13 mi E on SR 32; between the road & lake, upstream from dam's E embankment (signs). All year; 14-day limit. Sites without hookups, $10 ($5 with federal senior pass). 28 paved sites with elec/wtr, $13 base, $15 at premium locations during 3/1-10/31 ($6.50 & $7.50 with federal senior pass); $11 rest of year ($5.50 with federal senior pass). 3 sites with full hookups, $15 during 3/1-10/31 ($7.50 with federal senior pass), $13 rest of year ($6.50 with federal senior pass). Group camping area available. Picnic shelter & reservable outdoor wedding chapel, $25 (call 870-388-9556). Amphitheater. **GPS: 33.70429, -93.93908**

BEARD'S LAKE CAMPGROUND

From Ashdown, 12 mi E on SR 32; 1.5 mi W on access rd, below the dam. All year; 14-day limit. 3 shoreline tent sites & sites without hookups, $9 during 3/1-10/31 ($4.50 with federal senior pass); $8 rest of year ($4 with federal senior pass). 5 paved sites with elec/wtr, $13 during 3/1-10/31 ($6.50 with federal senior pass); $9 rest of year ($4.50 with federal senior pass). Hiking trail with boardwalk. Area inhabited by alligators. Pit toilets. Use dump, showers, playground, beach, flush toilets at Beard's Bluff. **GPS: 33.6958, -93.94398**

COTTONSHED LANDING CAMPGROUND

From Ashdown, 20 mi E on SR 32; N on SR 355 to Tollette; 8 mi W on CR 234 to Schaal, 2 mi S on access rd. All year; 14-day limit. 46 paved sites with elec/wtr, $13 base, $15 at prime locations during 3/1-10/31 ($6.50 & $7.50 with federal senior pass); $11 rest of year. Picnic shelter, $25 (for reservations, 870-287-71189). Fish cleaning station. **GPS: 33.79123, -93.96602**

PARALOMA LANDING CAMPGROUND

From Brownstown at jct with SR 317, 4 mi SE through Paraloma on SR 234. 34 paved sites with elec/wtr, $11 during 3/1-10/31 ($5.50 with federal senior pass); $8 rest of year ($4 with federal senior pass). Some pull-through sites. Fish cleaning station, pit toilets. **GPS: 33.786865, -94.009766**

RIVER RUN EAST CAMPGROUND

From Ashdown, 12 mi E on SR 32; below the dam on shore of Little River outlet channel. All year; 14-day limit. 8 gravel sites without hookups, $5 ($2.50 with federal senior pass). Pit toilets. **GPS: 33.697354, -93.943312**

RIVER RUN WEST CAMPGROUND

From Ashdown, 10 mi E on SR 32; below dam, W side of Little River outlet channel. All year; 14-day limit. 4 gravel sites without hookups, $5 ($2.50 with federal senior pass). Pit toilets. **GPS: 33.691306, -93.966513**

SARATOGA LANDING CAMPGROUND

From Saratoga, 1 mi S on SR 32; 1 mi W on access rd. All year; 14-day limit. 17 gravel sites without hookups, $5 ($2.50 with federal senior pass. Picnic shelter, pit toilets, fishing pier. **GPS: 33.7255, -93.922766**

WHITE CLIFFS CAMPGROUND

From Brownstown at jct with SR 234, 4 mi S on gravel SR 317. All year; 14-day limit. 18 gravel sites without hookups, $5 ($2.50 with federal senior pass. Group camping available. ORV area & hiking trail on adjacent property. Pit toilets. **GPS: 33.76082, -94.058544**

NIMROD LAKE (LR) 13

GPS: 34.9517, -93.06

This 3,550-acre lake is 8.3 mi SE of Ola on SR 7 and 66 mi NW of Little Rock in N-central Arkansas. Off-road vehicles prohibited. Campground checkout time 1 p.m. Three of the lake's campgrounds (Quarry Cove, County Line and Carter Cove) are on the lake. Sunlight Bay is on Wilson Slough upstream from the lake, and River Road is on the Fourche LaFavre River downstream from the dam. Camping available all year with reduction of services and facilities off-season. Carden Point is the only day use area; its facilities include a boat ramp, group shelter, picnicking, playground and beach. Interpretive programs. Project Office, Nimrod Lake, 3 Highway 7 S, Plainview, AR 72857-9600. (479) 272-4324.

CARTER COVE CAMPGROUND

From Plainview, 3.4 mi SE on SR 60, following signs; 0.8 mi S on access rd. All year; 14-day limit. 34 sites with elec/wtr, $14 ($7 with federal senior pass. RV limit 30 ft. Picnic shelter for up to 50 people & 26 vehicles. At reserved sites, 2-night minimum stay required on weekends, 3 nights on holiday weekends. Fish cleaning station. (479) 272-4983. NRRS (5/15-10/25). **GPS: 34.96111, -93.23861**

COUNTY LINE CAMPGROUND

From Plainview, 7 mi E on SR 60; S of road (signs). All year; 14-day limit. 20 sites with elec/wtr, $16 base, $18 at premium locations ($8 & $9 with federal senior pass). RV limit 30 ft. At reserved sites, 2-night minimum stay required on weekends, 3 nights on holiday weekends. Fish cleaning station. (479) 272-4945. NRRS (5/15-10/25). **GPS: 34.96333, -93.18805**

QUARRY COVE CAMPGROUND

From Ola, 9 mi SE on SR 7; 0.5 mi W on SR 60 to access rd. All year; 14-day limit 31 sites with elec/wtr, $14 ($7 with federal senior pass). RV limit 30 ft. Showers closed in winter. Picnic shelter, fish cleaning station, amphitheater. At reserved sites, 2-night minimum stay required on weekends, 3 nights on holiday weekends. NRRS 3/15-10/25. (479) 272-4233. **GPSS: 34.95611, -93.16556**

RIVER ROAD CAMPGROUND

From Ola, 9 mi SE on SR 7; 0.3 mi On River Rd; below dam on the Fourche Lefave River. All year; 14-day limit. 21 sites with elec (no wtr hookups), $13 ($6.50 with federal senior pass). RV limit 30 ft; 2 pull-through sites. Picnic shelter, nature trail. At reserved sites, 2-night minimum stay required on weekends, 3 nights on holiday weekends. (479) 272-4835. NRRS (3/15-10/25). **GPS: 34.95028, -93.15611**

SUNLIGHT BAY CAMPGROUND

From Plainview at jct with SR 28, 3.5 mi S on Sunlight Bay Rd. All year; 14-day limit. 29 sites with elec/wtr, $14 ($7 with federal senior pass). RV limit 30 ft. Picnic shelter, fish cleaning station. Showers closed in winter. At reserved sites, 2-night minimum stay required on weekends, 3 nights on holiday weekends. (479) 272-4234. NRRS (3/15-10/25). **GPS: 34.95472, -93.30389**

NORFORK LAKE (LR) 14
GPS: 36.25, -92.24

This 22,000-acre lake is 4 mi NE of Norfork on SR 177 near the Missouri state line and SE of Branson, Missouri. Off-road vehicles prohibited.

Campground checkout time 3 p.m. Campsites that are free in winter may have reduced amenities. Resource Manager, Norfolk Lake, P. O. Box 2070, Mountain Home, AR 72654-2070. (870) 425-2700. See Missouri listings.

BIDWELL POINT CAMPGROUND

From Mountain Home at jct with SR 201, 9 mi NE on US 62; 2 mi N across bridge on SR 101; on NE side (right). 4/1-9/30; 14-day limit. 2 sites without hookups, $14 ($7 with federal senior pass). 46 sites with 30-amp elec, $18 ($9 with federal senior pass). RV limit 40 ft. Picnic shelter with elec for up to 200 people & 50 vehicles, $52. At reserved sites, 2-night minimum stay required on weekends, 3 nights on holiday weekends. (870) 467-5375. NRRS (5/16-9/13) **GPS: 36.38611, -92.2375**

CALAMITY BEACH PARK

From Howards Ridge at jct with CR 526, 3 mi S on SR 201 (Pigeon Creek Rd); 3 mi E on CR 37; N on Calamity Beach access rd. All year; 14-day limit. Free primitive undesignated sites. Pit toilet, no drkg wtr. Get free camping permit from lake office.

CRANFIELD CAMPGROUND

From Mountain Home at jct with SR 201, 5.5 mi E on US 62 (signs); 1.6 mi N (left) on CR 34. 4/1-9/30; 14-day limit. 4/1-9/30; 14-day limit. 67 sites with 30-amp elec, $18 ($9 with federal senior pass). RV limit 35 ft; 6 pull-through sites, 2 handicap sites. Two picnic shelters for up to 60 people & 20 vehicles, $52. At reserved sites, 2-night minimum stay required on weekends, 3 nights on holiday weekends. Amphitheater, change shelter, phone, marina, canoeing, handicap accessible fishing area. (870) 492-4191. NRRS (5/16-9/13). **GPS: 36.40472, -92.32083**

CURLEY POINT PARK

From Elizabeth, 2 mi S on SR 87; 3 mi W on Kerley Point Rd. All year; 14-day limit. Free primitive camping at undesignated sites. No facilities, no drkg wtr. Get free camping permit from lake office.

GAMALIEL CAMPGROUND

From Mountain Home, 9 mi NE on US 62; 4.5 mi N on SR 101; 3 mi SE on CR 42. 4/1-9/30; 14-day limit. 64 sites with 30-amp elec, $16 base, $18 at premium locations ($8 & $9 with federal senior pass). RV limit 40 ft; 3 pul-through sites, 3 handicap sites. Picnic shelter for up to 100 people & 20 vehicles, $42. At reserved sites, 2-night minimum stay required on weekends, 3 nights on holiday weekends. (870) 467-5680. NRRS (5/16-9/13). **GPS: 36.42111, -93.22222**

HENDERSON CAMPGROUND

From Mountain Home at jct with SR 201, 10 mi E on US 62; cross lake bridge; E side (left, signs); on a peninsula in central area of lake. 4/1-9/30; 14-day limit. 38 sites with 30-amp elec, $16 ($8 with federal senior pass). RV limit 30 ft; 4 pull-through sites. No reservations. Picnic shelter $40-$42 (NRRS). Marine dump station. (870) 488-5282. **GPS: 36.37083, -92.23417**

JORDAN CAMPGROUND

From Jordan, 2.5 mi N on CR 64; at SE end of lake. 4/1-9/30; 14-day limit. 7 tent sites, $7 & $9 ($3.50 & $4.50 with federal senior pass); 31 sites with elec, $16 ($8 with federal senior pass). In off-season, some sites may be open & free. RV limit 30 ft. No reservations. (870) 499-7223. **GPS: 36.27, -92.19361**

JORDAN COVE PARK

From Jordan, 2.5 mi N on CR 64; just W of Jordan Campground. All year; 14-day limit. Free primitive camping at undesignated sites. No facilities, no drkg wtr. Get free camping permit from lake office.

JORDAN ISLAND

From Jordan, 2.5 mi N on CR 64 to Jordan Campground; launch boat, then N on Lake Norfork to sand-covered Jordan Island (formerly called Sandy Island). Free primitive tent camping; no facilities, no drkg wtr. Get free camping permit from lake office.

PANTHER BAY CAMPGROUND

From Mountain Home at jct with SR 201, 8.6 mi E on US 62; 1 mi N on SR 101; right on 1st access rd (signs). 4/1-9/30; 14-day limit. 7 sites without hookups, $9 ($4.50 with federal senior pass); 15 sites with elec, $18 ($9 with federal senior pass). Picnic shelter, marine dump station. (870) 492-4544. **GPS: 36.37657, -92.25921**

QUARRY COVE/DAM SITE A CAMPGROUND

From Norfork, 2.9 mi NE to Salesville on SR 5; 2 mi E on SR 177 (signs). All year; 14-day limit. 67 sites with elec, $18 ($9 with federal senior pass). RV limit 60 ft; 2 pull-through sites. Group camping area without elec for up to 150 people, $62. Picnic shelters, $40 & $52. Handicap accessible fishing area. 2-night minimum stay required on weekends, 3 nights on holiday weekends. (870) 499-7216. NRRS (5/16-9/13).Some sites closed in 2011 due to renovations. **GPS: 36.25833, -92.24056**

ROBINSON POINT CAMPGROUND

From Mountain Home at jct with SR 201, 9 mi E on US 62; 2.5 mi S (right) on CR 279 (signs). 4/1-10/31; 14-day limit. 102 sites with 30-amp elec, $18 ($9 with federal senior pass). RV limit 40 ft; 3 pull-through sites, 1 handicap site. Amphitheater. Picnic shelter for up to 36 people & 20 vehicles, $42. At reserved sites, 2-night minimum stay required on weekends, 3 nights on holiday weekends. (870) 492-6853. NRRS (5/17-9/13) **GPS: 36.35278, -92.23944**

OZARK LAKE (LR) 15
GPS: 35.4733, -93.81

This 10,600-acre lake has 173 mi of shoreline and is SW of Ozark, 39 mi E of Ft. Smith. Campground checkout time 2 p.m. Alcohol prohibited. Park Manager, Ozark Lake, 6042 Lock and Dam Road, Ozark, AR 7294. (479) 667-1100/2129 or 1-800-844-2129.

AUX ARC CAMPGROUND

From Ozark, 1.3 mi S on SR 23; 1 mi E on SR 309; left at Aux Arc access road. All year; 14-day limit. 4 sites without hookups, $10 ($5 with federal senior pass); 57 sites with elec $18, $20 for elec/wtr ($9 & $10 with federal senior pass. RV limit in excess of 65 ft. Three picnic shelters with elec, $50. At reserved sites, 2-night minimum stay required/weekends, 3 nights on holiday weekends. (479) 667-1100. NRRS (3/1-10/31).
GPS: 35.47028, -93.81806

CITADEL BLUFF CAMPGROUND

From Cecil, 1.6 mi N on SR 41. All year; 14-day limit. 25 primitive sites without hookups, $10 ($5 with federal senior pass). Picnic shelter, pit toilets, drkg wtr. RV limit 35'. **GPS: 35.462646, -93.945557**

CLEAR CREEK PARK

From Alma, 5.2 mi S on SR 162, following signs; 3.6 mi E (left) on Clear Creek Rd. All year; 14-day limit. 11 sites without hookups, $10 ($5 with federal senior pass); 25 sites with elec, $16 ($8 with federal senior pass). RV limit in excess of 65 ft; 4 pull-through sites. No reservations. Some sites may be open & free 11/1-2/28. Picnic shelter $50. Day use fees for picnicking, boat ramp, dump station.(479) 632-4882.
GPS: 35.43792, -94.18329

RIVER RIDGE PARK

From Cecil, 12 mi W on SR 96; 1.2 mi NE on Hoover's Ferry Rd. 4/1-9/30; 14-day limit. 18 primitive sites, free. Pit toilets, drkg wtr. **GPS: 35.443761, -94.071103**

SPRINGHILL PARK

From Ft. Smith at jct with I-540 exit 3, 7.3 mi S on SR 59 (signs). All year; 14-day limit. 3 sites without hookups, $10 ($5 with federal senior pass). 15 sites with 30-amp elec/wtr, $18; 10 sites with 50-amp elec (no wtr hookups), $18; 17 sites with 50-amp elec/wtr, $20 ($9 & $10 with federal senior pass). RV limit in excess of 65 ft. Some sites may have reduced fees & reduced services in winter. Group camping area. 5 picnic shelters, $50. Day use fees for picnicking, boat ramp, dump station. (479) 452-4598. **GPS: 35.343018, -94.296143**

VINE PRAIRIE PARK

From Mulberry, 1.7 mi S on SR 917. All year; 14-day limit. 7 sites without hookups, $10 ($5 with federal senior pass); 12 sites with elec, $16 ($8 with federal senior pass). Picnic shelter, $50. Day use fees for picnicking, boat ramp, dump. 479-997-8122. **GPS: 34.485596, -94.062744**

ARKANSAS RIVER AREA (LR)
WILBUR D. MILLS POOL, LOCK #2
ARKANSAS POST TO PINE BLUFF
GPS: 34.24, -91.96

Pine Bluff Project Office, P. O. Box 7835, Pine Bluff, AR 71611. (870) 534-0451.

MERRISACH LAKE PARK

From Tichnor at jct with SR 44, 8.2 mi S; exit NW near project office (signs). All year; 14-day limit. 70 sites. 5 sites without hookups, $11 base, $12 at premium locations ($5.50 & $6 with federal senior pass). Sites with 30-amp elec/wtr, $16, $18 at premium locations; sites with 50-amp elec/wtr, $19 ($8, $9 & $9.50 with federal senior pass). RV limit in excess of 65 ft. Picnic shelters, $30 without elec, $40 with elec. Interpretive trail. NRRS. **GPS: 34.0303, -91.2664**

NOTREBES BEND PARK

From Tichnor at jct with SR 44, 8.2 mi S across canal W of project office, then 5.5 mi W; on E side of dam. 4/1-10/30; 14-day limit. 30 sites with 50-amp elec/wtr, $19 ($9.50 with federal senior pass). RV limit 50 ft. Checkout time 2 p.m. Gate lock combination provided for late entry by registered campers. NRRS. **GPS: 33.98806, -91.30917**

PENDLETON BEND PARK

From Dumas, 9 mi N on US 65; 2 mi E on SR 212 (signs). All year; 14-day limit. 31 sites with elec, $16 base for 30-amp elec, $17 at premium locations, $19 for 50-amp elec/wtr ($8, $8.50 & $9.50 with federal senior pass). RV limit 40 ft; 2 pull-through sites. Picnic shelter for up to 75 people & 12 vehicles, $40. Gate lock combination provided for late entry by registered campers. Checkout time 2 p.m. (870) 479-3292. NRRS. **GPS: 33.98944, -91.35722**

WILBUR D. MILLS PARK

From Dumas, 9 mi N on US 65; 2 mi E on SR 212 (signs), then through Pendleton Bend Park. 3/4-10/31; 14-day limit. 21 sites with elec/wtr, $16 ($8 with federal senior pass). RV limit 60 ft. Checkout time 2 p.m. 1 handicap site. NRRS. **GPS: 33.97889, -91.30861**

ARKANSAS RIVER AREA
POOL 3, POOL 5 & TERRY LOCK & DAM
PINE BLUFF TO LITTLE ROCK (LR) 17
GPS: 34.24, -91.96

Pine Bluff Resident Office, P. O. Box 7835, Pine Bluff, AR 71611. (870) 534-0451.

RISING STAR PARK

From Linwood at jct with US 65, 3.6 mi E on Blankinship Rd, then follow signs. 3/1-10/31; 14-day limit. 24 sites with 50-amp elec/wtr, $19 ($9.50 with federal senior pass). RV limit 50 ft. Picnic shelter $60. NRRS (5/19-9/19). **GPS: 34.16889, -91.73667**

TAR CAMP PARK

From Redfield at jct with US 65/SR 46, 5.8 mi E, following signs.3/1-10/31; 14-day limit. 8 sites without hookups, $9 ($4.50 with federal senior pass); 45 sites with 50-amp elec/wtr, $19 ($9.50 with federal senior pass). RV limit 40 ft. Two picnic shelters for up to 60 people & 20 vehicles, $60. At reserved sites, 2-night minimum stay required on weekends, 3 nights on holiday weekends. NRRS (3/1-9/15). **GPS: 34.44972, -92.1125**

WILLOW BEACH PARK

From N of Little Rock on I-440, 2.5 mi E on US 165; S on Colonel Manard Rd, then 1 mi W on Blue Heron (signs). All year; 14-day limit. 21 sites with 50-amp elec/wtr, $19 ($9.50 with federal senior pass). RV limit 40 ft. Two picnic shelters for up to 60 people & 20 vehicles, $50 (no elec) & $60 (with elec). Handicap accessible fishing area. (501) 961-1332. NRRS (5/18-9/19). **GPS: 34.69917, -92.13722**

ARKANSAS RIVER AREA
TOAD SUCK FERRY & MURRAY L&D
LITTLE ROCK TO DARDANELLE (LR) 18
GPS: 34.79, -92.26

Checkout time is 2 p.m. Resource Manager, Toad Suck Ferry, Rt. 5, Box 199, Conway, AR 72032. (501) 329-2986.

CHEROKEE L&D #9 PARK

From Morrilton, 0.7 mi S on Cherokee St; 0.8 mi S on Quincy Rd (signs). 3/1-10/31; 14-day limit. 33 sites with wtr/elec, $14 for 30-amp elec/wtr; $20 for 50-amp elec/wtr. Two picnic shelters available all year (for reservations, office), $50. (501) 354-9155. **GPS: 35.13916, -92.740479**

CYPRESS CREEK CAMPGROUND

From Houston at jct with SR 216, 2 mi N on SR 113. 3/1-10/31; 14-day limit. Free. 9 sites no hookups. RV limit 40'. **GPS: 35.069576, -92.716021**

MAUMELLE PARK

From jct with I-430, 4 mi W on SR 10 (Cantrell Rd); 4 mi N on Pinnacle Valley Rd (signs). All year; 14-day limit. 98 sites. Sites $22 for 30-amp elec/wtr; $24 for 50-amp elec/wtr; $26 for 50-amp elec/wtr at waterfront sites ($11, $12 & $23 with federal senior pass). RV limit in excess of 65 ft; 3 pull-through sites, 1 handicap site. Eight picnic shelters, $50. At reserved sites, 2-night minimum stay required on weekends, 3 nights on holiday weekends. (501) 868-9477. NRRS. **GPS: 34.82944, -92.43194**

POINT REMOVE PARK

From Morrilton, 0.7 mi S on Cherokee St. 3/1-10/31. Free. 16 sites. **GPS: 35.123535, -92.785156**

SEQUOYA CAMPGROUND

From Morriton, 4 mi S on SR 9; 2 mi W on River View Rd. All year; 14-day limit. 14 sites with elec, $14. Picnic shelter, $50. **GPS: 35.17, -92.78**

TOAD SUCK FERRY CAMPGROUND

From near Conway at I-40 exit 129, 7 mi W on SR 60 (signs); 0.5 mi E on access road. 48 sites with wtr/elec, $18 for 30-amp elec, $$20 for 50-amp. RV limit in excess of 65 ft. Five picnic shelters, $50. At reserved sites, 2-night minimum stay required on weekends, 3 nights on holiday weekends. (501) 759-2005. NRRS (3/1-10/31).
GPS: 35.07389, -92.54472

TABLE ROCK LAKE (LR) 19
GPS: 36.48, -93.30

In N-central Arkansas S of Branson, Missouri, Table Rock is SR 165 W of US 65. Visitor center with exhibits, auditorium, audiovisual presentations. Resource Manager, Upper White River Project Office, 4600 State Road 165 Ste. A, Branson, MO 65616-8976. (417) 344-4101. See Missouri listings.

CRICKET CREEK CAMPGROUND

From Ridgedale, MO, 5.3 mi SW on SR 14 (signs). 4/1-9/15; 14-day limit. About 35 sites. Sites without hookups, $14 ($7 with federal senior pass); sites with elec, $18 ($9 with federal senior pass); sites with elec/wtr, $19 ($9.50 with federal senior pass). RV limit in excess of 65 ft; 4 pull-through sites. Non-campers pay $4 day use fee for boat ramp, dump station, picnicking, beach, sand volleyball. At reserved sites, 2-night minimum stay required on weekends, 3 nights on holiday weekends. (870) 426-3331. NRRS. **GPS: 36.4831, -93.3003.**

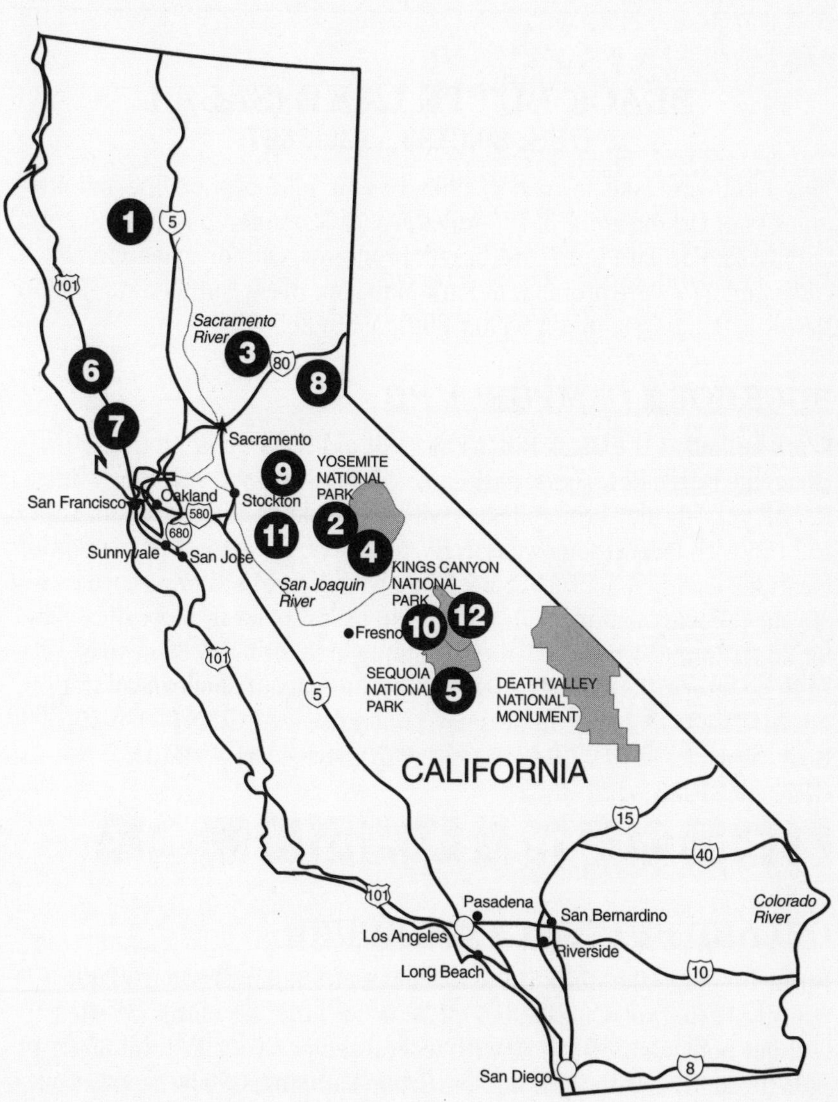

1
5
101
Sacramento River
3
80
6
8
7
Sacramento
9
YOSEMITE NATIONAL PARK
San Francisco
Oakland
Stockton
580
680
2
11
4
Sunnyvale
San Jose
KINGS CANYON NATIONAL PARK
San Joaquin River
12
10
Fresno
101
SEQUOIA NATIONAL PARK
5
DEATH VALLEY NATIONAL MONUMENT
5
CALIFORNIA
15
40
101
Pasadena
San Bernardino
Colorado River
Los Angeles
Riverside
Long Beach
10
8
San Diego

CALIFORNIA

State Capital: **Sacramento**
Nickname: **Golden State**
Statehood Year: **1850**

31ST STATE

BLACK BUTTE LAKE (SAC) 1
GPS: 39.8183, -122.3367

This 4,460-acre lake, formed in 1963, has 40 miles of shoreline and is 8 miles W of Orland and I-5, 100 miles NW of Sacramento in north-central California. For dam tours and ranger programs, call for scheduling. ORVs and ATV's are prohibited. Park Manager, Black Butte Lake, 19225 Newville Road, Orland, CA 95963-8901. (530) 865-4781.

BUCKHORN CAMPGROUND

From Orland at the Black Butte Lake exit of I-5, 14 mi W on CR 200 (Newville Rd), follow signs, past dam; 0.5 mi SW of jct with Black Butte Rd. All year; 14-day limit. 65 sites without hookups. 5 walk-to tent sites, $12 ($6 with federal senior pass). RV/tent sites, $12 base, $15 at premium locations during 4/1-10/31 ($6 & $7.50 with federal senior pass); $12 rest of year ($6 with senior pass). RV limit in excess of 65 ft; most sites okay for 35 ft; 28 pull-through. Group camping area for up to 80 people, $90-$120 by reservation. Picnic shelters, amphitheater, fish cleaning station, interpretive trail. Non-campers pay $5 day use fee. NRRS (4/1-9/30). Boat ramp closed in 2010 for renovation; check current status.
GPS: 39.81083, -122.36528

ORLAND BUTTES CAMPGROUND

From Orland at the Black Butte Lake exit of I-5, 6 mi W on CR 200; 3.3 mi SW (left) on CR 206; 0.5 mi W. 4/1-9/11; 14-day limit. 35 sites without hookups, $15 ($7.50 with federal senior pass). RV limit 35 ft; 18 pull-through. Limited lake access. Group camping, $90 by reservation. Amphitheater, fish cleaning station. NRRS. **GPS: 39.7725, -122.35167**

EASTMAN LAKE (SAC) 2
GPS: 37.2167, -119.9833

This 1,780-acre lake is 25 mi NE of Chowchilla, 55 mi N of Fresno. Day use fee for non-campers, $4. Park Manager, Eastman Lake, P. O. Box 67, Raymond, CA 93653-0067. (559) 689-3255.

CODORNIZ RECREATION AREA

From Raymond on SR 99, E on 26th Ave; N on Hwy 29 (signs). All year; 14-day limit. 88 sites. 3 tent sites, $16 ($8 with federal senior pass). 42 sites without hookups, $20 ($10 with federal senior pass). Sites with elec/wtr or full hookups $30 ($15 with federal senior pass). Primitive equestrian sites with wtr hookups, $10; may be reserved by equestrian groups & non-profit organizations. RV limit in excess of 65 ft; 14 pull-through sites. Picnic shelter, amphitheater, fish cleaning station, visitor center, bike/hiking/bridle trails, canoeing, disc golf, horseshoe pits, volleyball court, free wireless Internet service. NRRS.
GPS: 37.21583, -119.96861

Here are the recreation area's other camping areas:

Wildcat Group Camp, on the E side of the lake. 19 primitive sites (7 pull-through & 3 horse sites) with wtr for overflow, Scouts, non-profit groups & large family equestrian sites, $20 individual sites, $60 groups.

Equestrian Camp for groups of up to 60 people & 30 vehicles, $60. Amphitheater, corral, hitching posts, toilets, dump, drkng wtr, bridle trails access. Individual sites $10.

North Group Camp A for up to 40 people & 15 vehicles, $80. Showers, toilets, drkg wtr, dump, hiking trail access.

North Group Camp B for up to 100 people & 25 vehicles, $90. Showers, toilets, dump, drkg wtr, elec, hiking trail access.

South Group Camp for up to 160 people & 50 vehicles, $100. Showers, toilets, drkg wtr, dump, elec, hiking trail access, playground.

ENGLEBRIGHT LAKE (SAC) 3
GPS: 39.24, -121.26

815-acre lake with 24 mi of shoreline 21 miles E of Marysville on SR 20 and 75 mi NE of Sacramento. Group tours, ranger programs. Park Mgr., Englebright Lake, P. O. Box 6, Smartville, CA 95977-0006. (530) 432-6427.

BOAT IN CAMPING

From Marysville, 21 mi E on SR 20; left on Mooney Flat Rd, then 2.5 mi to Point Defiance Park. Boat-in to 100 free primitive shoreline sites. 5/1-9/30; 14-day limit. Tbls, fire grates, lantern pole, portable toilets. Drkg wtr near boat ramps. **GPS: 39.23, -121.26**

POINT DEFIANCE RECREATION AREA

From Marysvile, 21 mi E on SR 20; left on Mooney Flat Rd, then 2.5 mi to park. All year; 14-day limit. 7 primitive sites for groups up to 50 people, $50-$75. Picnic shelters, $50 Sunday-Thursday; Friday-Saturday, $75 (reservation required). **GPS: 39.67, -121.26**

HENSLEY LAKE (SAC) 4
GPS: 37.12, -119.88

This 1,500-acre lake is 17 mi NE of Madera on SR 400 and N of Fresno. Multi-use trails available. Contact office for tours and ranger programs. Resource Mgr., Hensley Lake, P. O. Box 85, Raymond, CA 93653. (559) 673-5151.

HIDDEN VIEW CAMPGROUND

From Chowchilla at jct with SR 99, follow Ave. 26 (signs). All year; 14-day limit. $20 at 40 sites no hookups ($10 with federal senior pass); $30 at 15 sites elec ($15 with federal senior pass. RV limit in excess of 65 ft; 17 pull-through, 1 handicap with wtr/elec (call for reservation). 2 group camping areas no hookups, $100. Self-guided nature trail. Non-campers pay $4 day use fee. 3-day minimum stay required on holiday weekends. NRRS. **GPS: 37.12472, -119.89722**

KAWEAH LAKE (SAC) 5
GPS: 36.44, -119.03

This 1,945-acre lake is 3 miles NE of Lemoncove on SR 198, SE of Fresno and 21 miles E of Visalia. Visitor center at Lemon Hill Park. Swimming permitted unless otherwise posted. Fee for non-camper use of showers, dump station. Contact office for scheduling group tours and ranger programs. Resource Manager, Kaweah Lake, P. O. Box 44270, Lemoncove, CA 93244-4270. (559) 597-2301.

HORSE CREEK CAMPGROUND

From dam, 3 mi E on SR 198; left side (signs). 10 mi from Sequoia National Park. All year; 14-day limit. 80 sites without hookups, $16 ($8 with federal senior pass). RV limit 35 ft; 35 pull-through sites, 1 handicap site. Overflow area open on major holidays. 3-day minimum stay on holiday weekends. Evening programs at amphitheater between MD & LD. Fish cleaning station, interpretive trails, visitor center. Non-campers pay $4 day use fee. (559) 561-3155. NRRS.
GPS: 36.3906, -118.9547

LAKE MENDOCINO (SF) 6
GPS: 39.1989, -123.1833

Mendocino is a 3,500 ft. long and 160 ft. high, 1,822-acre lake 2 miles NE of Ukiah on Lake Mendocino Dr, off US RT 101. It is 1.5 miles E of Calpella off SR 20 and 120 mi N of San Francisco. Equestrian trail at S end of the lake, ORVs prohibited. Campground checkout time is 11 a.m. Over 300 campsites. Camping at the Kaweyo Staging Area is by permit only. Park Manager, Lake Mendocino, 1160 Lake Mendocino Drive, Ukiah, CA 95482-9404. (707) 462-7581.

BU-SHAY CAMPGROUND

From Ukiah, go 5 mi N on US RT 101, 2.7 mi E on SR 20, after crossing the Russian River bridge turn left 1 mi. Over 100 sites, $20. Three group camping areas up to 80 people and 20 vehicles, Little Bear accommodating up to 120 people and Tata accommodating up to 104 people, from $140 to $200 (NRRS), picnic shelters are available, coin operated showers, no 3rd vehicle permitted and an amphitheater with summer evening shows on Friday and Saturday. 164 sites. RV limit 40'. Open from May 15th to Sept. 26th. NRRS. **GPS: 39.23, -123.15.**

CHEKAKA RECREATION AREA

From Ukiah, 2 mi N on US 101 to Lake Mendocino exit; N (left) at N State St; E (right) to Lake Mendocino Dr; top of hill on right (signs). All year; 14-day limit. 20 sites without hookups, $16 ($8 with federal senior pass). RV limit 43 ft. No showers or flush toilets. Two picnic shelters: OVR for up to 50 people & 25 vehicles, and JOR for up to 50 people & 20 vehicles, both $40. 18 hole disc golf course, hiking trail, horse staging area. NRRS (5/1-9/29) **GPS: 39.2, -123.18**

KYEN CAMPGROUND & DAY USE AREA

From Ukiah, 5 mi N on US 101; 1 mi E (right) on Hwy 20; 0.8 mi E on Marina Dr. All year; 14-day limit. 101 sites without hookups, $20 base, $22 at premium waterfront locations ($10 & $11 with federal senior pass). RV limit 35 ft; 2 pull-through sites. Visitor's center, amphitheater, coin showers. 4 picnic shelters, $30-$40. At reserved sites, PSA and PSC without electric for up to 50 people and 20 vehicles are $30, and PSB and OAKG with electric for up to 50 people and 20 vehicles are $35. RV limit 35'. At reserved sites, 2-day minimum stay required on weekends, 3 days on holiday weekends. NRRS (5/1-9/29) **GPS: 39.23667, -123.17778**

MITI PARK

Accessible by boat-in only on the E side of the dam. 5/1-9/30; 14-day limit. 10 primitive tent sites, $8. **GPS: 40.78, -123.22**

LAKE SONOMA (SF) 7
GPS: 38.71, -123.00

This 2,700-acre lake has 50 miles of shoreline and is 3 miles W of Geyserville from the Canyon Rd exit off US 101. Visitor center. Group tours & ranger programs scheduled by calling project office. 40 miles of trails for hikers, horseback riders and mountain bikers. Campground checkout time is noon. A fish hatchery at dam, operated by the state. Park Manager, Lake Sonoma, 3333 Skaggs Springs Road, Geyserville, CA 95441-9644. (707) 433-9483.

LIBERTY GLEN CAMPGROUND

From Healdsburg at jct with Dry Creek Rd exit of US 101, 15 mi W (signs). All year; 14-day limit. 97 RV/tent sites, $16 ($8 with federal senior pass). 16 double sites, $32; 7 handicap sites. RV limit 46 ft. Group camping area for up to 150 people and 51 vehicles, $80. Amphitheater, chemical vault toilets. NRRS (4/1-9/30). **GPS: 38.70833, -123.00**

BOAT-IN OR HIKE-IN SITES

Access by boat or hiking trails from boat ramps or primary public areas around lake. All year; 14-day limit. $10. 15 primitive campgrounds include 2 group camping areas, Broken Bridge and Island View, both $40 during 10/1-3/31 and $56 during 4/1-9/30. Camps provide chemical vault toilets, tbls, fire rings, lantern holders. No drkg wtr. Two-day minimum stay on weekends during peak period of 4/1-9/30; 3-day minimum stay on holiday weekends. Register at lake visitor center. NRRS.

MARTIS CREEK LAKE (SAC) 8
GPS: 39.3267, -120.1117

This 770-acre lake is 6 miles SE of Truckee on SR 267 and 32 miles SW of Reno, Nevada on I-80. Martis Creek Lake was the first "catch and release trophy trout" lake established in the state. Contact office for group tours & ranger programs and also for reservations for handicap sites (530) 639-2342. Motorized (gas or electric) boats prohibited. Resource Manager, Martis Creek Lake, P. O. Box 6, Smartville, CA 95977-0006. **GPS: 39.32, -120.11**

ALPINE MEADOWS CAMPGROUND

N side of dam, 0.3 mi NE of SR 267. 5/15-10/15; 14-day limit. 25 sites without hookups, $18 ($9 with federal senior pass). RV limit 30 ft; 6 pull-through, 2 handicap. Amphitheater, phone.
GPS: 39.322998, -120.121094

NEW HOGAN LAKE (SAC) 9
GPS: 38.1517, -120.8117

A 4,400-acre lake with 50 miles of shoreline, New Hogan is 30 miles NE of Stockton off SR 26, 1 mil S on Hogan Dam Rd. Nature walks & ranger programs. Coin operated showers at campgrounds; checkout time 2 p.m. Park Manager, New Hogan Lake, 2713 Hogan Dam Road, Valley Springs, CA 95252-9510. (209) 772-1343.

ACORN CAMPGROUND

From Valley Springs, 0.5 mi S on SR 26; 1 mi S (left) on Hogan Dam Rd (signs); 0.7 mi E on Hogan Parkway. All year; 14-day limit. 128 sites without hookups, $14 on Sun-Thurs & $18 on Fri-Sat during 4/1-9/30; $14 every night during 10/1-3/31 ($7 & $9 with federal senior pass). RV limit in excess of 65 ft; 30 pull-through, 3 handicap sites. $10 fee for each vehicle parked at interior parking lot. Campfire programs, amphitheater, fish cleaning stations, group camping. Shower fee of 50 cents for 5 minutes. At reserved sites, 2-night minimum stay required on weekends, 3 nights on holiday weekends. NRRS (4/1-9/30). **GPS: 38.175, -120.79167**

COYOTE POINT GROUP CAMPGROUND

Access through Oak Knoll Campground. 4/1-10/31. Group area for up to 50 people, $100. Shower fee of 50 cents for 5 minutes in adjoining campground. Amphitheater, fish cleaning station. At reserved sites, 2-night minimum stay required on weekends, 3 nights on holiday weekends. Combination provided for gate lock for late entry by registered campers. **GPS: 37.98444, -120.84472**

DEER FLAT PARK

Accessible by boat only on the E side of the lake. Register at Acorn Campground. 5/1-9/30; 14-day limit. 30 primitive sites & onboard boat camping. All sites $10.

OAK KNOLL CAMPGROUND

From Valley Springs, 0.5 mi S on SR 26; 1 mi S on Hogan Dam Rd; 0.7 mi E on Hogan Parkway; 1.1 mi N on S. Petersburg Rd. 5/15-9/4; 14-day limit. 50 primitive sites, $10 base, $12 at premium locations ($5 & $6 with federal senior pass). RV limit in excess of 65 ft; 8 pull-through sites. Group camping (at Coyote Point), $100. Onboard camping (houseboats), $10. Fish cleaning station at Acorn Campground. Shower fee of 50 cents for 5 minutes. Amphitheater. At reserved sites, 2-night minimum stay required on weekends, 3 nights on holiday weekends. NRRS. **38.175, -120.79167**

PINE FLAT LAKE (SAC) 10
GPS: 36.8317, -119.325

This 13,000-acre lake has 67 miles of shoreline. It is 1 mile E of Piedra, 35 miles E of Fresno. Campground checkout time 2 p.m. Dam tours, ranger programs and group/handicap campsites (for scheduling and reservations, call (559) 787-2589). Park Manager, Pine Flat Lake, P. O. Box 117, Piedra, CA 93649-0117.

ISLAND PARK CAMPGROUND

From Piedra, 9.5 mi NE on Trimmer Springs Rd, then S (signs). All year; 14-day limit. 15 tent sites & 54 sites without hookups, $20 ($10 with federal senior pass). 22 sites with elec, $30 ($15 with federal senior pass). RV limit in excess of 65 ft. Two group camping areas, each for up to 75 people 20 vehicles, $100. Fish cleaning station, amphitheater, coin operated showers. Non-campers pay $3 day use fee for boat ramp. NRRS. **GPS: 36.83333, -119.31389**

STANISLAUS RIVER PARKS (SAC) 11
GPS: 37.77, -120.84

Below Melones Dam on Stanislaus River, E of San Francisco off SR 99. From Modesto turn on SR 108/120; 12 mi E of Oakdale, N on Kennedy Rd, then N on Sonora Rd; cross Stanislaus River; Knights Ferry Information Center is on right. Fishing and whitewater rafting & canoeing area. Camping by reservation only with camping permits issued at information center. Termed "environmental camping" by the Corps, access to sites is by boat, foot or bicycle. For reservations (1 to 2 weeks in advance), call (209) 881-3517. Park Manager, Stanislaus River Parks, 17968 Covered Bridge Road, Oakdake, CA 95361-9510.

HORSESHOE ROAD RECREATION AREA

From Knights Ferry, W on Sonoroa & Orange Blossom Roads to Horseshoe Rd. All year; 14-day limit. 16 tent sites, $10; group camping $38. Boat-in, walk-in or bike-in only for individual sites. **GPS: 37.81, -120.66**

MC HENRY AVENUE RECREATION AREA

From Modesto, 6 mi N on McHenry Ave across Stanislaus River; 1 mi W on River Rd; left at park sign. 1/1-10/31; 14-day limit. 4 tent sites, $10; group camping $38. Boat-in, walk-in or bike-in only for individual sites. **GPS: 37.72, -121.11**

VALLEY OAK

From Oakdale, 1.5 mi N on SR 120; left on Orange Blossom Rd; 3 mi E on Rodden Rd, then left. All year; 14-day limit. 10 sites, $10; group camping $38. Boat-in, walk-in or bike-in only for individual sites. **GPS: 37.78, -120.80**

SUCCESS LAKE (SAC) 12
GPS: 36.0583, -118.9183

This 2,450-acre lake is 8 miles E of Porterville on SR 190 (in theSierra Nevada foothills) N of Bakersfield. Swimming permitted. ORV prohibited. (559) 783/9200. Resource Manager, Success Lake, P. O. Box 1072, Porterville, CA 93258. (559) 784-0215.

TULE CAMPGROUND

From dam, 2 mi E on SR 190, then N (signs). All year; 14-day limit. 95 sites without hookups, $16 ($8 with federal senior pass); 9 sites with elec, $21 ($10.50 with federal senior pass. RV limit 65 ft; 27 pull-through sites, 2 handicap sites. Picnic shelter, amphitheater, fish cleaning station, campfire programs on Saturdays MD-LD. 3 day minimum stay required on holiday weekends. NRRS. **GPS: 36.08306, -118.91639**

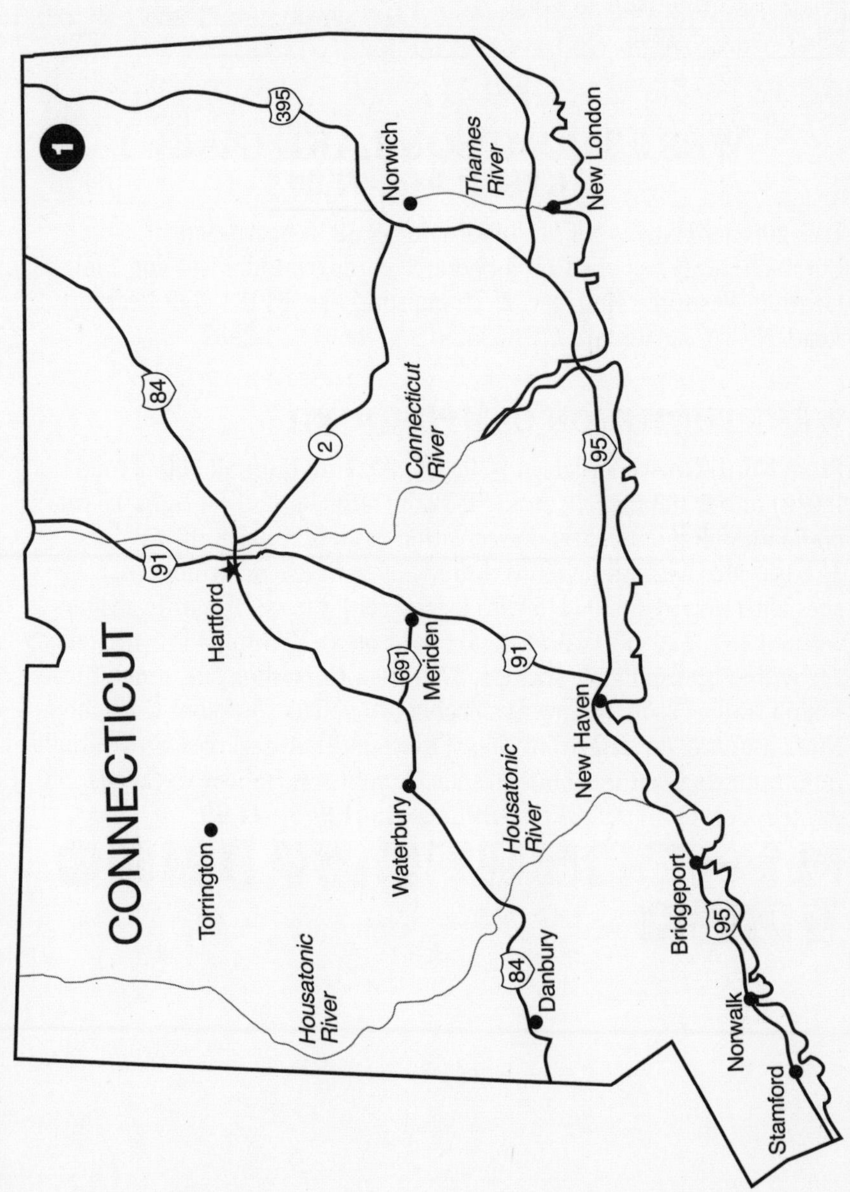
1
CONNECTICUT
395
Norwich
Thames River
New London
84
2
Connecticut River
95
91
Hartford
Meriden
691
91
New Haven
Housatonic River
Torrington
Waterbury
Bridgeport
95
Danbury
84
Housatonic River
Norwalk
Stamford

CONNECTICUT

State Capital: **Hartford**
Nickname: **Constitution State**
Statehood Year: **1788**

5TH STATE

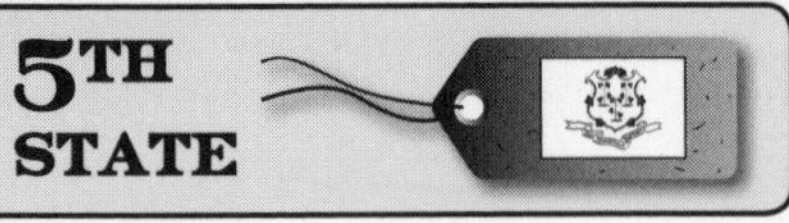

WEST THOMPSON LAKE (NAE) 1
GPS: 41.945, -71.90

This 200-acre lake is NE of Putnam off SR 12 in northeastern Connecticut. It has one Corps-operated campground. Field dog trial area location. Resource Manager, W Thompson Lake, RFD 1, 449 Reardon Road, N Grosvernordale, CT 06255-9801. (860) 923-2982.

WEST THOMPSON CAMPGROUND

From North Grosvenordale at I-395 exit 99, 1 mi E on SR 200; 2 mi S (right) on SR 193 (signs); cross SR 12 at traffic light; first right 0.5 mi on Reardon Rd; left 0.2 mi on recreation road. 5/20-9/20; 14-day limit. 11 basic sites without hookups, $15 ($7.50 with federal senior pass). 11 sites with elec/wtr, $30 ($15 with federal senior pass). 2 lean-to shelters without elec, $20 ($10 with federal senior pass). RV limit 45 ft. 1 handicap site with wtr/elec. Picnic shelters, $75-$100. Horseshoe pits, amphitheater, hiking trails, nature programs. Alcohol prohibited. Checkout time noon. No swimming, no waterfront sites. Firewood($). At reserved sites, 2-night minimum stay required on weekends, 3 nights on Holiday weekends. No day use fees. (860) 923-3121. NRRS. **GPS: 41.945, -71.90**

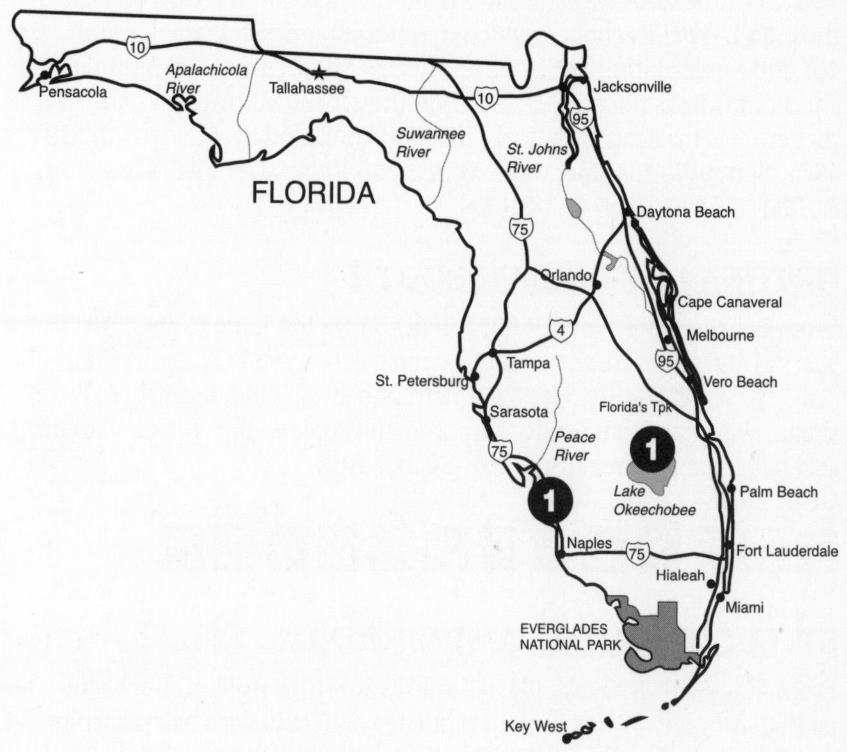
10
Apalachicola
River
Pensacola
Tallahassee
10
Jacksonville
95
Suwannee
River
St. Johns
River
FLORIDA
Daytona Beach
75
Orlando
Cape Canaveral
4
Melbourne
95
Tampa
St. Petersburg
Vero Beach
Florida's Tpk
Sarasota
Peace
River
75
1
1
Lake
Okeechobee
Palm Beach
Naples
75
Fort Lauderdale
Hialeah
Miami
EVERGLADES
NATIONAL PARK
Key West

FLORIDA

State Capital: **Tallahassee**
Nickname: **Sunshine State**
Statehood Year: **1845**

27TH STATE

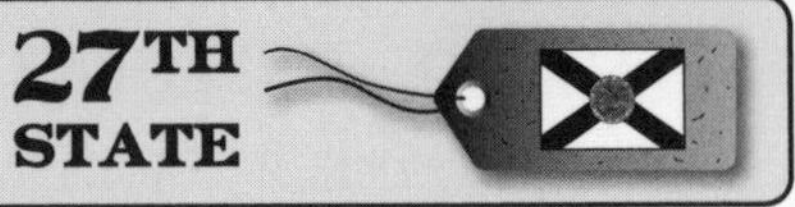

OKEECHOBEE WATERWAY (JX) 1
GPS: 26.756733, -80.917815

This 154-mile waterway stretches from Ft. Myers on the Gulf of Mexico through Lake Okeechobee, which is about 30 miles in diameter and, 467,000 acres, exiting at Stuart on the Atlantic Ocean. Campground checkout time is noon. Lock facility tours scheduled through park rangers. Visitor centers in Alva (239) 694-2582 and St. Lucie (772) 219-4575. South Florida Operations Office, 525 Ridgelawn Road, Clewiston, FL 33440-5399. (863) 983-8101.

ORTONA LOCK & DAM SOUTH

From Labelle, 8 mi E on SR 80; N (left) on Dalton Lane (signs). All year; 14-day limit. 51 sites with 50-amp elec/wtr, $24 ($12 with federal senior pass). RV limit 45 ft; 4 pull-through sites, 4 handicap sites. Picnic shelter with handicap facilities for 2 to 40 people & 15 vehicles. Handicap accessible fishing area. (863) 675-8400. NRRS.
GPS: 26.78722, -81.30861

ST. LUCIE SOUTH CAMPGROUND

From at jct with I-95 exit 101, 0.5 mi W on SR 76; right on Locks Rd (signs). All year; 14-day limit. 3 tent sites, $20 ($10 with federal senior pass); 8 sites with elec, $24 ($12 with federal senior pass); 4 sleep-onboard boat sites with hookups, $24 ($12 with federal senior pass). RV limit 45 ft. Picnic shelter for up to 20 people, $35. (772) 287-1382. NRRS. **GPS: 27.11028, -80.285**

W. P. FRANKLIN NORTH

From N of Fort Myers at jct with I-75 exit 25, 10 mi E on US 80; 4 mi N on SR 31; 3 mi E on SR 78; N on N. Franklin Rd (signs). All year; 14-day limit. 30 sites with 50-amp elec/wtr, $24 ($12 with federal senior pass); 8 sleep-onboard boat sites with hookups, $24. Two picnic shelters up to 30 people and 1 vehicle, $35. Handicap accessible fishing area. RV limit 35 ft; 1 pul-through site, 1 handicap site. (239) 694-8770. NRRS.
GPS: 26.7417, -81.69278

GEORGIA

75
2
Lake
Sidney
Lanier
6
3
1
85
4
Atlanta
20
Augusta
Chattahoochee
River
85
8
185
Macon
Oconee
River
Savannah
River
16
Columbus
Savannah
7
Ocmulgee
River
Altamaha
River
Chattahoochee
River
95
GEORGIA
75
Flint River
5

GEORGIA

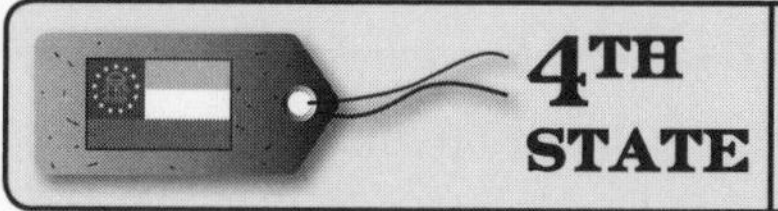

State Capital: **Atlanta**
Nickname: **Peach State**
Statehood Year: **1788**

ALLATOONA LAKE (MB) 1
GPS: 34.1633, -84.7283

A 12,000-acre lake with 270 miles of shoreline 30 miles NW of Atlanta off I-75, east of Cartersville in NW Georgia. Fee charged for visitors to 10:00 p.m. ORV prohibited. Master, Visa, Discover and American Express cards accepted at all campgrounds. Visitor center, historic & cultural site, interpretive programs, wildlife viewing. Group picnic shelter fees $50-$175. Operations Manager, Allatoona Lake, P. O. Box 487, Cartersville, GA 30120-0487. (678) 721-6700.

CLARK CREEK NORTH CAMPGROUND

From Atlanta, N on I-75; from exit 278, 2.3 mi N on Glade Rd (signs), cross lake bridge, then left. 4/22-9/6; 14-day limit. 24 sites with 50-amp elec/wtr, $28 ($14 with federal senior pass); 5 pull-through. RV limit 40'. 2 night stay on weekends, 3 nights on holiday weekends. NRRS.
GPS: 34.09722, -84.68056

CLARK CREEK SOUTH CAMPGROUND

From Atlanta, N on I-75; from exit 278, 2 mi N on Glade Rd (signs), then right before lake bridge. THIS CAMPGROUND IS CLOSED DURING 2011. 40 sites, 24 elec/wtr, 5 tent only sites, 1 handicap site with wtr/elec. Tent only sites and sites without hookups are $14; sites with water and electric hookups are $20; premium sites with water and electric are $22. RV limit 40'. 2-night stay on weekends, 3 nights on holiday weekends. Contact the office for information about re-opening. GPS: **34.07, -84.67**

MCKASKEY CREEK CAMPGROUND

From Cartersville at I-75 exit 290, 2 mi E (right) on SR 20 (signs); 1.5 mi S on Spur 20; 1.5 mi E on CR (McKaskey Creek Rd). 3/25-9/6; 14-day limit. 19 tent sites, $16 & $18 ($8 & $9 with federal senior pass); 32 sites with 50-amp elec/wtr, $22 ($11 with federal senior pass), $28 at premium locations. RV limit 40'. At reserved sites, 2-night stay required on weekends, 3 nights on holiday weekends. NRRS. **GPS: 34.19, -84.71806**

MCKINNEY CAMPGROUND

From Atlanta, N on I-75 to exit 278; 3 mi E on Glade Rd past Clark Creek to second 4-way stop sign (signs); 1 mi N (left) on King's Camp Rd; left at forks. All year; 14-day limit. 150 sites with 50-amp elec/wtr, $24 ($12 with federal senior pass), $28 at premium locations; 35 pull-through. RV limit 40'. At reserved sites, 2-night stay required on weekends, 3 nights on holiday weekends. **GPS: 34.10694, -84.69556**

OLD 41 #3 CAMPGROUND

From Atlanta, N on I-75 to exit 283; .07 mi W to stop light; .08 mi right on SR 92 (Lake Acworth Dr), crossing the overpass, then right to bottom of overpass & 2.5 mi left following signs. 4/22-9/6; 14-day limit. 4/22-9/6; 14-day limit. 50 sites with 50-amp elec/wtr, base fee $24 ($12 with federal senior pass); premium locations $32 ($16 with federal senior pass); double sites $56. RV limit 50'; 4 pull-through. At reserved sites, 2-night stay required on weekends, 3 nights on holiday weekends. NRRS. **GPS: 34.08833, -84.71056**

PAYNE CAMPGROUND

From Atlanta, N on I-75 to exit 277; 2 mi E on SR 92; N (left) on Old Alabama Rd to dead end, then 1.5 mi E (right) on Kellogg Creek Rd following signs. 3/25-9/6; 14-day limit. 11 sites without hookups, $16 & $18 ($8 & $9 with federal senior pass); 49 sites with 50-amp elec/wtr,

$24 base ($12 with federal senior pass), $28 at premium locations ($14 with federal senior pass), $56 at double sites. RV limit 40'. At reserved sites, 2-night stay required on weekends, 3 nights stay on holiday weekends. NRRS. **GPS: 34.12083, -84.57917**

SWEETWATER CAMPGROUND

S of Canton at jct with SR 5, 5 mi W on SR 20 across Knox Bridge, then 2 mi S. 3/25-9/6; 14-day limit. 42 tent sites, $18 ($9 with federal senior pass); 118 sites with 50-amp elec/wtr, $24 base ($12 with federal senior pass), $28 at premium sites ($14 with federal senior pass), $56 at double sites; 23 pull-through. Group camping up to 54 people, 9 sites w/picnic shelter, $250. RV limit in excess of 65'. At reserved sites, 2-night stay required/weekends, 3 nights/holiday weekends. NRRS. **GPS: 34.19444, -84.57889**

UPPER STAMP CREEK CAMPGROUND

From Cartersville at I-75 exit 290, 4 mi E on SR 20; 1.3 mi S on Wilderness Rd (signs); dirt road to left. 4/22-9/5; 14-day limit. 2 tent sites, $18 ($9 with federal senior pass); 18 sites with 50-amp elec/wtr, base fee $22 ($11 with federal senior pass), $26 at premium sites ($13 with federal senior pass). RV limit 30'. At reserved sites, 2-night stay required on weekends, 3 nights stay on holiday weekends. NRRS. **GPS: 34.20278, -84.67667**

VICTORIA CAMPGROUND

From Atlanta, I-75 N to I-575N exit 7; 3 mi W on Old Alabama Rd; 3.5 mi N (right) on Bells Ferry Rd; 3 mi W (left) on Victoria Landing Dr. 3/25-10/10; 14-day limit. 74 sites with 50-amp elec/wtr, $20 base ($10 with federal senior pass), $26 at premium locations ($13 with federal senior pass), $28 full hookups ($14 with federal senior pass); 27 pull-through. RV limit 65'. At reserved sites, 2-night stay required on weekends, 3 nights on holiday weekends. NRRS. **GPS: 34.15139, -86.1944**

CARTERS LAKE (MB) 2
GPS: 34.6133, -84.685

A 3,200-acre lake 27 miles N of Cartersville on US 411, N of jct. with SR 136 and SW of Ellijay in NW Georgia. Visitor center. Day use facilities: Damsite Park -- boat ramp, picnicking, group shelter; Doll Mountain Park -- boat ramp, picnicking, group shelter; Northbank Park -- picnicking, group shelter, playground, interpretive trail; Reregulation Dam -- picnicking, group shelter, interpretive trail; Woodring Park -- boat ramp, picnicking, group shelter, interpretive trail. Shelters are $30 & $50. $4 day use fee charged at most areas. Site Manager, Carter Lake, P. O. Box 96, Oakman, GA 30732-0096. (706) 334-2248.

BOAT IN CAMPGROUND

From dam boat launch, E to peninsula via boat or hike 2 mi to sites on the Amadahy Trail from Woodring Branch Campground access rd. All year; 14-day limit. 12 free primitive tent sites. Pit toilets, no drkg wtr.

DOLL MOUNTAIN CAMPGROUND

From Ellijay, S on Old Hwy 5; S on SR 382, then W; on S side of lake. CAUTION: Steep downhill grade to campground. 4/1-10/30; 14-day limit. No hookups $16, including 26 tent ($8 with federal senior pass); sites with elec/wtr, $18 base ($9 with federal senior pass); sites with 50-amp elec/wtr, $20 & $24 ($10 & $12 with federal senior pass). RV limit 40 ft; 5 pull-through. Picnic shelter, amphitheater. Night-time emergency exit provided. At reserved sites, 2-night stay required/weekends, 3 nights/ holiday weekends. (706) 276-4413. NRRS. **GPS: 34.51333, -84.62389**

HARRIS BRANCH CAMPGROUND

From Gordon, 5.5 mi E on SR 136; 0.7 mi E on SR 382, then NW; on S side of lake. Open about 5/1-9/6; 14-day limit. 10 sites without hookups, $16 ($8 with federal senior pass). Group camping area, $60 (contact office for info. and reservations). (706) 276-4545. **GPS: 34.60, -84.63**

RIDGEWAY CAMPGROUND

From Ellijay, approximately 5 mi W on SR 282; access on the left. All year; 14-day limit. 20 primitive sites, $10 (self-register). Hiking & mountain biking trails. Pit toilets. **GPS: 34.63, -84.67**

WOODRING BRANCH CAMPGROUND

From Ellijay, 11 mi W on SR 282/US 76, following signs; on N side of lake. 4/1-10/30; 14-day limit. 12 sites in primitive camping area, $10 ($5 with federal senior pass); 11 tent sites, $14 & $16 ($7 & $8 with federal senior pass). 31 sites with elec/wtr, $20 for 30-amp elec, $22 for 50-amp elec ($10 & $11 with federal senior pass). RV limit 40 ft. Picnic shelter, amphitheater. At reserved sites, 2-night stay required on weekends, 3 nights on holiday weekends. (706) 276-6050. NRRS. **GPS: 34.67056, -84.55**

HARTWELL LAKE (SV) 3
GPS: 34.46, -82.19

A 56,000 acre lake with 962 miles of shoreline, Hartwell is 5 miles N of the City of Hartwell on US 29 and SW of Greenville, SC on state line. Guided tours of dam and power plant available. Checkout time is 2 p.m. Alcohol prohibited. ORV, golf carts and motorized scooters also prohibited. The Corps operates 9 campgrounds and 15 major day use areas on this lake. Day use fees charged. Day use facilities: Apple Island Access -- boat ramp; Ashbury Park -- boat ramp, picnicking; Big Oaks Rec. Area -- boat ramp, picnicking, group shelter, playground, trails; Broyles Park -- boat ramp, picnicking, group shelter, playground, beach; Camp Creek Access -- boat ramp; Carters Ferry Access -- boat ramp; Cleveland Access -- boat ramp; Crawford South Ferry Access -- boat ramp; Denver Access -- boat ramp; Double Spring Access -- boat ramp; Duncan Branc Access -- boat ramp; Durham Access -- boat ramp; Eighteen Mile Access -- boat ramp; Elrod Ferry Park -- boat ramp, picnicking, group shelter; playground, beach; Fair Play Park -- boat ramp, picnicking, group shelter, playground, beach; Friendship Park

-- boat ramp, picnicking, playground, beach; Green Pond Access -- boat ramp; Hartwell Park -- group sheter; Jarrett Ramp Access -- boat ramp; Jenkins Ferry -- boat ramp; Lawrence Bridge Park -- boat ramp, picnicking; Long Point Rec. Area -- boat ramp, picnicking, group shelter, playground; Martins Creek Access -- boat ramp; Mary Ann Branch Access -- boat ramp; Mullins Ford -- boat ramp, picnicking; Poplar Springs Park -- boat ramp, picnicking, group shelter; Powderbag Creek Access -- boat ramp; Richland Creek Access -- boat ramp; River Forks Park -- boat ramp, picnicking, group shelter, playground, beach; Rock Springs Access -- boat ramp; Singing Pines Park -- boat ramp, picnicking, group shelter, playground, beach; SC River Area -- trails; Spring Branch -- boat ramp; Stephens County -- boat ramp, picnicking; Tabor Access -- boat ramp; Townville Park -- boat ramp; Twelve Mile Park -- boat ramp, picnicking, group sheltre, playground, beach; Walker Creek Access -- boat ramp; Weldon Island Park -- boat ramp, picnicking, group shelter. Recent improvements: new restrooms at Friendship Rec. Area boat ramp, ramp area repaved; new courtesy dock at Townville Access; new courtesy dock at Spring Branch; comfort station replaced at Watsadler, Springfield & Twin Lakes Campgrounds; new comfort station & upgraded electrical service at Crescent Group Camp. Visitor center, interpretive programs. Project Manager, Hartwell Lake and Powerplant, P. O. Box 278, Hartwell, Ga. 30643-0278. (706) 856-0300/(888) 893-0678. See SC listing.

GEORGIA RIVER RECREATION AREA

From Hartwell, 6.5 mi N on US 29; on Savannah River just below dam. 5/1-9/30; 14-day limit. 15 primitive sites, $6 ($3 with federal senior pass). Some sites may be open & free off-season. Small RVs welcome, but sites most suitable for folding trailers, pickup campers & tents. Register at lake visitor center on Hwy 29. **GPS: 34.40, -82.70**

MILLTOWN CAMPGROUND

From Hartwell, 4 mi N on SR 51; 4 mi E on New Prospect Rd, followING signs. 5/1-9/6; 14-day limit. 25 primitive sites, no hookups, $10 ($5 with federal senior pass). RV limit 36'. Three group camping areas, $50-$60. Courtesy dock. NRRS. **GPS: 34.40972, -82.87583**

PAYNES CREEK CAMPGROUND

From Hartwell, 10 mi N on SR 51 to Reed Creek; turn left and follow signs; on Tugaloo River. 5/1-9/8; 14-day limit. 43 sites with 50-amp elec/wtr, $20 ($10 with federal senior pass); double sites $44. RV limit 60'. 37 sites at waterfront. NRRS. **GPS: 34.47927, -82.97528**

WATSADLERS CAMPGROUND

From Hartwell, 5.5 mi N on US 29, following signs; near Hartwell Dam, overlooking lake. All year; 14-day limit. 51 sites with 50-amp elec/wtr, $22 during 4/1-9/30 & $20 during 10/1-3/31 ($11 & $10 with federal senior pass); double sites $46. RV limit 50'. 49 sites are lakefront; 17 pull-through. NRRS. **GPS: 34.34389, -82.84139**

J. STROM THURMOND LAKE (SV) 4
GPS: 33.69, -82.35

A 70,000-acre lake with 1,200 mi of shoreline adjacent to Clarks Hill and NW of Augusta on the SC state line (US 221 crosses top of dam). Exhibits on display at visitor center. Checkout time 2 p.m. Alcoholic beverages prohibited. $4 day use fees charged. Day use activities: Calhoun Falls Park -- boat ramp; Chamberlain Ferry Park -- boat ramp; Cherokee Park -- boat ramp, picnicking, group shelter, playground, beach; Clarks Hill Park -- boat ramp, picnicking, group shelter, beach; Dordon Creek -- boat ramp; Double Branches -- boat ramp; Gill Point Park -- boa ramp, picnicking, group shelter, beach; Ket Creek -- boat ramp; Lake Springs Park -- boat ramp, picnicking, group shelter, playground, beach, interpretive trail; Leathersville -- boat ramp; Modoc Ramp -- boat ramp; Mt. Pleasant -- boat ramp; Murray Creek -- boat ramp; Parksville Park -- boat ramp, picnicking, group shelter, playground, beach, hiking trail; Parkway -- boat ramp; Scots Ferry -- boat ramp; West Dam Park -- picnicking, group shelter, playground, beach. Resource Manager, J. Strom Thurmond Lake, Route 1, Box 12, Clarks Hill, SC 29821-9701. (864) 333-1100/(800) 533-3478. See SC listing.

BIG HART CAMPGROUND

From Thomson, 3 mi N on US 78 past jct with SR 43; 4 mi E (right) on Russell Landing Rd (signs); at confluence of Big Creek & Hart Creek on W end of lake. 4/1-10/31; 14-day limit. 31 sites with 50-amp elec/wtr, $20 base, $22 at premium locations ($10 & $11 with federal senior pass). RV limit 60'. Group camping 7 50-amp elec/wtr RV sites, $154. Group picnic shelter, $75. At reserved sites, 2-night stay required on weekends,3 nights on holiday weekends. (706) 595-8613. NRRS. **GPS: 33.6225, -82.5103**

BROAD RIVER CAMPGROUND

From I-85 exit 173, 30 mi S on SR 17, then 11 mi toward Calhoun on SR 72; 10 mi right on SR 79 across the Broad River on left; on S shore of Broad River at confluence with Savannah River. 3/1-9/5; 14-day limit. 31 sites 30-amp elec/wtr, $18 & $20 ($9 & $10 with federal senior pass); double sites $36, triple sites $54. RV limit in excess of 65'; 17 pull-through. Fish cleaning station, courtesy dock. At reserved sites, 2-night stay required/weekends, 3 nights on holiday weekends. Open from March 1st to September 4th. (706) 359-2053. NRRS. **GPS: 33.96167, -82.575**

BUSSEY POINT CAMPGROUND

From Lincolnton, S on SR 47 to SR 220 NE; exit S at Kenna on gravel rd; at entrance to Bussey Point Wilderness Recreation Area, a peninsula on the lake. All year; 14-day limit. 10 primitive sites plus 4 sites for equestrian camping, $6 self-registration. Pit toilets, drkg wtr, 12.5-mi trail for hiking, biking, horseback riding. Picnic shelter. No reservations. **GPS: 33.71, -82.26**

CLAY HILL CAMPGROUND

From Woodlawn, 3 mi S on SR 43; on the E side, N shore of Little River. All year; 14-day limit. 7 primitive sites, $12 ($6 with federal senior pass), 10 sites with 30-amp wtr/elec, $16 ($8 with federal senior pass). RV limit 25'. (706) 359-7495. **GPS: 33.67, -82.45**

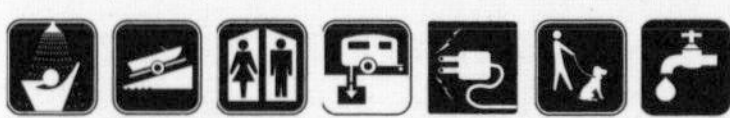

HESTER'S FERRY CAMPGROUND

From Lincolnton at jct with US 378, 12 mi N on SR 79; 2 mi E on Hwy 44 (signs); on Fishing Creek. 4/1-10/31; 14-day limit. 10 primitive sites, $16 ($8 with federal senior pass); 16 sites with 30-amp elec/wtr, $18 ($9 with federal senior pass); 9 pull-through. RV limit 40'. At reserved sites, 2-night stay required on weekends, 3 nights on holiday weekends. 31st. (706) 359-2746. NRRS (no reservations in Oct). **GPS: 33.9425, -82.55028**

PETERSBURG CAMPGROUND

From Pollards Corner, 2 mi NE on US 221, then E. All year; 14-day limit. 8 sites without hookups, $14 ($7 with federal senior pass); 85 sites with elec/wtr, $16 ($8 with federal senior pass), $22 with 50-amp elec/wtr ($11 with federal senior pass). RV limit 45'; 54 pull-through. Picnic shelters, $50. At reserves sites, 2-night stay required/weekends, 3 nights on holiday weekends. Fish cleaning station, picnic shelters, fishing dock, hiking trail, phone. (706) 541-9464. NRRS. **GPS: 33.66194, -82.26083**

RAYSVILLE CAMPGROUND

From Woodlawn, 7 mi S on SR 43, then W; at Little River. 3/1-10/31; 14-day limit. 55 sites with 50-amp elec/wtr, $20 ($10 with federal senior pass), $22 at premium locations ($11 with federal senior pass). RV limit 40'; 32 pull-through sites. At reserved sites, 2-night stay required on weekends, 3 nights on holiday weekends. Fish cleaning station, picnic shelters. (706) 595-6759. NRRS. **GPS: 33.64417, -82.47722**

RIDGE ROAD CAMPGROUND

From Highway 221 at Pollards Corner, 4 mi NW on SR 47 toward Lincolnton, then 5 mi NE on Ridge Rd to the campground. 4/1-9/30; 14-day limit. 6 sites without hookups, $16 ($8 with federal senior pass); 63 sites with 50-amp elec/wtr $20, premium locations $22 ($10 & $11 with federal senior pass); double sites $38. RV limit 50'; 27 pull-through sites. Fish cleaning station. At reserved sites, 2-day stay required on weekends, 3 days on holiday weekends. (706) 541-0282. NRRS. **GPS: 33.68, -82.25861**

WINFIELD CAMPGROUND

From Pollards Corner, 10 mi W on SR 150; 5 mi N on Winfield Rd; on Little River near Mistletoe State Park. 3/1-9/29; 14-day limit. 80 sites with 50-amp elec/wtr, $20 ($10 with federal senior pass), $22 at premium locations ($11 with federal senior pass). RV limit 65'; 35 pull-through sites. At reserved sites, 2-night stay required on weekends, 3 nights on holiday weekends. (706) 541-0147. NRRS.
GPS: 33.65194, -82.42194

LAKE SEMINOLE (MB) 5
GPS: 30.711131, -84.847172

A 37,500-acre lake with 376 mi of shoreline, N of Chattahoochee, Florida, in SW Georgia on the state line off US 90. Campground checkout time 3 p.m. Alcohol prohibited. Visitors permitted to 9:30 p.m. for a fee. Visitor center, picnicking. Day use facilities: Chattahoochee Park -- boat ramp, picnicking, group shelter, playground; Cypress Pond Park -- boat ramp, picnicking; Desser Park -- boat ramp, picnicking; Fairchilds Park -- boat ramp, picnicking; Rays Lake Park -- boat ramp, group picnicking; Reynoldsville Park -- boat ramp, picnicking. $3 boat launch fee charged at some parks. Resource Site Manager, Lake Seminole, P. O. Box 96, Chattahoochee, FL 32324-0096. (229) 662-2001.

EAST BANK CAMPGROUND

From Chattahoochee, Florida at jct with US 90, 1.5 mi N on Bolivar St (Booster Club Rd); left on East Bank Rd; near Jim Woodruff Dam. All year; 14-da limit. 2 tent sites, $12 ($6 with federal senior pass); 62 sites with 50-amp elec/wtr, $20 ($10 with federal senior pass); double sites $40. RV limit in excess of 65'. Horseshoe pits, picnic shelter, courtesy dock, phone. (229) 622-9273. NRRS. **GPS: 30.71806, -84.86111**

FACEVILLE LANDING CAMPGROUND

From Bainbridge, 14 mi S on SR 97, then N on Faceville Landing Rd. All year; 14-day limit. 7 primitive sites, 4 for tents, $6. RV limit 40'. Picnic shelter, courtesy dock, pit toilets. **GPS: 30.77, -84.84**

HALES LANDING CAMPGROUND

From Bainbridge at jct with US 84, 3.8 mi SW on SR 253; 2 mi SW on Ten Mile Still Rd, following signs, then S. All year; 14-day limit. 26 sites with 50-amp elec/wtr, $16 ($8 with federal senior pass). Picnic shelter, 1 handicap site, courtesy dock. **GPS: 30.88, -84.66**

RIVER JUNCTION CAMPGROUND

From Chattahoochee, Florida, at jct with US 90, 2 mi N on Bolivar St (Booster Club Rd); left at sign. All year; 14-day limit. 11 sites with elec/wtr, $16 ($8 with federal senior pass). Group camping for scouts. RV limit 40'. **GPS: 30.75, -84.84**

LAKE SIDNEY LANIER (MB) 6
GPS: 34.16, -84.07

A 38,000 acre lake with 690 miles of shoreline, located W of I-985 exit 4, 35 miles NE of Atlanta in north-central Georgia. Alcoholic beverages prohibited. Campground checkout time 3 p.m. Visitors to 9:30 p.m. for a fee. Chestnut Ridge and Shoal Creek Campgrounds were leased to Lake Lanier Islands Resort and no longer operate as part of the Corps parks system. Van Pugh South day use park was converted into a campground in 2010 and is still managed as a Corps campground. $3 or $4 day use fees are charged at the following parks: Buford, East Bank, Lower Pool West, Lower Pool East, Lanier Park, Burton Mill, Van Pugh North, Balus Creek, Little Hall, Vann's Tavern, Six Mile, Tidwell & West Bank.

Parks around the lake operated by other government agencies include: Forsythe County's Young Deer Park -- picnicking, swimming, boat ramp, playground; Shady Grove Campground -- swimming beach, boat ramp, picnic shelters, playground; Charleston Park -- 3 boat ramps, picnicking. Hall County's Charleston Park -- 3 boat ramps, picnicking; Clarks Bridge Park -- boat launch, canoeing, kayaking, beach, picnicking, fishing; Laurel Park -- beach, biking, boat launch, nature trail, picnicking, playground, ball fields; River Forks Park -- campground, beach, boat ramp, biking, dump station, playground, hiking, picnicking, playground; Lanier Park -- boat ramp, picnicking, swimming; Longwood Park -- picnicking, playground; Holly Park -- boat ramp, picnicking. Dawson County's War Hill Park -- campground, picnicking, boat ramps. Lumpkin County Park -- ball fields, picnicking.

The lake's project headquarters includes a visitor center, interpretive programs, picnicking. Lanier Project Manager, Lake Sidney Lanier, P. O. Box 567, Buford, GA 30515-0567. (770) 945-9531.

BALD RIDGE CREEK CAMPGROUND

From Cumming, N on SR 400 to exit 16; right on Pilgrim Mill Rd; right on Sinclair Shoals Rd; left on Bald Ridge Rd. 3/16-11/19; 14-day limit. 82 sites with 50-amp elec/wtr, $32 ($16 with federal senior pass). RV limit in excess of 65 ft; 9 pull-through sites. 2-night stay on weekends, 3 nights on holiday weekends. (770) 889-1591. NRRS. **GPS: 34.20, -84.09**

BOLDING MILL CAMPGROUND

From Cumming, N on SR 400 to exit 17, then NE on SR 306; right on HWy 53; left on Old Sardis Rd; left on Chestatee Rd. 4/13-9/10; 14-day limit. 9 tent sites, $18 ($9 with federal senior pass); 88 sites with 50-amp elec/wtr, $32 ($16 with federal senior pass). RV limit in excess of 65'. 2-night stay on weekends, 3 nights on holiday weekends. (770) 532-3650. NRRS. **GPS: 34.34167, -83.94972**

CHESTNUT RIDGE CAMPGROUND

This campground is no longer part of the Corps of Engineers park system and has been leased to the private Lake Lanier Islands Resort.

DUCKETT MILL CAMPGROUND

From Cumming N on SR 400 to exit 17; right on Hwy 306; right on Hwy 53; right on Duckett Mill Rd. 4/13-9/10; 14-day limit. 14 tent sites, $18 ($9 with federal senior pass); 97 sites with 50-amp elec/wtr, $32 ($16 with federal senior pass). 2-night stay required on weekends, 3 nights on holiday weekends. (770) 532-9802. NRRS. **GPS: 34.305, -83.9325**

OLD FEDERAL CAMPGROUND

From I-985N exit 8, left on SR 347 (Friendship Rd); right on McEver Rd; left on Jim Crow Rd (signs). 3/16-11/19; 14-day limit. 25 tent sites, $22 ($11 with federal senior pass); 59 sites with elec/wtr, $27 for 30-amp elec, $32 for 50-amp elec ($13.50 & $16 with federal senior pass). 2-night stay required on weekends, 3 nights on holiday weekends. (770) 967-6757. NRRS. **GPS: 34.22222, -83.94944**

SAWNEE CAMPGROUND

From Cumming at jct of SR 400N exit 14, E (left) on Hwy 20; left on Sanders Rd; at lst stop sign, 3.5 mi right on Buford Dam Rd; on left. 10 tent sites, $22 ($11 with federal senior pass); 42 sites with elec/wtr, $30

& $32 ($15 & $16 with federal senior pass). RV limit 40'. 2-night stay required on weekends, 3 nights on holiday weekends. (770) 887-0592. NRRS. **GPS: 34.17667, -84.07528**

SHOAL CREEK CAMPGROUND

This campground is no longer part of the Corps of Engineers park system and has been leased to Lake Lanier Islands Resort.

TOTO CREEK CAMPGROUND

From Cumming, N on SR 400; right on SR 136; right at stop sign; left before crossing bridge. About 4/15-9/15; 14-day limit. 10 primitive sites, $22 ($11 with federal senior pass). **GPS: 34.16, -84.07**

VAN PUGH SOUTH CAMPGROUND

From I-985 exit 8, left on Hwy 347/Friendship Rd; right on McEver Rd; left on Gaines Ferry Rd, follow signs. About 4/15-9/15; 14-day limit. Former day use park now operated as campground. 18 tent sites, $22 ($12 with federal senior pass); 37 RV sites with elec/wtr, $30 & $32 ($15 & $16 with federal senior pass). Sites have tbls, fire rings, grills.
GPS: 34.18444, -83.9056

WALTER F. GEORGE LAKE (MB) 7
GPS: 31.6267, -85.0633

A 45,000-acre lake with 640 miles of shoreline located on Chattahoochee River at the Alabama/Georgia state line W of Albany. The dam is near Ft. Gaines off SR 39. Visitors to 9:30 p.m. for a fee. Campground checkout time is 3 p.m. Day use facilities: Cheneyhatchee Creek -- boat ramp; Cool Branch -- boat ramp, marina; East Bank Damsite -- boat ramp, picnicking, group shelter, playground; Highland Park -- boat ramp, group picnicking, playground, beach. Picnic shelters are $35 daily except $50 at Highland Park shelter. Day use fees charged for beaches, boat launches. Eight county & municipal parks around the lake also have facilities.

Camping also available at Coheelee County Park, Florence Landing & Marina, and Lakepoint Resort Campground. Visitor center, historic & cultural site, interpretive programs. Resource Site Manager, Walter F. George Lake, route. 1, Box 176, Ft. Gaines, GA 31751-9722. (229) 768-2516. See AL listing.

COTTON HILL CAMPGROUND

From Ft. Gaines, 7 mi N on SR 39, then W following signs. All year; 14-day limit. 10 tent sites, $18 ($9 with federal senior pass); 94 sites with wtr/elec, $20. RV limit 40'; 10 pull-through sites. At reserved sites, 2-night stay required on weekends, 3 nights on holiday weekends. Picnic shelter, fish cleaning station, 2 playgrounds, phones. (229) 768-3061. NRRS. NOTE: Campground was closed part of 2010 for renovation; check status before arriving. **GPS: 31.67444, -85.06417**

ROOD CREEK CAMPGROUND

From Georgetown at jct with US 27, 9.5 mi N on SR 39, across Rood Creek, then W. 3/1-10/31; 14-day limit. Free primitive camping. 34 sites. fire rings, lantern posts, pit toilets. **GPS: 32.03, -85.04**

WEST POINT LAKE (MB) 8
GPS: 32.9183, -85.1883

A 25,900-acre lake with 500 miles of shoreline SW of Atlanta and NW of I-85 on the Georgia/Alabama state line N of West Point off US 29. Power house visitor facility and dam tours, interpretive programs. Day use facilities: Alligator Creek Park -- boat ramp, picnicking, group shelter, hiking trail; Anderson Park -- picnicking, group shelter, playground; Clark Park -- boat ramp, picnicking; Dewberry Park -- boat ramp; Eagleview Park -- picnicking; group shelter, playground; East Cook Recreation Area -- boat ramp, picnicking, group shelter, playground, beach, hiking trail; Evansville Park -- boat ramp, picnicking; Georgia Park -- boat ramp; Glass Bridge Park -- boat ramp, picnicking, group shelter; Half Moon Creek Park -- picnicking; Hardley Creek Park -- picnicking, group shelter, playground; Horace King Park -- boat ramp, picnicking, group shelter; Liberty Hill Park -- boat ramp; Long Cane Park -- boat ramp, picnicking, group shelter, hiking trail; McGee Bridge Park, boat ramp, picnicking, group shelter; Potts Road Park -- boat ramp; Rocky Point Recreation Area -- boat ramp, picnicking, group shelter, playground, beach, hiking trail; Sunny Point Park -- boat ramp, picnicking, group shelter, trails; Veasey Creek Park -- boat ramp; Wehadkee Park -- boat ramp; Whitewater Park -- boat ramp; Yellowjacket Recreation Area -- boat ramp, picnicking, playground, beach. Resource Manager, West Point Lake, 500 Resource Managers Drive, West Point, GA 31833-9517. (706) 883-6749/645-2937. See AL listing.

AMITY CAMPGROUND

From Lanett, 7 mi N on CR 212. All year; 14-day limit. 3 tent sites, $16 ($8 with federal senior pass); 55 sites with elec/wtr, $24 ($12 with federal senior pass). Interpretive trail, amphitheater. At reserved sites, 2-night stay required on weekends, 3 nights on holiday weekends.
(334) 499-2404. NRRS during 3/11-11/30. **GPS: 32.97083, -85.22222**

HOLIDAY CAMPGROUND

From LaGrange, 7 mi W on SR 109, follow signs; 2.3 mi S on Thompson Rd. 2/25-9/25; 14-day limit. 37 tent sites & 6 RV/tent sites without hookups, $16 ($8 with federal senior pass); 92 sites with elec/wtr, $24 ($12 with federal senior pass). Three group camping areas -- one with 10 primitive tent sites, $16; one with 8 RV/tent sites with elec, $22, and the third with 14 RV sites & 5 tent sites, $170. RV limit 65'. At reserved sites, 2-night stay required on weekends, 3 nights on holiday weekends.
(706) 884-6818. NRRS. **GPS: 33.02611, -85.17889**

INDIAN SPRINGS GROUP CAMPGROUND

From La Grange, 8 mi W on SR 109; N side near Rock Mills Rd. Contact the host at Whitetail campground at (706) 884-8972 for status. All year; 14-day limit. Four group tent camping areas, $50-$110. NRRS. NOTE: Campground was closed in 2010; check status before arriving.
GPS: 33.04, -85.18

RINGER CAMPGROUND

From LaGrange, 8.7 mi N on US 27, then W. All year; 14-day limit. 37 free primitive sites. RV limit 20'. Nature trail. **GPS: 32.91, -85.19**

R. SHAEFER HEARD CAMPGROUND

From West Point, 4 mi N on US 29 to dam road; left at signs. 2/25-9/25; 14-day limit. 117 sites with elec/wtr, $24 ($12 with federal senior pass); 10 sites with decks, 7 pull-through. Double sites $48. RV limit in excess of 65 ft. At reserved sites, 2-night stay required/weekends, 3 nights on holiday weekends. Amphitheater. (706) 645-2404. NRRS.
GPS: 39.92722, -85.16389

WHITETAIL RIDGE CAMPGROUND

From LaGrange, 7 mi W on SR 109; 0.8 mi S on Thompson Rd; on left. 3/18-11/27; 14-day limit. 58 sites with elec/wtr, $24 ($12 with federal senior pass); 4 pull-through. Double sites $48. RV limit in excess of 65'. At reserved sites, 2-night stay required on weekends, 3 nights on holiday weekends. (706) 882-8972. NRRS. **GPS: 33.02222, -85.19167**

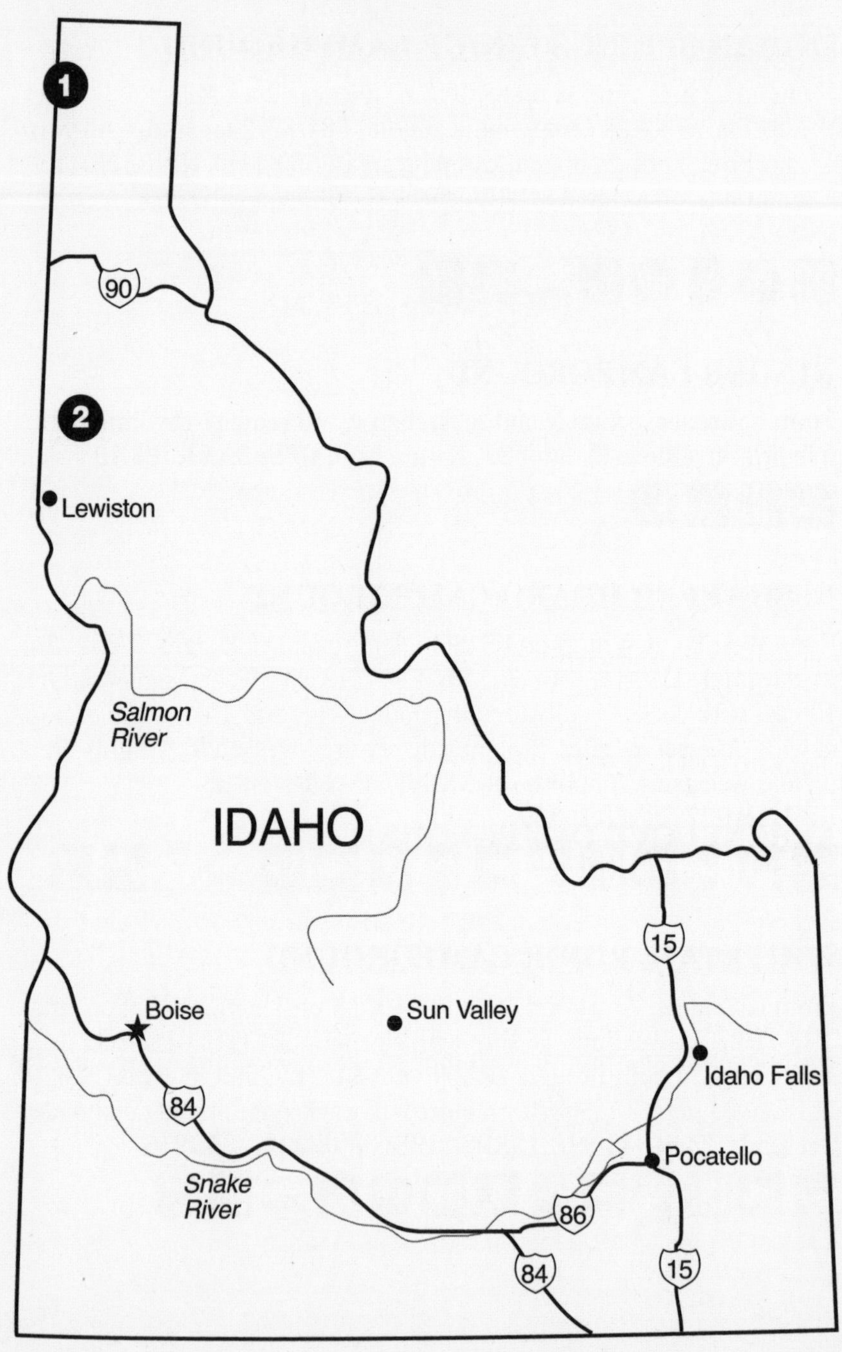
1
90
2
Lewiston
Salmon River
IDAHO
15
Boise
Sun Valley
Idaho Falls
84
Pocatello
Snake River
86
84
15

IDAHO

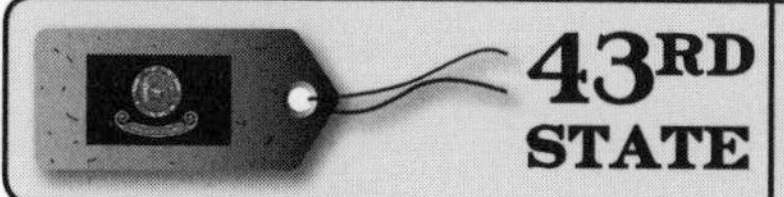

43RD STATE

State Capital: **Boise**
Nickname: **Gem State**
Statehood Year: **1890**

ALBENI FALLS DAM (LAKE PEND OREILLE) (SEA) 1
GPS: 48.25, -116.54

Located in Panhandle of NW Idaho across from Newport, Washington, and S of US 2, 4 mi W of Priest River. 140-plus campsites in four campgrounds. Fee charged for second vehicle overnight. No unlicensed vehicles permitted. 25-cent fee for showers. Checkout time 2 p.m. Visitor center, historic & cultural site, interpretive programs. Other Rec. areas: Johnson Creek Rec., leased to State of Idaho for free primitive camping (3-day limit) & boat launch (pit toilet, no drkg wtr); Vista Rec. Area, visitor center, movie theater, picnicking, amphitheater, restrooms; Morton Slough Access Area, leased to state for picnicking & boat ramp (pit toilets, no drkg wtr); Trestle Creek Rec. Area, picnicking, swimming, boat ramp, pit toilet. For recorded campground status, call (208) 437-5517. Resource Manager, Albeni Falls Project, 2576 E Highway 2, Oldtown, ID 83822-9243. (208) 437-3133.

ALBENI COVE CAMPGROUND

From Newport, SE on SR 41; 3 mi E (left) on Fourth St (part gravel); stay on the dirt road, veering left at the forks; directly across from dam. Rough access, not suitable for large RVs. 5/14-9/10; 14-day limit. 5 walk-to tent sites, $18 ($9 with federal senior pass); 10 RV/tent sites without hookups, $18 ($9 with federal senior pass. RV limit 20'. Fee for firewood. Bird watching, interpretive programs, jet skiing, kayaking, phone. NRRS.
GPS: 48.17722, -116.9975

PRIEST RIVER RECREATION AREA

From Priest River at jct with SR 57, 1 mi E on US 2; turn right; at confluence of Priest & Pend Oreille Rivers. 5/14-9/10; 14-day limit. 20 RV sites without hookups (8 pull-through), $16 ($8 with federal senior pass);

5 bike-in tent sites, $4 ($2 with federal senior pass). Showers 25 cents; no day use fees; dump, boat ramp, swimming areas, picnicking open to non-campers. Picnic shelter $35. Amphitheater. RV limit 60'. NRRS. **GPS: 48.17917, -116.88889**

RILEY CREEK RECREATION AREA

From Priest River Park, 9 mi E on US 2 to LaClede; 1 mi S on Riley Creek Rd. 5/14-9/24; 14-day limit. 67 sites with elec/wtr, $24 ($12 with federal senior pass). No entrance or day use fees; beach, trails, bike ramp,, dump, playground, picnicking free to non-campers. Coin showers. Two picnic shelters, $35. Amphitheater, horseshoe pits, bike trail, bird watching, campfire programs, canoeing, group grill, information center, interpretive programs, jet skiing, kayaking, phone, play field. RV limit 40'. NRRS. **GPS: 48.16111, -116.77028**

SPRINGY POINT RECREATION AREA

From Sandpoint at jct with US 2, S on US 95 across long bridge; 3 mi W on Lakeshore Dr, N of rd. 5/14-9/24; 14-day limit. 38 sites without hookups, including 1 walk-in tent site & 7 pull-through RV sites, $18 ($9 with federal senior pass). Coin shower, phone. NRRS.
GPS: 48.2375, -116.58333

DWORSHAK RESERVOIR (WW) 2
GPS: 46.51, -116.2961

A 54-mi lake located 5 mi NE of Orofino on SR 7 E of Lewiston & N of US 12 in NW Idaho. Noted for Kokanee salmon, rainbow trout and smallmouth bass. Guided group tours, audio-visual programs, displays, visitor center, fish hatchery. Day use facilities include Big Eddy Rec. Area, boat ramp, marina, picnicking, group shelter, playground, beach, hiking trail; Bruce's Eddy Rec. Area, boat ramp; Dam Viewpoint, picnicking; Merrys Bay, picnicking, hiking trails. For reservoir information call 1-800-321-3198. Resource Manager, P. O. Box 48, Ahsahka, ID 83520-0048. (208) 476-1255/1261/ 1-800-321-3198.

CANYON CREEK CAMPGROUND

From Orofino, 11 mi NE off Elk River, Wells Bench & Eureka Ridge Rds (gravel, signs). 17 free primitive RV/tent sites. RV limit 22'. Open from spring through fall; 14-day limit. Pit toilets. **GPS: 48.35, -116.75**

COLD SPRINGS GROUP CAMPGROUND

On S shore of lake across from Dent Acres boat ramp. Boat-in or hike-in access only. Free primitive tent camping area. Open from spring through fall; 14-day limit. Fire pits, grills, tbls, pit toilets.

DAM VIEW RECREATION AREA

From Orofino, 5 mi W on SR 7 to Dworshak entrance, follow signs 2 mi; turn on Big Eddy Rd. Open spring through fall; 14-day limit. primitive sites. Chemical toilets, fire pits, no drkg wtr.

DENT ACRES CAMPGROUND

From Orofino, 20 mi NE on Elk River Rd via Wells Bench Rd (signs). 4/7-11/30; 14-day limit. 49 pull-through sites with 50-amp elec/wtr, $18 during peak season of 5/19-9/5 ($9 with federal senior pass); $10 during 4/7-5/18 & 9/6-11/30 ($5 with federal senior pass). RV limit 35 ft. Picnic shelter for up to 100 people & 26 vehicles, $25. Fish cleaning station (closed in winter), marine dump station, ice & firewood($). (208) 476-9029. NRRS during 5/20-9/7. **GPS: 46.6361, -116.21833**

DENT ACRES GROUP CAMPGROUND

From Orofino, 18 mi NE on Elk River Rd via Wells Bench Rd (2 mi from Dent Acres campground). 5/1-9/30. 3-acre tent camping area for up to 200 people and 48 vehicles, $50. Pit toilets Picnic shelter with elec.

GRANDAD CREEK CAMPGROUND

From project office, 68 mi N on Silver Creek Rd & Musselman Rd (both gravel); no signs. 10 free primitive sites. Pit toilets, no drkg wtr. Open spring through fall, subject to weather conditions.

MINI CAMPS CAMPGROUND

Accessible by boat-in or hiking trail, marked by signs, at various locations around the lake. Group camping with maps available. 121 free primitive tent sites. Open spring through fall. Pit toilets, no drkg wtr.

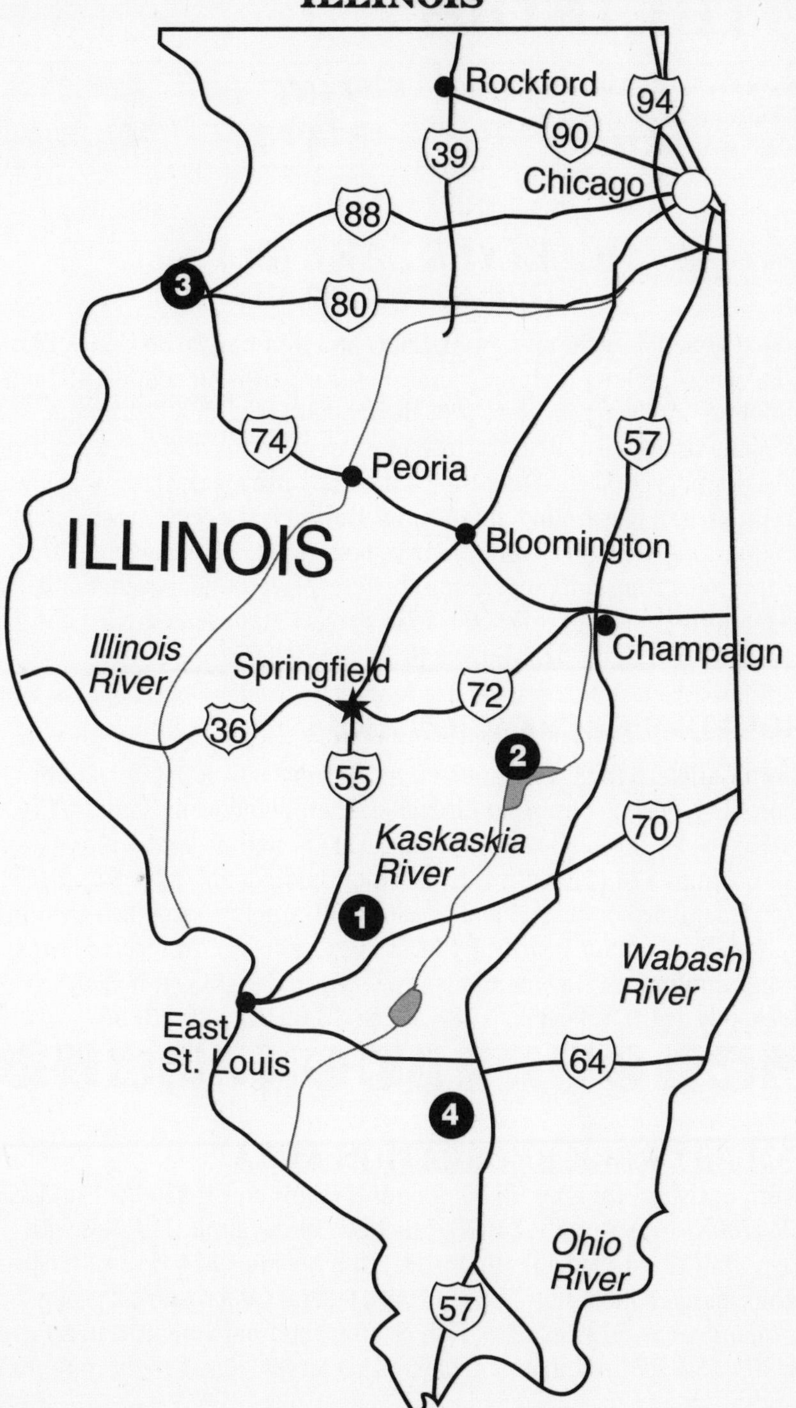

Rockford
94
90
39
Chicago
88
3
80
74
Peoria
57
ILLINOIS
Bloomington
Champaign
Illinois River
Springfield
72
36
2
55
70
Kaskaskia River
1
Wabash River
East St. Louis
64
4
Ohio River
57

ILLINOIS

State Capital: **Springfield**
Nickname: **Prairie State**
Statehood Year: **1818**

21ST STATE

CARLYLE LAKE (SL) 1
GPS: 37.7167, -89.0183

A 26,000-acre lake 50 mi E of St. Louis and N of Carlyle on US 50. Dam E Lakeview parking lot has a handicap fishing pier. All comfort stations, buildings and camping areas provide handicap facilities. Dam tours, seaplane usage, visitor center, interpretive programs, historic & cultural sites. Campground checkout time 4 p.m. Day use areas: Dam W Spillway, group shelter, playground, interpretive trails, visitor center with exhibits & aquarium; General Dean Rec. Area, boat ramp; Keyesport Rec. Area, boat ramp, group camping, group shelters, playground, beach. For daily lake information, call (618) 594-4637. Project Manager, Carlyle Lake, 801 Lake Rd., Carlyle, IL 62231-9703. (618) 594-2484/5253.

BOULDER RECREATION AREA

From Carlyle, 6 mi E on US 50; 3.5 mi N (sign) on CR 2500E; 0.5 mi E on CR 1700N; 2.4 mi N on CR 2550E, then W following signs. 4/15-10/15; 14-day limit. 83 sites with elec, $14 ($7 with federal senior pass); full hookups $24 ($12 with federal senior pass); double sites $28 ($14 with federal senior pass). Picnic shelter $30, amphitheater, fish cleaning station. Boat rentals nearby. RV limit in excess of 65'. At reserved sites, 2-night minimum stay required on weekends, 3 nights on holiday weekends. (618) 594-5253. NRRS. **GPS: 38.69167, -89.23306**

COLES CREEK RECREATION AREA

From Carlyle, 6 mi E on US 50; 3.5 mi N (sign) on CR 2500E; 1 mi W on CR 1700N; 1 mi S on CR 2400E. 5/1-9/30; 14-day limit. 119 sites with elec, $14 ($7 with federal senior pass); full hookups $24 ($12 with federal senior pass); double sites $28 ($14 with federal senior pass); 2 group camping areas, $125 & $225. Fish cleaning station, amphitheater. Picnic shelter $30. RV limit in excess of 65'. At reserves sites, 2 night minimum stay required on weekends, 3 nights on holiday weekends. (618) 226-3211. NRRS. **GPS: 38.65444, -89.26722**

DAM WEST RECREATION AREA

From Carlyle, 1 mi N on CR 1800E. 4/1-11/1; 14-day limit. 109 sites with elec, $12-$18 ($6-$9 with federal senior pass); full hookups $24 ($12 with federal senior pass); double sites $36; ($48 with full hookups). RV limit in excess of 65'. Picnic shelter $30. Fish cleaning station, amphitheater. Boat rentals nearby. At reserved sites, 2-night minimum required stay on weekends, 3 nights on holiday weekends. (618) 594-4410. NRRS. **GPS: 38.62778, -90.35933**

EAST SPILLWAY RECREATION AREA

Below dam. 5/1-9/30; 14-day limit. 5 sites without hookups, $10 ($5 with federal senior pass); 10 sites with elec, $12 ($6 with federal senior pass). Picnic shelter $30.

LOTUS GROUP CAMPGROUND

Within the Coles Creek Rec. Area. 5/1-9/30; 14-day limit. Group camping area for up to 80 people & 25 vehicles with 10 mini shelters, 4 bunk beds in each, and a sheltered dining area that seats 30 people, $75. Fish cleaning station. This campground requires a 2 night minimum stay on weekends and a 3 night stay on holiday weekends. NRRS.

MCNAIR GROUP CAMPGROUND

Within the Dam E Rec. area. 5/1-9/30; 14-day limit. 44 sites, $10 without hookups ($5 with federal senior pass), $14 with elec ($7 with federal senior pass). Also 4 group camping areas with elec & picnic shelters, $50-$175. Fish cleaning station. When not reserved, single sites are available. At reserved sites, 2-night minimum stay required on weekends, 3 nights on holiday weekends. NRRS. **GPS: 38.630615, -89.29248**

LAKE SHELBYVILLE (SL) 2
GPS: 39.41, -88.7767

An 11,100-acre lake NE of Shelbyville, 31 mi S of Decatur and SW of I-57 from Matoon. Visitor center has interpretive audiovisual programs and exhibits. Dam tours on weekends from Memorial Day weekend through Labor Day; they start at the visitor center at 3 p.m. Saturday and 11 a.m. Sunday. Equestrian trail nearby. Checkout time 4 p.m. Unreserved picnic shelters are free. Day use facilities: Camp Campbell Environmental Study Area -- group picnicking, shelter, hiking trails; Dam E Park -- picnicking, shelter ($30), playground; Dam W Park -- boat ramp, picnicking, shelter ($30), playground, beach ($1 per person), trails; Lithia Springs Chautauqua -- picnicking; Okaw Bluff -- hiking trails; Spillway Area -- picnicking, shelter ($30), playground; Whitley Creek Park -- boat ramp, picnicking; Dam W Overlook -- Shelter ($30), large group shelter ($50); Dam W Beach -- shelter ($30); Wilborn Creek -- beach ($1). Day use $4; $3 at most boat ramps. Daily lake information, recording (217) 774-2020. Operations Manager, Lake Shelbyville, RR #4, Box 128B, Shelbyville, IL 62565-9804. (217) 774-3951/3313.

COON CREEK CAMPGROUND

From Findlay, 2.8 mi S; 0.2 mi W on CR 1900; 1.7 mi S on CR 2075; on W side of lake. About 4/1-10/15; 14-day limit. 208 sites with wtr/elec, $18 ($9 with federal senior pass); 6 full hookups $24 ($12 with federal senior pass); double sites $48. 30 pull-through. RV limit in excess of 65'. Fish cleaning station, amphitheater, horseshoe pits, phone, nature trail. 2-night minimum stay/weekends, 3 nights/holiday weekends. Non-campers $3 for boat ramp. (217) 774-2233. NRRS. **GPS: 39.45139, -88.7625**

FORREST W. "BO" WOOD CAMPGROUND

From Sullivan, 2.6 mi S on SR 32; 0.5 mi W at sign. About 4/15-10/30; 14-day limit. 77 sites with elec (more being built), $18 ($9 with federal senior pass), full hookups $24 ($12 with federal senior pass); double sites $36. RV limit in excess of 65'. Picnic shelter ($30), amphitheater, fish cleaning station. 2-night minimum stay/weekends, 3 nights/holiday weekends. Non-campers $3 for boat ramp. NRRS **GPS: 39.55139, -88.62222**

LITHIA SPRINGS CAMPGROUND

From Shelbyville, 3.2 mi E on SR 16; 2.1 mi N on CR 2200E; 1.4 mi W; on E side of lake. About 4/15-10/30; 14-day limit. 115 sites with elec, $18 ($9 with federal senior pass); $22 with full hookups ($11 with federal senior pass); double sites $36. 4 pull-through sites. RV limit in excess of 65'. Picnic shelter ($30), amphitheater, horseshoe pits, fish cleaning station. 2-night minimum stay/weekends, 3 nights/holiday weekends. Non-campers pay $3 for boat ramp. NRRS. **GPS: 39.43444, -88.76**

LONE POINT CAMPGROUND

From Findlay, 2.8 mi S; 0.5 mi E on CR 1785; 0.8 mi S on CR 2150; 0.5 mi E on CR 1725; 0.5 mi S on CR 2175 (E of Coon Creek Rd). About 5/15-9/15; 14-day limit. 2 tent sites, 5 RV/tent sites & 85 sites with elec, $16 ($8 with federal senior pass); double sites $32 ($16 with federal senior pass). 4 group camping areas, $80-$160. RV limit in excess of 65 ft. Amphitheater, fish cleaning station, picnic shelter ($30), phone, 11-mi backpack trail. 2-night minimum stay on weekends, 3 nights on holiday weekends. Non-campers pay $3 for boat ramp. Open from May 3rd to September 3rd. NRRS. **GPS: 39.45222, -88.74028**

OKAW BLUFF GROUP CAMPGROUND

From Sullivan, 4.7 mi S on SR 32. About 3/1-11/30; 14-day limit. 2 group camping areas, $140. 2 houses for up to 34 persons; bunk beds, no linens; kitchen with utensils, showers, ice machine, picnic tables, outdoor grills, Rec. facilities, meeting room($75). For information and reservation, call (217) 774-3951.

OPOSSUM CREEK CAMPGROUND

From Shelbyville, 3.4 mi N on SR 128; 0.9 mi E on CR 1650N; 0.5 mi S on CR 1880E; 1.2 mi E on CR 1600N. About 5/15-LD; 14-day limit. 21 tent sites, 57 RV/tent sites with elec, $16 ($8 with federal senior pass); double sites $32. RV limit in excess of 65'. Fish cleaning station, phone. 2-night minimum stay on weekends, 3 nights on holiday weekends. NRRS. **GPS: 39.44556, -88.7725**

WILBORN CREEK GROUP CAMPGROUND

From Bethany, 2.5 mi SE on SR 121; 3.5 mi S to sign, then 0.75 mi W. About 5/27-LD; 14-day limit. Small group camping area for up to 80 people, about 10 RVs & 25 tents. No elec. $120. Fish cleaning station, nearby beach. 2-night minimum stay on weekends, 3 nights on holiday weekends. Campers use showers at Bo Wood Campground (8 mi). Non-campers pay $3 for boat ramp, $1 per person for swimming beach. (217) 774-3951. Reservations required; NRRS. **GPS: 39.57556, -88.70333**

MISSISSIPPI RIVER PUA (RI) 3
GPS: 44.95, -93.10

Mississippi River Visitor Center is N of SR 92 between I-74 and US 67 on the Rock Island Arsenal, an island just N of Rodman Ave near Government Bridge. Observation area for locking operations, exhibits, theater with seasonal hours, instructional programs. At campgrounds, free sites during winter may have reduced amenities. IL day use areas include: Big Slough Rec. area -- boat ramp ($3), fishing, picnicking; Cattail Slough Rec. Area, boat ramp ($3), fishing; Canton Chute Rec. Area -- pit toilets, boat ramp; Lock & Dam 21 -- boat & wildlife observation deck, picnicking, toilets, tours of lock. For info., contact park rangers. No's 1-3, L&D #11, Dubuque, IA 52001, (563) 582-0881. No's 4-10, P. O. Box 398, Thomson, IL 61285, (815) 259-3628. No's 12-17, L&D #16, 1611-2nd Ave., Muscatine, IA 52761, (563) 263-7913. No's 18-23, L&D #21, Quincy, IL 62301, (217) 228-0890. Visitor center, PO Box 2004, Rock Island, IL 61204-2004 (309) 794-5338. See IA, MO, WI listings.

NO. 12. ANDALUSIA SLOUGH RECREATION AREA

From Andalusia, across river S of Davenport, IA, 2 mi W on SR 92; along the river. All year; 14-day limit. Rd.-style primitive camping, $4 during 5/15-10/15 ($2 with federal senior pass); free rest of year. 16 sites, some pull-through. Picnic shelter, wtr hydrants, pit toilets. **GPS: 41.4392, -90.7754**

NO. 19. BEAR CREEK RECREATION AREA

From Quincy, 12 mi N on SR 96 to Marcelline; 1.5 mi on Bolton Rd; 3 mi W across levee. All year; 14-day limit. 40 free primitive. Picnic shelter. **GPS: 40.111816, -91.47949**

NO. 15. BLANCHARD ISLAND RECREATION AREA

From Muscatine at the Iowa bridge, 1.5 mi E on SR 92; 4 mi S; second right past Copperas Creek Bridge; off the river's main channel. All year; 14-day limit. 34 sites. $4 during 5/15-10/15 ($2 with federal senior pass); free rest of year. Volunteer host. **GPS: 41.3481, -91.0557**

NO. 2. BLANDING LANDING RECREATION AREA

From Galena at jct with US 20, S on county rd to Blanding, then W. About 5/15-10/25; 14-day limit. 7 sites without elec, $10 ($5 with federal senior pass); 30 sites with elec, $14 ($7 with federal senior pass). No wtr hookups. RV limit 50'. Picnic shelter $25. Amphitheater, phone. At reserved sites, 2-night minimum stay required on weekends, 3 nights on holiday weekends. (815) 591-2326. NRRS. **GPS: 42.2858, -90.4033**

NO. 9. FISHERMAN'S CORNER RECREATION AREA

From Hampton, 1 mi N on SR 84 or from I 80, 1 mi S SR 84; near L&D #14. About 4/9-10/24; 14-day limit. 5 tent sites, $10 ($5 with federal senior pass); 29 RV/tent sites with elec. 30-amp sites $16 ($8 with federal senior pass), 50-amp sites $18 ($9 with federal senior pass). RV limit in excess of 65'. Amphitheater, horseshoe pits. At reserved sites, 2-night minimum stay required/weekends, 3 nights/holiday weekends. Good view of river barges, lock & dam. (309) 496-2720. NRRS.
GPS: 41.56972, -90.39

NO. 21. JOHN HAY RECREATION AREA

On Hwy 106 near E Hannibal. All year; 14-day limit. 8 free primitive sites. Picnic shelter.

NO. 7. LOCK & DAM #13 RECREATION AREA

From Fulton, 2 mi N on SR 84; W on Lock Rd (signs). All year; 14-day limit. 6 free primitive sites, $3 day use fee for boat ramp during 5/1-11/30 ($1.50 with federal senior pass); free rest of year. Picnic shelter, observation deck overlooking lock chamber. **GPS: 41.498438, -90.154297**

NO. 22. PARK & FISH RECREATION AREA

From Hull, 0.7 mi W on US 36; 6.1 mi S; on Illinois side of L&D #22. All year; 14-day limit. 6 free primitive sites. A picnic shelter.

NO. 5. THOMSON CAUSEWAY RECREATION AREA

From Thomson, W 4-5 blocks on Main St; S on Lewis Ave, following signs; on island in river's back-water. About 4/8-10/24; 14-day limit. 5 tent sites, $10 ($5 with federal senior pass); 76 sites with elec, $16 or $18 at premium locations ($8 & $9 with federal senior pass). 4 pull-through sites. RV limit in excess of 65'. Two picnic shelters, $25. Amphitheater. At reserved sites, 2-night minimum stay required on weekends, 3 nights on holiday weekends. For 2011, new & renovated shower facilities, sewer line added, dump station renovated. (815) 259-3628. NRRS.
GPS: 41.95167, -90.11083

RAND LAKE (SL) 4

GPS: 38.0383, -88.97

A 18,900-acre lake located N of Benton on SR 14 W of I-57 in S-central Illinois. Checkout time 4 p.m, Visitor center offers exhibits, interpretive programs, live snake display. Boat rentals nearby. Day use areas: Dam W Area -- boat ramp($), picnicking, shelter, playground, trails; Gun Creek Wildlife Area -- boat ramp; Ina Access Area -- boat ramp($); Jackie Branch -- boat ramp; N Marcum Day Use Area -- boat ramp, picnicking, shelter($25), playground, beach, trails; Turnip Patch Access -- boat ramp($). New visitor center features exhibits, aquarium, snake display, demonstration wetland garden, demonstration wildlife garden, demonstration bee hives, picnicking, shelter, playground, interpretive trails. For daily lake information, recording (618) 629-1828. Project Manager, Rend Lake, 12220 Rend City Rd., Benton, IL 62812-9803. (618) 724-2493.

DALE MILLER YOUTH GROUP AREA

From I-57 exit 71, 2.5 mi W on SR 14; 2.5 mi N on Rend City Rd; E (right) on Rend Lake Dam Rd; N (left) on Trail Head Lane. 4/1-10/30. Group camping for up to 200 people and 50 vehicles, $75-$150. 5 cabins with bunk beds (sleep 8); RV & tent sites available. 2-night minimum stay on weekends, 3 nights on holiday weekends. Amphitheater, picnic shelters. Boat rentals nearby. ORV prohibited w/o prior approval. NRRS.

GUN CREEK RECREATION AREA

From Benton, 6 mi N on I-57 to exit 77; 0.2 mi W on SR 154; S on Gun Creek Trail & 0.5 mi W on Golf Course Dr. About 3/15-11/30; 14-day limit. 100 sites with elec, $16 ($8 with federal senior pass). RV limit 65'. Picnic shelter $25. Amphitheater, interactive programs. At reserved sites, 2-day minimum stay required on weekends, 3 days on holiday weekends. (618) 629-2338. NRRS. **GPS: 38.07861, -88.93028**

NORTH SANDUSKY RECREATION AREA

From Benton, 6 mi N on I-57 to exit 77; 6 mi W on SR 154; S on Rend City Rd to stop sign; on S side of intersection. About 3/15-11/1; 14-day limit. 118 sites with elec/wtr, $16 base ($8 with federal senior pass); full hookups $24 ($12 with federal senior pass). Shagbark group camping with elec, $100. RV limit 65'. Picnic shelter $25. Campground store, bike trails. 2-day minimum stay on weekends, 3 days on holiday weekends. (618) 625-6115. NRRS. **GPS: 38.07888, -89.00556**

SOUTH MARCUM RECREATION AREA

From Benton at I-57 exit 71, 2.5 mi W on SR 14; 2.5 mi N on Rend City Rd; E on Rend Lake Dam Rd, N on Trail Head Lane. 4/1-10/30; 14-day limit. 14 walk-to tent sites, $12 ($6 with federal senior pass); 146 sites with elec/wtr, $16 ($8 with federal senior pass), $22 full hookups ($11 with federal senior pass), double sites $40. RV limit in excess of 65'. Picnic shelter ($25), amphitheater. Boat rentals, horseback riding nearby. 2-day minimum stay on weekends, 3 days on holiday weekends. (618) 435-3549. NRRS. Campground was closed in 2010 for extensive renovation; check current status before visit. **GPS: 38.0375, -88.93611**

SOUTH SANDUSKY CAMPGROUND

From Benton at I-57 exit 71, 2.5 mi W on SR 14; 6 miN on Rend City Rd. 4/1-11/1; 14-day limit. 8 walk-to tent sites, $12 ($6 with federal senior pass); 119 sites with elec/wtr, $16 ($8 with federal senior pass); full hookups $24 ($12 with federal senior pass). Picnic shelter $25. Amphitheater. Boat rentals, horseback riding nearby. RV limit 65'. 2-day minimum stay on weekends, 3 days on holiday weekends. (618) 625-3011. NRRS. **GPS: 38.06028, -89.00472**

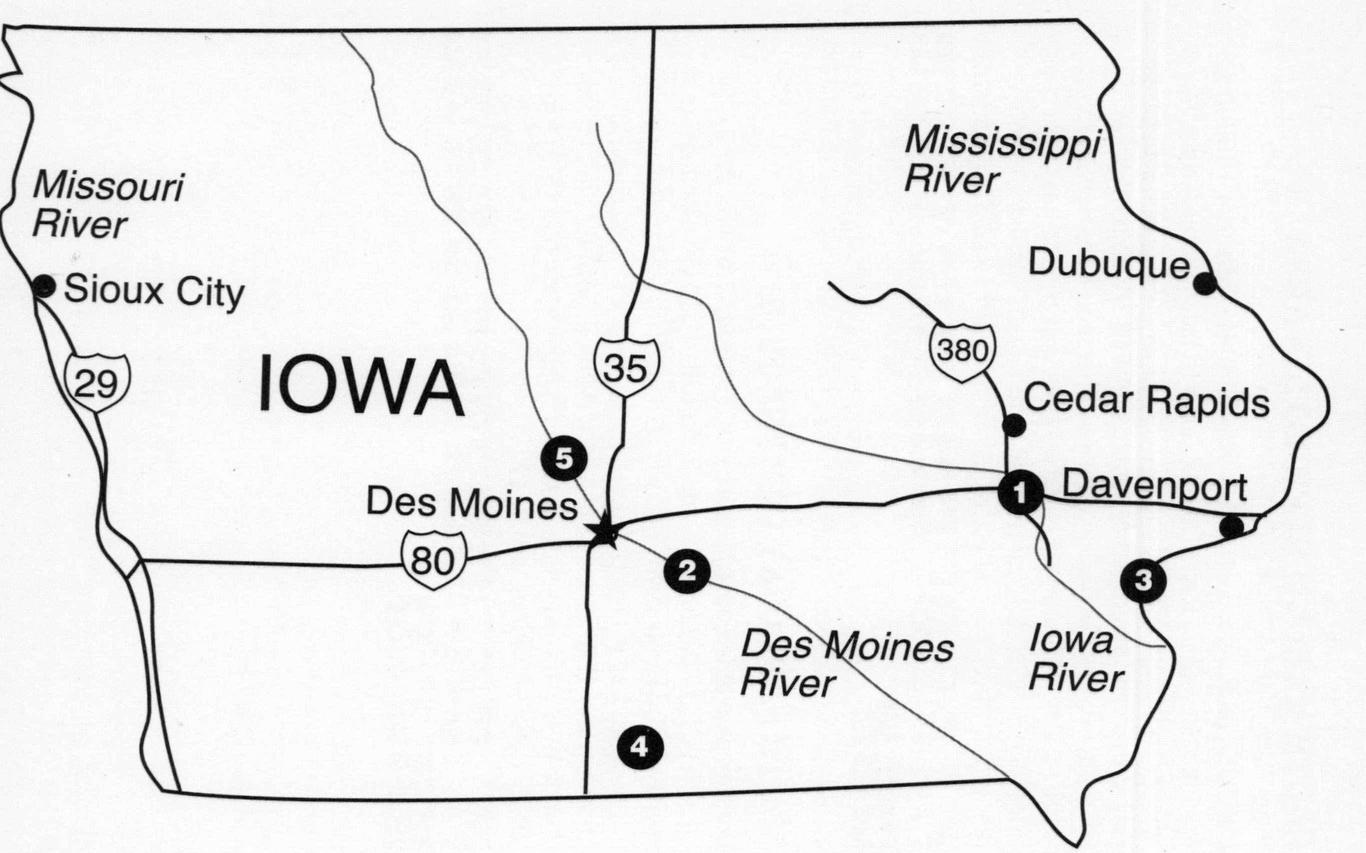
Missouri River
Sioux City
29
IOWA
35
5
Des Moines
80
2
4
Des Moines River
Mississippi River
Dubuque
380
Cedar Rapids
1
Davenport
3
Iowa River

IOWA

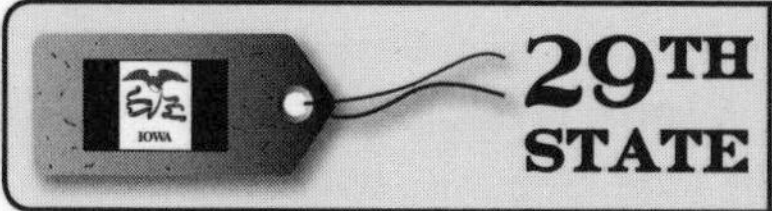

State Capital: **Des Moines**
Nickname: **Hawkeye State**
Statehood Year: **1846**

CORALVILLE LAKE (RI) 1
GPS: 41.723772, -91.522174

A 5,430-acre lake 3 mi N of Coralville/Iowa City. Off exit 244 of I-80, 55 mi W of Davenport. Visitor center with displays on history & natural resources of lake area; includes replica eagle's nest, fossils, 12-minute movie about flood of 1993. Campground checkout time 5 p.m. ORV prohibited. Day use areas: Curtis Bridge -- boat ramp; Mehaffey Bridge -- boar ramp($3); Square Point -- hiking; Turkey Creek Recreation Area -- picnic shelter, playground, hiking, disc golf; Sugar Bottoms Day Use Area -- disc golf, mountain biking trails; Sandy Beach Day Use Area -- boat ramp($3). Park Manager, Coralville Lake, 2850 Prairie du Chien Rd., NE, Iowa City, IA 52240-7820. (319) 338-3543.

DAM COMPLEX

This complex comprises Cottonwood, Linder Point, Tail Waters E and W, and W Overlook campgrounds. Requires a 2-day minimum stay on weekends and 3 days on holiday weekends at reserved sites. Visitor center, disc golf course at Turkey Creek, Devonian Fossil Gorge, interpretive trail. 60% of sites reservable. NRRS.

COTTONWOOD CAMPGROUND

On W side of spillway. 4/15-10/14; 14-day limit. 15 walk-in tent sites. $12 ($6 with federal senior pass). NRRS. **GPS: 41.43351, -91.32081**

LINDER POINT CAMPGROUND

On W side of dam, N of access rd. 4/15-10/14; 14-day limit. 26 sites (9 with 50-amp elec), 9 full hookups, some walk-in sites. Walk-in tent sites & tent sites without elec, $12 ($6 with federal senior pass); RV/tent sites without elec, $12-$14 ($6-$7 with federal senior pass); sites with elec, $16 ($8 with federal senior pass); premium sites with elec, $20 ($10 with federal senior pass); sites with full hookups, $24 ($12 with federal senior pass). RV limit in excess of 65'. **GPS: 41.43405. -9132545**

SANDY BEACH CAMPGROUND

From I-380 at exit 10, E on 120th St; S on Curtis Bridge Rd; E on Sandy Rd, follow signs. 5/1-9/30; 14-day limit. 60 sites. 10 primitive walk-to tent sites, $12 ($6 with federal senior pass); 48 sites with elec, $18 ($9 with federal senior pass); 2 sites with full hookups, $22 ($11 with federal senior pass). RV limit in excess of 65'. Horseshoe pits, phone, shelter. 2-day minimum stay on weekends, 3 days on holiday weekends. NRRS. **GPS: 41.81361, -91.59528**

SUGAR BOTTOM CAMPGROUND

From I-80, N on I-380 to exit 4, then E on Penn St to N Front St. (Mehaffey Bridge Rd); cross Mehaffey bridge, then 1.3 mi S (right). 5/1-9/30; 14-day limit. 17 walk-to tent sites, $12 ($6 with federal senior pass); 224 sites with elec, including 13 full hookups, 33 pull-through. Base rate with elec, $16; premium sites with elec, $18; 50-amp elec sites, $20; full hookups $24 (rates $8, $9, $10 & $12 with federal senior pass). RV limit in excess of 65'. Amphitheater, horseshoe pits, disc golf course, mountain bike trails. Four group camping areas, $72-$180. 2-day minimum stay on weekends, 3 days on holiday weekends. NRRS.
GPS: 41.75639, -91.55917

TAIL WATER EAST CAMPGROUND

Below dam on E side of the outlet. 4/15-10/14; 14-day limit. 28 sites, 22 with electric (5 with 50-amp) & 5 walk-in tent sites. 1 pull-through RV site. Tent sites $12 ($6 with federal senior pass); sites without elec, $12-$14 ($6-$7 with federal senior pass); sites with elec $16 ($8 with federal senior pass); premium sites with elec, $20 ($10 with federal senior pass); sites with 50-amp elec, $20. RV limit in excess of 65'. Fish cleaning station. **GPS: 41.43255, -91.31673**

TAIL WATER WEST CAMPGROUND

Below dam on W side of the outlet. 4/15-10/15; 14-day limit. 30 sites (9 walk-in tent sites). Tent sites $12 ($6 with federal senior pass); sites without elec, $12-$14 ($6-$7 with federal senior pass); sites with elec, $16 ($8 with federal senior pass); sites with 50-amp elec $20 ($10 with federal senior pass); full hookups $24 ($12 with federal senior pass). Picnic shelter, fish cleaning station. During 2010, 20 sites upgraded to concrete pads with hookups, some full hookups. **GPS: 41.43334, -91.31758**

WEST OVERLOOK CAMPGROUND

On W side of dam, N of dam access rd. 4/15-10/15. 89 sites with electric (1 handicap site, 1 pull-through), $16 ($8 with federal senior pass); premium sites with elec, $20 ($10 with federal senior pass). Picnic shelter, fish cleaning station. **GPS: 41.43535, -91.32133**

LAKE RED ROCK (RI) 2
GPS: 41.3708, -92.9794

A 15,000-acre lake 4 mi SW of Pella off SR 163, SE of Des Moines in southwestern Iowa. Visitor center, interpretive programs, campfire programs. Checkout time 4 p.m. Day use areas: Fifield Recreation Area -- picnic shelter ($30), playground; N Tailwater -- shelter ($30), playground; S Overlook -- boat ramp, shelter ($30); S Tailwater -- shelter ($30). For camping/lake information, recording, call (641) 828-7522. Operations Manager, Lake Red Rock, 1105 Highway T-15, Knoxville, IA 50138-9522. (641) 828-7522/628-8690.

HOWELL STATION RECREATION AREA

From Pella at jct with SR 163, 1 mi W on SR 28; 5 mi SW on CR T-15; E on Idaho; S on 198th Pl, then S following signs. 4/14-10/31; 14-day limit. 143 sites with elec, 66 with 50-amp, $20 ($10 with federal senior pass). Amphitheater with weekend programs during MD-LD, fish cleaning station. RV limit in excess of 65 ft. No reservations until flood recovery work completed. **GPS: 41.365, -92.97361**

IVAN'S RECREATION AREA

Below the dam on S side of the outlet. Usually open about 4/15-10/1, but closed until further notice for flood damage reconstruction. 22 sites, $16 ($8 with federal senior pass). Fish cleaning station.

NORTH OVERLOOK CAMPGROUND

From jct with CR G-28, 3 mi S on CR T-15. 4/21-9/26; 14-day limit. 9 basic tent sites, $10 ($5 with federal senior pass); 46 sites with elec, $16 ($8 with federal senior pass). Picnic shelter($30), amphitheater with weekend programs MD-LD. RV limit in excess of 65'. 2-day minimum/weekends, 3 days/holiday weekends. NRRS. **GPS: 41.380371, -92.969971**

WALLASHUCK CAMPGROUND

From Pella, 4 mi W on CR G-28; 2 mi S on 190th Ave. 4/21-10/10; 14-day limit. 83 sites with elec, 23 with 50-amp, $16 ($8 with federal senior pass). RV limit in excess of 65'. Amphitheater offers campfire programs MD-LD. Fish cleaning station. 2-day minimum stay on weekends, 3 days on holiday weekends. NRRS. **GPS: 41.4, -92.99417**

WHITEBREAST CAMPGROUND

From Knoxville, 8 mi NE on CR T-15; 2 mi N on CR S-71; on S side of lake. 4/21-9/26; 14-day limit. 109 sites with elec, $16 ($8 with federal senior pass). Two group camping areas, one for up to 96 people & 24 vehicles, $192; the other for up to 56 people & 14 vehicles, $112. Picnic shelter ($30), amphitheater, fish cleaning station. RV limit 60'. 2-day minimum stay/weekends, 3 days/holiday weekends. NRRS. **GPS: 41.36417, -93.025**

MISSISSIPPI RIVER PUA (RI) 3
GPS: 42.53, -90.65

Campsites that are free during the winter may have reduced amenities. Day use facilities: Lock & Dam 11 -- river & wildlife viewing deck, picnicking, Sunday tours of lock; Lock & Dam 14 -- fishing pier, nature trail, picnic shelters; Lock & Dam 16 -- bird watching, observation deck, picnicking, Sunday lock tours; Kilpeck Landing -- boat ramp, picnicking. For information, contact Park Rangers: No's 1-3, L&D #11, 2530 Kerper Blvd., Suite #3,Dubuque, IA 52001, (563) 582-0881. No's 4-10, P. O. Box 398, Thomson, IL 61285, (815) 259-3628. No's 12-17, L&D #16, 1611-2nd Avenue, Muscatine, IA 52761, (563) 263-7913. See IL, MO & WI listings.

NO. 6. BULGER'S HOLLOW RECREATION AREA

From Clinton, 3 mi N on US 67; 1 mi E on 170th St; at widest point on the river. All year; 14-day limit. 9 tent sites, 17 RV sites. $4 during 5/15-10/15 ($2 with federal senior pass); some sites free rest of year. Pit toilets, drkg wtr, picnic shelter($25), horseshoe pits. Volunteer host. **GPS: 41.93457, -90.181641**

NO. 13. CLARKS FERRY RECREATION AREA

From Muscatine, 15 mi E on SR 22 (signs); on river's main channel. 4/8-10/9; 14-day limit. 27 sites with elec, $16 ($8 with federal senior pass), $18 at premium locations ($9 with federal senior pass). Picnic shelter($25), amphitheater, horseshoe pits. 2-day minimum stay on weekends, 3 days on holiday weekends. (563) 381-4043. NRRS. **GPS: 41.46639, -90.80944**

NO. 17. FERRY LANDING RECREATION AREA

From Muscatine, 25 mi S on US 61, then E on SR 99, following signs for L&D #17; at mouth of Iowa River. All year; 14-day limit. 20 free primitive sites. Pit toilets, no drkg wtr. **GPS: 41.161621, -91.007568**

NO. 3. PLEASANT CREEK RECREATION AREA

From Dubuque, 24 mi S on US 52 following signs for L&D #12; on river's main channel. All year; 14-day limit. 55 primitive sites, $4 during 5/15-10/15 ($2 with federal senior pass), free rest of year. Day use $3. Self registration. **GPS: 42.209961, -90.379639**

NO. 14. SHADY CREEK RECREATION AREA

From Muscatine, 10 mi E on SR 22 (signs). 5/6-10/22; 14-day limit. 39 sites with elec, $16 ($8 with federal senior pass); $18 at premium locations. RV limit in excess of 65'. Picnic shelter $25. Horseshoe pits, amphitheater. 2-day minimum stay on weekends, 3 days on holiday weekends. 16-acre park. (563) 262-8090. NRRS. **GPS: 41.4475, -90.87722**

RATHBUN LAKE (KC) 4

GPS: 40.8283, -92.8767

An 11,000-acre lake 7 mi N of Centerville off SR 5, 85 mi SE of Des Moines in southeastern Iowa near the Missouri state line. A fish hatchery is below the dam. The area around the lake has more than 700 campsites. For information call (641) 647-2464. Resource Manager, Rathbun Lake, 20112 Highway J-5-T, Centerville, IA 52544-8308.

BRIDGEVIEW CAMPGROUND

From Moravia, 10 mi W on Highway 142, follow signs. 5/1-9/29; 14-day limit. 11 sites without elec, $12 ($6 with federal senior pass); 95 sites with elec, $16 ($8 with federal senior pass), $18 at premium sites with 50-amp elec ($9 with federal senior pass), $32 at 7 double sites. 6 pull-through. RV limit in excess of 65'. Picnic shelter for up to 24 people and 12 vehicles, $25. Fish cleaning station. All-terrain vehicle park nearby. At reserved sites, 2-day stay required on weekends, 3 days on holiday weekends. NRRS. **GPS: 40.87861, -93.02667**

BUCK CREEK CAMPGROUND

From Centerville, 5 mi N on Highway 5; 4 mi NW on CR J-29; 2 mi N on CR J-5-T, following signs. 5/1-9/29; 14-day limit. 42 sites with elec, $16 ($8 with federal senior pass), $18 at premium sites with 50-amp elec ($9 with federal senior pass). 10 pull-through sites. RV limit in excess of 65 ft. Picnic shelter, fish cleaning station. At reserved sites, 2-day stay required on weekends, 3 days on holiday weekends. NRRS.
GPS: 40.86278, -92.86778

ISLAND VIEW CAMPGROUND

From Centerville, 2.5 mi N on SR 5; 3.8 mi NW on CR J-29; 0.2 mi N on CR J-5-T. 187 sites with elec. $16 at 30-amp sites ($8 with federal senior pass), $32 at double sites ($16 with federal senior pass); $18 at 50-amp premium sites ($9 with federal senior pass). RV limit in excess of 65'. Group camping area, $125-$250. 3 picnic shelters, $25-$50. At reserved sites, 2-day stay required on weekends, 3 days stay on holiday weekends. NRRS. **GPS: 40.85028, -92.91833**

PRAIRIE RIDGE CAMPGROUND

From Moravia, 4 mi W on Highway J-18; 2.5 mi S on 200th Ave, following signs. 5/1-9/29; 14-day limit. 54 sites with 50-amp elec, $18 ($9 with federal senior pass. RV limit in excess of 65'. Group camping area for up to 72 people & 18 vehicles, $50 Sunday-Thursday, $100 on Friday and Saturday. Picnic shelter for up to 40 people and 12 vehicles, $25. Fish cleaning station. At reserved sites, 2 day stay required on weekends, 3 days on holiday weekends. NRRS. **GPS: 40.87694, -92.88722**

ROLLING COVE CAMPGROUND

From Centerville, W on Highway 2; 6 mi N on CR T-14; 2.5 mi W; 2.5 mi N on 150th Ave; 1 mi E on 435th St, following signs. 5/1-9/29; 14-day limit. 45 sites without elec, $12. RV limit in excess of 65'. No reservations. Fish cleaning station. **GPS: 40.844727, -92.972656**

SAYLORVILLE LAKE (RI) 5
GPS: 41.7036, -93.6811

A 5,950-acre lake N of Des Moines & Johnston. Exit 131 off I-35/80, on Merle Hay Rd, then N on NW Beaver Dr. Visitor center (515) 964-0672. Neal Smith Trail runs 23.7 mi from Big Creek Beach to Des Moines. Day use areas: Cottonwood -- picnicking, playground, trails, 9 picnic shelters ($50); Lakeview -- boat ramp, picnicking, shelter; Oak Grove -- beach, picnicking, playground, trails, 2 shelters ($50); Sandpiper Recreation Area -- boat ramp, marina, picnicking, playgrond, beach, hiking trail, shelter ($110); Walnut Ridge -- picnicking, playground, hiking, shelter ($50). For lake information/recording, call (515) 276-0433. Park Manager, Saylorville Lake, 5600 northwest 78th Avenue, Johnston, IA 50131. (515) 276-4656/270-6173.

ACORN VALLEY CAMPGROUND

From I-35/80 N of Des Moines, exit 131 onto Johnson/Saylorville Rd, then 2.8 mi N on Merle Hay Rd through Johnston; from 4-way stop sign, 3.7 mi NW (left) on Beaver Dr; just past the National Weather

Service Building, turn right onto NW Corydon Dr, then right into the campground. MD-LD; 14-day limit. 66 walk-to tent sites, $12 ($6 with federal senior pass); sites with elec, $16 ($8 with federal senior pass); premium sites with elec, $18 ($9 with federal senior pass); sites with elec/wtr, $22 ($11 with federal senior pass). RV limit 65'. Picnic shelter. Interpretive programs, recycle center, small pond. (515) 276-0429. NRRS. **GPS: 41.73778, -93.72361**

BOB SHETLER CAMPGROUND

From I-35/80 N of Des Moines, exit 131 onto Johnson/Saylorville Rd., then 2.8 mi N on Merle Hay Rd through Johnston; from 4-way stop sign, 1 mi NW (left) on Beaver Dr; at large concrete water storage tank on right, turn right for 0.8 mi NW on 78th Ave; right at T-intersection for 0.4 mi. 5/1-9/30; 14-day limit. 67 sites with elec; 8 pull-through. $16 ($8 with federal senior pass). RV limit in excess of 65'. 2 picnic shelters $50. Fish cleaning station, phone, biking trail. (515) 276-0873. NRRS. **GPS: 41.70167, -93.68528**

CHERRY GLEN CAMPGROUND

From I-35/80 exit 90 N of Des Moines, 2.4 mi on Highway 160 to its end; continue 4.1 mi on Highway 415 N; at campground sign, left turn lane, then 0.6 mi on NW 94th Ave. 4/15-10/15; 14-day limit. 125 sites with elec, $22 ($11 with federal senior pass). RV limit in excess of 65'. Picnic shelter $50. Fish cleaning station, bike rentals nearby. (515) 964-8792. NRRS. **GPS: 41.73139, -93.68**

PRAIRIE FLOWER RECREATION AREA

From I-35 exit 90 N of Des Moines, 2.4 mi on Highway 160 to its end; continue 5.6 mi on Highway 415N; at campground sign, left turn lane, then 0.2 mi on NW Lake Dr. 5/1-10/15; 14-day limit. 153 sites with elec. Base fee $16 ($8 with federal senior pass); premium sites with elec, $18 ($9 with federal senior pass); wtr/elec sites $20 ($10 with federal senior pass); full hookups & 50-amp elec, $24 ($12 with federal senior pass). RV limit in excess of 65'. Ten group camping areas, $64-$252: Elderbery and Knapweed -- up to 24 people & 8 vehicles; Fleabane -- up to 36 people & 12 vehicles; May Weed & June Berry -- up to 48 people & 16 vehicles; Ox-eye -- up to 60 people & 20 vehicles; Nipplewart -- up to 72 people & 24 vehicles; Goldenrod & Ironwood -- up to 84 people & 28 vehicles; Leadplant -- 50-amp elec, up to 84 people & 58 vehicles. Bike rentals nearby. (515) 984-6925. NRRS. **GPS: 41.74833, -93.6875**

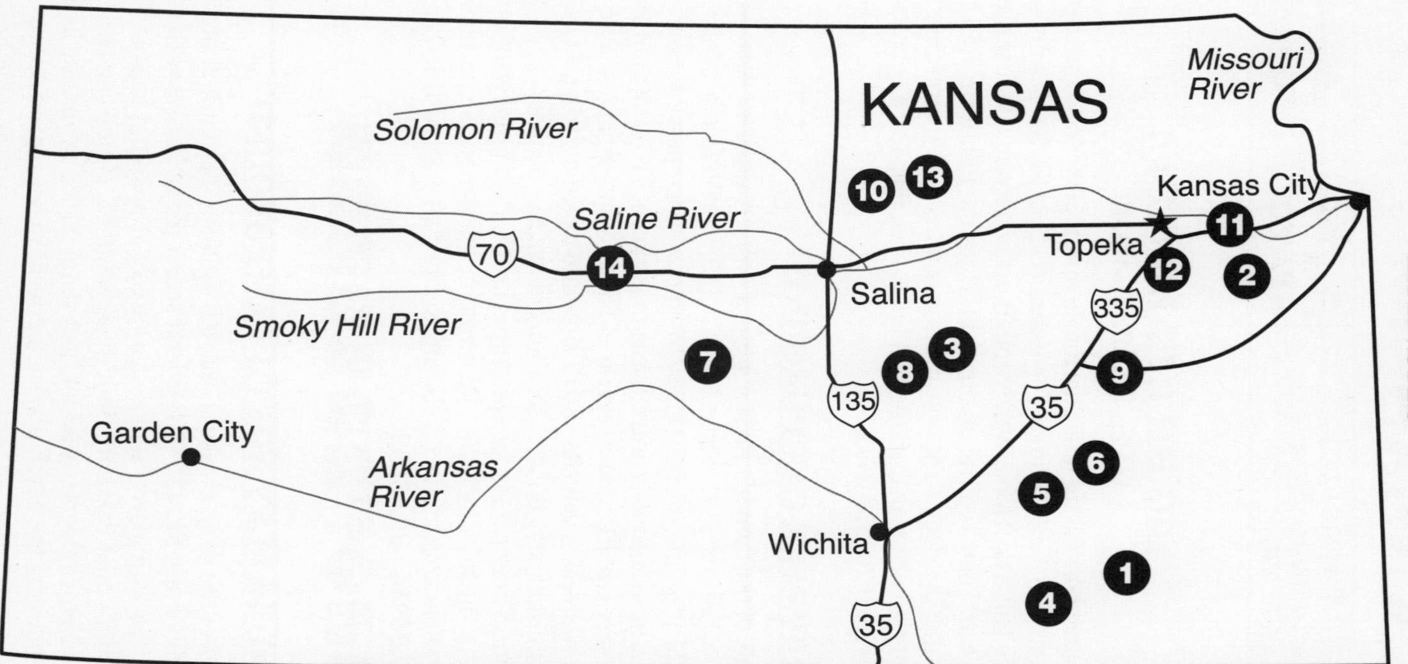

KANSAS
Missouri River
Kansas City
Topeka
Salina
Wichita
Garden City
Solomon River
Saline River
Smoky Hill River
Arkansas River
70
335
35
135
35
1
2
3
4
5
6
7
8
9
10
11
12
13
14

KANSAS

State Capital: **Topeka**
Nickname: **Sunflower State**
Statehood Year: **1861**

34TH STATE

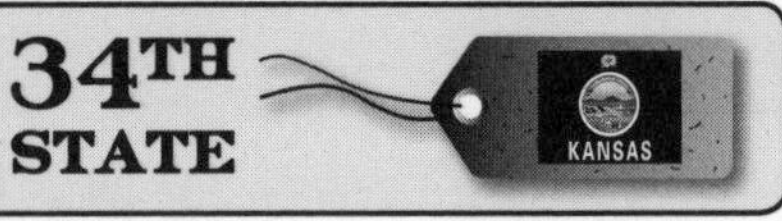

BIG HILL LAKE (TU) 1
GPS: 37.2683, -95.47

A 1,240-acre lake 4.5 mi E of Cherryvale on CR 5000 and 11 mi SW of Parsons and US 400, 160 mi SW of Kansas City in SE Kansas. Includes 17-mi Big Hill Lake Horse Trail through varied terrain. Day use areas: Downstream Point -- picnic shelter $30; Highway 160 Horse Trail -- boat ramp, trails; Overlook Park -- picnicking, shelter $30, interpretive trail, fishing dock. Lake Manager, Big Hill Lake, P. O. Box 426, Cherryvale, KS 67335-0426. (620) 336-2741.

CHERRYVALE CAMPGROUND

On W side of the dam 0.3 mi N of project office (signs). All year; 14-da limit. 23 sites with elec/wtr, $17 base ($8.50 with federal senior pass), $22 at premium sites ($11 with federal senior pass). Lower rates may be available during off-season period of 11/1-3/30, but with reduced services. RV limit in excess of 65'. Group camping area for up to 75 people & 9 vehicles with 7 sites and a picnic shelter, $148. 3-day minimum stay on weekends for groups. Non-campers pay $3 for boat ramp, $1 per person for swimming beach. Park underwent major repairs during 2010, including Rd. work, new water and sewer hookups, upgrading electrical service to 50 amps. Open all year. NRRS.
GPS: 37.26944, -95.45833

MOUND VALLEY NORTH CAMPGROUND

On E side of the dam; at lake shore. 4/1-10/30; 14-day limit. 8 sites without hookups, $12 ($6 with federal senior pass); 74 sites with elec, $16 base ($8 with federal senior pass) & $20 at premium locations ($10 with federal senior pass). RV limit in excess of 65'. Group camping areas, $10-$40. Non-campers pay $3 for boat ramp, $1 for swimming beach. Change house at the beach. Park underwent major repairs during 2010, including Rd. work, new water hookups, upgrade of electrical service to 50 amps. (620) 328-2050. NRRS. **GPS: 37.26944, -95.45833**

TIMBER HILL CAMPGROUND

From E side of the dam, 3 mi N, then W on gravel rd. About 3/26-11/1; 14-day limit. 20 sites without elec, some pull-through. $10. Drkg wtr, pit toilets, fishing dock. Non-campers pay $3 for boat ramp.
GPS: 37.296387, -95.446289

CLINTON LAKE (KC) 2
GPS: 38.9233, -95.33

A 7,000-acre lake with 85 mi of shoreline located 1 mi SW of Lawrence, W of US 59 & 45 mi W of Kansas City. Visitor center. Resource Manager, Clinton Lake, 872 N. 1402 Rd., Lawrence, KS 66049-9176.
(785) 843-7665.

ASH GROUP CAMPGROUND

Near Hickory/Walnut parks. 5/1-9/30. Undesignated-site group camping areas for 10 to 75 persons & 26 vehicles, $50. Picnic shelter, fish cleaning station, horseshoe pits. Pit toilets; shower at Hickory/Walnut Campground. NRRS (through Hickory/Walnut Campground).
GPS: 38.9125, -95.3744

BLOOMINGTON EAST PARK

From Lawrence, 4 mi W on Highway 40 (6th St); 5 mi W (left) on CRoad 442 to Stull; 6 mi S (left) on CR 1023; 4 mi NE (left) on CR 6 through Clinton, then follow signs. Contains Cedar Ridge, Hickory and Walnut campgrounds.

BLOOMINGTON WEST GROUP CAMPGROUND

From Lawrence, 4 mi W on Hwy 40 (6th St); 5 mi W (left) on CR 442 to Stull; 6 mi S (left) on CR 1023; 4 mi NE (left) on CR 4: 0.5 mi E (right) on CR 1200N, then first gravel Rd. on left (near N corner of Clinton). Group camping area with sites (no hookups) for 25-150 people, $100. Sheltered dining area, canoeing, courtesy dock, jet skiing, ball fields, swings, horseshoe pits. NRRS.

GPS: 38.92833, -95.39028

CEDAR RIDGE CAMPGROUND

4/1-10/15; 14-day limit. 84 sites (61 pull-through & 13 offering 50-amp service) with wtr/elec, $18 ($9 with federal senior pass). RV limit in excess of 65'. Horseshoe pits, fish cleaning station. NRRS.

GPS: 38.91278, -95.37472

ELM GROUP CAMPGROUND

Near Hickory/Walnut campgrounds. 5/1-9/30; 14-day limit. Undesignated-site group camping areas for 10-75 persons & 26 vehicles, $50. Picnic shelter, volleyball court, pit toilets, drkg wtr. Pick up gate keys at the Walnut Creek Campground. NRRS.

HICKORY/WALNUT CAMPGROUND

5/1-9/30; 14-day limit. 127 sites without hookups, $10 at Oak Loop, $12 other sites ($5 & $6 with federal senior pass). 94 sites with elec, $16 ($8 with federal senior pass). RV limit in excess of 65'. Amphitheater, fish cleaning station, phone, evening programs. NRRS.

GPS: 38.9125, -95.37444

ROCKHAVEN CAMPGROUND

From Stull, 6 mi S on SR 1023; 3 mi E on SR 458; 0.8 mi N on gravel CR 700E. 4/1-10/30; 14-day limit. Equestrian (horse & mule) camping. 50 sites w/o hookups, $6 self-registration, $8 if ranger collects ($3 & $4 with federal senior pass). 2 pit toilets. Day use parking area for non-campers.
GPS: 38.890137, -95.365234

WOODRIDGE CAMPGROUND

From Stull, 3.4 mi S on CR 1023; 1 mi E on CR 2, 0.4 mi B on gravel CR 350E. All year; 14-day limit. Free primitive trail tent camping on 450 acres along 4.5-mi trail. Fire rings.

COUNCIL GROVE LAKE (TU) 3
GPS: 38.698372, -96.50116

A 3,310 acre lake 1.5 mi NW of Council Grove off US 56 and SR 177, 101 mi SW of Kansas City. All-terrain vehicle area below the dam. Checkout time 4 p.m. Swimming permitted unless otherwise posted. Day use facilities include ORV trail at Outlet Park, hiking trails at Woodridge Park. Some campsites free during winter with reduced amenities; wtr/elec service off 11/1-3/31, but hydrants provided at Neosha Park and the lake office. 50-amp electrical upgrades made at Canning Creek, Santa Fe Trail and Richey Cove Campgrounds. Lake Manager, Council Grove Lake, 945 Lake Rd., Council Grove, KS 66846-9322. (620) 767-5195.

CANNING CREEK COVE CAMPGROUND

From Council Grove, 1.5 mi N on SR 177; W across Dam Rd, then 2 mi right on City Lake Rd. All year; 14-day limit. 4 sites without hookups, $10-$12 during 4/1-10/30 ($5 & $6 with federal senior pass), free off-season. 5 sites with elec, $16 & $17 ($8 & $8.50 with federal senior pass; 32 sites with elec/wtr, $17 for 30-amp ($8.50 with federal senior pass), $18 at premium locations ($9 with federal senior pass), $20 with 50-amp ($10 with federal senior pass). RV limit in excess of 65'. Picnic shelters $10. Non-campers pay day use fee for boat ramp, picnicking,

dump. Three group camping areas, $80-$200 (2-night minimum stay). At reserved sites, 2-day minimum stay required on weekends, 3 days on holiday weekends. (620) 767-6745. NRRS during 4/14-9/30.
GPS: 38.69222, -96.53389

CUSTER PARK

From Council Grove at jct with US 56, 3.5 mi N on SR 55/177, then W. 3/1-11/30; 14-day limit. 10 sites without hookups, $7 ($3.50 with federal senior pass). Non-campers pay day use fee for boat ramp.

KANSAS VIEW CAMPGROUND

From Council Grove at jct with US 56, 1.5 mi N on SR 57/177, then W. All year; 14-day limit. 5 primitive sites, $7 ($3.50 with federal senior pass) during 4/1-11/1; some sites free rest of year. Group camping area $30. Free picnic shelter.

KIT CARSON COVE CAMPGROUND

From Council Grove at jct with US 56, 2 mi N on SR 177/57, then W. All year; 14-day limit. 1 site without hookups, $8 ($4 with federal senior pass); 14 sites with wtr/elec, $14 during 3/1-10/31. During winter, some sites free without services. Non-campers pay day use fee at boat ramp.
GPS: 38.695313, -96.495605

MARINA COVE CAMPGROUND

From Council Grove, 1.5 mi N on SR 177; 1 mi W on Dam Rd; 1.5 mi W; on right. All year; 14-day limit. During 4/1-10/31, 1 primitive site $8 ($4 with federal senior pass), 3 sites with elec, $12 ($6 with federal senior pass). Rest of year, some sites free without services. Fish cleaning station. Non-campers pay day use fee for boat ramp.

NEOSHO CAMPGROUND

From Council Grove, 1.5 mi N on SR 177; 1 mi W on Dam Rd; 1 mi right to City Lake Rd, then 0.3 mi W; on right. All year; 14-day limit. 7 sites with elec, $12 during 4/1-10/31 ($6 with federal senior pass), 1 site with elec/wtr, $14 ($7 with federal senior pass). Off-season, some sites free without hookups. Get wtr from campground hydrant. Non-campers pay day use fee for boat ramp. **GPS: 38.68042, -96.517822**

RICHEY COVE CAMPGROUND

From Council Grove at jct with US 56, 2.8 mi on SR 57/177, W side. All year; 14-day limit. 2 primitive tent sites, $12 ($6 with federal senior pass). 11 sites with elec, $16 during 4/1-10/31 ($8 with federal senior pass). 21 sites with wtr/elec, $18 during 4/1-10/31 ($9 with federal senior pass); full hookups $22. Wtr/elec off during 11/1-3/31; some sites free. RV limit in excess of 65'. Group camping area for up to 50 people & 16 vehicles, $100 with 2-night minimum stay. At reserved single sites, 2-day minimum stay required on weekends, 3 days on holiday weekends. (620) 767-5800. NRRS during 4/15-9/30. **GPS: 38.70917, -96.50333**

SANTA FE TRAIL CAMPGROUND

From Council Grove, 1.5 mi N on SR 177; 1 mi W on Dam Rd; 1 mi W on City Lake Rd, then 1 mi W, on right. 3/1-12/1; 14-day limit. 2 sites without hookups, $11-$12 ($5-$6 with federal senior pass); 5 sites with elec, no wtr hookups, $16 ($8 with federal senior pass); 28 sites with wtr/elec, $17 ($8.50 with federal senior pass); full hookups $22 ($11 with federal senior pass. No wtr service after 11/1. Group camping area for up to 50 people & 32 vehicles, $140 with a 2-night minimum stay. At reserved sites, 2-day minimum stay required on weekends, 3 days on holiday weekends. Non-campers pay day use fee for boat ramp. (620) 767-7125. NRRS during 4/15-9/30. **GPS: 38.68333, -95.51667**

ELK CITY LAKE (TU) 4
GPS: 37.2817, -96.7833

A 4,122-acre lake 5 mi NW of Independence and US 160, 127 mi E of Wichita in southern Kansas. Lake Manager, P. O. Box 426, Cherryvale, KS 67335-0426. (620) 336-2741.

CARD CREEK RECREATION AREA

From Elk City at jct with SR 39, 7 mi SE on US 160; 1.3 mi N & 1.7 mi NW. All year; 14-day limit. 4 primitive tent sites, $12 ($6 with federal senior pass), free during 11/1-3/31; 15 RV sites with elec, some pull-through, $16 ($8 with federal senior pass), lower fees during 11/1-3/31 but reduced services. New shower & restrooms. Picnic shelter $30. **GPS: 37.25708, -95.848145**

OUTLET CHANNEL RECREATION AREA

From Elk City, 7 mi NW of Independence on county rd below dam, W side of spillway. All year; 14-day limit. 13 sites without hookups, $10 ($5 with federal senior pass) during 3/26-11/1; free rest of year, but no wtr. 3 sites with elec, $14 ($7 with federal senior pass) during 3/26-11/1; free rest of yr, but no elec or wtr. Picnic shelter $30. New playground & concrete pit toilets. **GPS: 37.280377, -95.782517**

FALL RIVER LAKE (TU) 5
GPS: 37.64667, -96.07

A 2,450-acre lake 4 mi NW of Fall River off US 400, 70 mi E of Wichita. All-terrain vehicles, golf carts must be street legal with tags and lights. Visitor center. Lake Manager, Fall River Lake, Rt.. 1, Box 243E, Fall River, KS 67047-9738. (620) 658-4445.

DAMSITE RECREATION AREA

From US 400 at jct with Highway 99, 7.8 mi E, 0.9 mi N, 2.4 mi E, on right. All year; 14-day limit. 12 sites without hookups, $13 ($6.50 with federal senior pass) during 4/1-10/31. 8 sites with elec, $17 during 4/1-10/31 ($8.50 with federal senior pass), lower fees during off-season. 13 sites with elec/wtr, $19 during 4/1-10/31 ($9.50 with federal senior pass), lower fees during off-season. 1 handicap site with wtr/elec, $21 ($11.50 with federal senior or disabled pass). RV limit in excess of 65'. Nature trails, interpretive programs, canoeing, jet skiing. Group camping area for up to 150 people & 30 vehicles, $84. Picnic shelter free. NRRS during 4/1-10/30. **GPS: 37.65, -96.06639**

ROCK RIDGE NORTH RECREATION AREA

From US 400 jct with Highway 99, 7.8 mi E, 1.7 mi N, 1.5 mi W (low water crossing), 0.9 mi E. 4/1-10/31; 14-day limit. 19 sites without hookups, $9 ($4.50 with federal senior pass); 23 sites with elec, $13 ($6.50 with federal senior pass); 2 sites with elec/wtr, $16 ($8 with federal senior pass). Some winters, some sites open at lower fees, but park closed 10/31 in 2010. **GPS: 37.66157, -96.10509**

WHITE HALL BAY CAMPGROUND

From US 400 at milemarker 344 (Z 50 Rd), 0.09 mi N (left); 2.8 mi E (right) across the dam; 0.8 mi N (left); 0.7 mi W (left); 1.7 mi N (right) to low-water crossing, then continue N for 0.1 mi; 0.4 mi W; 1.1 mi S to park. 4/1-10/31; 14-day limit. 1 site without hookups, $13 ($6.50 with federal senior pass); 14 sites with elec, no wtr, $17 ($8.50 with federal senior pass); 11 sites with wtr/elec, $19 or $21 with 50-amp elec ($9.50 & $10.50 with federal senior pass). Some winters, some sites open at lower fees, but park closed 10/31 in 2010. RV limit in excess of 65'. Group camping areas with elec, $50-$84. NRRS. **GPS: 37.66667, -96.06639**

JOHN REDMOND DAM & RESERVIOR (TU) 6

GPS: 38.2417, -95.755

A 9,400-acre lake 6 mi N and W of Burlington off US 75, 110 mi SW of Kansas City. Off-Rd. vehicle area at Otter Creek provides 140 acres for dirt bikes and all- terrain vehicles. Lake Manager, John Redmond Dam, 1565 Embankment Rd. southwest, Burlington, KS 66839-8911. (620) 364-8613.

DAMSITE AREA CAMPGROUND

From New Strawn, 1 mi SW. All year; 14-day limit. 4 sites w/o hookups, $10 ($5 with federal senior pass); 22 sites with elec/wtr, some pull-through, $15 ($7.50 with federal senior pass). During 11/1-3/31, some sites usually available free, but in 2010, all sites were closed. Three picnic shelters for up to 50 people & 26 vehicles, $10. 3 group camping areas with elec, $30-$80. At reserved sites, 2-day minimum stay required on weekends. Nature trail, horseshoe pits, Hickory Creek bridle/mountain biking trail. No day use fees charged. Open all year. **GPS: 38.25, -95.75**

HARTFORD RAMP PARK

From Hartford, 0.5 mi E on gravel Rd.. Free primitive camping. Undesignated sites. Pit toilets.

RIVERSIDE EAST CAMPGROUND

From Burlington, 3.5 mi N on Highway 75; 1.5 mi W on Embankment Rd (signs). 4/1-10/31; 14-day limit. 53 sites with elec/wtr, $15 ($7.50 with federal senior pass); 6 pull-through. RV limit in excess of 65'. At reserved sites, 2-day stay required on weekends. Two picnic shelters, $10. Interpretive trail, bike trail. No day use fees. NRRS during 4/29-9/28. **GPS: 38.23333, -95.75**

RIVERSIDE WEST CAMPGROUND

From Burlington, 3.5 mi N on Hwy 75; 1.5 mi W on Embankment Rd (signs). 4/1-10/31; 14-day limit. Sites without elec, $8 ($4 with federal senior pass); 37 sites with elec (21 also with wtr, and 50-amp elec recently added to 13 sites), $15 ($7.50 with federal senior pass). Picnic shelter for up to 100 people & 30 vehicles, $10. Universal access ramp to fishing dock. RV limit in excess of 65'. At reserved sites, 2-day minimum stay required on weekends. No day use fees. NRRS during 4/29-9/28.
GPS: 38.22917, -95.7667

WEST WINGWALL

Located below the dam. 4/1-10/31; 14-day limit. 6 sites without hookups, $10 ($5 with federal senior pass. No day use fees.

KANOPOLIS LAKE (KC) 7
GPS: 38.6217, -97.97

A 3,400-acre lake with 41 mi of shoreline located 31 mi SW of Salina off Highway 141, 85 mi NW of Wichita. Historical & cultural site, visitor center. Operations Manager, Kanopolis Lake, 105 Riverside Drive, Marquette, KS 67464-7464. (785) 546-2294.

BOLDT BLUFF CAMPGROUND

From dam, go 2 mi S on K-141, 5 mi W on Avenue T (gravel), 3 mi N on 25th Rd. (gravel), 2 mi E on Avenue Q. All year; Primitive camping area with no designated sites. Camping is free.

RIVERSIDE CAMPGROUND

From Salina, 10 mi W on Hwy 140; 14 mi S on Hwy 141; 0.5 mi E; at SE end of dam. All year; 14-day limit. 23 sites without hookups, $12 during peak season of 5/1-9/30 ($6 with federal senior pass), free rest of year. 9 sites with elec, $18 during 5/1-9/30 ($9 with federal senior pass), $6 for elec rest of year. RV limit in excess of 65'. At reserved sites, 2-day minimum stay required on weekends, 3 days on holiday weekends. NRRS. **GPS: 38.59972, -97.93333**

VENANGO CAMPGROUND

From dam, N on Hwy 141, on left; at NW end of dam. All year; 14-day limit. 114 sites without hookups, $12 during peak season of 5/1-9/30 ($6 with federal senior pass), free rest of year. 87 sites wit elec, $18 with wtr during 5/1-9/30 ($9 with federal senior pass), $16 with elec but no wtr ($8 with federal senior pass), $6 for elec rest of year. Primitive group camping area for up to 50 people & 21 vehicles with shelter house ($30). Four picnic shelters, $20. RV limit in excess of 65'. At reserved sites, 2-day minimum stay required on weekends, 3 days on holiday weekends. ATV trail, nature trail. NRRS. **GPS: 38.63306, -97.9875**

YANKEE RUN

From dam, 2 mi S on K-141; 5 mi W on grave Avenue T; 3 mi N on gravel 25th Rd; 1 mi E on Avenue Q; 1 mi N on gravel 26th Rd. All year; 14-day limit. Free primitive camping at undesignated sites. Pit toilet, trails. **GPS: 38.6430636, -98.0169947**

MARION RESERVOIR (TU) 8
GPS: 38.3683, -97.0833

A 6,200-acre lake 3 mi NW of Marion off US 56, 46 mi NE of Wichita, Marion features 171 campsites at four parks. Unregistered vehicles, all-terrain vehicles, golf carts prohibited. 1-mi Willow Walk Nature Trail at Cottonwood Point. Non-campers pay day use fee for campground boat ramps, but undeveloped ramps at Durham Cove & Broken Ridge are free. Lake Manager, Marion Reservoir, 2105 Pawnee Rd., Marion, KS 66861-9740. (620) 382-2101.

COTTONWOOD POINT CAMPGROUND

From Marion, 3 mi W on US 56; 2 mi N on Old Mill Rd (signs). 3/15-11/15; 14-day limit. 53 sites with 30-amp elec, $17 ($8.50 with federal senior pass); 41 sites with 50-amp elec/wtr, $20 ($10 with federal senior pass); 7 pull-through. Some sites might be open & free without utilities off-season. RV limit 50'. Two group camping areas with elec, $80; 2 picnic shelters, $20. NRRS during 4/10-10/15. At reserved sites, 2-day stay required on weekends, 3 days on holiday weekends. NOTE: This campground is being expanded and renovated during 2011, and periodic closures might be necessary. Closures will be posted at the park entrance. No reservations will be accepted during the 2011 season until work is finished. For updated information, call lake office at 620-382-2101. **GPS: 38.38889, -97.08889**

FRENCH CREEK COVE PUBLIC USE AREA

From Marion, 7 mi W on US 56; 1 mi N on Limestone Rd; 1 mi E on 210th St. All year; 14-day limit. 20 sites with elec, $12 during 3/15-11/15 ($6 with federal senior pass); rest of year, some sites free but reduced services. Non-campers pay day use fee for boat ramp, picnicking. **GPS: 38.8889, -97.1461**

HILLSBORO COVE CAMPGROUND

From Marion, 4 mi W on US 56; N on Nighthawk, then E. All year; 14-day limit. 37 sites with elec, $17 during 3/15-11/14 ($8.50 with federal senior pass); 15 sites with wtr/elec, $19 during 3/15-11/14 ($9.50 with federal senior pass). 8 pull-through sites. Some sites open & free without utilities off-season, but park was closed during winter of 2010. Group camping area for up to 80 people & 15 vehicles, $80. RV limit 50'. At reserved sites, 2-day minimum stay required on weekends, 3 days on holiday weekends. NRRS during 4/10-10/15. **GPS: 38.38278, -97.09972**

MARION COVE CAMPGROUND

From Marion, 3 mi W on US 56; 1 mi N on Pawnee, past project office, on left. All year; 14-day limit. 2 RV sites, 4 tent sites, $8 ($4 with federal senior pass) during 3/15-11/15; some sites free with reduced services rest of year. **GPS: 38.380541, -97.075455**

MELVERN LAKE (KC) 9
GPS: 38.515, -95.705

A 6,900-acre lake with 101 mi of shoreline on eastern edge of the state's Flinthills region. It is 3.5 mi W of Melvern on SR 31 and W of US 75, N of I-35 and 39 mi S of Topeka. Historic and cultural site, visitor center with interpretive programs, displays, exhibits. Group tours provided upon request. All campgrounds are open and free during the winter, but no facilities or utilities are available. Project Office, Melvern Lake, 31051 Melvern Parkway, Melvern, KS 66510-9759. (785) 549-3318.

ARROW ROCK PARK

From Olivet at jct with US 75, 1 mi W on CR K-276; 1 mi N on S Fairlawn Rd; 1 mi W on Arrow Rock Pkwy. All year; 14-day limit. 26 sites without hookups, $12 during 5/1-9/30 ($6 with federal senior pass), free rest of year. 19 sites with 30-amp elec, $17 ($18 with elec/wtr) during 5/1-9/30 ($8.50 & $9 with federal senior pass), some free rest of year with reduced amenities. 5 pull-through sites. RV limit in excess of 65'. At reserved sites, 2-day minimum stay required on weekends, 3 days on holiday weekends. NRRS durig 5/1-9/30. **GPS: 38.49056, -95.75944**

COEUR D'ALENE PARK

From Melvern at jct with US 75, 1 mi S on Melvern Lake Pkwy; 1 mi NW on Coeur D'Alene Pkwy; at SE corner of lake. All year; 14-day limit. 25 sites without hookups, $12 during 5/1-9/30 ($6 with federal senior pass), free rest of year. 33 sites with 30-amp elec/wtr, $17 during 5/1-9/30 ($8.50 with federal senior pass), some free rest of year. 1 handicap site with 50-amp elec/wtr/sewer, $20. RV limit 50'. Picnic shelters ($20), horseshoe pits, fish cleaning station, 2 nature trails, several playgrounds. At reserved sites, 2-day minimum stay required on weekends, 3 days on holiday weekends. NRRS during 5/1-9/30. **GPS: 38.49667, -95.71806**

OUTLET PARK

From Melvern at jct with US 75, 0.3 mi W on Merlvern Lake Pkwy; 0.3 mi W on Cutoff Rd; 0.5 mi N on River Pond Pkwy, below dam. All year; 14-day limit. 61 sites with 30-amp elec/wtr, $18 during 5/1-9/30 ($9 with federal senior pass). 51 sites with 50-amp elec, $20 during 5/1-9/30 ($10 with federal senior pass). 89 sites with full hookups, $22 during 5/1-9/30 ($11 with federal senior pass). Some sites free off-season, but no utilities. RV limit in excess of 65'. Youth group camping. Picnic shelter for up to 100 people & 25 vehicles, $18-$22. Amphitheater, horseshoe pits, fish cleaning station, interpretive trail, change house at the beach, 90-acre fishing pond, phones, pedestrian/biking trails, historic suspension bridge. Gasoline engines prohibited on the lake. At reserved sites, 2-day minimum stay required on weekends, 3 days on MD & LD weekends. NRRS during 5/1-9/30. **GPS: 38.51306, -95.0639**

SUN DANCE PARK

From Lebo at jct of I-35 & US 50, 4.5 mi N; at SW corner of lake. All year; 14-day limit. Free. 30 primitive gravel sites. No day use fee for picnicking or boat ramp. **GPS: 38.479101, -95.859574**

TURKEY POINT PARK

From Osage City, S on CR K-170; 2 mi E on 301st St; 1 mi S on Indian Hills; 0.5 mi S on Turkey Point Pkwy. All year; 14-day limit. 14 sites without hookups, $12 during 5/1-9/30 ($6 with federal senior pass), free off-season. 16 sites with 30-amp elec/wtr, $17 during 5/1-9/30 ($8.50

with federal senior pass; some sites free off-season but no utilities. 18 sites with 50-amp elec/wtr, $19 during 5/1-9/30 ($9.50 with federal senior pass), some sites free off-season but no utilities. 3 pull-through sites. RV limit 65'. Group camping area for up to 100 people & 30 vehicles with shelter, $40. Fish cleaning station, horseshoe pits. At reserved sites, 2-day minimum stay required on weekends, 3 days on MD and LD weekends. NRRS during 5/1-9/30. **GPS: 38.49889, -95.78944**

MILFORD LAKE (KC) 10
GPS: 39.0833, -96.895

A 15,700-acre lake 5 mi NW of Junction City/I-70 on Hwy K-57 W of US 77, 65 mi W of Topeka. Project Office/Information Center has displays and exhibits. along with a 24 hour accessible brochure information area. 11 free picnic shelters can be reserved for $25. Day use areas: School Creek ORV Areas -- an off-Rd. vehicle area for vehicles less than 50" wide only; E Rolling Hills Park -- boat ramp, picnic shelter, playground, beach, interpretive trail; N Overlook Park -- picnic shelter, playground; Outlet Park -- boat ramp, picnic shelter, playground, beach, bridle trails. Free campsites during winter may have reduced amenities. Other Milford camping includes Clay County Park, Flagstop RV Park, Milford State Park, Thunderbird Marina. Project Manager, Milford Lake, 4020 W Highway K/57, Junction City, KS 66441-8997. (785) 238-4643.

CURTIS CREEK PARK

From Junction City at I-70 exit 290, 5 mi N on Milford Lake Rd; 6 mi W on CR 837. 4/15-9/30; 14-day limit. 8 tent sites & 20 RV sites without hookups, $12 ($6 with federal senior pass; 48 sites with elec, $16 ($8 with federal senior pass), $18 for elec/wtr sites ($9 with federal senior pass. RV limit in excess of 65'. At reserved sites, 2-day minimum stay required on weekends, 3 days on holiday weekends. Non-campers pay $3 for boat ramp, dump. NRRS. **GPS: 39.09278, -96.955**

FARNUM CREEK PARK

From Milford at I-70 exit 295, 11 mi N on US 77. 4/15-9/30; 14-day limit. 3 tent sites & 30 RV sites without hookups, $12 ($6 with federal senior pass); 46 sites with elec, $18 ($9 with federal senior pass); 5 pull-through sites. RV limit 60'. At reserved sites, 2-day minimum stay required on weekends, 3 days on holiday weekends. Non-campers pay $3 for dump station, boat ramp. Fish cleaning station. NRRS beginning in 2011. **GPS: 39.07778, -95.89167**

SCHOOL CREEK PARK

From Wakefield, 1 mi W on SR 82. All year; 14-day limit. 56 sites, 12 primitive. During 4/15-9/30, $10 ($5 with federal senior pass); off-season, some sites are free. RV limit 30'. ORV trail. **GPS: 39.142578, -96.936768**

TIMBER CREEK PARK

From Wakefield, 1 mi E on SR 82. All year; 14-day limit. 36 sites, $10 during 4/15-9/30 ($5 with federal senior pass). Some sites free off-season. Nature trail. **GPS: 39.213623, -96.971924**

WEST ROLLING HILLS CAMPGROUND

From Junction City at I-70 exit 290, 5 mi N on Hwy 244 (Milford Lake Rd). 4/15-9/30; 14-day limit. 12 tent sites & 6 RV sites without hookups, $12 ($6 with federal senior pass). 38 sites with elec/wtr -- 30-amp sites $18, 50-amp sites $19 ($9 & $9.50 with federal senior pass). 3 pull-through sites. RV limit in excess of 65'. Some free primitive campsites also available. Non-campers pay $3 for boat ramp, dump, picnicking. Fish cleaning station. At reserved sites, 2-day minimum stay required on weekends, 3 days on holiday weekends. NRRS. **GPS: 39.075, -96.92333**

PERRY LAKE (KC) 11

GPS: 39.1117, -95.425

An 11,150-acre lake 3 mi NW of Perry off US 24, 15 mi NE of Topeka. Unregistered vehicles, off-Rd. vehicles, motorcycles, golf carts prohibited. 30-mi National Recreation Trail follows eastern shoreline. Visitor center. Day use facilities: Outlet Park -- picnicking, ORV trail; Perry Park -- boat ramp, picnicking, playground, beach; Thompsonville Park -- picnicking. Project Manager, Perry Lake, 10419 Perry Park Drive, Perry, KS 66073-9717. (785) 597-5144.

LONGVIEW PARK

From Oskaloosa, 5.5 mi W on SR 92; 2.1 mi S on Ferguson Rd; 1.5 mi W on 86th St. 5/1-9/30; 14-day limit. 6 walk-to tent sites & 13 RV/tent sites without hookups, $12 ($6 with federal senior pass); 26 sites with elec, $16 ($8 with federal senior pass). Group walk-to tent camping area for up to 100 people, $30. RV limit in excess of 65'. At reserved sites, 2-day minimum stay required on weekends, 3 days on holiday weekends. Perry Hiking Trail. NRRS. **GPS: 39.18472, -95.44444**

OLD TOWN PARK

From Oskaloosa, 6 mi W on SR 92; on the S side before the bridge (signs); at E side of lake. All year; 14-day limit. 43 sites without hookups, $12 during 5/1-9/30 ($6 with federal senior pass), $10 rest of year, self-pay ($5 with federal senior pass). 33 sites with elec/wtr, $17 during 5/1-9/30 ($8.50 with federal senior pass), some $10 without utilities off-season. Picnic shelter for up to 100 people & 20 vehicles, $20. RV limit in excess of 65'. At reserved sites, 2-day minimum stay required on weekends, 3 days on MD & LD weekends. NRRS during 5/1-9/30. **GPS: 39.225, -95.4375**

ROCK CREEK PARK

From Perry at jct with Hwy 24, 3 mi N on SR 237; E to Rock Creek Park Rd; on W side of lake. All year; 14-day limit. 20 walk-to tent sites & 56 RV/tent sites without hookups, $12 during 5/1-9/30 ($6 with federal senior pass); $10 during rest of year, self-pay ($5 with federal senior pass). Sites with 30-amp elec/wtr, $17 during peak season ($8.50 with federal senior pass); 50-amp elec/wtr sites $18 during peak season ($9 with federal senior pass). Some sites $10 off-season self-pay, but no utilities ($5 with federal senior pass). Some free primitive camping in designated area. RV limit in excess of 65'. Picnic shelter for up to 100 people & 6 vehicles, $30. At reserved sites, 2-day minimum stay required on weekends, 3 days on MD & LD weekends. Fish cleaning station. NRRS 5/1-9/30. **GPS: 39.12083, -95.45417**

SLOUGH CREEK PARK

From Perry at jct with Hwy 24, 7 mi N on Ferguson Rd; 1 mi SE on Slough Creek Rd; on E side of lake. 4/15-10/15; 14-day limit. 18 walk-to tent sites & 121 sites without hookups, $12 ($6 with federal senior pass); sites with elec but no wtr hookups, $16; 30-amp elec/wtr sites $17; 50-amp elec/wtr sites $18 ($8, $8.50 & $9 with federal senior pass). 15 pull-through sites. Two group camping areas, $30. RV limit in excess of 65'. At reserved sites, 2 day minimum stay required on weekends, 3 days on holiday weekends. 2.5-mi interpretive trail & 30-mi Perry Hiking Trail, fish cleaning stations. NRRS. **GPS: 39.13472, -95.43056**

POMONA LAKE (KC) 12
GPS: 38.6517, -95.5567

A 4000-acre lake 17 mi W of Ottawa on SR 268/68; 1 mi N on Pomona Dam Rd. 35 mi S of Topeka. Visitor center. Camping fees increased in 1011 after installing new showers, primitive toilets, paving roads and upgrading sites to 50-amp electric service. Project Manager, Pomona Lake, 5260 Pomona Dam Rd., Vassar, KS 66543-9743. (785) 453-2201.

CARBOLYN PARK

From Lyndon, 4.5 mi N on US 75; E before Dragoon Creek bridge (signs); on W side of lake. 5/1-9/30; 14-day limit. 3 sites without elec, $12 ($6

with federal senior pass); 26 sites with elec, $16 ($8 with federal senior pass). RV limit 55'. At reserved sites, 2-day minimum stay required on weekends, 3 days on holiday weekends. Picnic shelter. NRRS.
GPS: 38.675, 95.67917

CEDAR PARK

From Michigan Valley, 2 mi W on E 213th St; 1 mi N on S. Shawnee Heights Rd; 3 mi W on E. 205th St, then follow signs; on N side of lake. All year; 14-day limit. 8 free primitive sites. Rock boat ramp.
GPS: 38.654053, -95.580811

MICHIGAN VALLEY PARK

From Michigan Valley, 1 mi S, then 1 mi W; on NW side of dam. 5/1-9/30; 14-day limit. 38 primitive sites $14 ($7 with federal senior pass); sites with 30-amp elec, $18 ($9 with federal senior pass); 8 prime pull-through sites with 50-amp elec/wtr, $20 ($10 with federal senior pass); 9 sites with wtr/elec/sewer, $22 ($11 with federal senior pass). Wigeler group camping area for up to 100 people & 2 vehicles, $40 (may be reserved only through NRRS during 5/1-10/31). Three picnic shelters, $30, $40 & $60. RV limit in excess of 65'. At reserved sites, 2-day minimum stay required on weekends, 3 days on holiday weekends. Amphitheater, fishing dock. NRRS. **GPS: 38.66472, -95.54889**

OUTLET AREA PARK

From Michigan Valley, 2 mi S; 1.5 mi W on gravel rd; below dam along 110 Mi Creek on S side of lake. All year; 14-day limit. 34 sites with elec/wtr, $18 during 4/1-10/31 ($9 with federal senior pass), $12 off-season ($6 with federal senior pass). Picnic shelters $30. Interpretive nature trail, amphitheater. NRRS (4/1-10/31). **GPS: 38.64583, -95.55972**

WOLF CREEK PARK

From Michigan Valley, 1 mi S, 1 mi W to dam, then 1 mi NW; on N side of lake. 5/1-9/30 33 sites without elec, $14 ($7 with federal senior pass); 46 sites with elec, $18 ($9 with federal senior pass). Group camping area with 23 elec/wtr sites, $125-$150, open 4/1-9/30. RV limit 65'. At reserved sites, 2-day minimum stay required on weekends, 3 days on holiday weekends. 18-hole disc golf course. NRRS. **GPS: 38.67639, -95.56806**

110 MILE PARK

From Michigan Valley, 2 mi W on E. 213th St; 1 mi N on S. Shawnee Heights Rd; 1.5 mi W on E. 205th St (signs); on N side of lake. All year; 14-day limit. Free. 25 primitive sites. No wtr during 10/1-4/30. Group equestrian camping area may be reserved through lake office. Short walking trail & 33-mi trail for hikers, bikers, horse riders. **GPS: 38.673096, -95.581543**

TUTTLE CREEK LAKE (KC) 13
GPS: 39.2567, -96.59

A 12,570-acre lake 5 mi N of Manhattan on US 24 and SR 13, 55 mi W of Topeka. Off-Rd. vehicle and cycle area. Campsites that are free sites during winter may have reduced amenities. The state of Kansas also operates campgrounds around the lake as part of Tuttle Creek State Park -- Randolph Park on the NE side; River Pond Park below the dam; Spillway Park on E side of lake; Fancy Creek Park on NW end of lake, and Rocky Ford Campground on S side of lake. County-operated Carnahan Creek Park on the E side offers free random camping. Project Manager, Tuttle Creek Lake, 5020 Tuttle Creek Boulevard, Manhattan, KS 66502-8812. (785) 539-8511.

STOCKDALE PARK

From dam, 6 mi W on US 24/77; 1.5 mi on CR 895; 2.5 mi E (right) on CR 396. 188 acres. All year; 14-day limit. 10 RV/tent sites without hookups & 2 walk-in tent sites, $12 during 4/15-9/30 ($6 with federal senior pass);

3 pull-through sites. Random camping $8 ($4 with federal senior pass). During 10/1-4/14, some sites free. RV limit in excess of 65'. At reserved sites, 2-day minimum stay required/weekends, 3 days/holiday weekends. Picnic shelter. NRRS during 4/15-9/30. **GPS: 39.30611, -96.65222**

TUTTLE CREEK COVE PARK

From the dam at the project office, 0.1 mi E on SR 13; 2.5 mi N on CR 897; on W side of lake. 252 acres. All year; 14-day limit. 17 sites without hookups, $12 during 4/15-10/31 ($6 with federal senior pass); 39 sites with wtr/elec, $18 during 4/15-10/31 ($9 with federal senior pass); 5 pull-through sites. Some sites open & free off-season, but no utilities. Picnic shelter. NRRS (4/15-10/31). **GPS: 39.27694, -96.63028**

WILSON LAKE (KC) 14
GPS: 36.9683, -98.495

A 9000-acre lake 7 mi S of Lucas on SR 232, 135 mi NW of Wichita. ORV prohibited. Campsites that are free sites during winter may have reduced amenities. State of Kansas operates Wilson & Otoe State Park campgrounds. Visitor center. Day use fees charged to non-campers. Resource Manager, Wilson Lake, 4860 Outlet Boulevard, Sylvan Grove, KS 67481. (785) 658-2551.

LUCAS PARK

From Wilson at I-70 exit 206, 9 mi N on SR 232; park on left; on N side of lake. 32 RV/tent sites without hookups, $12 during 5/1-9/30 ($6 with federal senior pass), free rest of year. 54 sites with elec (no wtr), $16 during 5/1-9/30 ($8 with federal senior pass). 16 sites with elec/wtr, $18 during 5/1-9/30 ($9 with federal senior pass). Walk-to tent sites $12 ($6 with federal senior pass). Premium double sites with elec, $36 ($18 with federal senior pass). Free camping off-season, but $8 utility fee charged at sites with elec; no showers off-season. Group camping area with 20 sites (15 with elec), $150. RV limit in excess of 65'. At reserved sites, 2-day minimum stay required on weekends, 3 days on holiday weekends. NRRS during 4/15-9/30. **GPS: 39.95556, -98.51944**

MINOOKA PARK

From Dorrance at I-70 exit 199, 7 mi N on Dorrance Rd (signs); on S side of lake. All year; 14-day limit. 41 sites without hookups, $12 during 5/1-9/30 ($6 with federal senior pass), free rest of year. 66 sites with elec, $16 during 5/1-9/30 ($8 with federal senior pass). 52 sites with elec/wtr, $18 during 5/1-9/30 ($9 with federal senior pass). Free camping off-season, but $8 utility fee charged at sites with elec; no showers off-season. RV limit in excess of 65'. Group camping area with 12 sites (6 with elec, 6 with elec/wtr, $150. Picnic shelter $20. Fish cleaning station, amphitheater. At reserved sites, 2-day minimum stay required on weekends, 3- days on holiday weekends. Open all year. NRRS during 4/15-9/30. **GPS: 38.93278, -98.575**

SYLVAN PARK

From Lucas, 7 mi S on SR 232; below the dam on N side of spillway. All year; 14-day limit. 3 sites without hookups, $12 during 5/1-9/30 ($6 with federal senior pass), free rest of year. 24 sites with elec/wtr, $18 during 5/1-9/30 ($9 with federal senior pass), free off-season but $10 utility fee charged at sites with elec; no showers off-season. Group camping area with 8 elec/wtr RV sites, $100. Picnic shelter for up to 50 people and 20 vehicles, $20. RV limit in excess of 65'. At reserved sites, 2-day minimum stay required on weekends, 3 days on holiday weekends. Horseshoe pits, visitor center. NRRS during 5/1-9/30. **GPS: 38.96833, -98.49167**

KENTUCKY

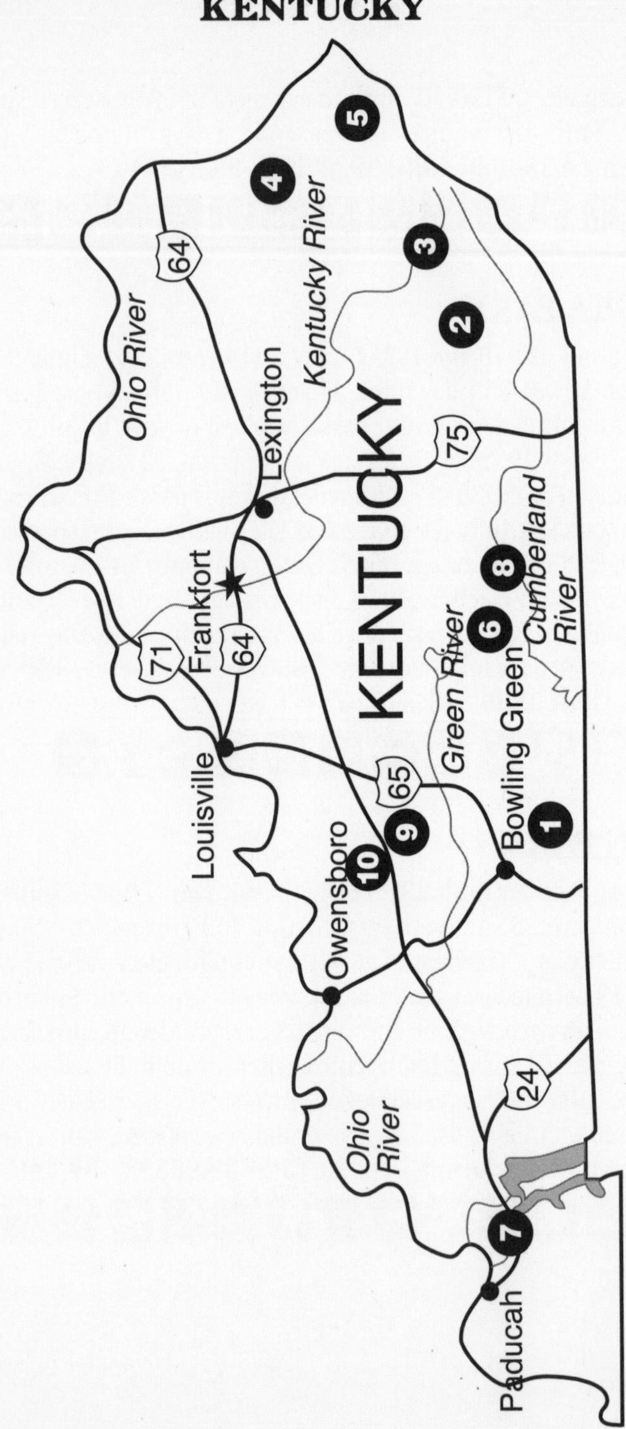

KENTUCKY
Ohio River
Kentucky River
Lexington
Frankfort
Louisville
Owensboro
Bowling Green
Green River
Cumberland River
Ohio River
Paducah
64
64
71
75
65
24
1
2
3
4
5
6
7
8
9
10

KENTUCKY

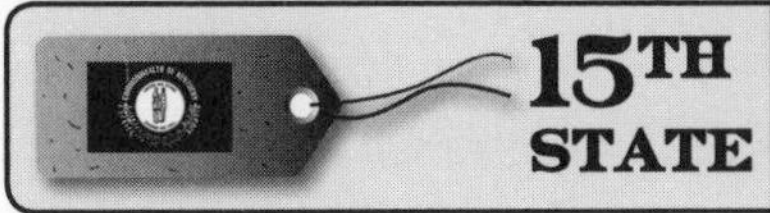

15TH STATE	State Capital: **Frankfort** Nickname: **Bluegrass State** Statehood Year: **1792**

Louisville District - All fee campgrounds may charge a visitor fee. Nashville District - Fees may be higher on weekends. A visitors fee may be charged.

BARREN RIVER LAKE (LO) 1
GPS: 36.8967, -86.125

A 10,000-acre lake 20 mi E of Bowling Green and 1.5 mi SW of Finney on SR 252 or SR 1533. Alcohol and off-Rd. vehicles prohibited. Campground checkout time 5 p.m. Camping also at Barren River State Park and Walnut Creek Campground Visitors to 9:30 p.m. Visitor center. Day use facilities include: Browns Ford Park -- boat ramp; Peninsula Park -- boat ramp, marina; Port Oliver Rec. Area -- boat ramp; Quarry Rd. Park -- picnicking, beach, hiking trail. Park Manager, Barren River Lake, 11088 Finney Rd., Glasgow, KY 42141-9642. (270) 646-2055.

BAILEY'S POINT CAMPGROUND

From Cedar Springs at jct with US 231/31E, 2 mi N on SR 252; 1.5 mi E on CR 517 (signs). 4/15-10/22; 14-day limit. 53 sites without elec, $16 ($8 with federal senior pass), $17 wtr hookup ($8.50 with federal senior pass). 148 sites with elec/wtr $22 ($11 with federal senior pass). RV limit in excess of 65'. 3-night minimum stay on holiday weekends. Interpretive trail, amphitheater, horseshoe pits, firewood, picnic shelter, phone. (270) 622-6959. NRRS. **GPS: 36.89083, -86.09528**

BEAVER CREEK CAMPGROUND

From Rocky Hill, 2.5 mi E on SR 252, across lake bridge, then 1.4 mi SW. 4/15-9/15; 14-day limit. 12 primitive sites, $10. Pit toilet.

TAILWATER CAMPGROUND

Below the dam. From jct of SRds 252/1533, N to entrance rd at S end of dam; follow signs. 5/6-9/10; 14-day limit. 45 sites with elec/wtr, $18 ($9 with federal senior pass). Off-seaon, some sites may be free with reduced services. RV limit in excess of 65'. Group primitive tent camping area for up to 100 people, $50. Picnic shelter for up to 100 people and 25 vehicles. Amphitheater, horseshoe pits. 3-night minimum stay on holiday weekends. (270) 622-7732. NRRS during 5/6-9/10.
GPS: 36.89444, -86.13306

THE NARROWS CAMPGROUND

From Lucas, 1.7 mi W, following signs. 5/6-9/10; 14-day limit. 86 sites with elec/wtr, $22 ($11 with federal senior pass). RV limit in excess of 65'. 3-night minimum stay on holiday weekends. Amphitheater, marina, interpretive trail, horseshoe pits, picnic shelter, boat rentals nearby. (270) 646-3094. NRRS. **GPS: 36.90417, -86.07083**

BUCKHORN LAKE (LO) 2
GPS: 37.34, -83.4717

A 1,230-acre lake 28 mi W of Hazard and N of Daniel Boone National Forest on SR 28, 0.5 mi from Buckhorn in southeastern Kentucky. Alcohol prohibited by local law. Historic & cultural site. Day use facilities: Buckhorn Lake Dam -- boat ramp; Confluence Rec. Area -- boat ramp, picnicking, picnic shelter with wtr/elec $30, playground; Leatherwood Rec. Area -- boat ramp, shelter $30, playground; Tailwater Rec. Area -- picnicking, playground, hiking trail. Resource Manager, Buckhorn Lake, Buckhorn, KY 41721. (606) 398-7251.

BUCKHORN BOAT-IN CAMPS

Accessible by boat only, near the emergency spillway, dock provided. 5/1-9/7; 14-day limit 15 primitive shoreline tent sites, $10. 3-night minimum stay required on holiday weekends. Pit toilets, trash stations, drkg wtr, security lighting, lantern posts, sand paths, playground.

BUCKHORN CAMPGROUND

On W side of Stilling Basin below dam, adjacent to Tailwater Rec. Area. 5/1-9/29; 14-day limit. 4 walk-in tent sites & 18 primitive & overflow sites, $10 & $12 ($5 & $6 with federal senior pass); 23 sites with elec/wtr (optional CATV) $20 ($10 with federal senior pass), $30 at double sites. RV limit 50'. 2 horseshoe pits, phone, firewood. 3-night minimum stay on holiday weekends. (606) 398-7220. NRRS. **GPS: 37.35083, -83.47278**

TRACE BRANCH CAMPGROUND

From Krypton, 1.3 mi S on SR 451; 2.1 mi SW on Campbell Creek Rd. 5/1-9/29; 14-day limit. 13 paved primitive sites (8 along shoreline), $12 ($6 with federal senior pass); 15 sites with elec/wtr, $22 ($11 with federal senior pass). RV limit 50'. Horseshoe pits, volleyball net, firewood. 3-night minimum stay on holiday weekends. NRRS.
GPS: 37.24167, -83.37278

CARR CREEK LAKE (LO) 3
GPS: 37.2233, -83.0567

A 710-acre lake 16 mi E of Hazard on SR 15 NW of Jefferson National Forest and E of Daniel Boone National Forest in southeastern Kentucky. Visitor center, wildlife viewing. Short nature trail at dam area & 6-mi Sugar Branch hiking trail. Camping also at Carr Creek State Park. Resource Manager, Carr Fork Lake, 843 Sassafras Creek Rd., Sassafras, KY 41759-8806. (606) 642-3308/3307.

LITTCARR CAMPGROUND

From the dam at jct with SR 1089, 5.2 mi E on SR 15; 2.4 mi NE on SR 160, then N on E side of SR 160. 4/29-10/11; 14-day limit. 31 sites with elec/wtr, $20 ($10 with federal senior pass); 14 sites with full hookups, $26 ($13 with federal senior pass). RV limit 50'. Picnic shelter, horseshoe pits. 3-night minimum stay on holiday weekends. (606) 642-3052. NRRS. **GPS: 37.2375, -82.94972**

LITTCARR #1 CAMPGROUND

From the dam at jct with SR 15, 2.4 mi NE on SR 160. 4/1-10/15; 14-day limit. 6 primitive sites, $12 ($6 with federal senior pass). Horseshoe pits.

DEWEY LAKE (HU) 4
GPS: 37.7367, -82.73

A 1,100-acre lake 10 mi S of Van Lear on SR 302/3 in eastern Kentucky SW of Huntington, W Virginia. For lake information call (606) 886-6398. Modern campsites at nearby Jenny Wiley State Park. Off-Rd. vehicles prohibited. Resource Manager, Dewey Lake, HC 70, Box 540, Van Lear, KY 41265. (606) 886-6709/789-4521.

SHORELINE CAMPGROUNDS I & II

Boat-in only access (boat rentals nearby). 5/1-10/31; 14-day limit. 30 primitive sites, 15 at each campground. All sites are $7.

FISHTRAP LAKE (HU) 5
GPS: 37.7367, -82.73

A 1,130-acre lake 10 mi S of Pikeville on US 460 in SE Kentucky near the Virginia/W Virginia state lines. Checkout time 4 p.m. Visitor center, interpretive programs, picnicking. For lake information, call (606) 437-9426. Resource Manager, Fishtrap Lake, 2204 Fishtrap Rd., Shelbiana, KY 41562. (606) 437-7496.

GRAPEVINE CAMPGROUND

From Phyllis, 0.5 mi W on SR 194. MD-LD; 14-day limit. 18 sites without hookups, $8 ($4 with federal senior pass); 10 sites with wtr/elec, $12 ($6 with federal senior pass). Three picnic shelters for up to 100 people and 50 vehicles, $50. (606) 835-4564.

GREEN RIVER LAKE (LO) 6
GPS: 37.245, -85.3417

An 8,210-acre lake 9 mi S of Campbellsville on SR 55, 95 mi S of Louisville. Alcohol prohibited by local law. Off-Rd. vehicles prohibited. Outside the campgrounds, day use facilities include boat ramp, picnic shelter and playground at Tailwater Park. Visitor center, historic & cultural site, interpretive programs. Park Manager, Green River Lake, 544 Lake Rd., Campbellsville, KY 42718-9705. (270) 465-4463.

HOLMES BEND CAMPGROUND

From Columbia at SR 206 exit 49, 1.2 mi N on SR 55; 1 mi NE on SR 551; 3.8 mi N on Holmes Bend Rd. 4/15-10/30; 14-day limit. 23 sites without hookups, $17 ($8.50 with federal senior pass); 101 sites with elec, 41 with wtr, $23 ($11.50 with federal senior pass). A picnic shelter, firewood, ice, and an amphitheater are available. RV limit in excess of 65'. 3-night minimum stay on holiday weekends. Interpretive trail, hiking trail, picnic shelter, amphitheater; boat rentals nearby. (270) 384-4623. NRRS. **GPS: 37.21389, -85.26667**

PIKES RIDGE CAMPGROUND

From Knifley, 4.8 mi NW on SR 76; SW on Pikes Ridge Rd (signs). 4/15-9/24; 14-day limit. 40 sites without hookup, $15 ($7.50 with federal senior pass); 21 sites with elec/wtr, $21 ($10.50 with federal senior pass). RV limit in excess of 65'. Picnic shelter for up to 100 people. 3-night minimum stay on holiday weekends. Interpretive trails. (270) 465-6488. NRRS. **GPS: 37.28056, -85.29167**

SMITH RIDGE CAMPGROUND

From Campbellsville, 1 mi E on Hwy 70; 3 mi S on SR 372; W (right) on County Park Rd (signs). 4/15-9/24; 14-day limit. 18 sites without hookups, $17 ($8.50 with federal senior pass); 62 sites with elec/wtr, $23 ($11.50 with federal senior pass). RV limit in excess of 65'. Group camping area for up to 100 people. 3-night minimum stay on holiday weekends. (270) 789-2743. NRRS. **GPS: 37.29583, -85.31**

WILSON CREEK CAMPGROUND

From Campbellsville, 4 mi E on SR 70; 7 mi E on SR 76; on right. All year; 4-day limit. 5 free primitive sites.

LAKE BARKLEY (NV) 7
GPS: 37.0217, -88.22

A 57,920-acre lake SE of I-24/US 62 near Gilbertsville, E of Paducah and S into Tennessee. Campground checkout time 3 p.m. Visitor center with display on early lifestyles and river usage, interpretive programs. Historic & cultural site. Day use facilities: Boyds Landing -- boat ramp, picnicking; Buzzard Rock -- boat ramp; Cadiz Rec. Area -- boat ramp, picnicking, picnic shelter, playground; Calhoun Hill -- boat ramp; Coleman Bridge -- boat ramp; Tailwater Left Bank -- boat ramp; Tailwater Right Bank -- boat ramp, picnic shelter; Devils Elbow -- boat ramp; Dry Creek -- ORV area; Hallaway Hills -- boat ramp; Mayberry Branch -- boat ramp; Eddyville -- boat ramp, picnicking; Old Kuttawa -- boat ramp, picnicking, shelter, playground, beach, hiking trails; Rivers Bend -- boat ramp; Rivers End -- boat ramp; Rockcastle -- boat ramp, picnicking, shelter, beach; Saline Creek -- boat ramp; Tobacco Port -- boat ramp. Resource Manager, Lake Barkley, Box 218, Highway 62, Grand Rivers, KY 42045-0218. (270) 362-4236. See Tennessee listings.

CANAL CAMPGROUND

From Paducah, E on I-24 to jct with "The Trace" (at Land Between the Lakes); 3 mi S on The Trace, then E. 3/25-10/30; 14-day limit. 113 sites with wtr/elec, 15 pull-through, base rate $16 ($8 with federal senior pass). Sites with 50-amp elec/wtr, $19 ($9.50 with federal senior pass); premium sites with wtr/elec, $24 ($12 with federal senior pass); full hookups $29 ($14.50 with federal senior pass). RV limit in excess of 65'. Group camping area for up to 64 people and 30 vehicles with shelter, $160. 3-night minimum stay on holiday weekends. Amphitheater. (270) 362-4840. NRRS. **GPS: 36.99556, -88.20972**

EUREKA CAMPGROUND

Across the spillway on E side of dam. 4/29-9/5; 14-day limit. 26 sites with elec; 3 pull-through. Sites with elec/wtr, $16 ($8 with federal senior pass); sites with wtr/elec, $17 ($8.50 with federal senior pass); premium sites with wtr/elec, $23 ($11.50 with federal senior pass. RV limit in excess of 65'. Group picnic shelter with elec, $35. 2-night minimum stay on weekends, 3 nights on holiday weekends. Biking trail, hiking trail, phone. (270) 388-9459. NRRS. **GPS: 37.02056, -88.22361**

HURRICANE CREEK CAMPGROUND

From Cadiz, 7.5 mi N on SR 139; 6.5 mi W on SR 276; 0.3 mi N on SR 724, then W. 4/29-10/30; 14-day limit. 6 walk-to tent sites, $10 & $12 ($5 & $6 with federal senior pass); 2 tent sites with elec, $16 & $18 ($8 & $9 with federal senior pass); 45 sites with 50-amp elec/wtr, $16 base, $22 at premium locations ($8 & $11 with federal senior pass). 11 pull-through sites. RV limit in excess of 65'. 2- night minimum stay on weekends, 3 nights on holiday weekends. (270) 522-8821. NRRS. **GPS: 36.92, -87.97583**

LAKE CUMBERLAND (NV) 8
GPS: 36.8717, -85.145

A 50,000-acre lake S of Lexington near the TN state line and S of the Cumberland Pkwy. Wolf Creek Dam is on US 127, 4.2 mi S of the jct. of SR 55/US 127. Visitor center with exhibits. Historic & cultural site, interpretive programs. in the office. Day use facilities: Farmers Mill Park -- boat ramp; Halcomb Landing -- boat ramp; Lakeview Park -- boat ramp; Mill Springs -- picnicking, shelter, old mill; Seventy-Six Falls Park -- picnicking, shelter, trails. Primitive shoreline tent camping is free at 53 designated camping areas; carry-out trash, bury waste; no toilets; 14-day limit. Resource Manager, Lake Cumberland, 855 Boat Dock Rd., Somerset, KY 42501-0450. (606) 679-6337/6338.

CUMBERLAND POINT RECREATION AREA

From Nancy, 0.2 mi E on SR 80; 1 mi S on SR 235; 8 mi SE on SR 761. 30 acres. 4/1-10/31; 14-day limit. 28 sites with elec/wtr, $18 ($9 with federal senior pass); 1 premium site, $20. RV limit in excess of 65'. Group picnic shelter for up to 300 people & 100 vehicles, $50. Sites $4 higher on holidays.2-night minimum stay on weekends, 3 nights on holiday weekends. Amphitheater, horseshoe pits. (606) 871-7886. NRRS.
GPS: 36.96556, -84.43222

FALL CREEK RECREATION AREA

From Monticello, 0.4 mi NW on SR 92; 1.5 mi NE on SR 90; 6 mi N on SR 1275, then northwest. 5/1-10/30; 14-day limit. Newly renovated facilities & sites. 10 sites with elec/wtr, $20 ($10 with federal senior pass). Picnic shelter.(606) 348-6042.

FISHING CREEK RECREATION AREA

From Somerset at jct with US 27, 5.5 mi W on SR 80; exit prior to lake bridge, then 2 mi N on Hwy 1248 (signs). 5/13-9/18; 14-day limit. 20 tent sites with elec, $15 ($7.50 with federal senior pass); 10 RV/tent sites with elec/wtr, $18 ($9 with federal senior pass); 16 premium sites with wtr/elec, $21 ($10.50 with federal senior pass). RV limit in excess of 65'. At reserved sites, 2-night minimum stay required on weekends, 3 nights on holiday weekends. Fees $4 higher on holidays. New playground. (606) 679-5174. NRRS. **GPS: 37.04972, -84.68333**

KENDALL RECREATION AREA

From Jamestown, 10 mi S on US 127; right on Kendall Rd before crossing dam, follow signs. 3/18-11/6 (some sites open all year); 14-day limit. 6 tent sites $15 ($7.50 with federal senior pass); 112 sites with elec/wtr, $19 ($9.50 with federal senior pass), $21 at premium locations ($10.50 with federal senior pass). Fees $4 higher on holidays. RV limit in excess of 65 ft. Picnic shelter with elec for up to 600 people & 100 vehicles, $50. At reserved sites, 2-night minimum stay required on weekends, 3 nights/ holiday weekends. Horseshoe pits, fish cleaning station, hiking trail, 2 playgrounds. (270) 343-4660. NRRS. **GPS: 36.86806, -85.1475**

WAITSBORO RECREATION AREA

From Somerset, 5 mi S on US 27, then W (right) on Waitsboro Rd, following signs. 4/1-10/31; 14-day limit. 4 basic tent sites, $14 ($7 with federal senior pass); 1 tent site with elec & RV sites with elec/wtr, $19 ($9.50 with federal senior pass); premium RV sites, $20 ($10 with federal senior pass). Sites $4 higher on holidays. Two picnic shelters for up to 15 people, $50. RV limit in excess of 65'. At reserves sites, 2-night minimum stay required on weekends, 3 nights on holiday weekends. (606) 561-5513. NRRS. **GPS: 37.04972, -84.68333**

NOLIN LAKE (LO) 9
GPS: 37.30246, -86.261902

A 5,795-acre lake 2 mi N of Mammoth Cave National Park on SR 13/52. It is 15 mi N of Brownsville on SR 259, 22 mi S on Leitchfield on SR 259. Alcohol prohibited by local law. Camping also available at Nolin Lake State Park. Day use facilities: Iberia Park -- boat ramp, picnic shelter, playground, beach; Tailwater Park -- boat ramp, picnic shelter, playground; Vanmeter Park -- boat ramp. $3 fee charged at 5 boat ramps; $50 at picnic shelters. Park Manager, Nolin Lake, 2150 Nolin Dam Rd., P. O. Box 339, Bee Springs, KY 42207-0289. (270) 286-4511.

DOG CREEK CAMPGROUND

From Munfordville, 18 mi W on SR 88; 1 mi S on SR 1015 (signs). Open about 4/15-9/30; 14-day limit. 70 sites, 46 without hookups for $15 ($7.50 with federal senior pass), $19 at premium locations ($8.50 with federal senior pass); 24 sites with elec/wtr, $22 ($11 with federal senior pass). RV limit in excess of 65'. 3-night minimum stay required on holiday weekends. Picnic shelter, watchable wildlife area. Beach open only to campers. (270) 524-5454. NRRS. **GPS: 37.3208, -86.27**

MOUTARDIER CAMPGROUND

From Leitchfield, 16 mi S on SR 259 (signs); 2 mi SE on SR 2067. Open about 4/15-10/30; 14-day limit. 86 sites without hookups, $15 ($7.50 with federal senior pass), $19 at premium locations ($9.50 with federal senior pass). 81 sites with elec/wtr, $21-$22 ($10.50-$11 with federal senior pass). RV limit in excess of 65'. Picnic shelter, horseshoe pits, fish cleaning station. 3-night minimum stay on holiday weekends. Boat rentals nearby. (270) 286-4230. NRRS. **GPS: 37.31639, -86.23306**

WAX CAMPGROUND

From Munfordville, 20 mi W on SR 88. Open about 4/15-9/30; 14-day limit. Open about 4/15-9/30; 14-day limit. 46 sites without hookups ($15 ($7.50 with federal senior pass), $19 at premium locations ($9.50 with federal senior pass). 24 sites with elec/wtr, $22 ($11 with federal senior pass). 7 pull-through sites. RV limit in excess of 65'. Boat rentals nearby. Picnic shelter, horseshoe pits, fish cleaning station. 3-night minimum stay on holiday weekends. (270) 242-7578. NRRS.
GPS: 37.32083, -86.12917

ROUGH RIVER LAKE (LO) 10
GPS: 37.589207, -86.510468

A 5,100-acre lake 1.4 mi N of Falls of Rough Post Office on SR 79, 51 mi N of Bowling Green. Alcohol prohibited by local law. Off-Rd. vehicles also prohibited. Campground checkout time 4:30 p.m. Horse trails nearby. Sites open during winter may have reduced amenities. A large number are lakeside sites. Visitor center. Park Manager, Rough River Lake, 14500 Falls of Rough Rd., Falls of Rough, KY 40119-9801. (270) 257-2061.

AXTEL CAMPGROUND

From Harned, 9 mi S on SR 259; 0.5 mi W on SR 79, on left. Open about 3/25-10/31; 14-day limit. 115 sites without elec, 55 at $15 & 60 premium locations at $16 ($7.50 & $8 with federal senior pass). 43 sites with elec/wtr $22 or $24 at premium locations ($11 & $12 with federal senior pass). RV limit 45'. 3-night minimum stay on holiday weekends. Boat rentals nearby. Picnic shelter. (270) 257-2584. NRRS during 4/15-10/30.
GPS: 37.625, -86.44972

CAVE CREEK CAMPGROUND

From the dam, 2.9 mi S on SR 79; 0.8 mi E on SR 736. Open about 4/30-9/19; 14-day limit. 70 sites without hookups, 36 at $10 & 34 prime location sites, $12 ($5 & $6 with federal senior pass). 16 sites with elec/wtr, $14 ($7 with federal senior pass). RV limit 40'. 3-night minimum stay on holiday weekends. Fishing pier. (270) 879-4304. NRRS during 5/23-9/11. **GPS: 37.575, -86.49167**

LAUREL BRANCH CAMPGROUND

From Mc Daniels, 1 mi NW on SR 259; 0.4 mi SW on SR 110 (signs). All year; 14-day limit. During 3/26-11/1, 52 sites without hookups, $14 ($7 with federal senior pass); 25 sites with elec/wtr, $19 ($9.50 with federal senior pass. Off-season, some sites open at reduced rates. RV limit 40'. At reserved sites, 2-night minimum stay required on weekends, 3 nights on holiday weekends. (270) 257-8839. NRRS during 5/4-10/30.
GPS: 37.60833, -86.45833

NORTH FORK CAMPGROUND

From Mc Daniels, 2 mi N on SR 259. About 4/30-9/15; 14-day limit. 56 sites without hookups, $17 ($8.50 with federal senior pass); 50 sites with wtr/elec, $20 ($10 with federal senior pass. RV limit 60'. Picnic shelter, fishing dock. 3-night minimum stay on holiday weekends. (270) 257-8139. NRRS during 5/5-9/11. **GPS: 37.63306, -86.44167**

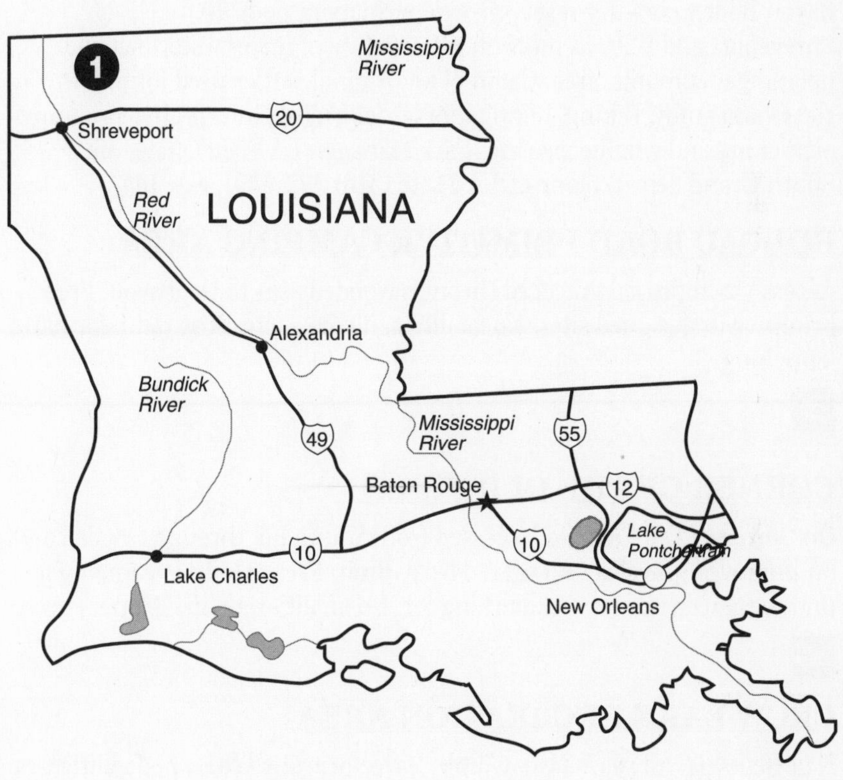
1
Mississippi River
20
Shreveport
Red River
LOUISIANA
Alexandria
Bundick River
49
Mississippi River
55
Baton Rouge
12
10
10
Lake Pontchartrain
Lake Charles
New Orleans

LOUISIANA

State Capital: **Baton Rouge**
Nickname: **Pelican State**
Statehood Year: **1812**

18TH STATE

BAYOU BODCAU RESERVOIR (VK) 1
GPS: 32.705, -93.5133

Bayou Bodcau is a dry reservoir w/o permanent pool. 20 mi NE of Shreveport and I-20, 18 mi N on SR 157. Site of major waterfowl and upland game mgmt. area. Cabin of an original settler used for public classroom study. Biking, hiking, horseback riding, interpretive programs, picnicking and wildlife viewing. Park Manager, LA Field Office, 3505 South Grand Street, Monroe, LA 7120. (318) 322-6391, ext. 104.

BODCAU ROAD PRIMITIVE CAMPING AREA

Access via improved gravel rd through wooded area to the bayou. Free primitive undesigned sites. No facilities, no drkg wtr. Boat ramp for hand launching.

CORNER OF THE OLD FIELD

On Corner of Old Field Rd, accessed from Young Rd, through wooded area on improved gravel rd. All year; 14-day limit. Free primitive camping at undesignated sites on rock parking lot. No facilities, no drkg wtr.

CROW LAKE RECREATION AREA

N of Bellevue. All year; 14-day limit. 2 free primitive sites, no facilities, no drkg wtr. Rock boat ramp.

DELLA FIELD PRIMITIVE AREA

Access via improved gravel rd to bayou. All year; 14-day limit Free primitive undesignated sites. No facilities, no drkg wtr. Boat ramp for hand launching.

HIGHWAY 157 PRIMITIVE AREA

Near Springhill; free primitive camping on rock parking lot. No facilities, no drkg wtr. All year; 14-day limit. Gravel boat ramp.

HIGHWAY 160 PRIMITIVE AREA

From Hwy 160 bridge onto gravel rd to site. Free primitive camping at undesignated sites. No facilities, no drkg wtr. Concrete boat ramp.

HIGHWAY 2 PRIMITIVE CAMPING AREA

Near Sarepta. All year; 14-day limit. Free primitive camping a undesignated sites. No facilities, no drkg wtr. Concrete boat ramp.

HORSE CAMPGROUND

On the N end of the dam near the spillway. Large groups should call for a permit and information. More than 50 mi of horse trails available. Free primitive camping. Open all year; 14-day limit.

IVAN LAKE RECREATION AREA

From Bellevue, 2 mi N on county rd; overlooks Ivan Lake. All year; 14-day limit. Free. 4 primitive sites. Pit toilets, fire rings, no drkg wtr. Boat ramp nearby.

PARDEE CALLOWAY PRIMITIVE AREA

Access via improved gravel rd from Old Cotton Valley Rd. Free primitive camping at undesignated sites. No facilities, no drkg wtr. Rock boat ramp.

RAINEY WELLS RECREATION AREA

N of Bellevue on county rd. All year; 14-day limit. 2 free primitive sites. No facilities, no drkg wtr. Rock boat ramp.

TOM MERRILL RECREATION AREA

From Haughton/Fillmore exit of I-20, 15 mi N on SR 157; 3 mi E at Bellevue (Bodcau Dam Rd, sign). All year; 14-day limit. 20 sites with elec/wtr, $12 ($6 with federal senior pass); sites without hookups, $6 ($3 with federal senior pass). RV limit 20'. Durdiln Hill Trail starts at this campground and extends 6 mi for hikers & mountain bikers. Picnic shelter, $35. **GPS: 32.705779, -93.51692**

SOUTH ABUTMENT EAST RECREATION AREA

From Bellevue, 2 mi N on county rd; on the upstream side of the dam. All year; 14-day limit. 12 primitive sites, $6. Toilet, no drkg wtr.

TEAGUE LAKE PRIMITIVE CAMPING AREA

Access via improved gravel rd to the bayou. All year; 14-day limit. Free primitive camping pad. No facilities, no drkg wtr. Gravel boat ramp.

WENK'S LANDING

From Minden on I-20, go 17 mi north on U.S. Rt. 371 through Cotton Valley, on left before Sarepta (signs). Primitive camping in designated areas only. Camping is free. Open all year.

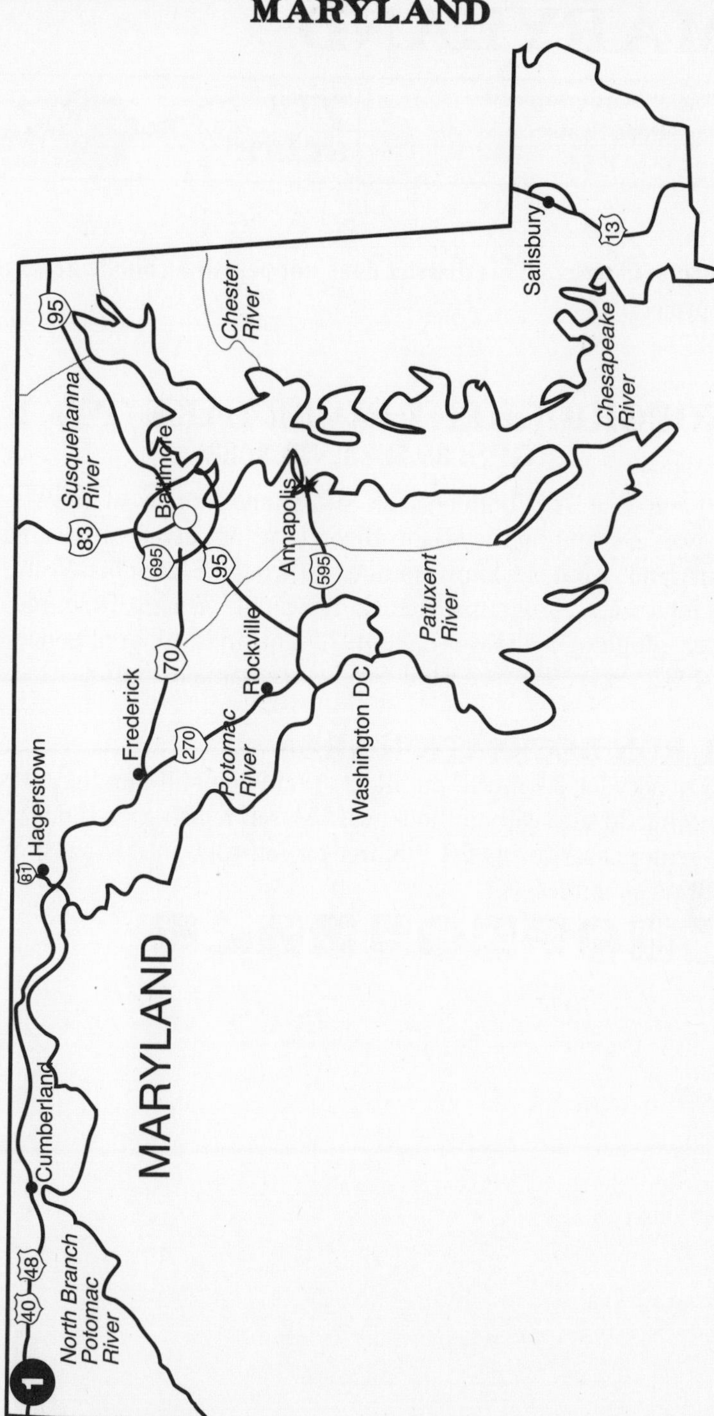
MARYLAND
1
40
48
North Branch Potomac River
Cumberland
81
Hagerstown
Frederick
270
Potomac River
Rockville
70
Washington DC
695
Baltimore
83
Susquehanna River
95
595
Annapolis
Patuxent River
Chester River
Chesapeake River
Salisbury
13

MARYLAND

State Capital: **Annapolis**
Nickname: **Free State**
Statehood Year: **1788**

7TH STATE

Pittsburgh Disttrict - This district does not permit alcoholic beverages at any project.

YOUGHIOGHENY RIVER LAKE (PT) 1
GPS: 39.7983, -79.3683

A 2,840-acre lake S of Confluence off SR 281 and N of US 40 in SW Pennsylvania, spanning the Mason-Dixon Line between Pennsylvania and Maryland. Trout stockings from April through September. Visitor center, interpretive programs, picnicking, wildlife viewing. Resource Manager, Youghiogheny River Lake, 497 Flanigan Road, Confluence, PA 15424-1932. (814) 395-3242/3166. See Pennsylvania listings.

MILL RUN RECREATION AREA

From Friendsville, 3.7 mi NE on SR 53; 1 mi W on Mill Run Rd. All year; 14-day limit. 30 sites without hookups, $13, self-registration ($6.50 with federal senior pass) during 5/1-9/8; free for self-contained RVs rest of year but no amenities.

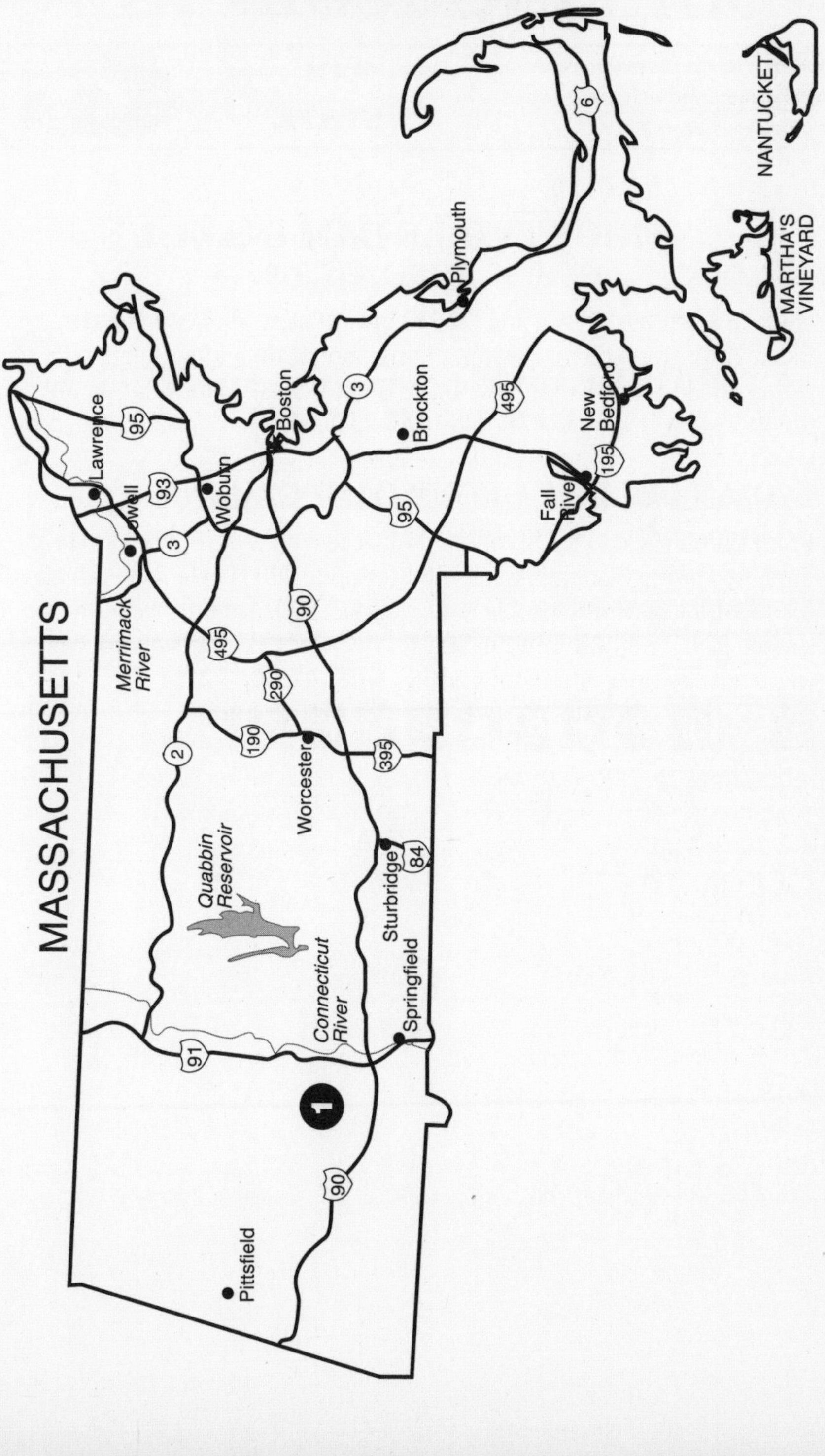

MASSACHUSETTS

Merrimack River
Lawrence
Lowell
Woburn
Boston
Brockton
Plymouth
New Bedford
Fall River
Worcester
Sturbridge
Springfield
Pittsfield
Quabbin Reservoir
Connecticut River
MARTHA'S VINEYARD
NANTUCKET
95
93
3
495
90
290
190
395
2
84
91
6
195
1

MASSACHUSETTS

State Capital: **Boston**
Nickname: **Bay State**
Statehood Year: **1788**

6TH STATE

KNIGHTVILLE DAM (NAE) 1
GPS: 42.261811, -72.876434

Four mi S of Chesterfield and SR 143 in west-central Massachusetts. Picnicking, group picnic shelter, hiking, mountain biking, horseback riding. 2,430 acres. Knightville Dam, RR 1, Box 285, Huntington, MA 01050-9942. (413) 667-3430/(508) 249-2547.

INDIAN HOLLOW GROUP CAMPGROUND

From Chesterfield, 4 mi SE on SR 143; access on S St. 5/20-9/12; 14-day limit Two group camping areas: GN1 for up to 100 people & 31 vehicles, $85; GS1 for up to 100 people & 41 vehicles, $90. Amphitheater. Picnic shelter $50. 2-night minimum stay on weekends, 3 nights on holiday weekends. By reservation only. NRRS. **GPS: 42.34, -72.84**

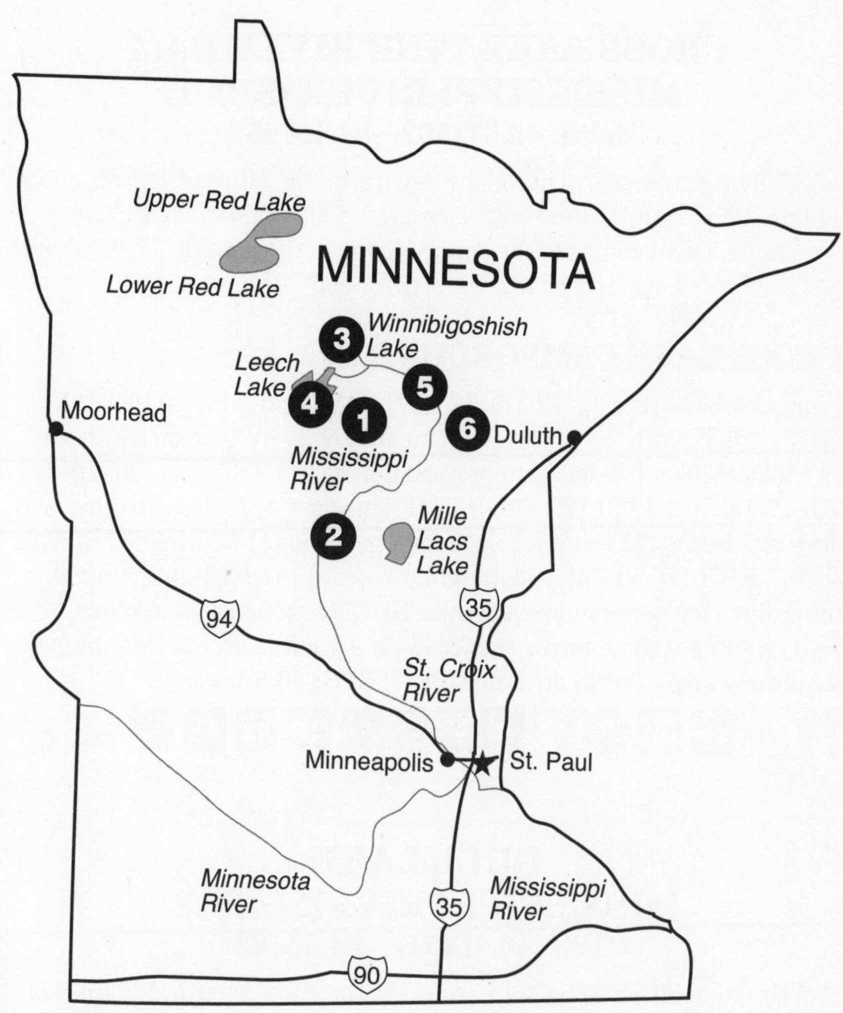

Upper Red Lake
MINNESOTA
Lower Red Lake
3
Winnibigoshish Lake
Leech Lake
5
4
1
6
Moorhead
Duluth
Mississippi River
2
Mille Lacs Lake
35
94
St. Croix River
Minneapolis
St. Paul
Minnesota River
35
Mississippi River
90

MINNESOTA

State Capital: **St. Paul**
Nickname: **North Star State**
Statehood Year: **1858**

32ND STATE

CROSS LAKE/PINE RIVER DAM MISSISSIPPI RIVER (SP) 1

GPS: 46.671502, -94.110957

A 13,660-acre lake with 119 mi of shoreline off SR 210, on CR 3/66, about 100 mi SW of Duluth. Interpretive programs. Campground checkout time noon. ORV prohibited. Resource Manager, Cross Lake, 35507 CR 66, Box 36, Cross Lake, MN 56422-0036. (218) 692-2025.

CROSS LAKE CAMPGROUND

From Crosby at jct with SR 210, 12 mi N on SR 6; 6 mi W on CR 11; NE on CR 3. 4/1-10/31; 14-day limit. 6 tent sites & 30 RV/tent sites without elec, $20 ($10 with federal senior pass) during 5/1-9/30; fees $10 during 4/1-4/30 & 10/1-10/31 ($5 with federal senior pass). 73 ites with elec, $26 during 5/1-9/30 ($13 with federal senior pass) but $13 during 4/1-4/30 & 10/1-10/31 ($6.50 with federal senior pass. At reserved sites, 2-night minimum stay required on weekends, 3 nights on holiday weekends. Fish cleaning station, picnic shelter ($40), handicap accessible fishing & swimming areas. NRRS during 5/1-9/16. **GPS: 46.66, -94.10**

GULL LAKE MISSISSIPPI RIVER (SP) 2

GPS: 46.413541, -94.35462

N of Brainerd off SR 371, Gull Lake is 115 mi SW of Duluth, 130 mi N of Minneapolis. Burial mound display. Campground checkout time noon. ORV prohibited. Resource Manager, Gull Lake, 10867 E Gull Lake Drive, Brainerd, MN 56401-9413. (218) 829-3334.

GULL LAKE RECREATION AREA

From Brainerd, 10 mi NW on SR 371; W on CR 125 to dam; on Gull River at outlet of lake. All year; 14-day limit. 37 sites with elec, $26 during 5/1-9/30 ($13 with federal senior pass); $13 during 10/1-4/30 ($6.50 with federal senior pass). Showers open 5/1-10/1; wtr available 4/15-11/1. Group picnic shelter with elec for up to 40 people & 10 vehicles, is $40. At reserved sites, 2-night minimum stay required on weekends, 3 nights on holiday weekends. Fish cleaning station, interpretive trail, handicap accessible swimming area, phone. NRRS (5/1-9/30).
GPS: 46.41083, -94.35139

LAKE WINNIBIGOSHISH MISSISSIPPI RIVER (SP) 3
GPS: 47.253718, -93.584633

A 67,000 acre lake, Big Winnie, as it's called, is NW of Deer River & N of US 2, off SR 46, 102 mi NW of Duluth. ORV prohibited. Campground checkout time noon. Resource Manager, Lake Winnibigoshish, 34385 Highway 2, Grand Rapids, MN 55744-9663. (218) 326-6128.

WINNIE DAM RECREATION AREA

From Deer River, 1 mi NW on US 2; 12 mi N (right) on SR 46; 2 mi W (left) on CR 9 (signs). 5/1-10/31; 14-day limit. 22 sites with elec, $18 & $22 ($9 & $11 with federal senior pass. RV limit in excess of 65'. Picnic shelter, fish cleaning station. At reserved sites, 2-night minimum stay required on weekends, 3 nights on holiday weekends. NRRS during 5/1-9/15. **GPS: 47.43, -94.04917**

LEECH LAKE (SP) 4
GPS: 47.26, -94.20

A 126,000-acre lake E of Walker on SR 371, Leech is 35 mi W of Grand Rapids, 120 mi W of Duluth and 30 mi SW of Deer River. Interpretive programs, snowmobile trail. Campground checkout time noon. ORV prohibited. Resource Manager, Leech Lake, P. O. Box 111, Federal Dam, MN 56641-0111. (218) 654-3145.

LEECH LAKE CAMPGROUND

From Cass Lake at jct with US 2, 8 mi S on Hwy 8; on SW side of dam. 5/1-10/31; 14-day limit. 4 walk-to tent sites, $12 ($6 with federal senior pass); 73 sites with elec, $24 ($12 with federal senior pass). RV limit in excess of 65'; 3 pull-through. Group shelter, $35. At reserved sites, 2-night minimum stay required on weekends, 3 nights on holiday weekends. Fish cleaning station, horseshoe pits, interpretive programs, marina, nature trails, phone, shuffleboard. (218) 654-3145, Ext. 2. NRRS during 5/1-9/30. **GPS: 47.24472, -94.23**

POKEGAMA LAKE MISSISSIPPI HEADWATERS (SP) 5
GPS: 47.25, -93.58

A 16,000-acre lake W of Grand Rapids off US 2 and 169, 82 mi NW of Duluth. Campground checkout time noon. ORV prohibited. Resource Manager, Pokegama Lake, 34385 Highway 2, Grand Rapids, MN 55744-9663. (218) 326-6128.

POKEGAMA DAM CAMPGROUND

From Grand Rapids, 2 mi W on US 2; S (left, following signs) of road. 4/1-10/31; 14-day limit. 2 tent sites, $13 ($6.50 with federal senior pass); 19 sies with elec, $26 ($13 with federal senior pass). RV limit in excess of 65'. Picnic shelter for up to 50 people & 50 vehicles, $40. At reserved

sites, 2-night minimum stay required on weekends, 3 nights on holiday weekends. Fish cleaning station. NRRS during 5/1-9/15.
GPS: 47.25, -93.58333

SANDY LAKE MISSISSIPPI RIVER (SP) 6
GPS: 46.7883, -98.3283

A 9,400-acre lake off SR 65 N of McGregor, Sandy Lake **(also known as Big Sandy)** is 60 mi W of Duluth. Interpretive facility and interpretive programs. An old lock house has been turned into interpretive display. Sandy Lake Rec. Area is on the canoe Rt. that linked Lake Superior with the Mississippi River during the fur trading period. Campground checkout time noon. ORV prohibited. Resource Manager, Big Sandy Lake, 22205 531st Lane, Mc Gregor, MN 55760-0192. (218) 426-3482.

SANDY LAKE RECREATION AREA

From McGregor, 13 mi N on SR 65, then S; at the outlet of Sandy Lake. 4/1-10/31; 14-day limit. 8 walk-to tent sites, $16 ($8 with federal senior pass); 48 sites with elec, $24 ($12 with federal senior pass); double sites with elec, $48 ($24 with federal senior pass). Two group camping areas for up to 25 people & 3 vehicles, $60. Picnic shelters with elec for up to 40 people & 20 vehicles, $25-$35. RV limit in excess of 65'; 8 pull-through sites. Some sites may have lower fees during April & October. At reserved sites, 2-night minimum stay required on weekends, 3 nights on holiday weekends. Fish cleaning station, museum, horseshoe pits. NRRS during 5/1-9/30. **GPS: 46.78833, -93.32833**

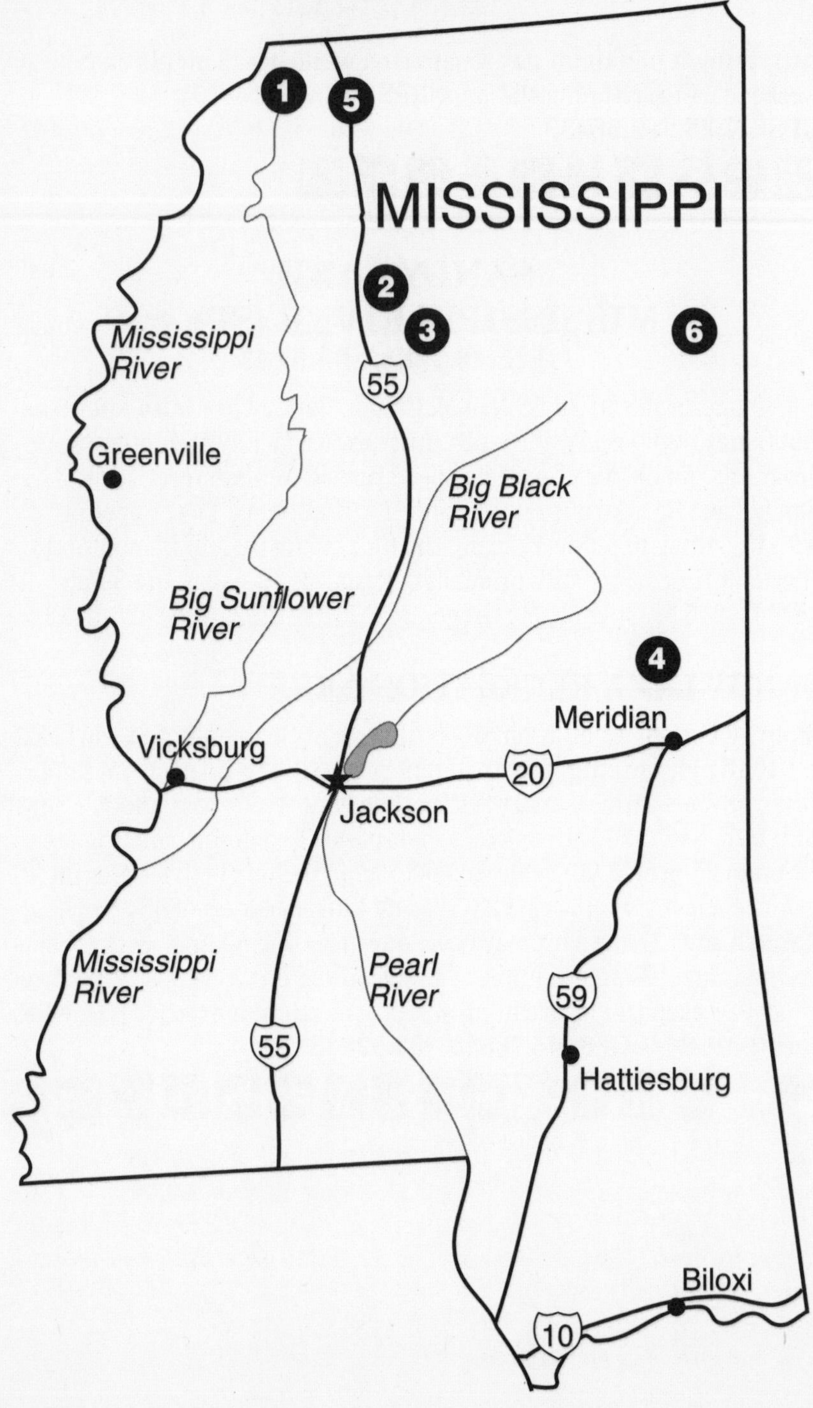
1
5
MISSISSIPPI
2
3
6
Mississippi River
55
Greenville
Big Black River
Big Sunflower River
4
Meridian
Vicksburg
20
Jackson
Mississippi River
Pearl River
59
55
Hattiesburg
Biloxi
10

MISSISSIPPI

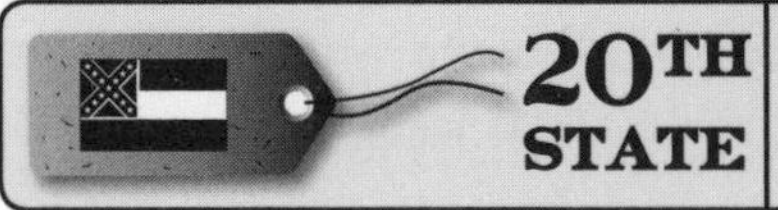

State Capital: **Jackson**
Nickname: **Magnolia State**
Statehood Year: **1817**

ARKABUTLA LAKE (VK) 1
GPS: 34.7567, -90.1233

This 12,730-acre lake is N of Arkabutla on SR 301, 30 mi S of Memphis, TN. Visitors to 10 p.m., and campground checkout time is 4 p.m. Sites that are free during winter may have reduced amenities. Day use facilities: Bayou Point Park -- boat ramp, picnicking, group shelter, playground; Coldwater Point Park -- boat ramp, picnicking; Hwy. 51 Landing -- boat ramp, picnicking; Plantation Point -- picnicking; Sunfish Bay -- trails. Visitor center. Resource Mgr. Arkabutla Lake Field Office, 3905 Arkabutla Dam Road, Coldwater, MS 38618-9737. (662) 562-6261.

DUB PATTON RECREATION AREA

From Arkabutla, N on Scenic Loop 304 across the dam; on N side (signs). All year; 14-day limit. 8 tent sites with elec & 51 RV/tent sites with elec, $18 base, $20 at premium locations during 3/1-10/31 ($9 & $10 with federal senior pass); $16 base, $18 at premium locations during 11/1-2/28 ($8 & $9 with federal senior pass). RV limit 50 ft. Two picnic shelters for up to 100 people & 30 vehicles, $30 (not available off-season). Amphitheater, nature trails. NRRS during 3/1-10/31. **GPS: 34.77444, -90.11472**

HERNANDO POINT CAMPGROUND

From Coldwater, W on I-55 to US 51, then N across lake to Wheeler Rd; 6 mi W, following signs. All year; 14-day limit. 83 sites with elec/wtr, $18 base, $20 at premium locations during 3/1-10/31 ($9 & $10 with federal senior pass); $16 base, $18 at premium locations during 11/1-2/28 ($8 & $9 with federal senior pass). RV limit in excess of 65'. Picnic shelter for up to 100 people & 30 vehicles, $30 (not available off-season). Amphitheater. NRRS during 3/1-10/31. **GPS: 34.73361, -90.06889**

KELLY'S CROSSING CAMPGROUND

From Arkabutla, 0.3 mi E, then 3 mi N. All year; 14-day limit. 24 primitive sites, $16 during 3/1-10/31 ($8 with federal senior pass); free during 11/1-2/28. RV limit 20'. Pit toilets.

SOUTH OUTLET CHANNEL CAMPGROUND

From Arkabutla, 4.5 mi N on Scenic Loop Rd, below dam (signs). All year; 14-day limit. 22 sites without hookups, $16 during 3/1-10/31 ($8 with federal senior pass); free during 11/1-2/28. RV limit 20'. Pit toilets. Picnic shelter ($30).

PLEASANT HILL CAMPGROUND

From Hernando, 5 mi W on SR 304; 5 mi S on Fogg Rd. All year; 14-day limit. 10 sites without hookups, $16 during 3/1-10/31 ($8 with federal senior pass); free during 11/1-2/28. RV limit 20'. Pit toilets.

SOUTH ABUTMENT CAMPGROUND

From Arkabutla, N to dam on Scenic Loop 304 (signs); just S of dam. All year; 14-day limit. 80 sites with elec, $18 base, $20 at premium locations during 3/1-10/31 ($9 & $10 with federal senior pass)); $16 base, $18 at premium locations during 11/1-2/28 ($8 & $9 with federal senior pass). RV limit 60'. Group camping area with 2 sites, $50; picnic shelter with elec for up to 100 people & 30 vehicles, $30. NRRS during 3/1-10/31. Note: At last report, campground was closed for renovations; check status before arriving: 662-562-6261. **GPS: 34.74667, -90.1325**

ENID LAKE (VK) 2
GPS: 34.1583, -89.8217

This 15,560-acre lake is 26 mi N of Grenada and 1.7 mi E of Enid off I-55 exit 233 on SR 233. It is 65 mi S of Memphis, Tennessee. Visitors to 10 p.m. Besides Corps-managed facilities, camping also is available at George Payne Cossar State Park. Visitor center, interpretive programs. Resource Manager, Enid Lake, 931 County Road 36, Enid, MS 38927. (662) 563-4571.

BYNUM CREEK LANDING

From Water Valley at jct with SR 7, 8.3 mi NW on SR 315; 2.8 mi SW; 2.4 mi SE on all-weather rd. All year; 14-day limit. 5 primitive sites, free. RV limit 20'. Pit toilets.

CHICKASAW HILL CAMPGROUND

From Pope, 8.8 mi SE, then 1.6 mi SW; on N side of lake. All year; 14-day limit. 7 tent sites & 44 RV/tent sites with elec/wtr, $14 during 3/1-10/31 ($7 with federal senior pass); $10 during 11/1-2/28 ($5 with federal senior pass). RV limit 65'. Picnic shelter $30. Amphitheater. Reserved sites, 2-night minimum stay required/weekends, 3 nights/holiday weekends. NRRS during 3/1-10/31. Note: Last report, campground closed for renovation; check status prior to arrival. (662) 563-4571. **GPS: 34.16389, -89.82222**

FORD'S WELL RECREATION AREA

From I-55 exit 227 S of Enid, E on SR 32 to CR 557, N to campground. All year; 14-day limit. 12 sites with elec/wtr, $10 for campers using the 17-mi Spyglass Equestrian Trail. New in 2010, Ford's Well features hitching rails, horse wash station & overlook with hitching rails; joint effort involving Corps, state parks department & a private equestrian club. Gazebo, picnic shelter, fire rings, grills.

LONG BRANCH CAMPGROUND

From I-55 exit 227 S of Enid, 3.8 mi NE on SR 32; 1.9 mi N. All year; 14-day limit. 14 primitive sites, $6 during 3/1-10/31 ($3 with federal senior pass); $5 during 11/1-2/28 ($2.50 with federal senior pass). RV limit 20'. Pit toilets. No reservations.

PERSIMMON HILL CAMPGROUND

From I-55 exit 233, 1 mi E on CR 36 to dam; at S end of dam (signs). All year; 14-day limit. 72 sites with elec, $16 base, $18 at premium locations during 3/1-10/31 ($8 & $9 with federal senior pass); $10 base, $12 at premium locations during 11/1-2/28 ($5 & $6 with federal senior pass). RV limit 65 ft; 2 pull-through sites. Picnic shelters, $30. At reserved sites, 2-night minimum stay required on weekends, 3 nights on holiday weekends. NRRS during 3/1-10/31. **GPS: 34.13556, -89.88611**

PLUM POINT CAMPGROUND

From Pope, 5.3 mi SE, then 3.7 mi SE on all-weather rd. All year; 14-day limit. 10 primitive sites, $6 during 3/1-10/31 ($3 with federal senior pass); $5 during 11/1-2/28 ($2.50 with federal senior pass). RV limit 20'. Pit toilets. No reservations.

POINT PLEASANT CAMPGROUND

From I-55 exit 227 S of Enid, 6.3 mi NE on SR 32, then NW. All year; 14-day limit. 3 primitive sites, free. RV limit 20'. Pit toilets. No reservations.

WALLACE CREEK CAMPGROUND

From I-55 exit 233, 2.5 mi E on CR 36 to the dam; across the spillway on W side of the dam (signs). All year; 14-day limit. 99 sites with elec/wtr, $16 base, $18 at premium locations during 3/1-10/31 ($8 & $9 with federal senior pass); $10 base, $12 at premium locations during 11/1-2/28 ($5 & $6 with federal senior pass). RV limit 65'; 7 pull-through sites. At reserved sites, 2-night minimum stay required on weekends, 3 nights on holiday weekends. Hiking trail, interpretive trail, amphitheater, fish cleaning station, phone, ORV trail, picnic shelters. NRRS during 3/1-10/31. **GPS: 34.16111, -89.89167**

WATER VALLEY LANDING CAMPGROUND

From Water Valley at jct with SR 315, 2 mi S on SR 7; 5.3 mi W on SR 32; 3.2 mi NW; on S side of lake. 3/1-10/31; 14-day limit. 29 sites with elec/wtr, $14 ($7 with federal senior pass). RV limit 60'. Picnic shelter, $30. At reserved sites, 2-night minimum stay required on weekends, 3 nights on holiday weekends. NRRS. **GPS: 34.14306, -89.76389**

GRENADA LAKE (VK) 3
GPS: 33.8083, -89.7717

A 35,820-acre lake with 148 mi of shoreline, Grenada is 2 mi NE of Grenada, off I-55 exit 206, then E on SR 8. It is 99 mi S of Memphis, TN. Visitor center with displays, interpretive programs & exhibits. Sports complex area located below dam. Campsites that are free sites during winter may have reduced amenities. Day use facilities: Cape Retreat -- picnicking, beach; Choctaw Landing -- boat ramp, picnicking; Dam Area Central -- picnicking, group shelter, playground, interpretive trail; Lower Torrance --boat ramp; Piney Woods -- boat ramp; S Abutment A -- boat ramp, picnicking, group shelter, playground, interpretive trail; S Graysport -- boat ramp. Resource Manager, Grenada Lake Field Office, P. O. Box 903, Grenada, MS 38902-0903. (662) 226-1679/5911.

BRYANT CAMPGROUND

From I-55 exit 55 N of Grenada, NE on SR 7, then SE on county rd to campground. All year; 14-day limit. 5 free primitive sites. Pit toilet, no drkg wtr.

CHOCTAW CAMPGROUND

From Gore Springs at SR 8, N on Graysport Crossing Rd across lake bridge, past N Graysport Campground; N (left) on Gums Crossing Rd; SW (left) on Rounsville Church Rd. All year; 14-day limit. 5 free primitive sites. Pit toilet, no drkg wtr.

GUMS CROSSING CAMPGROUND

From Gore Springs at SR 8, N on Graysport Crossing Rd across lake bridge, past N Graysport Campground, then N on CR 221 to river. All year; 14-day limit. 14 free primitive sites. Pit toilet, no drkg wtr.

NORTH ABUTMENT CAMPGROUND

From I-55 exit 55 N of Grenada, 5 mi NE on SR 7, then S past the primitive campground; at N end of dam. All year; 14-day limit. 56 sites with wtr/elec, $18 ($9 with federal senior pass). RV limit 40'; 4 pull-through sites. Picnic shelter, $30. Amphitheater, fish cleaning station. At reserved sites, 2-night minimum stay required on weekends, 3 night on holiday weekends. NRRS. **GPS: 33.84, -89.77**

NORTH GRAYSPORT CAMPGROUND

From Gore Springs at jct with SR 8, 5.8 mi N across bridge; on E side of lake between rivers. All year; 14-day limit. 51 sites with elec/wtr, $14 ($7 with federal senior pass). RV limit 55'. At reserved sites, 2-night minimum stay required on weekends, 3 nights on holiday weekends. Amphitheater. (662) 226-1679. NRRS. **GPS: 33.84417, -89.60361**

OLD FORT CAMPGROUND

From the dam, on S side. All year; 14-day limit. 21 primitive sites, $6 ($3 with federal senior pass). RV limit 20'. Picnic shelter, $30. Pit toilets. No reservations.

SKUNA-TURKEY CREEK CAMPGROUND

From Coffeeville, 4.5 mi SE on SR 330; 2.1 mi S; 3.8 mi W. All year; 14-day limit. 6 free primitive sites. RV limit 20'. Pit toilets.

OKATIBBEE LAKE (MB) 4
GPS: 34.307144, -88.681641

A 4,000-acre lake with 28 mi of shoreline 10 mi N of I-20/I-59 and NW of Meridian off SR 19, 20 mi W of the Alabama state line. Visitor center. Day use facilities: Collinsville Park -- boat ramp, picnicking, group shelter, playground, beach; E Bank Park -- picnicking, group shelter, trails; Pine Springs Park -- boat ramp, picnicking, group shelter, playground, beach; W Bank Park -- boat ramp, picnicking, group shelter, playground, beach. Day use fees are charged: $4 at beaches, $3 at boat ramps. Okatibbee Water Park campground is operated by the Pat Harrison Waterway District; federal senior passes are accepted. Project Manager, Okatibbee Lake, P. O. Box 98, Collinsville, MS 39325-0098. (601) 626-8431.

GIN CREEK CAMPGROUND

From Collinsville at jct with SR 19, 2.8 mi N on CR 17 (W Lauderdale School Rd) past "T"; 1 mi E, on right. All year; 14-day limit. 7 primitive sites, $8 ($4 with federal senior pass).

TWILTLEY BRANCH CAMPGROUND

From Collinsville at jct with SR 19, 1 mi E on CR 17; exit 1.7 mi E & S. All year; 14-day limit. 12 RV/tent sites no hookups, $12 ($6 with federal senior pass); 49 sites with elec/wtr, $18 base, $20 at premium ($9 & $10 with federal senior pass). RV limit in excess of 65'; 4 pull-through, 62 handicap. 3 group camping areas: sites 63 & 64 for up to 24 people & 9 vehicles; site 65 for up to 48 people & 24 vehicles, $30-$60. Picnic shelter. At reserved sites, 2-night minimum stay required/weekends, 3 nights/ holiday weekends. (601) 626-8068. NRRS. **GPS: 32.49583, -88.80972**

SARDIS LAKE (VK) 5
GPS: 34.4, -89.7883

A 32,100-acre lake NE of Batesville and I-55 exit 246 on SR 35, 9 mi SE of Sardis and 50 mi S of Memphis, Tennessee. Campground checkout time 2 p.m. Campsites that are free during winter may have reduced amenities. Visitor center, interpretive programs. Day use facilities: Coles Point -- boat ramp; Coontown Crossing -- boat ramp, picnicking; Cypress Point -- picnicking, group shelter, playground, beach; Engineers Point -- boat ramp, picnicking, group shelter; Lespedeza Point -- boat ramp. Project Manager, Sardis Lake Field Office, 29949 Hwy. 315, Sardis, MS 38666-3066. (662) 563-4531.

BEACH POINT CAMPGROUND

From Sardis at jct with I-55 exit, 8 mi E on SR 315. All year; 14-day limit. 14 primitive sites, $8 during 4/1-9/30 ($4 with federal senior pass), free during 10/1-3/31. RV limit 20 ft. Flush & pit toilets.

CLEAR CREEK CAMPGROUND

From Oxford at jct with SR 7, 10.5 mi NW on SR 314, then 2 mi SW. All year; 14-day limit. 52 sites with wtr/elec, $10 ($5 with federal senior pass). RV limit 65 ft. Picnic shelter, $30. At reserves sites, 2-night minimum stay required on weekends, 3 nights on holiday weekends. NRRS during 4/1-9/30. **GPS: 34.42694, -89.70972**

HURRICANE LANDING CAMPGROUND

From Abbeville, 3.6 mi W (left) at sign on Hurriciane Landing Rd. All year; 14-day limit. 20 primitive sites, $16 during 4/1-9/30 ($8 with federal senior pass); $8 during 10/1-3/31 ($4 with federal senior pass). RV limit 20'. Flush & pit toilets. No reservations.

OAK GROVE CAMPGROUND

From Batesville at I-55 exit 246, E on SR 35; below the dam on Lower Lake. All year; 14-day limit. 82 sites with elec/wtr, $16 ($8 with federal senior pass). Amphitheater, picnic shelter. No reservations.

PATS BLUFF CAMPGROUND

From Batesville at I-55 exit 243A, 9 mi on Hwy 6, then N on county rd; watch for signs. 4/1-9/30; 14-day limit. 14 primitive sites, $8 ($4 with federal senior pass). RV limit 20'. Picnic shelter, $30. Note: At last report, the campground was closed for renovations and site upgrades with wtr & elec; check current status before visiting. (662) 563-4531.

SLEEPY BEND CAMPGROUND

From I-55 exit 252 or 246, E to Lower Lake below John Kyle State Park. All year; 14-day limit. 50 primitive sites, $8 during 4/1-9/30 ($4 with federal senior pass); free 10/1-3/31. RV limit 20'. Flush & pit toilets.

TENNESSEE-TOMBIGBEE WATERWAY (MB) 6

GPS: 33.52, -88.51

The Tennessee-Tombigbee Waterway is a navigable link between the lower Tennessee Valley and the Gulf of Mexico. Stretching 234 mi from Demopolis, Alabama, to Pickwick Lake in the NE corner of Mississippi, this man-make channel has a series of ten locks and dams forming ten pools. Fishing piers are available. Off-road vehicles prohibited. Jamie L. Whitten Historical Center, Fulton, MS (662) 862-5414 and the Bay Springs Resource & Visitor Center, Bay Springs Lake, near Dennis, MS (662) 423-1287, open daily except during winter months and on some federal holidays. Interpretive exhibits, artifacts, 120-seat auditorium with audiovisual equipment, group tours, (662) 862-5414. Campground checkout time 3 p.m., visitor vehicles to 9 p.m. Registered campers may use any of the day use areas on the waterway without paying fees which are charged to non-campers. Contact Resource Manager, Waterway Management Center, 3606 W Plymouth Road, Columbus, MS 39701. (662) 327-2142. See entries in Alabama.

BLUE BLUFF RECREATION AREA

From Aberdeen at jct with Commerce St (Hwy 145), N on Meridian (from center of downtown), cross railroad tracks and bridge, then 1st right following signs; at Aberdeen Lake. All year; 14-day limit. 92 sites with elec/wtr, $16 base, $18 for full hookups & waterfront sites ($8 & $9 with federal senior pass). RV limit in excess of 65'. At reserved sites, 2-night minimum stay required on weekends, 3 nights on holidays. Information center, interpretive programs, guided interpretive walks, amphitheater, multi-use court, phone, wildlife viewing, fish cleaning station, picnic shelter, handicap accessible fishing. (662) 369-2832. NRRS during 3/1-10/31. **GPS: 33.84444, -88.53222**

DEWAYNE HAYES RECREATION AREA

From Columbus, 4 mi N on US 45; 1.5 mi W on SR 373; 2 mi SW on Stenson Creek Rd; 0.5 mi left on Barton's Ferry Rd; at Columbus Lake. All year; 14-day limit. 10 walk-to tent sites, $10 ($5 with federal senior pass); 100 RV/tent sites with elec/wtr, $16 base, $18 at premium locations ($8 & $9 with federal senior pass); 25 full hookups, $20 ($10 with federal senior pass). RV limit in excess of 65 ft. At reserved sites, 2-night minimum stay required on weekends, 3 nights on holidays. Fish cleaning station, picnic shelter, interactive water sprayground, information center, interpretive programs, interpretive trail, guided interpretive walks, game courts. (662) 434-6939. NRRS during 3/1-10/31. **GPS: 33.60028, -88.47139**

PICKENSVILLE RECREATION AREA

From Pickensville at jct with SR 14, 0.75 mi W on Hwy 86; at Aliceville Lake. All year; 14-day limit. 176 sites with elec/wtr, $16 base, $20 at premium sites ($8 & $10 with federal senior pass). RV limit in excess of 65'. At reserved sites, 2-night minimum stay required on weekends, 3 nights on holiday weekends. Bike trail, fish cleaning station, interpretive programs, guided interpretive walks, multi-use courts, phone, picnic shelters. 205-373-8820. NRRS during 3/1-10/31. **GPS: 33.22639, -88.27667**

PINEY GROVE RECREATION AREA

From Tishomingo, W on SR 25; S on SR 30, then SE; on Bay Springs Lake. 5/1-11/30; 14-day limit. 141 sites with elec/wtr, $18 base, $20 at premium locations ($9 & $10 with federal senior pass). RV limit in excess of 65'; 6 pull-through. 10 primitive tent sites with boat-in access are free (no drkg wtr). At reserved sites, 2-night minimum stay required/weekends, 3 nights/holidays. Picnic shelters, fish cleaning station, amphitheater, interpretive trail. (662) 862-7070. NRRS. **GPS: 34.56889, -88.32722**

TOWN CREEK CAMPGROUND

From Columbus at jct with US 45N, W on SR 50; 1 mi W of Tenn-Tom Bridge on SR 50; 1.5 mi N; right on J. Witherspoon Rd; on Columbus Lake. All year (but campground was closed 12/1-3/1 during winter of 2010-11); 14-day limit. 10 walk-to tent sites, $10 ($5 with federal senior pass); 100 RV/tent sites with wtr/elec, $16 base, $18 full hookups ($8 & $9 with federal senior pass). RV limit in excess of 65'. At reserved sites, 2-night minimum stay required on weekends, 3 nights on holidays. Fish cleaning station, bike trail, interpretive programs, guided interpretive walks, phone. (662)494-4885. NRRS during 3/1-10/31. **GPS: 33.60833, -88.50417**

WHITTEN CAMPGROUND

Adjacent to the City of Fulton at Fulton Pool. From jct with US 78, N on Hwy 25; W on Main St to Waterway, then 2 mi N (signs). All year; 14-day limit. 60 sites with elec/wtr, $18 base, $20 at premium locations. RV limit in excess of 65'; 3 pull-through sites. At reserved sites, 2-night minimum stay required on weekends, 3 nights on holiday weekends. Picnic shelters, amphitheater, interpretive trail, phone, nature trails, game courts. (662) 862-7070. NRRS. **GPS: 34.28972, -88.41583**

MISSOURI
29
35
5
4
Independence
Kansas City
Missouri River
70
St. Louis
Jefferson City
Osage
River
3
Lake
of the Ozarks
44
Mississippi
River
7
8
Springfield
Gasconade
River
2
10
55
9
1
6

MISSOURI

State Capital: **Jefferson City**
Nickname: **Show-Me State**
Statehood Year: **1821**

24TH STATE

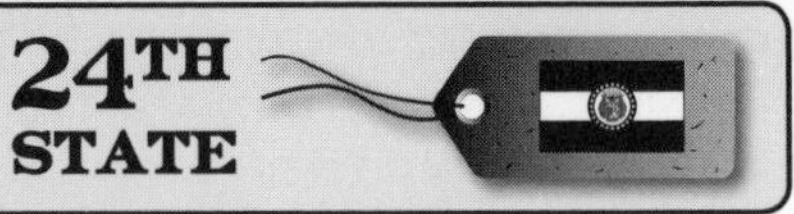

Little Rock District - Where posted, a fee is charged for use of dump station by non-campers. An extra fee may be charged for sites with water hookups.

BULL SHOALS LAKE (LR) 1
GPS: 36.3633, -92.5433

This 45,440-acre lake is 15 mi W of Mountain Home, Arkansas, on SR 178 and SE of Branson near the Missouri state line. ORV prohibited. Campground checkout time 3 p.m. Campsites that are free off-season may have reduced amenities. Resource Manager, Bull Shoals Lake, P. O. Box 367, Mountain Home, AR 72653. (870) 425-2700. See AR listings.

BEAVER CREEK CAMPGROUND

From Kissee Mills (sign), 2.5 mi S on Rt. O. 4/1-10/31; 14-day limit. 36 sites with elec, $16 base, $18 at premium 50-amp sites ($8 & $9 with federal senior pass). Group picnic shelter for up to 50 people & 1 vehicle, $42. RV limit 40 ft. At reserved sites, 2-night minimum stay on weekends, 3 nights on holiday weekends. (870) 546-3708. NRRS during 5/17-9/13. **GPS: 36.6433, 93.0322**

PONTIAC CAMPGROUND

From Arkansas line at jct with US 160, 4.7 mi S on SR 5; 7.3 mi SW to to Pontiac on Rt. W; 0.2 mi S; on bluff overlooking lake. 4/1-10/31; 14-day limit. 3 sites without hookups, $15 ($7.50 with federal senior pass); 29 sites with elec, $18 ($9 with federal senior pass); double sites $34. RV limit 40'. Picnic shelter for up to 50 people & 10 vehicles, $42. At reserved sites, 2-night minimum stay on weekends, 3 nights on holiday weekends. (870) 679-2222. NRRS during 5/17-9/13. **GPS: 36.51, -92.60806**

RIVER RUN CAMPGROUND

From Forsyth, E on SR 60 across bridge, then S across bridge (sign) & W; on upper end of lake. 4/1-9/30; 14-day limit. 32 sites with elec, $18 ($9 with federal senior pass. RV limit 40'. At reserved sites, 2-night minimum stay required on weekends, 3 nights on holiday weekends. (870) 546-3646). No reservations. **GPS: 36.679932, -93.10174**

THEODOSIA CAMPGROUND

From Isabella (sign), 3 mi W on US 160, across bridge, then S (left). 4/1-10/31; 14-day limit. 2 sites without hookups, $14 ($7 with federal senior pass); 31 sites with elec, $18 ($9 with federal senior pass); double sites $34 ($17 with federal senior pass). RV limit 45'. Picnic shelter, $4s. At reserved sites, 2-night minimum stay required on weekends, 3 nights on holiday weekends. (870) 273-4626. NRRS during 5/17-9/13 if renovations are finished. Note: This park was renovated in 2010. **GPS: 36.57333, -92.65361**

CLEARWATER LAKE (LR) 2
GPS: 37.367, 90.7717

A 1,600-acre lake 5 mi SW of Piedmont on CR HH off SR 34, E of Springfield and NW of Mark Twain National Forest in southeastern Missouri. Primitive camping permitted project-wide with a permit. Non-campers charged day use fees for dump station. Campsites that are free off-season may have reduced amenities. Visitor center, interpretive programs. Operations Manager, Clearwater Lake, RR 3, Box 3559D, Piedmont, MO 63957-9559. (573) 233-7777.

BLUFF VIEW CAMPGROUND

From Piedmont at jct with SR 34, 0.9 mi N on SR 49; 6.9 mi W on CR AA. All year; 14-day limit. 14 sites without elec, $14 ($7 with federal senior pass) during 5/15-9/15; free rest of year, but no services. 41 sites with elec (20 wtr hookups), $16 base & $20 with 50-amp elec/wtr ($8 & $10 with federal senior pass) during 5/15-9/15; free rest of year, but no utilities. RV limit in excess of 65'. Picnic shelter for up to 40 people & 9 vehicles, $40. At reserved sites, 2-night minimum stay required on weekends, 3 nights on holidays. Canoeing, interpretive trail, marina, boat rental. NRRS during 5/15-9/15. **GPS: 37.18194, -90.78944**

HIGHWAY K CAMPGROUND

From Annapolis, 5 mi SW on CR K; after bridge, on W side (signs); above lake on Back River. All year; 14-day limit. 21 sites without hookups, $14 ($7 with federal senior pass) during 4/1-10/31; some sites free rest of year but limited amenities. 65 sites with elec (22 with wtr hookups), $16 base & $20 with 50-amp elec/wtr ($8 & $10 with federal senior pass) during 4/1-10/31; some sites free rest of year, but no utilities. RV limit 60'; 2 pull-through. Picnic shelter for up to 40 people & 16 vehicles, $50. At reserved sites, 2-night minimum stay required on weekends, 3 nights on holidays. NRRS during 5/15-9/15. Canoeing, phone. **GPS: 37.32417, -90.7667**

PIEDMONT PARK

From Piedmont, 7 mi SW on SR 34; 5.6 mi SW on CR HH; 1.5 mi NE on Lake Rd (signs); on ridge above lake. All year; 14-day limit. 8 sites without hookups, $14 ($7 with federal senior pass) during 4/15-9/30; some sites free rest of year but limited amenities. 79 sites with elec (8 with wtr hookups), $16 base & $20 with 50-amp elec/wtr ($8 & $10 with federal senior pass) during 4/15-9/30; some sites free rest of year, but no utilities. RV limit in excess of 65 ft; 7 pull-through sites. Group camping area with elec for up to 40 people & 10 vehicles, $40. Two picnic shelters for up to 50 people & 11 vehicles, $50. At reserved sites, 2-night minimum stay required on weekends, 3 nights on holidays. Marina, phone, canoeing. NRRS during 5/15-9/15. **GPS: 37.1425, -90.77028**

RIVER ROAD CAMPGROUND

From Piedmont, 6 mi SW on SR 34; 5.6 mi SW on CR HH; below dam on shore of Black River. All year; 14-day limit. 12 sites without hookups,

$14 ($7 with federal senior pass) during 3/15-10/31; some sites free rest of year, but limited amenities. 97 sites with elec (no wtr hookups), $16 base & $20 with 50-amp elec ($8 & $10 with federal senior pass) during 3/15-10/31; some sites free rest of year but no utilities. RV limit in excess of 65'; 11 pull-through sites. Three picnic shelters: S1 & S2 for up to 50 people & 16 vehicles, and Zebo for up to 50 people & 9 vehicles, $50. At reserved sites, 2-night minimum stay required on weekends, 3 nights on holidays. Interpretive trail, phone, hiking trail, canoeing. NRRS during 5/15-9/15. **GPS: 37.13361, -90.76694**

WEBB CREEK CAMPGROUND

From Ellington, 2.6 mi SW on SR 21; 10.3 mi SE on CR H. All year; 14-day limit. 10 sites without hookups, $14 during 5/15-9/15 ($7 with federal senior pass); some sites free rest of year, but limited amenities. 25 sites with elec (some pull-through), $16 during 5/15-9/15 ($8 with federal senior pass); some sites free rest of year, but no utilities. Picnic shelter, overflow camping. No reservations. **GPS: 37.151123, -90.812756**

HARRY S TRUMAN LAKE (KC) 3
GPS: 38.2548, -93.4080

This 55,600-acre lake is near Warsaw on US 65, 94 mi SE of Kansas City. Visitor center open 3/1-10/31 with exhibit area, theater, interpretive programs. Campground checkout time 6 p.m. Corps day use facilities: Bledsoe Ferry -- boat ramp, picnicking, group shelter; Cooper Creek -- boat ramp; Crowes Crossing -- boat ramp; Fairfield -- boat ramp; Sac River -- boat ramp. Facilities not managed by the Corps include: Harry S Truman State Park; Osceola Campground (City of Osceola); Sterett Creek Park -- campground, boat ramp, marina, restaurant, playground (concession); Resource Manager, Harry S. Truman Lake, Rt.. 2, Box 29A, Warsaw, MO 65355-9603. (660) 438-7317.

BERRY BEND PARK

From Warsaw, 4.4 mi W on SR 7; 3 mi W on CR Z; 1.8 mi S on Berry Bend Rd; on Osage arm of lake, a peninsula in bend of river; equestrian camp on the N. All year; 14-day limit. 82 sites without hookups, $14 during 4/15-10/15 ($7 with federal senior pass); $8 rest of year but reduced amenities ($4 with federal senior pass). 114 sites with elec, $18 during 4/15-10/15 ($9 with federal senior pass); $8 rest of year but reduced amenities. RV limit in excess of 65'; 4 pull-through sites. Picnic shelter, amphitheater, horseshoe pits, change house. At reserved sites, 2-night minimum stay required on weekends, 3 nights on holiday weekends. (660) 438-3872. NRRS (4/15-10/15). **GPS: 38.1997, -93.51**

BERRY BEND EQUESTRIAN PARK

From Warsaw, 4.4 mi W on SR 7; 3 mi W on CR Z; 1.8 mi S on Berry Bend Rd; on Osage arm of lake, N of Berry Bend Park. Campers must have a horse. All year; 14-day limit. 65 sites without hookups, $12 base & $14 at premium locations during 4/15-10/15 ($6 & $7 with federal senior pass); $8 rest of year but reduced amenities. 24 sites with elec, $16 base & $18 at premium locations during 4/15-10/15 ($8 & $9 with federal senior pass). RV limit in excess of 65 ft. Two picnic shelters with elec for up to 64 people & 30 vehicles, $25. Group camping area available. Call for special rules on horses (660) 438-3812). At reserved sites 2-night minimum required stay on weekends, 3 nights on holiday weekends. Corrals, overhead tie posts, all-season wtr hydrants, hiking/bridle trails. NRRS (April 15th to October 14th). **GPS: 38.19972, -93.51**

BUCKSAW PARK

From Clinton, 7.8 mi E on SR 7; 2.5 mi S on CR U (signs); on Grand River arm of lake. All year; 14-day limit. 178 sites without hookups, $14 during 4/15-10/15($7 with federal senior pass); $8 rest of year but reduced amenities. 129 sites with elec, some with 50-amp elec/wtr, $18 base & $22 for 50-amp sites during 4/15-10/15 ($9 & $11 with federal senior pass); rest of year, $8 & $22 but reduced amenities ($4 & $11 with federal senior pass). RV limit in excess of 65 ft. Amphitheater, fish cleaning station, change house, boat rentals nearby, handicap accessible swimming area. At reserved sites, 2-night minimum stay required on weekends, 3 nights on holiday weekends. (660) 447-3402. NRRS (4/15-10/15). **GPS: 38.26, -93.60556**

LONG SHOAL PARK

From Warsaw, 4.4 mi W on SR 7 (signs); on Grand River arm of lake. All year; 14-day limit. 23 sites without hookups, $14 during 4/15-10/15 ($7 with federal senior pass); $8 rest of year but reduced amenities ($4 with federal senior pass). 95 sites with elec, $18 during 4/15-10/15 ($9 with federal senior pass); $8 rest of year but no utilities ($4 with federal senior pass). RV limit in excess of 65'; 3 pull-through. Picnic shelter up to 48 people & 25 vehicles, $20. Boat rentals nearby, change house, marina. At reserved sites, 2-night minimum stay required/weekends, 3 nights/holiday weekends. (660) 438-2342. NRRS (4/15-10/15). **GPS: 38.27611, -93.46972**

OSAGE BLUFF CAMPGROUND

From Warsaw at jct with SR 7, 3 mi S on US 65; 3 mi SW on SR 83, then 1 mi W on SR 295 following signs; at confluence of Osage & Pomme De Terre Rivers. All year; 14-day limit. 27 sites without hookups, $14 during 4/15-10/15 ($7 with federal senior pass); $8 rest of year but reduced amenities ($4 with federal senior pass). 41 sites with elec, $18 during 4/15-10/15 ($9 with federal senior pass); $8 rest of year but no utilities ($4 with federal senior pass). RV limit in excess of 65 ft. Boat rentals nearby. At reserved sites, 2-night minimum stay required on weekends, 3 nights on holiday weekends. NRRS (4/15-10/15). **GPS: 38.19056, -93.39333**

SPARROWFOOT PARK

From Clinton, 6 mi S on SR 13; 1.5 mi E, following signs; near confluence of Grand River & Deepwater Creek. 18 sites without hookups, $12 base, $14 at premium locations during 4/15-10/15 ($6 & $7 with federal senior pass); $8 rest of year but reduced amenities ($4 with federal senior pass). 93 sites with elec, $16 base & $20 at premium locations during 4/15-10/15 ($8 & $10 with federal senior pass); $8 rest of year but no utilities ($4 with federal senior pass). RV limit in excess of 65'; 3 pull-through sites. Three picnic shelters for up to 48 people & 30 vehicles, $20. Horseshoe pits, change house. At reserved sites, 2-night minimum stay required on weekends, 3 nights on holiday weekends. NRRS (4/15-10/15). **GPS: 38.29639, -93.72639**

TALLEY BEND CAMPGROUND

From Lowry City at jct with SR 13, 7 mi E on CR C; at the S side across bridge (signs); on Osage arm of lake. About 65 sites without hookups, $12 base & $14 at premium locations during 4/15-9/30 ($6 & $7 with federal senior pass); $8 rest of year but reduced amenities ($4 with federal senior pass). 109 sites with elec, $18 during 4/15-9/30 ($9 with federal senior pass); $8 rest of year but no utilities ($4 with federal senior pass). RV limit in excess of 65'; 8 pull-through sites. At reserved sites, 2-night minimum stay required on weekends, 3 nights on holiday weekends. NRRS (4/15-9/30). **GPS: 38.13778, -93.61722**

THIBAUT POINT PARK

From Warsaw, 4.3 mi N on US 65; 2.8 mi W on CR T; 1 mi S on gravel CR 218; at confluence of Little Tebo & Sterett Creeks. All year; 14-day limit. 25 sites without hookups, $14 during 4/15-10/15 ($7 with federal senior pass); $8 rest of year but reduced amenities ($4 with federal senior pass). 26 sites with elec, $18 during 4/15-10/15 ($9 with federal senior pass); $8 rest of year but no utilities. RV limit in excess of 65'. 4 concrete sites for disabled, equipped with accessible grills, tbls, lantern holders (2 without elec); they are available to other campers if campground is full. Three group camping areas: Camp A with 19 elec sites, group shelter with elec, grill, 8 tbls, $100; Camp B with 20 sites without elec, group shelter with elec, grill & 8 tbls, $80; Camp C with open RV/tent camping & shelter with elec, grill, 8 tbls, $50. Two picnic shelters with elec for up to 64 people & 1 vehicle, $25. Horseshoe pits, change house. At reserved sites, 2-night minimum stay required on weekends, 3 nights on holiday weekends. (660) 438-2767. NRRS (4/15-10/15). **GPS: 38.29639, -93.39639**

WINDSOR CROSSING PARK

From Lincoln, 11.7 mi W on CR C; 2.3 mi S on CR PP; on the E side (signs) at Tebo Creek arm of lake. All year; 14-day limit. 47 sites without hookups, $10 during 4/15-9/30 ($5 with federal senior pass); $6 rest of year but reduced amenities ($3 with federal senior pass). RV limit in excess of 65'; 6 pull-through sites; 3 handicap sites with accessible grills, tbls, lantern holders. At reserved sites, 2-night minimum stay required on weekends, 3 nights on holiday weekends. (660) 477-9275. NRRS (4/15-9/30). **GPS: 38.36444, -93.545**

MARK TWAIN LAKE
CLARENCE CANNON DAM (SL) 4
GPS: 39.525, -91.6433

This 18,600-acre lake is 14 mi SE of Monroe City on CR J, 120 mi NW of St. Louis. Campground checkout time 4 p.m. Visitor center (open all year), self-guided tours of hydroelectric power plant on weekends from May through August and special events throughout summer; outdoor theater. David C. Berti shooting range is under three covered shelters which are handicap accessible. For lake information, 24 hours, recorded, call (573) 735-2619. Mark Twain Birth Place State Historical Site at lake. Corps-operated day use facilities: Bluff View Recreation Area -- boat ramp, picnicking, group shelter, playground; Elk Fork Park -- boat ramp; HF 10 Park -- playground, biking/hiking trails; HF 13 Park -- hiking, interpretive trails; HF 16 Park -- biking/hikng trails; Highway 24 Park -- boat ramp; Hoot Owl Hollow -- boat ramp, picnicking; John F. Spalding Recreation Area -- boat ramp, picnicking, group shelter, playground, beach, hiking/biking & interpretive trails; Middle Ford Park -- boat ramp; N Fork Recreation Area -- boat ramp; Robert Allen Recreation Area -- boat ramp, picnicking; Rt BB HF 60 Park -- boat ramp; Rt FF

HF 11 Park -- boat ramp; Rt N HF 11 Park -- boat ramp, biking/hiking trails; S Fork Recreation Area -- boat ramp, picnicking; WgSee Spillway Recreation Area -- boat ramp, picnicking, playground. Operations Manager, Mark Twain Lake, 20642 Highway J, Monroe City, MO 63456-9359. (573) 735-4097.

FRANK RUSSELL CAMPGROUND

From Monroe City at jct with US 36, 4 mi E on US 24/36; 9 mi S on CR J; 1 mi N of dam. 4/15-10/10; 14-day limit. 56 sites with elec, $18 ($9 with federal senior pass). RV limit in excess of 65'. Amphitheater. Horse corral with stalls on a first come first served basis. At reserved sites, 2-night minimum stay on weekends, 3 nights on holidays. NRRS (4/15-9/15). **GPS: 39.53556, -91.6475**

INDIAN CREEK CAMPGROUND

From Monroe City, go 6 mi S on United States Rt. 24, 1.7 mi S on Rt. HH. 4/1-11/24; 14-day limit. 20 tent sites, $8 ($4 with federal senior pass); primitive hike-in sites open 5/15-9/15. 12 RV/tent sites without hookups, $8 ($4 with federal senior pass). 215 sites with elec, $18 base, full hookups $24 ($9 & $12 with federal senior pass. RV limit in excess of 65'. Group camping area by reservation, $30-$100. Two picnic shelters for up to 100 people & 1 vehicle, $30. Fish cleaning station, amphitheater. At reserved sites, 2-night minimum stay required on weekends, 3 nights on holiday weekends. NRRS during 4/15-9/15. **GPS: 39.53917, -91.73306**

JOHN C. "JACK" BRISCOE GROUP CAMP

From the dam, S side, 0.5 mi on CR J. Six group camping areas, GRP1 & GRP4 for up to 32 people and 4 vehicles are $60 and GRP2, GRP5 & GRP6 for up to 24 people and 3 vehicles are $45, a picnic shelter for up to 125 people and 10 vehicles is $30. Visitor center, horseshoe pits. 20 sites, $16 each; minimum of 3 sites required. Check in at the Frank

Russell Recreation Area. RV limit 60'. 2-night minimum stay required on weekends, 3 nights on holidays. 4/20-9/10. NRRS.

RAY BEHRENS RECREATION AREA

From Perry at jct SR 154, 6.6 mi N on CR J, N side. 4/1-11/21; 14-day limit. 165 sites with elec/wtr, $18 base, $24 full hookups ($9 & $12 with federal senior pass). RV limit in excess of 65'. Picnic shelter for up to 125 people & 1 vehicle, $30. Amphitheater, fish cleaning station. At reserved sites, 2-night minimum stay required on weekends, 3 nights on holiday weekends. NRRS (4/15-10/24). **GPS: 39.51583, -91.66306**

MISSISSIPPI RIVER (PUA) (RI) 5

GPS: 39.90, -91.42

For information, contact park ranger, RR #4, L&D # 21, Quincy, IL 62301, (217) 228-0890. See Illinois, Iowa & Wisconsin listings.

FENWAY LANDING CAMPGROUND

From Canton, 4.5 mi N on US 61, then E on CR 454; camping area is just across the levee. All year; 14-day limit. 15 free sites.
GPS: 40.138281, -91.517334

NORFOLK LAKE (LR) 6

GPS: 36.45, -92.59

Located 4 mi northeast of Norfork, Arkansas, on Arkansas SR 177 near the Missouri state line. Resource Manager, Norfork Lake, P. O. Box 2070, Mountain Home, AR 72654. (501) 425-2700. See Arkansas listing.

TECUMSEH CAMPGROUND

At Tecumseh on both sides of the lake. 4/1-9/30; 14-day limit. 7 sites without hookups, $9 ($4.50 with federal senior pass). Pit toilets.
GPS: 36.586587, -93.286826

UDALL CAMPGROUND

From Udall, 1.5 mi W on CR O; 0.7 mi on access road. 4/1-9/30; 14-day limit. 7 sites no hookups, $9 ($4.50 with federal senior pass). Pit toilets.
GPS: 36.544592, -92.285376

POMME DE TERRE LAKE (KC) 7
GPS: 37.9017, -93.32

This 7,790-acre lake with 113 mi of shoreline is 3 mi S of Hermitage on SR 254, 140 mi SE of Kansas City. The lake has 10 campgrounds, six managed by the Corps. Two campgrounds -- Quarry Point and Hwy. 83 Parks -- are managed by concessionaires, and the State of Missouri has two campgrounds within Pomme de Terre State Park. Corps campsites that are free off-season may have reduced amenities. Reservation fee of $20 for picnic shelters. The Pomme de Terre Lake Internet site (produced by the Kansas City District) has virtually no useful information about individual Corps campgrounds. Resource Manager, Pomme de Terre Lake, Rt. 2, Box 2160, Hermitage, MO 65668-9509. (417) 745-6411.

DAMSITE CAMPGROUND

From Hermitage, 3 mi SE on SR 254, then W at Carson's Corner. All year; 14-day limit. 9 tent sites, $12 ($6 with federal senior pass). 26 RV/tent sites without hookups, $12 base, $14 at premium locations ($6 & $7 with federal senior pass). 80 sites with elec, $20 base, $22 with elec/wtr ($10 & $12 with federal senior pass). Lower fees and reduced amenities during 10/1-4/14. RV limit 45 ft. Two picnic shelters with elec, $20. Amphitheater, handicap accessible fishing area. At reserved sites, 2-night minimum stay required on weekends, 3 nights on holiday weekends. (417) 745-2244. NRRS (4/1-9/30). **GPS: 37.90472, -93.30778**

LIGHTFOOT LANDING CAMPGROUND

From Elkton, 2.3 mi S on SR 83; 3.4 mi E on CR RB. All year; 14-day limit. 5 tent sites, $12 ($6 with federal senior pass) during 4/15-10/15; free rest of year but reduced amenities. 6 RV/tent sites without hookups, $14 ($7 with federal senior pass). 29 sites with elec/wtr, $20 ($10 with federal senior pass). RV limit in excess of 65'; 6 pull-through sites. Three group camping areas without elec for up to 50 people 16 vehicles, $30. Picnic shelter for up to 50 people & 16 vehicles, heated fishing pier, horseshoe pits; boat rentals nearby. At reserved sites, 2-night minimum stay required on weekends, 3 nights on holiday weekends. (417) 282-6890. NRRS (4/16-9/30). **GPS: 37.82611, -93.36139**

NEMO LANDING PARK

From Nemo at jct with CR D, 1 mi SW on SR 64; just before bridge. All year; 14-day limit. 3 tent sites, $12 ($6 with federal senior pass) during 4/16-10/15; free rest of year but reduced amenities. 61 RV/tent sites without hookups, $12 base, $14 at premium locations during 4/16-10/15 ($6 & $7 with federal senior pass); some sites free off-season but limited amenities. 55 sites with elec/wtr, $16 base, $18 at premium locations with 30-amp elec; $20 at premium locations with 50-amp elec ($8, $9 & $10 with federal senior pass). Some sites with hookups may have lower fees & reduced amenities off-season. RV limit 60'. Picnic shelter, amphitheater. horseshoe pits; boat rentals nearby. At reserved sites, 2-night minimum stay required on weekends, 3 nights on holiday weekends. (417) 993-5529. NRRS (4/16-9/30). **GPS: 37.86611, -93.27389**

OUTLET PARK CAMPGROUND

From Hermitage, 3 mi SE on SR 254; W at Carson's Corner; below dam on W side of outlet. All year; 14-day limit. 14 RV/tent sites without hookups, $12 ($6 with federal senior pass); 14 sites with elec, $14 base, $20 at premium locations ($7 & $10 with federal senior pass). During 10/16-/15, some sites without hookups may be free but with reduced amenities. RV limit 50'; 10 pull-through sites. Group camping area with elec, $30. Picnic shelter, horseshoe pits. At reserved sites, 2-night minimum stay required on weekends, 3 nights on holidays. (417) 745-2290. NRRS (4/16-9/30). **GPS: 37.90278, -93.32917**

PITTSBURG LANDING CAMPGROUND

From Pittsburg at jct with CR J, 1 mi S on SR 64; 3 mi E on CR RA. All year; 14-day limit. 40 free primitive sites. Picnic shelter, pit toilets. **GPS: 37.836949, -93.261612**

WHEATLAND PARK CAMPGROUND

From Wheatland at jct with US 54, 4.2 mi S on SR 83; 2 mi E on SR 254; 1 mi S on SR 205. 9 tent sites, $12 during 4/16-10/15 ($6 with federal senior pass); free off-season but reduced amenities. 9 RV/tent sites without hookups, $12 base, $14 at premium locations ($6 & $7 with federal senior pass); during 10/16-4/15, some sites without hookups may be free but with reduced amenities. 67 sites with elec: sites with elec, $16 ($8 with federal senior pass); sites with 50-amp elec/wtr, $20 ($10 with federal senior pass). RV limit 35'; 8 pull-through sites. Picnic shelter for up to 75 people. $20. At reserved sites, 2-night minimum stay required on weekends, 3 nights on holiday weekends. Open all year. (417) 282-5267. NRRS (April 16th to October 15th). **GPS: 37.87556, -93.37444**

STOCKTON LAKE (KC) 8
GPS: 37.6917, -93.7583

This 24,900-acre lake has 298 mi of shoreline. It is on the E side of Stockton on SR 32, 136 mi SE of Kansas City. Campsites that are free off season may have reduced amenities. Visitor center Operations Manager, Stockton Lake, 16435 E Stockton Lake Drive, Stockton, MO 65785-9471. (417) 276-3113.

CEDAR RIDGE CAMPGROUND

From Bona at jct with SR 215, 0.5 mi N on SR 245; 0.7 mi N on CR RA; 340-acre park on Little Sac arm of lake. All year; 14-day limit. 33 sites without hookups, $12 bases, $14 at premium locations during 4/16-9/30 ($6 & $7 with federal senior pass); sites free off-season but no flush toilets or showers. 21 sites with elec, $14 base, $20 at premium locations during 4/16-9/30 ($7 & $10 with federal senior pass; sites free off-season but no utilities. RV limit 60'. Picnic shelter. At reserved sites, 2-night minimum stay required on weekends, 3 nights on holiday weekends. (417) 995-2045. NRRS (4/15-9/30). **GPS: 37.57556, -93.68139**

CRABTREE COVE CAMPGROUND

From Stockton at jct with SR 39, 3.5 mi E on SR 32, then SW; 168-acre park on NW corner of lake. 3/15-10/31; 14-day limit. 32 sites no hookups, $12 base, $14 at premium locations during 4/16-9/30 ($6 & $7 with federal senior pass); free or reduced fees during 3/15-4/15 & 10/1-10/31, but no wtr or elec amenities. 32 sites with elec, $16 base, $18 at premium locations during 4/16-9/30 ($8 & $9 with federal senior pass); free or reduced fees during 3/15-4/15 & 10/1-10/31, but no wtr or elec amenities. RV limit 50 ft; 3 pull-through; 2 handicap without elec, 1 handicap with elec. Picnic shelter, handicap accessible fishing area, overflow sites. At reserved sites, 2-night minimum stay required/weekends, 3 nights/ holiday weekends. NRRS (4/16-9/30). **GPS: 37.66972, -93.75306**

HAWKER POINT CAMPGROUND

From Stockton at jct with SR 32, 6.2 mi S on SR 39; 5.2 mi E on CR H; 518-acre park at N end of Big Sac arm of lake. All year; 14-day limit. 32 sites without hookups, $12 base, $14 at premium locations during 4/15-9/30 ($6 & $7 with federal senior pass); some sites free rest of year, but reduced services & no wtr available. 30 sites with elec, $16 base, $18 at premium locations during 4/15-9/30 ($8 & $9 with federal senior pass); some sites free rest of year, but no utilities. RV limit 60'. At reserved sites, 2-night minimum stay required on weekends, 3 nights on holiday weekends. (417) 276-7266. NRRS (4/16-9/30). **GPS: 37.60639, -93.78111**

MASTERS CAMPGROUND

From Fair Play at jct with SR 123, 3.7 mi W on SR 32; 2.6 mi S on CR RA, then W; 836-acre park on Little Sac arm of lake. All year; 14-day limit. 73 sites no hookups, $10 base, $14 at premium locations during 5/15-9/15 ($5 & $7 with federal senior pass); free rest of year, but no wtr services & reduced amenities. RV limit 60 ft. Group camping area w/o elec up to 34 people & 18 vehicles, $35. 8 overflow sites. At reserved sites, 2-night minimum stay required/weekends, 3 nights/holiday weekends. (417) 276-6847. NRRS during 5/15-9/15. **GPS: 37.59917, -93.68**

ORLEANS TRAIL NORTH & SOUTH CAMPGROUNDS

From SE edge of Stockton, 0.5 mi E on CR RB; 0.5 mi right on Blake St; 959-acre park on NW shore of lake. All year at N campground; 14-day limit. 118 sites without hookups, $12 during 5/9-9/15 ($6 with federal senior pass); free rest of year, but no wtr services & reduced amenities. RV limit 50 ft; 4 pull-through sites. 5 sites at equestrian trailhead. Group camping area for up to 90 people & 45 vehicles with 12 elec sites, $85-$110. Picnic shelter, $30-$35. At reserved sites, 2-night minimum stay required on weekends, 3 nights on holiday weekends. (417) 276-6948. NRRS (5/9-9/15). **GPS: 37.6544, -93.78306**

RUARK BLUFF EAST CAMPGROUND

From Greenfield at jct with US 160, 6.4 mi N on CR H, before the bridge; on Big Sac arm of lake. 87 sites without hookups, $12 base, $14 at premium locations during 4/16-9/30 ($6 & $7 with federal senior pass); free rest of year, but no wtr services & reduced amenities. 28 sites with elec, $16 base, $18 at premium locations during 4/16-9/30 ($8 & $9 with federal senior pass); some sites free rest of year, but no utilities

& reduced amenities. RV limit in excess of 65 ft; 4 pull-through sites. Handicap accessible fishing area. At reserved sites, 2-night minimum stay required on weekends, 3 nights on holiday weekends. (417) 637-5303. NRRS (4/16-9/30). **GPS: 37.52222, -93.80528**

RUARK BLUFF WEST CAMPGROUND

From Greenfield at jct with US 160, 6.4 mi N on CR H, before bridge; on Big Sac arm of lake. 4/16-9/29; 14-day limit. 40 sites without hookups, $12 base, $14 at premium locations ($6 & $7 with federal senior pass). 46 sites with elec, $16 base, $18 at premium locations ($8 & $9 with federal senior pass). RV limit 50 ft. Group camping area with for up to 75 people & 35 vehicles with 11 elec sites, $85 Mon-Thursday, $110 Fri-Sun & on holidays. At reserved sites, 2-night minimum stay required on weekends, 3 nights on holiday weekends. (417) 637-5279. NRRS during 4/16-9/29. **GPS: 37.52583, -93.80944**

TABLE ROCK LAKE (LR) 9
GPS: 36.595, 93.3083

A 43,100-acre lake 3.4 mi SW of Branson on SR 165, W of US 65. Visitor center with exhibits, auditorium audiovisual presentations, nature trail. ORV prohibited. Campground checkout time 3 p.m. Campsites that are free off-season may have reduced amenities. Other camping areas at the lake include Big Bay Recreation Area (Mark Twain National Forest) and Table Rock State Park. Resource Manager, Upper White River Project Office, 4600 State Road 165 Ste. A, Branson, MO 65616-8976. (417) 334-4101. See Arkansas listings.

AUNT'S CREEK CAMPGROUND

From W of Branson at jct with SR 76, 3.9 mi SW on SR 13; 2.7 mi W on CR 00 & CR 00-9 (signs); on James River arm of lake. 5/1-9/15; 14-day limit. 3 sites without hookups, $14 ($7 with federal senior pass); 52 sites with elec, $18 ($9 with federal senior pass); double sites $36. RV limit in excess of 65'; 6 pull-through sites. Picnic shelter for up to 60 people & 25 vehicles, $50. At reserved sites, 2-night minimum stay required. Non-campers pay $4 day use fee for picnicking, beach, boat ramp, dump station. (417) 739-2792. NRRS. **GPS: 36.67361, -93.45972**

BAXTER PARK

From Lampe at jct with SR 13, 4.8 mi W on CR H (signs); on White River arm of lake. 5/1-9/15; 14-day limit. 31 sites without hookups, $14 ($7 with federal senior pass); 25 sites with elec, $18 ($9 with federal senior pass); double sites $32. RV limit in excess of 65 ft; 2 pull-through sites. At reserved sites, 2-night minimum stay required. Non-campers pay $4 day use fee for picnicking, beach, boat ramp, dump station (417) 779-5370. NRRS. **GPS: 36.67361, -93.45972**

BIG M PARK

From Mano at jct with CR E, 1.3 mi SE on CR M (signs); on White River arm of lake. 5/1-9/15; 14-day limit. 39 sites without hookups, $14 ($7 with federal senior pass); 8 sites with elec, $18 ($9 with federal senior pass); 14 sites with full hookups, $20 ($10 with federal senior pass); 1 double sites with elec, $32. RV limit in excess of 65'. At reserved sites, 2-night minimum stay required. Picnic shelter, marina, sand volleyball court. Non-campers pay $4 day use fee for picnicking, boat ramp, beach, dump station. (417) 271-3190. NRRS. **GPS: 36.55835, -93.67627**

CAMPBELL POINT PARK

From Shell Knob at jct with CR 39-5, 5.1 mi SE on SR YY; on White River arm of lake. 4/1-9/15; 14-day limit. 14 sites no hookups, $14 ($7 with federal senior pass); 36 sites with elec, $18 ($9 with federal senior pass); 24 sites with elec/wtr, $19 ($9.50 with federal senior pass); 1 full-hookup $20 ($10 with federal senior pass). Weekly rate available. RV limit in excess of 65'; 4 pull-through sites. Picnic shelter for up to 60 people &

20 vehicles, $50. At reserved sites, 2-night minimum stay required. Non-campers pay $4 day use fee for dump station, picnicking, boat ramp, beach, sand volleyball. (417) 858-3903. NRRS. **GPS: 36.59583, -93.55028**

CAPE FAIR PARK

From Reeds Springs at jct with SR 248, 1.4 mi S on SR 13; 8 mi W on SR 76 to Cape Fair; SW on CR 76-82 (signs); on James River arm of lake. 4/1-10/31; 14-day limit. 13 sites without hookups, $14 ($7 with federal senior pass); 23 sites with elec, $18 ($9 with federal senior pass); 46 sites with elec/wtr, $19 ($9.50 with federal senior pass). RV limit in excess of 65 ft; 7 pull-through sites. Picnic shelter for up to 60 people & 25 vehicles, $50. At reserved sites, 2-day minimum stay required. Non-campers pay $4 day use fee for boat ramp, dump, beach, picnicking. (417) 538-2220. NRRS. **GPS: 36.7225, -93.53157**

EAGLE ROCK PARK

From Eagle Rock, 3 mi S on SR 86; right before bridge (signs); on White River arm of lake. 5/1-10/31; 14-day limit. 11 sites no hookups, $14 ($7 with federal senior pass); 24 sites with elec, $18 ($9 with federal senior pass); 1 site with elec/wtr, $19 ($9.50 with federal senior pass); 1 full-hookup $20 ($10 with federal senior pass). RV limit in excess of 65 ft; 6 pull-through; At reserved sites, 2-night minimum stay required. Non-campers pay $4 day use fee for boat ramp, dump station, beach, picnicking, sand volleyball court. (417) 271-3215. NRRS. **GPS: 36.52722, -93.73**

INDIAN POINT PARK

From W of Branson at jct with SR 13, 3 mi W on SR 76; 2.8 mi S on Indian Point Rd; on White River arm of lake. 4/1-10/31; 14-day limit. 2 sites without hookups, $14 ($7 with federal senior pass); 2 tent sites with elec & 19 RV/tent sites with elec, $18 ($9 with federal senior pass); 54 sites with elec/wtr, $19 ($9.50 with federal senior pass. RV limit in excess of 65 ft. Group camping area with elec for up to 64 people & 11 vehicles, $50. Picnic shelter with elec for up to 60 people & 25 vehicles, $50. Fish hatchery nearby. At reserved sites, 2-night minimum stay required. Non-campers pay $4 day use fee for boat ramp, dump station, beach, picnicking. (417) 338-2121. NRRS. **GPS: 36.63111, -93.34722**

LONG CREEK PARK

From Ridgedale at jct with US 65, 3 mi W on SR 86; S on CR 86/50 prior to bridge (signs); on Long Creek arm of lake. 4/1-9/15; 14-day limit. 4 RV/tent sites without hookups & 6 basic tent sites, $14 ($7 with federal senior pass); 4 tent sites with elec, $19 ($9.50 with federal senior pass); 24 RV/tent sites with elec, $18 ($9 with federal senior pass); 13 sites with elec/wtr, $19 ($9.50 with federal senior pass). RV limit 55 ft; 2 pull-through sites. Picnic shelter for up to 60 people & 25 vehicles, $50. At reserved sites, 2-night minimum stay required. (417) 334-8427. NRRS. **GPS: 36.52056, -93.30417**

MILL CREEK PARK

From Lampe, 4 mi N on SR 13; 1 mi W on CR RB; on White River arm of lake. 4/1-10/31; 14-day limit. 67 sites with elec/wtr, $19 ($9.50 with federal senior pass); double site $34. RV limit in excess of 65 ft; 19 pull-through sites. At reserved sites, 2-night minimum stay required. Non-campers pay $4 day use fee for boat ramp, dump station, picnicking, beach. Picnic shelter for up to 60 people & 18 vehicles, $50. (417) 779-5378. NRRS. **GPS: 36.59361, -93.44111**

OLD HIGHWAY 86 PARK

From Ridgedale at jct with US 65, 7.6 mi W on SR 86; N on SR UU; on White River arm of lake. 4/1-10/31; 14-day limit. 40 sites with elec, $18 ($9 with federal senior pass); 31 sites with elec/wtr, $19 ($9.50 with

federal senior pass). RV limit in excess of 65'. Two picnic shelters: SR1 up to 60 people & 22 vehicles, and SR2 for up to 60 people & 10 vehicles, $50. At reserved sites, 2-day minimum stay required. Non-campers pay $4 day use fee for boat ramp, beach, dump station, picnicking, sand volleyball court. (417) 779-5376. NRRS (May 1st to Oct. 30th.
GPS: 36.55944, -93.31944

VINEY CREEK PARK

From Golden, 4 mi N on SR J; on White River arm of lake. 5/1-9/15; 14-day limit. 1 tent site & 21 RV/tent sites without hookups, $14 ($7 with federal senior pass); 24 sites with elec/wtr, $19 ($9.50 with federal senior pass). RV limit 50 ft; 9 pull-through sites. At reserved sites, 2-night minimum stay required. Non-campers pay $4 day use fee for boat ramp, dump station, beach, picnicking. NRRS. **GPS: 36.56611, -93.67583**

VIOLA PARK

From Viola, 5 mi S on SR 39; W on SR 39/48; on White River arm of lake. 4/1-9/15; 14-day limit. 1 basic tent site & 18 RV/tent sites without hookups, $14 ($7 with federal senior pass); 15 sites with elec, $18 ($9 with federal senior pass); 22 sites with elec/wtr, $19 ($9.50 with federal senior pass). RV limit in excess of 65'; 2 pull-through sites. At reserved sites, 2-night minimum stay required. Non-campers pay $4 day use fee for boat ramp, dump station, beach, picnicking. (417) 858-3904. NRRS.
GPS: 36.56167, -93.59472

WAPPAPELLO LAKE (SL) 10
GPS: 36.93, -90.2783

This 8,400-acre lake is 16 mi NE of Poplar Bluff and N of US 60, E of US 67, on CR T, 150 mi S of St. Louis. Campground checkout time 4 p.m. Campers required to register at the office for free sites. Visitor center with picnicking, interpretation programs, special events during summer. Overflow camping below the dam open only when all Corps and private campgrounds in surrounding area are full; $3 fee for primitive sites. Daily lake information, (573) 222-8139/1-877-LAKEVIEW. Visitor Center, (573) 222-8773. Operations Manager, Wappapello Lake, 10992 Highway T, Wappapello, MO 63966-9603. (573) 222-8562.

BLUE SPRINGS CAMPGROUND

From dam, 17 mi N on CR D; 1.8 mi S on CR BB; 1.5 mi W on CR 531. All year; 14-day limit. 2 free primitive sites in parking area. No facilities except grills.

CHAONIA LANDING CAMPGROUND

From Poplar Bluff at jct with US 67, 3.5 mi E on SR 172; 2.8 mi NE on CR W. All year; 14-day limit. 12 sites without hookups, $9 ($4.50 with federal senior pass). RV limit 22'. **GPS: 36.5823, -90.2136**

GREENVILLE RECREATION AREA

From Greenville, 2.5 mi S on US 67, before bridge (signs). All year; 14-day limit. 111 sites. Sites without hookups, $14 ($7 with federal senior pass); 5 sites hike-in. 98 sites with 30-amp elec, $16 ($8 with federal senior pass); double sites $32 ($16 with federal senior pass). Overflow camping open when public & private campgrounds in area are full; $3 primitive sites, no facilities. 2-night minimum stay required at all sites on weekends. RV limit in excess of 65'. Picnic shelter up to 100 people & 55 vehicles, $50. 2 horseshoe pits, amphitheater, historic trail, interpretive trail. (573) 224-3884. NRRS during 3/18-11/21. **GPS: 37.10278, -90.45833**

ISLANDS CAMPING AREAS

Accessible by boat only. Located near dam, SW side, offshore from Wappapello State Park. 2 large islands. All year; 14-day limit. 6 primitive tent sites, $9 ($4.50 with federal senior pass. Honor pay at Rockwood Point boat ramp, Redman Creek fee both or project office. Pit toilets, fire rings.

JOHNSON TRACT NATURAL AREA

From Greenville, 1.3 mi S on US 67; 2 mi S on CR D to parking lot on W side across from intersection with CR 534. All year; 14-day limit. 2 free primitive hike-in sites.

LOST CREEK LANDING

From dam, 11 mi N on CR D; W on Corps Rd 9. All year; 14-day limit. 3 free primitive sites in parking area. No facilities except grills.
GPS: 37.0223, -90.3065

NOTHERN PRIMITIVE CAMPING ZONE

Free primitive camping available on all Corps public lands S of Hwy 34 to PA 34 on E side of the St. Francis River and all Corps public lands on the W side, N of where Highway FF intersects with Highway 67. All year; 14-day limit.

PEOPLES CREEK RECREATION AREA

From the dam, 1.7 mi N on CR D (signs). All year; 14-day limit. 56 sites with elec. Sites with 30-amp elec, $16 ($8 with federal senior pass); sites with full hookups & 50-amp elec, $20 ($10 with federal senior pass). RV limit in excess of 65 ft. 2-night minimum stay required at all sites on weekends. Group camping area. 4 picnic shelters, $50. NRRS.

Note: lower camping area was closed for renovation during 2010; upgrades include 50-amp elec, added water spigots, new shower house; check current status before visiting. 573-222-8562. **GPS: 36.943604, -90.275879**

POSSUM CREEK CAMPGROUND

From the dam, 3 mi N on CR D; 1.5 mi W on CR 521 and Rd 7. All year; 14-day limit. 2 free primitive sites at parking area. Pit toilet, grills.

REDMAN CREEK RECREATION AREA

From the dam, 1 mi S on CR T (signs). All year; 14-day limit. Sites with 30-amp elec, $16 ($8 with federal senior pass); full-hookup sites, $20 ($10 with federal senior pass), double sites $40. Primitive boat-in tent sites, $9 ($4.50 with federal senior pass). Three picnic shelters: SO1 for up to 85 people & 30 vehicles; SO2 for up to 600 people & 200 vehicles, and SO3 for up to 150 people & 48 vehicles, $50. 2-night minimum stay required at all sites on weekends. Fish cleaning station, horseshoe pits, nearby boat rentals, visitor's center, hiking trail. (573) 222-8233. NRRS. **GPS: 36.92278, -90.2875**

SULPHUR SPRINGS CAMPGROUND

From Greenville, 1.3 mi S on US 67; 3.2 mi S on CR D; W on Road 17. All year; 14-day limit. 4 free primitive sites at parking area. Pit toilets, grills.

OZARK TRAIL

The Ozark Trail transverses approximately 30 mi through the Wappapello Lake Project and passes within 100' of 19 designated parking areas S of U. S. Highway 67. Free primitive tent camping permitted on Corps land within 100' of the trail. No facilities.

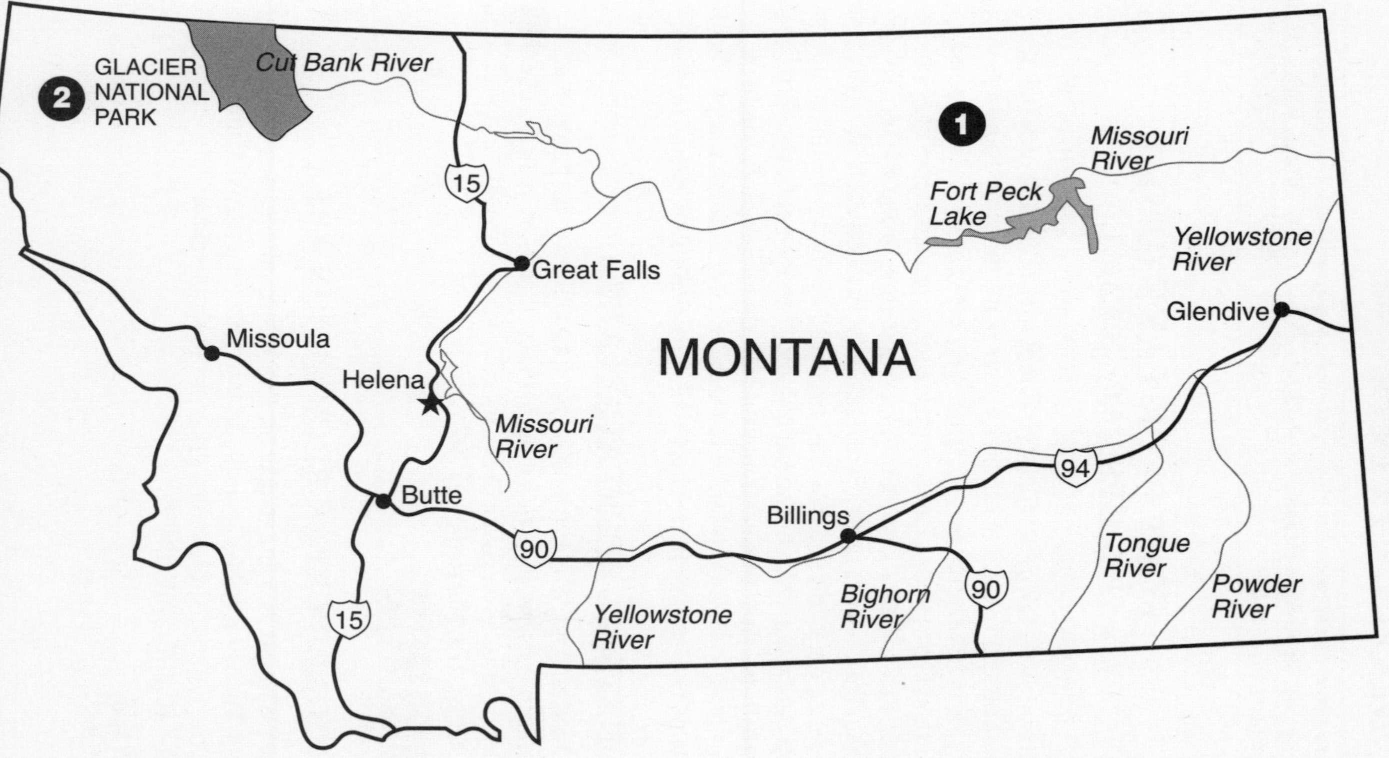
2
GLACIER NATIONAL PARK
Cut Bank River
1
Missouri River
Fort Peck Lake
Yellowstone River
Glendive
15
Great Falls
Missoula
MONTANA
Helena
Missouri River
Butte
94
Billings
90
Tongue River
Powder River
Bighorn River
90
15
Yellowstone River

MONTANA

State Capital: **Helena**
Nickname: **Treasure State**
Statehood Year: **1889**

41ST STATE

MONTANA

FORT PECK LAKE (OM) 1
GPS: 48.0, -106.4167

This 240,000-acre lake has 1,520 mi of shoreline and is 10 mi SW of Nashua on SR 117 in northeastern Montana, 112 mi W of N Dakota state line and 76 mi S of Canada. Power plant museum tours by appointment LD-MD; rest of year hourly every day 9-4:45. Day use facilities: First Dredge Park -- picnicking, group shelter, playground, beach; Flat Lake Park -- boat ramp, picnicking, group shelter; Nelson Dredge Park -- boat ramp; Second Dredge Park -- beach; Winter Harbor -- boat ramp. Camping areas not managed by the Corps include: James Kipp Recreational Area (Bureau of Land Management); Crooked Creek Recreational Area (concessionaire); Hell Creek Rec. Area (State of Montana); Rock Creek Marina (concessionaire). Lake Manager, Fort Peck Lake, P. O. Box 208, Ft. Peck, MT 59223-0208. (406) 526-3411/3224.

BONETRAIL RECREATION AREA

Recreation Area W of the dam on SR 24, 60 mi SW on gravel Willow Creek Rd (impassable when wet, dirt last 30 mi). All year; 14-day limit. 6 free primitive sites. RV limit 16'. Picnic shelter. Nearest dump station, 60 mi. **GPS: 47.69001, -107.17703**

CROOKED CREEK RECREATION AREA

From Winnett at S end of lake on Rt 20, N on all-weather gravel Drag Ridge Tr. All year; 14-day limit. 20 free primitive sites. RV limit 25'. Picnic shelter, pit toilets, fire rings, drkg wtr. Marina nearby.
GPS: 47.207, -107.55106

DEVILS CREEK RECREATION AREA

From dam, S on SR 24; W on SR 200 to Jordan, then 50 mi NW on gravel road through badlands of Hell Creek Gelogical Formation. All year; 14-day limit. 6 free primitive sites. RV limit 16'. Picnic shelter, pit toilets, fire rings, no drkg wtr. Nearest dump station, 50 mi.
GPS: 47.61806, -107.64306

DOWNSTREAM CAMPGROUND

W of spillway below dam near Fort Peck. About 4/25-11/1; 14-day limit. 1 walk-to tent site & 10 basic tent sites, $10 ($5 with federal senior pass). 71 sites with elec: 30-amp elec, $16, 50-amp elec, $18 ($8 & $9 with federal senior pass). No wtr hookups. RV limit in excess of 65'. Picnic shelters with elec, $20. Group camping area with elec for up to 200 people & 40 vehicles(includes 10 handicap sites), $164. 2-night minimum stay on weekends, 3 nights on holiday weekends. Fish cleaning station, interpretive center, fishing ponds, interpretive trail, phone. (406) 526-3224. NRRS during 5/13-9/6. **GPS: 48.00889, -106.42889**

DUCK CREEK RECREATION AREA

From W end of dam on SR 24, S following signs on paved rd to park. All year; 14-day limit. 9 free primitive sites. RV limit 40'. Pit toilets, fire rings, picnic shelter. **GPS: 47.978, -106.522**

FLAT LAKE RECREATION AREA

From Fort Peck, 5.7 mi S on SR 24. Al year; 14-da limit. 3 free primitive sites. Picnic shelter, pit toilets, fire rings, no drkg wtr. Nearest dump station 6 mi.

FLOODPLAIN RECREATION AREA

From E end of the dam on SR 24, N on SR 117 to just before the C.M. Russell National Wildlife Refuge office; on the right; 1 mi on paved rd, following signs. All year; 14-day limit. 5 free primitive sites. RV limit 50 ft. Fire rings, drkg wtr.

FOURCHETTE BAY RECREATION AREA

From Malta at jct with I-2, 60 mi S on gravel Hwy 191 (some spots impassable when wet). All year; 14-day limit. 44 free primitive sites. RV limit 20'. Picnic shelters, fire rings, pit toilets, no drkg wrt. Nearest dump station, 60 mi. **GPS: 47.3953, -107.39386**

MCGUIRE CREEK RECREATION AREA

From dam, 37 mi SE on SR 24 (dirt, impassable when wet); on W side at Big Dry arm of lake. All year; 14-day limit. 10 free primitive sites. RV limit 16'. Fire rings, pit toilets, no drkg wtr. Nearest dump station, 45 mi. **GPS: 47.3802, -106.14179**

NELSON CREEK RECREATION AREA

From Ft. Peck, 44 mi SE on SR 24; 7 mi W on all-weather gravel rd, following signs; at tip of Big Dry arm of lake within Hell Creek Geological Formation, called the bandlands. All year; 14-day limit. 16 free primitive sites. RV limit 40 ft. Picnic shelter, fire rings, drkg wtr. Nearest dump station, 45 mi. **GPS: 47.3423, -106.13449**

ROUNDHOUSE POINT CAMPGROUND

N of dam off Hwy 117. All year; 14-day limit. 3 free primitive sites. Fishing pier, pit toilets, walkway, fire rings. Nearest dump station 2 mi.

THE PINES RECREATION AREA

From near Fort Peck at jct with SR 117, 4 mi W on SR 24; 12 mi SW on Willow Creek Rd (all-weather gravel), then 15 mi S on gravel Pines Rd. All year; 14-day limit. 30 free primitive sites. RV limit 30 ft. Picnic shelter with elec & grill, fish cleaning station, fire rings, no drkg wtr. Nearest dump station, 33 mi. 25 primitive sites. All sites are free. RV limit 30'.

WEST END CAMPGROUND

2 mi off Hwy 24 on Duck Creek Rd; overlooking lake at W side of dam. MD-LD; 14-day limit. Primitive sites without hookups, $5 ($2.50 with federal senior pass); 13 sites with elec, $16 ($8 with federal senior pass). RV limit 35 ft. Picnic shelter, drkg wtr. Nearest dump station, 3 mi.
GPS: 47.997, -106.494

LAKE KOOCANUSA LIBBY DAM (SEA) 2
GPS: 48.42, -115.31

A 46,500-acre lake 17 mi NE of Libby in northwestern Montana on SR 37. Campsites available on project lands with some amenities. Visitor center provides powerhouse tours, interpretive programs, picnicking. Murray Springs Fish Hatchery. Libby Dam Project, 17115 Highway 37, Libby, MT 59923-9703. (406) 293-5577.

ALEXANDER CREEK CAMPGROUND

1 mi below dam on W shore of Kootenai River off gravel Powerhouse Rd, gravel. All year; 14-day limit. 2 free primitive sites.

BLACKWELL FLATS CAMPGROUND

3 mi below dam on W shore of Kootenai River, on gravel FR 228. All year; 14-day limit. 7 free primitive sites, some pull-through.

GPS: 48.369, -115.322

DUNN CREEK FLATS CAMPGROUND

2.5 mi below dam on E shore of Kootenai River, on gravel Rt 37. All year; 14-day limit. 13 free primitive sites, some pull-through sites.

GPS: 48.399, -115.309

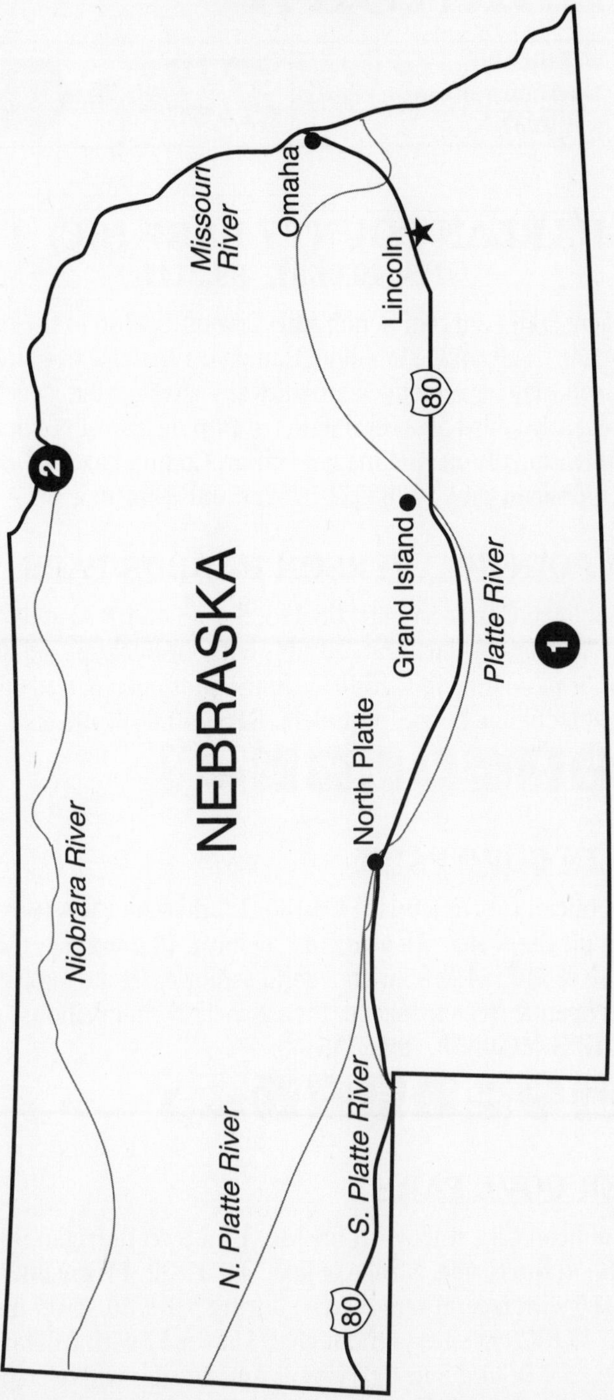

NEBRASKA

Omaha

Missouri River

Lincoln

80

Grand Island

Platte River

North Platte

Niobrara River

N. Platte River

S. Platte River

80

1

2

NEBRASKA

State Capital: **Lincoln**
Nickname: **Cornhusker State**
Statehood Year: **1867**

37TH STATE

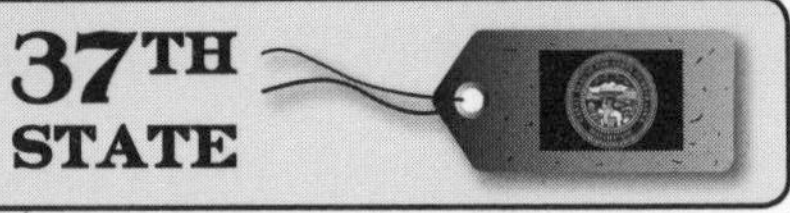

HARLAN COUNTY LAKE (KC) 1
GPS: 40.0667, -99.2117

A 13,250-acre lake 1 mi S of Republican City off US 136 in S-central Nebraska near the Kansas state line. Campsites that are free sites in the off season may have reduced amenities. Visitor center. New toilet facilities recently added at several parks. Camping also at N Shore Marina. Operations Project Manager, Harlan County Lake, 70788 Corps Road A, Republican City, NE 68971-9742. (308) 799-2105.

CEDAR POINT/PATTERSON HARBOR PARK

From Republican City at jct with US 136, 5 mi S on CR A; at dam on the S side. All year; 14-day limit. 30 sites without hookups, $8 ($4 with federal senior pass) during 5/15-9/15. Some sites open & free off-season. Picnic shelter, change house, pit toilets. **GPS: 40.045, -99.224**

GREMLIN COVE PARK

From Republican City at jct with US 136, 1.2 mi S on CR A (Berrigan Rd) to the dam on the N side. All year; 14-day limit. 70 gravel sites without hookups, $8 & $10 ($4 & $5 with federal senior pass) during 5/15-9/15. Some sites open & free off-season. Picnic shelter, change house, flush & pit toilets. **GPS: 40.0852, -99.2145**

HUNTER COVE PARK

From Republican City at jct with US 136, 1 mi S on Berrigan Rd; 0.5 mi W on CR B, on the N side, E edge of lake. 4/1-11/30; 14-day limit. 20 tent sites, $12 ($6 with federal senior pass) during 5/1-9/30, lower fees in Oct, Nov & Apr. 47 RV/tent sites without elec, $14 (or $7 with federal senior pass) during 5/1-9/30; $8 in Oct, Nov & Apr. 84 sites with elec, $18 &

$20 ($9 & $10 with federal senior pass) during 5/1-9/30; $8 in Oct, Nov & Apr. Holders of federal senior pass pay half rate off-season. RV limit in excess of 65 ft; 19 pull-through sites. 3-night minimum stay on holiday weekends. Boat rentals at N Shore Marina. Picnic shelters, amphitheater, fish cleaning station. Off-road vehicles prohibited. Non-campers pay $3 day use fee at boat ramp. NRRS 5/1-11/29. **GPS: 40.08306, -99.2325**

METHODIST COVE PARK

From Alma at jct with US 183, 2.5 mi W on S St; near W end of lake. 4/1-11/30; 14-day limit. 2 sites without hookups, $12 & $14 during 5/1-9/30 ($6 & $7 with federal senior pass), $8 in Oct, Nov & Apr ($4 with federal senior pass). 48 sites with elec, $20 & $22 during 5/1-9/30 ($10 & $11 with federal senior pass), $10 in Oct, Nov & Apr ($5 with federal senior pass). RV limit in excess of 65'. Fish cleaning station with grinder. Two group camping areas up to 75 people & 16 vehicles and picnic shelter for up to 125 people & 41 vehicles, $50. At reserved sites, 2-night minimum stay required on weekends, 3 nights on holiday weekends. Non-campers pay $3 day use fee for boat ramp. NRRS 5/1-9/30.
GPS: 40.08694, -99.31556

NORTH OUTLET PARK

From Republican City, 2 mi S on CR A, below dam on N side of the outlet. All year; 14-day limit. 30 sites without hookups, $8 during 5/15-9/15 ($4 with federal senior pass). During 9/15-5/14, some sites open & free. Picnic shelter, pit toilets. **GPS: 40.072998, -99.210205**

SOUTH OUTLET PARK

From Republican City, 2 mi S on CR A; 1 mi N on CR 1; below the dam. All year; 14-day limit. 30 sites no hookups, $8 during 5/15-9/15 ($4 with federal senior pass). During 9/15-5/14, some sites open & free. Pit toilets.
GPS: 40.070313, -99.208984

LEWIS & CLARK LAKE (OM) 2
GPS: 42.88, -97.48

Located 4 mi W of Yankton, S Dakota, on Hwy 50 at the Nebraska state line. Plant tours daily from 10 a.m. to 6 p.m. Memorial Day through Labor Day. Day use facilities: Overlook Park -- picnicking, group shelter, playground, hiking trail; Santee Park, boat ramp. Visitor center with exhibits on Missouri River region, dam construction; prairie garden. Lake Manager, Gavins Point Project, P. O. Box 710, Yankton, SD 57078. (402) 667-7873. See SD listing.

COTTONWOOD RECREATION AREA

From Yankton, S Dakota, 4 mi W on SR 52, then S on Dam Toe Rd; E of dam on downstream side. 4/21-10/16; 14-day limit. 77 sites with elec, $14 base, $16 at premium locations ($7 & $8 with federal senior pass. During off-season, some sites are open and free. RV limit in excess of 65'. At reserved sites, 2-night minimum stay required on weekends, 3 nights on holiday weekends. Fish cleaning station, picnic shelter. NRRS 5/21-10/16.

NEBRASKA TAILWATERS RECREATION AREA

From Yankton, S Dakota, 2 mi S on US 81, then 4 mi W on Nebraska SR 121; E of the dam on S side of river off Rt 121. 5/12-10/10; 14-day limit. 11 tent sites, $12 ($6 with federal senior pass); 31 sites with elec, $14 ($7 with federal senior pass). RV limit in excess of 65'. Fish cleaning station, picnic shelters. At reserved sites, 2-night minimum stay required on weekends, 3 nights on holiday weekends. NRRS.

GPS: 42.84889, -97.47028

Rio Grande River
1
2
Santa Fe
25
Gallup
Canadian River
40
40
Albuquerque
Gila River
25
NEW MEXICO
Pecos River
Carlsbad
Las Cruces
10
CARLSBAD CAVERNS NATIONAL PARK

NEW MEXICO

State Capital: **Santa Fe**
Nickname: **Land of Enchantment**
Statehood Year: **1912**

47TH STATE

ABIQUIU RESERVOIR (AQ) 1
GPS: 36.24, -106.43

A 5,200-acre lake 7 mi NW of Abiquiu off US 84 on SR 96, 60 mi NW of Santa Fe. The lake is 6,400 feet above sea level. Swimming permitted except where prohibited by signs. Visitor's center, picnicking. Day use facilities: Downstream Park -- picnicking; Overlook Park -- picnicking, interpretive trail; Rio Chama Recreation Area -- picnickng; Cerrito Recreation Area, picnicking. Operations Manager, Abiquiu Dam, P. O. Box 290, Abiquiu, NM 87510. (505) 685-4433.

RIANA CAMPGROUND

From Espanola, 30 mi N on US 84; 1 mi W on SR 96; on a bluff overlooking lake. All year; 14-day limit; fees during 4/15-10/15. 15 walk-to tent sites, $5 ($2.50 with federal senior pass); 24 sites without hookups, $10 ($5 with federal senior pass); 13 sites with wtr/elec, $14 ($7 with federal senior pass). Free primitive camping off-season. A group camping area and an amphitheater are available, and picnic shelters are $40 to $50. 54 sites, 15 tent only walk-in sites, 13 - 50 ampere, 2 pull through sites. From April 12th to October 12th, tent only sites are $5; sites without electric hookups are $10; sites with electric hookups are $14; from October 13th to April 11th, some sites are available and are free. Recreational vehicle maximum length is in excess of 65'. Open all year. (505) 685-4561. NRRS. **GPS: 36.23333, -106.43333**

COCHITI LAKE (AQ) 2
GPS: 35.625, -106.3333

A 1,200-acre lake 50 mi NE of Albuquerque and NW of I-25 on SR 22, 35 mi SW of Santa Fe. Visitor center with interpretive programs, picnicking. Ground fires and ORV prohibited. Swimming allowed except where prohibited by signs. Entire lake is a no-wake zone. Operations Manager, Cochiti Lake, 82 Dam Crest Road, Pena Blanca, NM 87041. (505) 465-0307.

COCHITI RECREATION AREA

From Albuquerque, N on I-25 to exit 259; W on SR 22 through Pena Blanca to project office. All year; 14-day limit. 32 sites no hookups, $12 ($6 with federal senior pass); 48 sites elec (no wtr), $20 ($10 with federal senior pass). 2 primary camping areas plus section for overflow and groups. RV limit in excess of 65'; 18 pull-through sites. Non-campers pay $3 day use fee for boat ramp. Fishing pier, covered shelters. 3-night minimum stay on holiday weekends. NRRS. **GPS; 35.64167, -106.325**

TETILLA PEAK RECREATION AREA

From Albuquerque, N on I-25 to exit 264; W on SR 16 to Tetilla Peak turnoff. 4/1-10/30; 14-day limit. 9 sites without hookups, $12 ($6 with federal senior pass); 36 sites with elec (no wtr hookups), $20 ($10 with federal senior pass). RV limit in excess of 65'; 7 pull-through sites, 35 handicap sites. Picnic shelters; no day use fees. 3-night minimum stay on holiday weekends. NRRS during 4/16-10/14.
GPS: 35.64722, -106.30444

NORTH CAROLINA

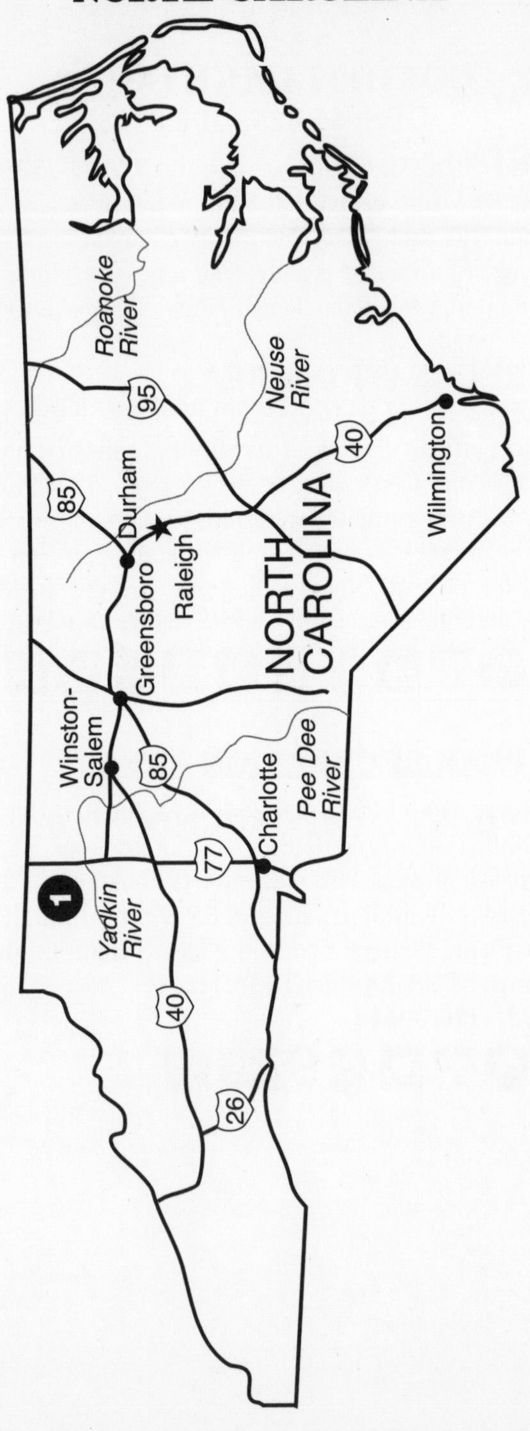

NORTH CAROLINA

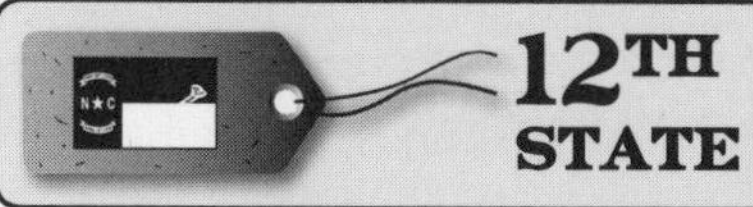

12TH STATE

State Capital: **Raleigh**
Nickname: **Tar Heel State**
Statehood Year: **1789**

W. KERR SCOTT RESERVOIR (WL) 1
GPS: 36.15, -81.2333

A 1,470-acre lake 3 mi W of Wilkesboro and S of US 421 off SR 268 in northwestern North Carolina. Visitors center, historic & cultural site, interpretive programs. Campground checkout time 3 p.m., visitors to 10 p.m. Off-road vehicles prohibited. Day use facilities: Berry Mountain Park -- picnicking, group shelter, playground, beach, trails; Boomer Road Park -- boat ramp, picnicking, group shelter, playground, beach; Dam Site Park -- boat ramp, picnicking, interpretive trail; Dark Mountain Park -- bike trail; Fish Dam Creek -- picnicking, group shelter, playground; Keowee Park -- boat ramp, picnicking, playground, group shelter; Mountain View -- hiking; Smitheys Creek Park -- boat ramp, picnicking, playground; Tailwater Access -- hiking trails. Boat launch fees $3, beach $4. Project Manager, W. Kerr Scott Dam, P. O. Box 182, Wilkesboro, NC 28697-0182. (336) 921-3390/3750.

BANDITS ROOST CAMPGROUND

From Wilkesboro at jct with US 421, 5.5 mi W on SR 268, then N on CR 1141. 4/1-10/31; 14-day limit. 17 tent sites, $18 & $19 ($9 & $9.50 with federal senior pass); 85 RV sites with elec/wtr, $22 base, $24 at premium sites ($11 & $12 with federal senior pass. RV limit in excess of 65'; 5 pull-through sitess. Group camping area with elec for up to 50 people & 2 vehicles, $75. Amphitheater, picnic shelter. (336) 921-3190. NRRS.
GPS: 36.11972, -81.24528

FORT HAMBY CAMPGROUND

From Wilkesboro, 5 mi N on US 421; 1.5 mi W (left) on S. Recreation Rd; on N side of lake. 4/15-10/31; 14-day limit. No hookups, $18 ($9 with federal senior pass); 32 sites with elec/wtr $22 ($11 with federal senior pass). RV limit in excess of 65'. Group camping area with elec, Robbers Den, up to 100 people & 32 vehicles, $125. Amphitheater, horseshoe pits. Alcohol prohibited. (336) 973-0104. NRRS. **GPS: 36.13833, -81.27111**

WARRIOR CREEK CAMPGROUND

From Wilkesboro, 8 mi W on SR 268 through Goshen, then N on CR 1180; on S side of lake. 4/15-10/15; 14-day limit. Tent sites $18 ($9 with federal senior pass); 53 sites with elec/wtr, $22 ($11 with federal senior pass. RV limit in excess of 65'. 2 group camping areas with elec, $85. (336) 921-2177. NRRS. **GPS: 36.11056, -81.30944**

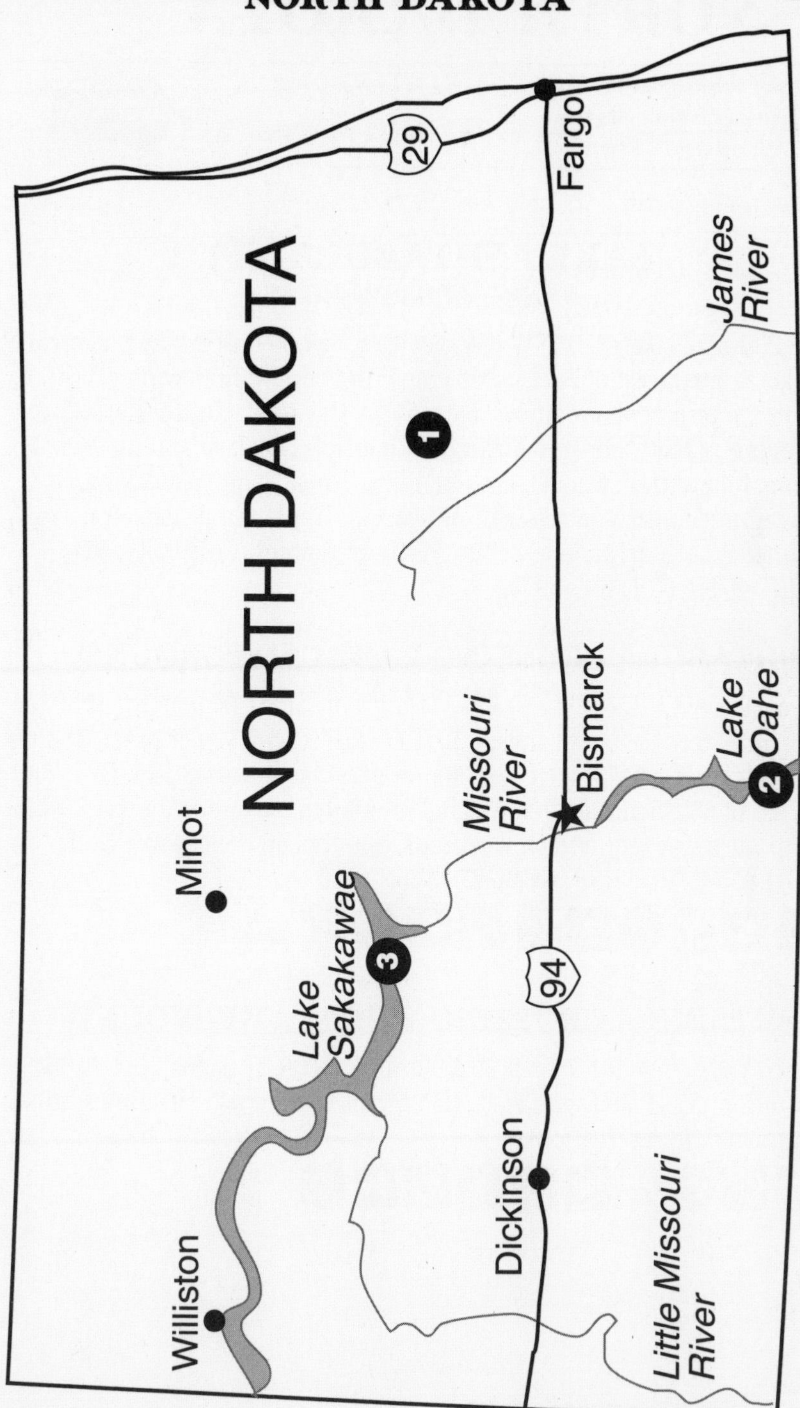
NORTH DAKOTA
Fargo
29
James River
1
Bismarck
Missouri River
Lake Oahe
2
Minot
3
Lake Sakakawae
94
Dickinson
Williston
Little Missouri River

NORTH DAKOTA

State Capital: **Bismarck**
Nickname: **Sioux State**
Statehood Year: **1889**

39TH STATE

LAKE ASHTABULA (SP) 1
GPS: 47.0367, -98.08

A 5,234-acre lake 11 mi NW of Valley City, exit 69 on I-94, in E-central N Dakota, northwest of Fargo. Snowmobiling permitted in winter. Visitor center, interpretive programs, picnicking. Day use facilities: Katie Olson Landing -- boat ramp, picnicking, hiking trails; Sibley Landing -- boat ramp, hiking trail; Sundstrom's Landing -- boat ramp, picnicking, playground. 3 designated swimming areas, 7 boat ramps Resource Manager, Lake Ashtabula, 2630 - 114th Avenue SE, Valley City, ND 58072-9795. (701) 845-2970.

ASHTABULA CROSSING EAST CAMPGROUND

From Valley City at I-94 exit 292, 14 mi N on CR 21 (signs). 5/1-9/30; 14-day limit. 5 walk-to tent sites, $22 ($11 with federal senior pass); 31 sites with elec, $22 ($11 with federal senior pass); double sites $44. RV limit in excess of 65'. Picnic shelter. Alcohol prohibited. At reserved sites, 2-night minimum stay required on weekends, 3 nights on holiday weekends. (701) 845-2970. NRRS. **GPS: 47.1375, -98.0**

ASHTABULA CROSSING WEST CAMPGROUND

From Valley City at I-94 exit 292, 14 mi N on CR 21 (signs). 5/1-10/31; 14-day limit. 41 sites with elec, $22. Picnic shelter, fish cleaning station, pit toilets. No reservations.

EGGERT'S LANDING CAMPGROUND

From the dam, E & N on SR 21, then W. 5/1-9/30; 14-day limit. 4 tent sites, $22; 2 sites without hookups, $22; 35 sites with elec, $22 ($11 with federal senior pass). RV limit in excess of 65'. Picnic shelter, fish cleaning station, firewood. 3-night minimum stay required on holiday weekends. Open from May 1st to September 30th. NRRS.
GPS: 47.09972, -98.01667

MEL RIEMAN CAMPGROUND

From Valley City at I-94 exit 292, under the railroad bridge, then 12 mi on CR 19. 5/1-9/30; 14-day limit. 27 sites, all $22 ($11 with federal senior pass). 3 tent sites, 3 RV sites without hookups, 15 sites with elec (3 pull-through). RV limit in excess of 65 ft. Picnic shelter, group camping area, fish cleaning station, horseshoe pits. NRRS. **GPS: 47.0375, -98.08333**

LAKE OAHE (OM) 2
GPS: 44.45, -100.3868

The lake has 2,250 mi of shoreline and is 6 mi N of Pierre, S Dakota, on SR 1804. Powerhouse tours daily during the summer. Park Manager, Lake Oahe, 28563 Powerhouse Rd., Room 105, Pierre, SD 57501-6174. Note: Most Corps campgrounds on the lake are now operated by the State of S Dakota as state park facilities. (605) 224-5862/(701) 255-0015.

BADGER BAY RECREATION AREA

From Linton, 13 mi W on SR 13; 17 mi N on SR 1804, then W. All year; 14-day limit. 6 free primitive sites. Pit toilets. Nearest dump station is 23 mi.

BEAVER CREEK RECREATION AREA

From Linton, 16 mi W on SR 13; 1 mi W & 2 mi S on SR 1804; on N side of Beaver Bay. 5/13-9/11; 14-day limit. 2 primitive areas with 21 sites, $5 & $10 ($2.50 & $5 with federal senior pass). 37 sites with elec, some pull-through, $14 ($7 with federal senior pass). Picnic shelter, fish cleaning station, sand volleyball, nature trail. At reserved sites, 2-night minimum stay required on weekends, 3 nights on holiday weekends.
(701) 255-0015. NRRS. GPS: **46.24972, -100.53333**

CATTAIL BAY RECREATION AREA

From Strasburg, 21 mi W on gravel Rd., 93rd St. All year; 14-day limit. 6 free primitive sites. Pit toilets. Nearest dump station is 15 mi.

HAZELTON RECREATION AREA

From Hazelton, 13 mi W on gravel 64th St to 63rd St. 5/13-9/11; 14-day limit. 18 primitive sites, $8 ($4 with federal senior pass); 12 new sites with elec, $10 ($5 with federal senior pass). RV limit 30'. Fish cleaning station. Nearest dump station 25 mi. NRRS. **GPS: 46.52056, -100.54333**

LAKE SAKAKAWEA (OM) 3
GPS: 45.5017, -101.4317

A 368,000-acre lake near Riverdale on SR 200, 75 mi N of Bismarck and W of US 83. Powerplant tours daily during summer. Off-Rd. vehicle area, national fish hatchery. Visitor center, interpretive programs, historic & cultural site. The lake has 35 recreation areas. Nesting area for least tern and piping plover and rest stop for whooping cranes.

Facilities not managed by the Corps: W Totten Trail Recreation Area -- boat ramps, pit toilet (McLean County); Sportsman's Centennial Park -- boat ramps, campground, playground, fish cleaning station, picnicking, group shelter, trails (McLean County); Ft. Stevenson State Park -- camping, boat ramp, dump, beach, volleyball court, picnicking; Indian Hills Recreation Area -- boat ramp, boat rental, camping, fish cleaning station, dump, showers, picnicking (Three Affiliated Tribes & State of N Dakota); Parshall Bay Recreation Area -- boat ramps, camping, fish cleaning station, group shelters, picnicking, playground, dump, showers (Montrail County Parks); Van Hook Recreation Area -- boat ramp, boat rental, camping, fish cleaning station, picnicking, group shelter, playground, dump, showers (Montrail County Parks); Pouch Point Recreation Area -- boat ramp, camping, group shelter, picnicking, playground, dump, showers (Three Affiliated Tribes); New Town Marina Recreation Area -- boat ramp, camping, fish cleaning station, picnicking, group shelter, playground, dump, showers (New Town Parks); White Earth Bay Recreation Area -- boat ramp, camping, group shelter, picnicking, playground, pit toilet; Little Beaver Bay Recreation Area -- boat ramp, camping, pit toilets, group shelter, picnicking (Williams County Water Resources District); Little Egypt Recreation Area -- camping, pit toilets (Williams County Water Resources District); White Tail Bay (Lund's Landing) Recreation Area -- boat ramp, boat rental, camping, picnicking, shower, flush & pit toilets (Williams County Water Resources District); Lewis and Clark State Park -- amphitheater, boat ramp, camping, fish cleaning station, hiking trail, dump, shower, picnicking, group shelter, playground; Lake Trenton Recreation Area -- boat ramp, camping, group shelter, picnicking, playground, showers, beach (Williams County Water Resources District); American Legion Park -- boat ramp, camping, group shelter, picnicking, pit toilets (American Legion Post 37); Tobacco Gardens -- boat ramp, camping, fish cleaning station, picnicking, group shelter, playground, dump, showers (McKenzie County Parks); Four Bears Recreation Area -- boat ramp, camping, fish cleaning station, group shelters, picnicking, playground, dump, showers (Three Affiliated Tribes); Skunk Creek Recreation Area -- boat ramp, camping, pit toilet (Three Affiliated Tribes); McKenzie Bay Recreation Area -- boat ramp, camping, boat rental, fish cleaning station, group shelter, picnicking, playground, dump, showers (Watford Cit Parks); Beaver Creek Bay Recreation Area -- boat ramp, camping, group shelters, picnicking, pit toilet (Zap Parks); Lake Shore Park -- boat ramp, boat rental, camping, fish cleaning station, group shelter, picnicking, playground, dump, showers (Beulah Parks); Beulah Bay Recreation Area -- boat ramp, camping, fish cleaning station, group shelter, picnicking, dump, showers (Beulah Parks); Hazen Bay Rec. Area -- boat ramp, camping, fish cleaning station, dump, group shelter, picnicking, showers (Hazen Parks); Lake Sakakawea State Park -- amphitheater, basketball court, boat ramp, boat rental, camping, fish cleaning station, hiking trail; group shelter, picnicking, playground, dump, showers, beach, volleyball court.

Corps-managed day use facilities: Tailwaters Recreation Area -- boat ramp, fish cleaning station, pit toilets; Spillway Pond Recreation Area -- boat ramp, picnicking, group shelter, flush toilets, playground, grills, beach; Spillway Overlook Recreation Area -- picnicking, group shelters, pit toilets; Riverdale Overlook Recreation Area -- picnicking, group shelter; Government Bay Rec. Area -- boat ramp, fish cleaning station, pit toilet; Little Missouri Bay Recreation Area is closed. Lake Manager, Lake Sakakawea, Box 527, Riverdale, ND 58565-0527. (701) 654-7411.

DEEPWATER RECREATION AREA

From jct with US 83, W on SR 37. 4/1-9/30; 14-day limit. 30 free primitive sites. Picnic shelter, pit toilets, drkg wtr.

DOUGLAS CREEK RECREATION AREA

From jct with US 83, 9 mi W of Garrison on SR 37; 7 mi S on gravel Rd.. All year; 14-day limit. 17 free primitive sites. RV limit 25'. Pit toilets, drkg wtr.

DOWNSTREAM CAMPGROUND

Below dam on W side of spillway; 0.75 mi W & 1 mi S of Riverdale. 5/6-9/30; 14-day limit. 16 tent sites, $10 & $12 ($5 & $6 with federal senior pass); 101 sites with elec, $14 & $16 ($7 & $8 with federal senior pass). RV limit in excess of 65'. Interpretive programs, amphitheater, fish cleaning station, horseshoe pits, picnic shelter. At reserved sites, 2-night minimum stay required on weekends, 3 nights on holiday weekends. (701) 654-7440. NRRS. **GPS: 47.49444, -101.40028**

EAST TOTTEN TRAIL RECREATION AREA

From Coleharbor, N on US 83 across lake bridge, then 0.2 mi E. 5/1-9/30; 14-day limit. 40 sites with elec, $14 & $16 ($7 & $8 with federal senior pass). RV limit 25'. Fish cleaning station, pit toilets.

WOLF CREEK RECREATION AREA

From project office, 1 mi E followING signs. All year; 14-day limit. 101 primitive sites, $10 ($5 with federal senior pass). Group camping area (contact office), fish cleaning station, picnic shelter, horseshoe pits, volleyball court. Pit toilets. No reservations.

OHIO

90
Toledo
80
90
Cleveland
76
Akron
1
Canton
75
71
OHIO
77
Great Miami
River
70
Columbus
Dayton
Ohio
River
Muskingum
River
Cincinnati
Ohio
River

OHIO

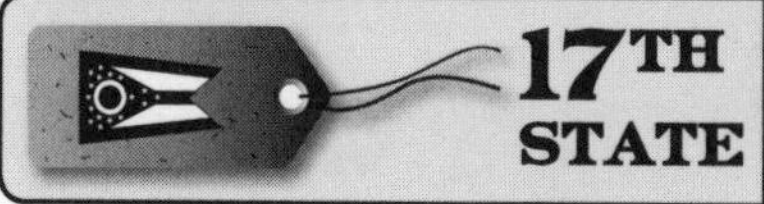

State Capital: **Columbus**
Nickname: **Buckeye State**
Statehood Year: **1803**

BERLIN LAKE (PT) 1
GPS: 41.0467, -81.0

A 3,590-acre lake near Deerfield on US 224 and Bedell Rd SE of Akron. Alcohol prohibited. Campfire programs at amphitheater the first Friday each month. For daily lake information, call (330) 547-5445. Resource Manager, Berlin Lake, 7400 Bedell Road, Berlin Center, OH 44401-9707. (330) 547-3781.

MILL CREEK RECREATION AREA

From I-76 exit 54, 5.5 mi S on SR 534; 2 mi E on US 224; 0.8 mi S on Bedell Rd. MD-LD; 14-day limit. 241 sites without hookups, $14 base, $18 at premium sites ($7 & $9 with federal senior pass); 107 sites with elec, $20 base, $24 with 50-amp elec ($10 & $12 with federal senior pass). RV limit in excess of 65'. Group tent camping area for up to 40 people & 8 vehicles, $20. Amphitheater, pavilion, interpretive program, kayaking, sailing, canoeing. At reserves sites, 2 night stay required on weekends, 3 nights on holiday weekends. (330)547-8180. NRRS.
GPS: 41.00694, -80.99806

OKLAHOMA

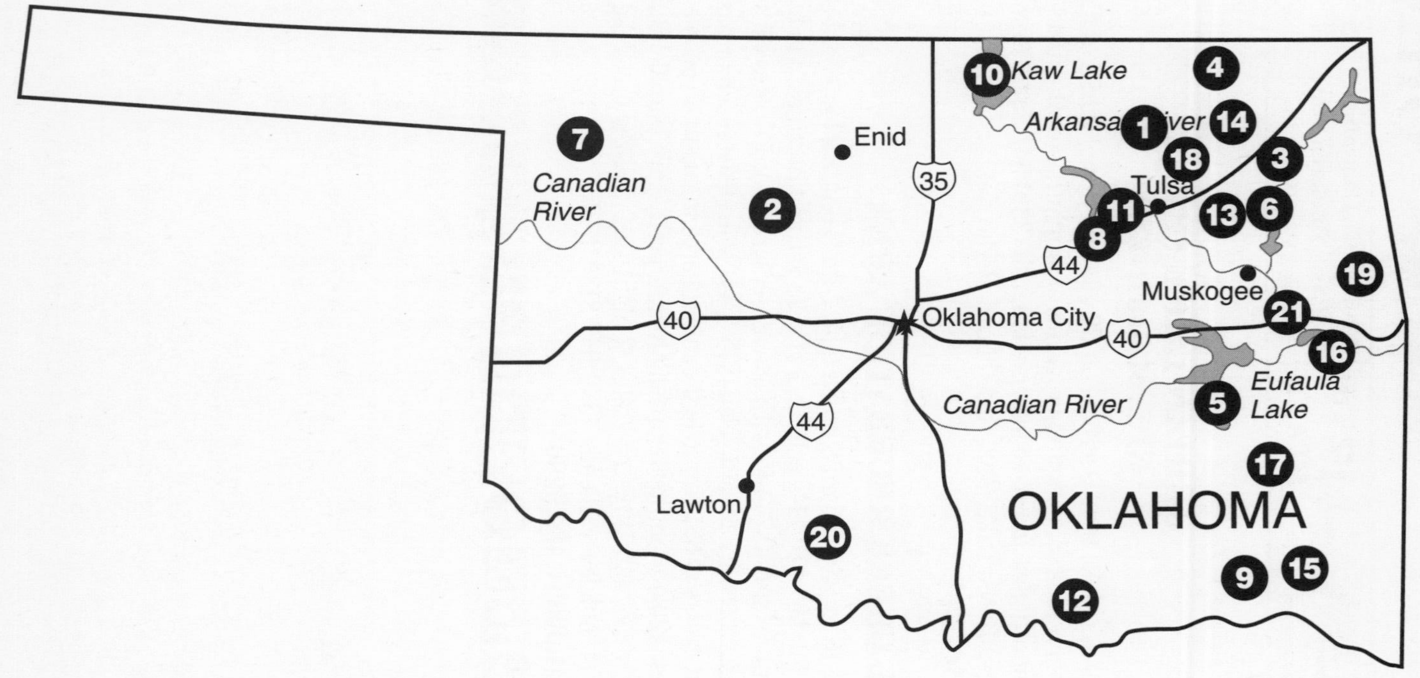

OKLAHOMA
Kaw Lake
Arkansas River
Enid
Tulsa
Muskogee
Oklahoma City
Canadian River
Canadian River
Eufaula Lake
Lawton
35
44
40
40
44
1
2
3
4
5
6
7
8
9
10
11
12
13
14
15
16
17
18
19
20
21

OKLAHOMA

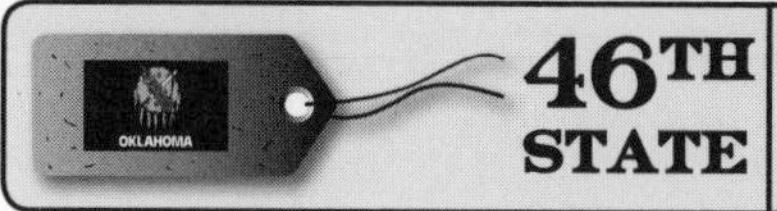

State Capital: **Oklahoma City**
Nickname: **Sooner State**
Statehood Year: **1907**

BIRCH LAKE (TU) 1
GPS: 36.535, -96.1583

This 1,137-acre lake is 20 mi SW of Bartlesville off SR 123/11 and 1.5 mi S of Barnsdall, 35 mi NW of Tulsa. Campground checkout time is 4 p.m. Lake Manager, Skiatook/Birch Lake, HC 67, Box 135, Skiatook, OK 74070-9103. (918) 396-3170.

BIRCH COVE A RECREATION AREA

From Barnsdall, 3.1 mi S across spillway, then 0.7 mi W, following signs. 4/1-10/31; 14-day limit. 85 sites with elec (no wtr hookups), $18 ($9 with federal senior pass); 5 pull-through, 3 handicap sites. RV limit in excess of 65'. Two picnic shelters: Egret for up to 100 people & 21 vehicles, $100, & Fly Catcher up to 60 people & 11 vehicles, $80. Amphitheater, change house, handicap accessible fishing area. Non-campers pay day use fee for boat ramp; beach & fishing dock not open to non-campers. NRRS. **GPS: 36.53444, -96.16222**

BIRCH COVE B RECREATION AREA

From Barnsdall, 3.1 mi S across spillway, then 0.7 mi W following signs. All year; 14-day limit. 12 sites with wtr/elec, $16 ($8 with federal senior pass). Beach, showers, playground, fishing dock at Birch Cove A open to registered campers. Non-campers pay day use fee for boat ramp.

TWIN COVE RECREATION AREA

From Barnsdall, 1.5 mi S near spillway. 4/1-9/30; 14-day limit. 11 sites no hookups, $10 ($5 with federal senior pass). Change house at beach. Group picnic shelters $25. Non-campers pay day use fee for beach, boat ramp.

CANTON LAKE (TU) 2
GPS: 36.0917, -98.5917

A 7,910-acre lake 75 mi NW of Oklahoma City and 2 mi N of Canton on SR 58A. The Corps operates 5 multi-use recreation areas. 3 parking areas with fishing jetties are at the dam. Visitor center, nature trail, outdoor amphitheater, active prairie dog town. Lake Manager, Canton Lake, HC 65, Box 120, Canton, OK 73724-0069. (580) 886-2989.

BIG BEND RECREATION AREA

From Canton, 1.8 mi W on SR 51; 4 mi N on secondary rd; on the N Canadian River. 3/15-10/31; 14-day limit. Big Bend has 2 camping areas. At Loop A, 13 sites without hookups, $14 ($7 with federal senior pass); sites $19 with 30-amp elec/wtr ($9.50 with federal senior pass) & $21 with 50-amp elec/wtr ($10.50 with federal senior pass). At Loop B, 10 sites without hookups, $14 ($7 with federal senior pass); 42 sites with elec/wtr, $19 ($9.50 with federal senior pass). Picnic shelter for up to 100 people & 21 vehicles, $40. RV limit 45'. During Nov & early March, some sites may be open and free without amenities; none open in 2010. 3-night minimum stay on holiday weekends. (580) 886-3576. Non-campers pay self-deposit day use fees for boat ramps. NRRS. **36.11833, -98.61444**

BLAINE PARK

From Canton, 0.7 mi W on SR 51; 1.7 mi N on SR 58A, below dam. 4/1-10/31; 14-day limit. 16 primitive sites, $10 ($5 with federal senior pass). Off-season, some sites are open & free, but no utilities (pit toilets). Non-campers pay day use fee for boat ramp.

CANADIAN RECREATION AREA

From Canton, 0.7 mi W on SR 51; 1.5 mi N on SR 58A; 0.8 mi W on secondary road. All year; 14-day limit. 56 sites with elec but no wtr hookups, $18 during 3/1-10/30 ($9 with federal senior pass), free rest of year but no utilities (pit toilets). 21 sites elec/wtr, $21 during 3/1-10/30 ($10.50 with federal senior pass), some free rest of year but no utilities.

10 sites have 50-amp elec in-season. RV limit in excess of 65 ft. Two group camping areas with elec: Cheyenne, for up to 110 people & 40 vehicles, $198; Arapaho, for up to 140 people & 40 vehicles, $252. Amphitheater. Picnic shelter for up to 100 people & 21 vehicles, $40. At reserved sites, 2-night minimum stay required on peak season weekends, 3 nights on holiday weekends. Non-campers pay day use fee for boat ramp. (580) 886-3454. NRRS during 4/15-9/30. **GPS: 36.09056, -98.60583**

FAIRVIEW GROUP CAMPGROUND

From Longdale, 0.5 mi N; 2.5 mi W on secondary road; on N Canadian River. 4/1-9/30; 14-day limit. Group camping area without elec for up to 100 people and 45 vehicles & 4 RVs with several tents, $50. Large shelter, 7 tbls, 4 gravel pads.

LONGDALE RECREATION AREA

From Longdale at jct with SR 58, 2 mi W on paved county rd. All year; 14-day limit. 37 RV/tent sites without hookups, $10 during 3/15-10/31 ($5 with federal senior pass), free off-season but no amenities (pit toilets). Self-pay during 9/11-10/31. Non-campers pay day use fees for boat ramp. RV limit 40'. At reserved sites, 2-night minimum stay required on weekends, 3 nights on holiday weekends. Picnic shelter for up to 100 people & 21 vehicles, $40. (580) 274-3454. NRRS (April 1st to September 7th). **GPS: 36.12917, -98.58139**

SANDY COVE RECREATION AREA

From Canton, 0.7 mi W on SR 51; 5 mi N on SR 58A; 1.2 mi W on county rd; on N Canadian River. 4/1-10/31; 14-day limit. 35 sites with elec (no wtr hookups), $17 ($8.50 with federal senior pass). RV limit 40'. Not open off-season. Picnic shelter for up to 100 people & 21 vehicles, $40. 3-night minimum stay on holiday weekends. No day use fees. (580) 274-3576. NRRS (May 1st to September 10th). **GPS: 36.10417, -98.56944**

CHOUTEAU LOCK & DAM NO. 17 (TU) 3
GPS: 35.8583, -95.3717

Located southeast of Tulsa and 4 mi NW of Okay on the Arkansas River, the lock and dam is part of the McClellan-Kerr Arkansas River navigation system. Boat ramps at Coal Creek and Tullahassee Loop Parks. Picnicking, horseback riding Lake Manager, Ft. Gibson, Fort Gibson Lake, State Highway 251A, Ft. Gibson, OK 74434-0370. (918) 682-4314. See Newt Graham L&D No. 18 later in the Oklahoma section.

AFTON LANDING RECREATION AREA

From Wagnor at jct with US 69, 5 mi SW on SR 51; 2 mi SE before bridge (signs). All year; 14-day limit. 2 sites without hookups, $14 ($7 with federal senior pass); $20 sites with elec/wtr, $18 & $20 ($9 & $10 with federal senior pass). Picnic shelter, $50. Non-campers pay day use fee for boat ramp & dump station.

COPAN LAKE (TU) 4
GPS: 36.91, -95.94

A 4,850-acre lake W of Copan, located 2 mi W of US 75 on SR 10, N of Tulsa near the Kansas state line. Campground checkout time 4 p.m. Day use areas: Copan Point -- boat ramp, picnicking, group shelter ($25), beach, hiking trails; Osage Plains Park, boat ramp. Lake Manager, HC 67, Box 135, Skiatook, OK 74070. (918) 396-3170.

POST OAK RECREATION AREA

From jct with US 75, W over dam; 1.2 mi N on SR 10; then E. 4/1-10/30; 14-day limit. 18 sites with elec/wtr, $16 base, $18 at handicap sites ($8 & $9 with federal senior or access pass). RV limit in excess of 65'. At reserved sites, 2-night minimum stay required on weekends, 3 nights on holiday weekends. New playground. No day use fees. (918) 532-4334. NRRS. **GPS: 36.90, -95.9583**

WASHINGTON COVE RECREATION AREA

From NW corner of Copan, 0.3 mi W; 0.5 mi N on secondary road (signs). 4/1-10/30; 14-day limit. 99 sites with elec/wtr, $16 ($8 with federal senior pass); $18 at 2 handicap sites. Group picnic shelter for up to 45 people & 20 vehicles, $25. RV limit in excess of 65'. At reserved sites, 2-night minimum stay required on weekends, 3 nights on holiday weekends. 21 new wtr hydrants. Non-campers pay day use fees. (918) 532-4129. NRRS. **GPS: 36.90, -95.95833**

EUFAULA LAKE (TU) 5
GPS: 35.3083, -95.3617

A 102,200-acre lake with 600 mi of shoreline, Eufaula is Oklahoma's largest lake. It is on the Canadian River, 12 mi E of Eufaula on SR 71 and 31 mi S of Muskogee. Powerhouse tours by appointment. Visitor center.

Recreation facilities not managed by the Corps of Engineers include: Eufaula Cove Marina (Eufaula City Park); Arrowhead Marina (concession); Arrowhead State Park (State of Oklahoma); (Belle Starr Marina (concession); Damsite S Marina (concession); Fountainhead Marina (concession); Highway 9 Landing (concession marina); Porum Landing Marina (Duchess Creek Marina); Eufaula Wildlife Management Area, Gaines Creek Unit -- primitive camping & boat ramp at Hickory Point area (State of Oklahoma).

Corps operated day use facilities: Cardinal Point -- boat ramp, picnicking, group shelter; Gaines Creek -- boat ramp; Hickory Point -- boat ramp, picnicking; Holiday Cove -- boat ramp, picnicking; Juniper Point -- boat ramp, picnicking. New bathrooms at Gentry Creek, Damsite E, Porum Landing, Elm Point & Oak Ridge Recreation Areas. Several boat ramps renovated. New pull-through sites with hookups at Belle Starr Rec. Area. 8 water hydrants added at Elm Point. Lake Manager, Eufaula Lake, Rt. 4, Box 5500, Stigler, OK 74462-9440. (918) 484-5135/799-5843/799-5843.

BELLE STAR RECREATION AREA

From I-40 S of Checotah, 7 mi S on US 69; 2 mi E on SR 150; 2 mi S, on right. 4/1-10/31; 14-day limit. 113 sites with wtr/elec, $16 for 30-amp elec, $18 for 50-amp ($8 & $9 with federal senior pass). RV limit in excess of 65'; 36 pull-through sites. Two picnic shelters: PS1 for up to 100 people & 21 vehicles; PS2 for up to 75 people & 21 vehicles, $50. Change house at beach. Non-campers pay day use fees for beach, dump, boat ramp. NRRS. **GPS: 35.3331, -95.50**

BROOKEN COVE RECREATION AREA

From E side of dam, 2 mi S on SR 71, then NW following signs. 4/1-10/31; 14-day limit. 60 sites with elec but no wtr hookups, $16 for 30-amp elec, $18 for 50-amp ($8 & $9 with federal senior pass); 8 pull-through sites. RV limit 60'. 2 group picnic shelters: PS1 for up to 75 people & 21 vehicles; PS2 for up to 100 people & 21 vehicles ($50). Non-campers pay day use fee for boat ramp. NRRS. **GPS: 35.29028, -95.38444**

DAMSITE EAST RECREATION AREA

On NE side, below dam. 4/1-10/31; 14-day limit. 10 sites with elec, $11. During off-season, some sites may be open & free but no amenities.

DAMSITE SOUTH RECREATION AREA

Across dam from Damsite E, then W (6 mi N of Enterprise on Hwy 71, following signs). 4/1-10/31; 14-day limit. 1 walk-to tent site, 4 primitive tent sites & 20 RV/tent sites without hookups, $11 ($5.50 with federal senior pass). 32 sites with elec but no wtr hookups, $16 ($8 with federal senior pass). RV limit 55'. Non-campers pay day use fee for boat ramp, beach, dump. Group picnic shelter with wtr/elec for up to 100 people & 21 vehicles, $50. Change house at beach. NRRS. **GPS: 35.29417, -95.3675**

ELM POINT RECREATION AREA

From McAlester at jct with US 69, 12 mi NE on SR 31, then NW. 3/1-10/31; 14-day limit. 3 primitive sites, $7 ($3.50 with federal senior pass); 14 sites with elec, no wtr hookups, $11 ($5.50 with federal senior pass). Off-season, sites may be open & free but no utilities. No reservations.

GAINES CREEK RECREATION AREA

From Oak Ridge Park, E across lake bridge on SR 9A, then S on secondary road. All year; 14-day limit. Free primitive camping in area managed by State of Oklahoma as part of Eufaula Wildlife Management Area. No facilities, no drkg wtr.

GENTRY CREEK RECREATION AREA

From Checotah, 9 mi W on US 266, then S following signs. 4/1-10/31; 14-day limit. 3 tent sites & 13 RV/tent sites without hookups, $11 ($5.50 with federal senior pass); 15 sites with elec, $16 & $18 ($8 & $9 with federal senior pass). RV limit 50'; 3 pull-through sites. NRRS.
GPS: 35.5006, -95.66444

HICKORY POINT RECREATION AREA

From McAlister at jct with US 69, 4 mi E on SR 31; 6 mi E, then N before bridge. All year; 14-day limit. 10 free primitive sites. Managed by State of OK as part of Eufaula Wildlife Mgmt. Area. No facilities, no drkg wtr.

HIGHWAY 9 LANDING RECREATION AREA

From Eufaula at jct with US 69, 9 mi SE on SR 9, then N. 4/1-9/30; 14-day limit. 3 campgrounds offer variety of sites. E Campground, 4 sites without hookups $7 & 5 sites with elec, $11 ($3.50 & $5.50 with federal senior pass). N Campground, 2 sites without hookups, $10 & $11, and 33 sites with elec, $16 ($5, $5.50 & $8 with federal senior pass). S Campground, 3 sites without hookups, $11; 27 sites with elec, $16 ($5.50 & $8 with federal senior pass). Picnic shelter for up to 100 people & 21 vehicles, $50. RV limit in excess of 65'; 6 pull-through sites. Entire campground closed during 2011 for renovations. Call for future status, (918) 799-5843. NRRS. **GPS: 35.24, -95.49222**

HIGHWAY 31 LANDING GROUP CAMPGROUND

From McAlister at jct with US 270, 5 mi NE on SR 31, N side. All year; 14-day limit. Free primitive group camping area. **GPS: 34.96, -95.64**

MILL CREEK BAY RECREATION AREA

From Eufaula, 6 mi W on SR 9; 2 mi S. 3/1-10/31; 14-day limit. 12 primitive sites, $7 ($3.50 with federal senior pass). Non-campers pay day use fee for boat ramp. Pit toilets, picnic shelter.

OAK RIDGE RECREATION AREA

From Eufaula at jct with US 69, 6 mi S, then NE on SR 9A. 3/1-10/31; 14-day limit. 5 primitive sites without hookups, $7 ($3.50 with federal senior pass); 8 sites with elec, no wtr hookups, $11 ($5.50 with federal senior pass. Off-season, some sites may be open & free but no amenities.

PORUM LANDING RECREATION AREA

From Porum, 6 mi W on SR 150. 4/1-10/31; 14-day limit. 4 sites without hookups, $11 ($5.50 with federal senior pass); 45 sites with elec, $16 ($8 with federal senior pass). RV limit 60'; 6 pull-through sites. Picnic shelter for up to 100 people & 21 vehicles, $50. NRRS. **GPS: 35.35083, -95.38306**

FORT GIBSON LAKE (TU) 6
GPS: 35.98, -95.29

A 19,900-acre lake 5 mi NW of Ft. Gibson on SR 251A from the Muskogee Turnpike. Campsites that are free in the off-season may have reduced amenities. Day-use facilities include boat ramps at Big Hollow, Mallard Bay, Mission Bend, Spring Creek and Wagoner City Park. Major rehabilitation work recently completed at Taylor Ferry S and Flat Rock Creek. Facilities not operated by the Corps of Engineers include Chouteau Bend Marina (concession); Dam Site Marina (concession); Jackson Bay Marina (concession); Long Bay Marina (concession); Mazie Landing Marina (concession); Paradise Cove Marina (concession); Pryor Creek Marina (concession); Taylor Ferry Marina (concession); Whitehorn Cove Marina (concession); Sequoyah Bay State Park; Sequoyah State Park. Lake Manager, Fort Gibson Lake, 8568 State Highway 251A, Ft. Gibson, OK 74434-0370. (918) 682-4314/6618.

BLUE BILL POINT CAMPGROUND

From Wagoner at jct with SR 51, 6 mi N on US 69; 3 mi E/NE following signs. All year; 14-day limit. 3 primitive sites without hookups, $14 ($7 with federal senior pass) during 3/1-10/31; free off-season. 40 sites with elec/wtr: $17 for 30-amp elec, $20 for 50-amp elec ($8.50 & $10 with federal senior pass); during 11/1-2/28, some sites may be open and free without utilities. 8 handicap sites with 50-amp elec/wtr. RV limit in excess of 65 ft. Picnic shelter with elec for up to 100 people & 20 vehicles, $50. Non-campers pay day use fee for boat ramp, dump station. NRRS during 3/1-10/31. **GPS: 36.0425, -95.33444**

DAMSITE CAMPGROUND

From Okay, 6 mi E on SR 251A, below dam on W side of outlet. All year; 14-day limit. 47 sites with elec/wtr, $18 & $20 ($9 & $10 with federal senior pass); some sites open and free during 11/1-2/28, but no utilities. RV limit in excess of 65'. Two group picnic shelters for up to 100 people & 20 vehicles, $50. Non-campers pay day use fee for boat ramp, dump station. NRRS during 3/1-10/31. **GPS: 35.86778, -95.23361**

FLAT ROCK CREEK CAMPGROUND

From Maize, 3 mi S on US 69, then 5 mi E & S. All year; 14-day limit. 2 primitive sites without hookups, $14 during 3/1-10/31 ($7 with federal senior pass), free rest of year. 36 sites with elec/wtr, $18 & $20 during 3/1-10/31 ($9 & $10 with federal senior pass); rest of year, some sites open and free without utilities. RV limit in excess of 65'. Picnic shelter for up to 100 people & 20 vehicles, $50. Non-campers pay day use fee for boat ramp, dump station. NRRS during 3/1-10/31. GPS: 36.04556, -95.32694. NOTE: Repair of flood-damaged roads to begin early in 2011, and campground will be closed until work is done. Tentative re-opening is MD weekend of 2011; check with campground for update (918) 476-6766.

ROCKY POINT CAMPGROUND

From Wagoner at jct with SR 51, 5 mi N on US 69; 1.8 mi E; 1 mi N, following signs. All year; 14-day limit. 4 sites without hookups, $14 ($7 with federal senior pass) during 3/1-10/31; free rest of year. 60 sites with wtr/elec, $18 & $20 ($9 & $10 with federal senior pass) during 3/1-10/31; some sites free off-season but no utilities. RV limit in excess of 65'. Picnic shelter for up to 100 people & 20 vehicles, $50. Change house at beach. Non-campers pay day use fee for beach, boat ramp, dump station. NRRS during 3/1-10/31. **GPS: 36.03306, -95.31639**

TAYLOR FERRY SOUTH CAMPGROUND

From Wagoner at jct with US 69, 8 mi E on SR 51; S before bridge. All year; 14-day limit. 6 sites without hookups, $14 during 3/1-10/31 ($7 with federal senior pass); some sites free off-season. 92 sites with elec/wtr: 30-amp elec sites, $18 ($9 with federal senior pass); 50-amp sites $20 ($10 with federal senior pass. RV limit in excess of 65'. Picnic shelters. Non-campers pay day use fee for boat ramp, dump station. (918) 485-4792. NRRS during 3/1-10/31. **GPS: 35.94083, -95.27611**

WILDWOOD CAMPGROUND

From Hulbert, 4 mi W on SR 80. All year; 14-day limit. 30 sites with elec/wtr: 30-amp sites $18, 50-amp sites $20 ($9 & $10 with federal senior pass). Some sites may be open & free off-season but no utilities. RV limit in excess of 65'; 9 pull-through sites. Picnic shelter for up to 100 people & 20 vehicles, $50. Non-campers pay day use fee for boat ramp, dump station. NRRS during 3/1-10/31. **GPS: 35.91806, -95.21444**

FORT SUPPLY LAKE (TU) 7
GPS: 36.55, -99.5667

An 1,820-acre lake 15 mi NW of Woodward on US 183, 1 mi SE of Fort Supply in northwestERN Oklahoma near the panhandle. Visitor center features exhibits of Indian arrowheads, old camp supply artifacts, wildlife display. Lake Manager, Fort Supply Lake, HC 65, Box 120, Canton, OK 73724. (580) 766-2701.

BEAVER POINT CAMPGROUND

Near the dam. All year; 14-day limit. 16 primitive sites, $9 ($4.50 with federal senior pass). Non-campers pay day use fee for boat ramp.

SUPPLY PARK CAMPGROUND

From Ft. Supply, 1 mi S, on W side of the dam. All year; 14-day limit. 16 sites without hookups, $13 during 4/1-10/30 ($6.50 with federal senior pass); $11 during 11/1-3/31 ($5.50 with federal senior pass). 82 sites with elec: 30-amp elec sites $18 during 4/1-10/30 & $13 during 11/1-3/31 ($9 & $6.50 with federal senior pass); 50-amp elec sites $20 during 4/1-10/30 & $14 during 11/1-3/31 ($10 & $7 with senior pass). Off-season fees by self-deposit; showers & waterborne restrooms closed off-season until 4/1; pit toilets open. RV limit in excess of 65'; 14 pull-through sites. Non-campers pay day use fees (self-deposit) for boat ramp, beach). Non-camper fee also for using dump station. Picnic shelter for up to 100 people & 21 vehicles, $35. Group camping area with elec, $144. Handicap accessible fishing area. 2-night minimum stay on holidays. 14 sites recently upgraded to 50-amp elec. Non-campers pay day use fees for beach, boat ramp, dump station. (580) 755-2001. NRRS during 5/1-9/14. **GPS: 36.5, -99.58333**

HEYBURN LAKE (TU) 8
GPS: 35.9467, -96.305

A 920-acre lake 13 mi SW of Sapulpa, 2 mi from US 66 and 26 mi SW of Tulsa off I-44. Lake Manager, Heyburn Lake, 27349 W Heyburn Lake Road, Kellyville, OK 74039-9615. (918) 247-6391/6397.

HEYBURN CAMPGROUND

From Bristow, 9 mi E; left on 257th W Av; follow paved rd 3 mi to W side of dam. 4/1-10/31; 14-day limit. 46 sites with wtr/elec: 30-amp sites $14, 50-amp sites $15, premium sites with close lake access, $16 ($7, $7.50 & $8 with federal senior pass). 10 pull-through, 1 handicap. Group camping area for up to 200 people & 50 vehicles, $100. Picnic shelter, change house. At reserved sites, 2-night minimum stay required/weekends, 3 nights/holiday weekends. Non-campers pay day use fee for beach, boat ramp, dump. (918) 247-6601. NRRS during 3/30-9/28. **GPS: 35.95167, -96.28028**

SHEPPARD POINT CAMPGROUND

From Bristow at jct of SR 48, 3.5 mi E on SR 33; at 305th W. Ave, follow signs S; on N side of lake. 4/1-10/31; 14-day limit. 17 tent sites, $10 ($5 with federal senior pass); 21 RV/tent sites with elec/wtr, $14 base, $16 at premium locations ($7 & $8 with federal senior pass). RV limit in excess of 65'. 2 group picnic shelters: 001 for up to 100 people & 50 vehicles, $50; 002 for up to 50 people & 50 vehicles, $25. At reserved sites, 2-night minimum stay required on weekends, 3 nights on holiday weekends. (918) 247-4551. NRRS during 4/1-9/28. **GPS: 35.95694, -96.31528**

SUNSET BAY CAMPGROUND

From Bristow, 9 mi E; left on 257th W Ave; follow paved rd to NE side of dam. All year; 14-day limit. 14 sites without hookups, $7 during 4/25-9/25 ($3.50 with federal senior pass). Sites may be open & free off-season. Non-campers pay day use fee for boat ramp, beach, dump station.

HUGO LAKE (TU) 9
GPS: 34.0167, -95.3767

A 13,250-acre lake 6 mi E of Hugo on US 70 about 30 mi N of Paris, Texas, in southeastern Oklahoma. In addition to the campgrounds, boat ramps are at Frazier Point, Salt Creek, Sawyer Bluff and Wilson Point, which also has picnic facilities, a playground and beach. Lake Manager, Hugo Lake, P. O. Box 99, Sawyer, OK 74756-0099. (580) 326-3345.

GROUP CAMPGROUND

From Sawyer at jct with US 70, 3.5 mi N on SR 147, then l mi W & 0.6 mi S (2.6 mi on county road). 5/1-9/30; 14-day limit Four group camping areas, $75. Each area has a group shelter, elec/wtr hookups for 5 RVs. Reserve by calling project office. Change house at beach.

KIAMICHI PARK

From Hugo, 6.8 mi E on US 70; 1 mi N on county rd (signs). 3/1-12/31; 14-day limit. 2 sites without hookups, $12 ($6 with federal senior pass); 20 sites with elec, no wtr, $14 ($7 with federal senior pass); 66 sites with elec/wtr, $15 ($7.50 with federal senior pass); 5 sites with full hookups, $22 ($11 with federal senior pass). RV limit in excess of 65 ft. Two picnic shelters, $25. At reserved sites, 2-night minimum stay required on weekends, 3 nights on holiday weekends. Nature trail, equestrian trail, change house at beach. Non-campers pay day use fee for boat ramp, beach, dump station. One camping loop remains open in winter for archery deer hunters. NRRS during 3/30-9/28. **GPS: 34.0025, -95.40157**

RATTAN LANDING CAMPGROUND

From Rattan, 4 mi W on SR 3/7, then S. All year; 14-day limit. 13 sites with elec/wtr, $12 ($6 with federal senior pass). Non-campers pay day use fee for boat ramp. All campsites in the park were scheduled to be paved late in 2010.

VIRGIL POINT CAMPGROUND

From Sawyer at jct with US 70, 2.5 mi N SR 147, then W. All year; 14-day limit. 52 sits with elec/wtr, $15 & $22 ($7.50 & $11 with federal senior pass). RV limit 55'. At reserved sites, 2-night minimum stay required on weekends, 3 nights on holiday weekends. NRRS during 3/30-9/28. **GPS: 34.03556, -95.36861**

KAW LAKE (TU) 10
GPS: 36.7017, -96.933

A 17,000-acre lake 8 mi E of Ponca City off US 60, 70 mi NE of Enid. Campground checkout time 4 p.m. Day use facilities: Burbank Landing -- boat ramp; Fisherman's Bend -- picnicking; Pioneer Park -- boat ramp, marina, picnicking, group shelter, beach; Traders Bend -- Boat ramp. Two concessions operate marinas: McFadden Cove and Pioneer Cove. Lake Manager, Kaw Lake, 9400 Lake Road, Ponca City, OK 74604-9629. (580) 762-7323.

BEAR CREEK COVE RECREATION AREA

From Newkirk, 7 mi E on improved county rd, then 3 mi S. 5/1-11/30; 14-day limit. 22 sites with elec/wtr, $15 ($7.50 with federal senior pass). RV limit 40'. Picnic shelter. At reserved sites, 2-night minimum stay required on weekends, 3 nights on holiday weekends. (580) 362-4189. NRRS during 5/1-9/15. **GPS: 36.4950, -96.5456**

COON CREEK COVE RECREATION AREA

From Ponca City, 4 mi N, 6 mi E on SR 11, then 1 mi N & 2 mi E on county rd. 3/1-11/30; 14-day limit. 12 primitive sites, $10 ($5 with federal senior pass); 54 sites with elec/wtr, $16 & $18 ($8 & $9 with federal senior pass). RV limit 55'. At reserved sites, 2-night minimum stay required on weekends, 3 nights on holidays. Non-campers pay day use fee for boat ramp. (580) 362-2466. NRRS during 4/1-9/30.
GPS: 36.4721, -96.5527

MCFADDEN COVE RECREATION AREA

From Ponca City, 7 mi E; on N side. 3/1-11/30; 14-day limit. 15 sites with elec, no wtr hookups, $12 ($6 with federal senior pass). Picnic shelter, marine dump station. Non-campers pay day use fee at boat ramp. No reservations. **GPS: 36.7037, -97.079234**

OSAGE COVE RECREATION AREA

From Ponca City, 9 mi E across dam, then 2 mi N (signs). 3/1-11/30; 14-day limit. 94 sites with elec, no wtr hookups, $18 ($9 with federal senior pass). RV limit 60'. Three group camping areas with elec for up to 40 people, $75-$100. Picnic shelter, amphitheater, nature trail. Non-campers pay day use fee for boat ramp. At reserved sites, 2-night minimum stay required on weekends, 3 nights on holiday weekends. (580) 762-9408. NRRS (4/1-9/30). **GPS: 36.69944, -96.92167**

SANDY PARK

From Ponca City, 9 mi E; 0.5 mi below the dam on E side. 4/1-10/1; 14-day limit. 12 sites with elec, no wtr hookups, $12 ($6 with federal senior pass). Non-campers pay day use fee at beach, not boat ramp.

SARGE CREEK COVE RECREATION AREA

From Kaw City, 2.8 mi E on SR 11 (signs). 3/1-11/30; 14-day limit. 51 sites with elec/wtr, $18 ($9 with federal senior pass). RV limit 60'. Group camping area for up to 60 people & 20 vehicles, $100. Picnic shelter, amphitheater, equestrian trail, ATV trail. At reserved sites, 2-night minimum stay required on weekends, 3 nights on holiday weekends. (580) 269-2303. NRRS (4/1-9/30). **GPS: 36.4630, -96.802533**

WASHUNGA BAY RECREATION AREA

From Kaw City, 2.6 mi E on SR 11; 0.6 mi N, 4.5 mi W on improved road (signs). 3/1-11/30; 14-day limit. 11 sites without hookups, $12 ($6 with federal senior pass); 20 sites with elec/wtr, $18 ($9 with federal senior pass). RV limit 60'. At reserved sites, 2-night minimum stay required on weekends, 3 nights stay on holiday weekends. (580) 269-2220. NRRS (5/1-9/15). **GPS: 36.7917023, -96.8419782**

KEYSTONE LAKE (TU) 11

GPS: 36.15, -96.2533

A 26,000-acre lake 15 mi W of Tulsa on US 412 and SR 51. Powerhouse tours by reservation. The lake has 16 recreation areas, 11 boat ramps, 2 ORV areas, 5 trails. Day use facilities: Swift County Park -- boat ramp below dam; Cowskin Bay N -- boat ramp; Osage Ramp -- boat ramp; Pawnee Cove -- boat ramp, New Mannford Ramp -- boat ramp (City of Mannford); Keystone Ramp -- boat ramp, picnicking, beach. Privately operated facilities include Keyport Marina & Westport Marina. The State of Oklahoma operates Keystone & Walnut Creek State Parks. Visitor center. Lake Manager, Keystone Lake, 23115 W Wekiwa Road, Sand Springs, OK 74063-9312. (918) 865-2621.

APPALACHIA BAY CAMPGROUND

From Sand Springs, 10.1 mi W on US 64, then S; on W side of US 64. All year; 14-day limit. 18 primitive sites, $8 ($4 with federal senior pass). ATV trail. Non-campers pay day use fee for boat ramp, beach.
GPS: 36.1109, -96.1725

BRUSH CREEK CAMPGROUND

From Sand Springs, 8 mi W on US 64; below dam, N side of spillway. All year; 14-day limit. 20 sites with elec/wtr, $15-$20 ($7.50-$10 with federal senior pass. Non-campers pay day use fee for dump station.

COWSKIN BAY SOUTH CAMPGROUND

Adjacent to NW corner of Westport. All year; 14-day limit. 30 free primitive undesignated sites. **GPS: 36.23174, -96.36529**

KEYSTONE RAMP RECREATION AREA

From Mannford, 4.8 mi E on SR 5, then N. All year; 14-day limit. 6 primitive undesignated sites, free. Pit toilets, no drkg wtr. No day use fees.

SALT CREEK NORTH CAMPGROUND

From Mannford, E across lake bridge on SR 51, then N. 4/1-10/30; 14-day limit. 13 sites without hookups, $10 ($5 with federal senior pass); 112 sites with elec, $15 base, $17 at premium locations ($7.50 & $8.50 with federal senior pass). RV limit in excess of 65'. Two group picnic shelters: A75 for up to 40 people & 11 vehicles, $25 without elec; B05 for up to 60 people & 21 vehicles, $60 with elec. 2 dump stations, amphitheater, change house. (918) 865-2845). NRRS (April 1st to September 15th).
GPS: 36.14861, -96.25306

WASHINGTON IRVING SOUTH CAMPGROUND

From Sand Springs, 10.1 mi W on US 64, across lake bridge, then E; on AK River arm of lake. 4/1-10/31; 14-day limit. 2 primitive sites, $10 ($5 with federal senior pass); 38 sites with elec, no wtr hookups, $15 base, $17 at premium sites ($7.50 & $8.50 with federal senior pass). RV limit in excess of 65'. At reserves sites, 2-night minimum stay required on weekends. (918) 243-7673. Nature trail. Non-campers pay day use fees for boat ramp, beach, dump station. NRRS (4/1-9/15). **GPS: 36.21111, -96.25556**

LAKE TEXOMA (TU) 12
GPS: 33.76, -96.46

Located 5 mi N of Denison, Texas in S-central Oklahoma on the state line. Off-road vehicles prohibited. Lake Manager, Lake Texoma, 351 Corps Road, Denison, TX 75020. (903) 465-4990. See Texas listings.

BUNCOMBE CREEK CAMPGROUND

From Kingston, 4 mi W on SR 32; 7 mi S on SR 99; 2 mi E (signs). All year; 14-day limit. 54 sites with elec/wtr, including 1 handicap site, $16 ($8 with federal senior pass), $20 at premium sites ($10 with federal senior pass). During 11/1-3/31, sites with elec are $12 ($6 with federal senior pass) without wtr hookups; payment by honor deposit. RV limit 45'. Nature trail, picnic shelter. (580) 564-2901. NRRS (4/1-9/30). **GPS: 33.89806, -96.81306**

BURNS RUN EAST CAMPGROUND

From Denison, TX, 8 mi N on SR 91 across dam; left first exit; on W side. All year; 14-day limit. 9 primitive tent sites, $15 ($7.50 with federal senior pass); 44 sites with elec/wtr, $20 base, $24 at premium sites ($10 & $12 with federal senior pass). During 11/1-3/31, sites with elec are $12 ($6 with federal senior pass) without wtr hookups; payment by honor deposit. RV limit in excess of 65'. Picnic shelter with elec for up to 100

people & 20 vehicles, $50. Nature trail. Non-campers pay day use fee for boat ramp, dump station. (580) 965-4660. NRRS (4/1-9/30).
GPS: 33.85139, -96.57472

BURNS RUN WEST CAMPGROUND

From Denison, TX, 8 mi N on SR 91, across bridge, then 3 mi W. 4/1-9/30; 14-day limit. 12 tent sites, $12 ($6 with federal senior pass); 105 sites with elec/wtr, $20 base ($10 with federal senior pass), $24 full hookups ($12 with federal senior pass). During 11/1-3/31, sites with elec are $12 ($6 with federal senior pass) without wtr hookups; payment by honor deposit. RV limit in excess of 65'; 43 pull-through. 2 picnic shelters with elec: GS1 for up to 100 people & 20 vehicles, and SRW for up to 100 people & 25 vehicles, $50. 5 group camping areas with elec for up to 50 people & 8 vehicles, $100. Non-campers pay day use fee for boat ramp, dump station. (580) 965-4922. NRRS (4/1-9/30). **GPS: 33.85556, -96.59111**

CANEY CREEK CAMPGROUND

From Kingston, 3 mi S on Donahoo St (Rock Creek Rd); 2 mi E on Lassiter Rd; 2 mi E & E. All year; 14-day limit. 10 tent sites, $15 ($7.50 with federal senior pass); 42 sites with elec/wtr, $20 base, $22 at premium sites ($10 & $11 with federal senior pass). During 11/1-3/31, sites with elec are $12 ($6 with federal senior pass) without wtr hookups; payment by honor deposit. RV limit in excess of 65'. Picnic shelter with elec for up to 100 people & 20 vehicles, $50. Non-campers pay day use fee at dump station. (580) 564-2632. NRRS (4/1-9/30). Note: new 50-amp elec service planned. **GPS: 33.92806, -96.70167**

DAMSITE

From Denison, TX, 5 mi N on SR 75A; Oklahoma side of dam. All year; 14-day limit. 6 sites without hookups, $7. are $7. Pit toilets, no drkg wtr.

JOHNSON CREEK CAMPGROUND

From Durant, 10 mi W on US 70; on N side of road at causeway. All year; 14-day limit. 54 sites with elec/wtr, $20 ($10 with federal senior pass); double sites $40. During 11/1-3/31, sites are $12 with elec but no wtr hookups ($6 with federal senior pass); payment by honor deposit. RV limit in excess of 65'. Picnic shelter with elec for up to 50 people & 20 vehicles, $50. Non-campers pay day use fee for dump station, boat ramp. (580) 924-7316. NRRS (4/15-9/30). **GPS: 33.99917, -96.56944**

LAKESIDE CAMPGROUND

From Durant, 9 mi W on US 70; 4 mi S on Streetman Rd. All year; 14-day limit. 4 tent sites, $15 ($7.50 with federal senior pass); 127 sites with elec/wtr, $20 & $22 ($10 & $11 with federal senior pass). During 11/1-3/31, sites with elec & no wtr hookups are $12 ($6 with federal senior pass); payment by honor deposit. RV limit in excess of 65'. Picnic shelter with elec up to 100 people & 20 vehicles, $50. Equestrian trail. Non-campers pay day use fee for boat ramp, dump station. (580) 920-0176. NRRS (4/15-9/30). Note: new 50-amp elec service is planned. **GPS: 33.9375, -96.55056**

PLATTER FLATS CAMPGROUND

From Colbert at jct with US 69/75, N exit overpass; 4 mi W (past 4-way stop sign), then 3 mi W. All year; 14-day limit. 10 sites without hookups, $12 ($6 with federal senior pass); 29 sites with wtr hookups, $12 ($6 with federal senior pass); 58 equestrian sites with wtr hookups, $12-$15 ($6-$7.50 with federal senior pass); 8 sites with elec but no wtr hookups, $20 ($10 with federal senior pass); 36 sites with elec/wtr $22 ($11 with federal senior pass); equestrian sites with elec/wtr, $20-$22 ($10-$11 with federal senior pass. During 11/1-3/31, sites with elec & no wtr hookups are $12 ($6 with federal senior pass); payment by honor deposit. RV limit in excess of 65'. Two picnic shelters, must be reserved, $50. Equestrian trails. (580) 434-5864. NRRS (4/1-9/30). Note: new 50-amp elec service is planned. **GPS: 33.92167, -96.54472**

NEWT GRAHAM L&D NO. 18 (TU) 13
GPS: 36.05, -95.5383

On the Arkansas River navigation system, 7 mi S of Inola and E of Tulsa. Five park areas include boat ramps, campsites, picnic areas. Lock Engineer, Rt. 2, Box 21, Gore, OK 74435-9404. (918) 775-4475.

BLUFF LANDING CAMPGROUND

From Wagnor, 11 mi SE on Muskogee Turnpike; E on 71st St (signs). All year; 14-day limit. 7 sites without hookups, $14 ($7 with federal senior pass); 25 sites with wtr/elec, $18 & $20 ($9 & $10 with federal senior pass. During 11/1-3/31, some sites available free or at reduced rates. Non-campers pay day use fee for boat ramp, dump station.

OOLOGAH LAKE (TU) 14
GPS: 36.4233, -95.6783

A 29,500-acre lake 2 mi SE of Oologah on SR 88, 25 mi NE of Tulsa and NW of I-44. Campground checkout time 4 p.m. Day use facilities include boat ramps at Allens Point, Big Creek Park, Clemont I Park, Eastside Ramp, Lighting Creek, Rosebud Bay, Vada Point and Winganon Ramp. Overlook Park has picnicking. Equestrian trail. Project Officer, P. O. Box 700, Oologah, OK 74053-0700. (918) 443-2250.

BIG CREEK RAMP CAMPGROUND

From Nowata, 5.1 mi E on US 60, then 2 mi N. All year; 14-day limit. 16 free primitive sites. Pit toilets.

BLUE CREEK RECREATION AREA

From Foyil, 6 mi W on SR 28A; 1.2 mi N; 1.5 mi W on gravel road (signs). 4/1-10/31; 14-day limit. 1 tent site, $12 ($6 with federal senior pass); 36 RV/tent sites without hookups, $14 ($7 with federal senior pass); 22 sites with elec, no wtr hookups, $18 ($9 with federal senior pass). RV limit in excess of 65'. Picnic shelter for up to 100 people & 20 vehicles, $50. Bridle trail. Non-campers pay day use fee for dump station, boat ramp. (918) 341-4244. NRRS (4/1-9/30). **GPS: 36.45222, -95.5925**

HAWTHORN BLUFF RECREATION AREA

From Oologah at jct with US 169, 1.5 mi E on SR 93 (signs). 4/1-10/31; 14-day limit. 24 sites without hookups, $16 ($8 with federal senior pass); 65 sites with elec, no wtr hookups, $20 ($10 with federal senior pass). RV limit in excess of 65'. Three group picnic shelters for up to 100 people & 50 vehicles, $50. At reserved sites, 2-night minimum stay required on weekends, 3 nights on holiday weekends. Hiking trail, interpretive trail, phone, amphitheater, change house. Non-campers pay day use fees for boat ramp, dump station, beach. (918) 443-2319. NRRS (4/1-9/30). **GPS: 36.43222, -95.68083**

REDBUD BAY RECREATION AREA

From Oologah, 3.2 mi E on SR 88; at E side of dam. 4/1-10/31; 14-day limit. 12 sites with elec/wtr, $16 ($8 with federal senior pass). Marine dump station & consessioniare services. No reservations. Non-campers pay day use fee for boat ramp.

SPENCER CREEK RECREATION AREA

From Foyil, 11 mi N on paved/gravel roads, following signs. 57 sites without hookups, $14 ($7 with federal senior pass); 28 sites with elec, no wtr hookups, $18 ($9 with federal senior pass). RV limit in excess of 65'. Group picnic shelter, $50. At reserved sites, 2-night minimum stay required on weekends, 3 nights on holiday weekends. Non-campers pay day use fees for boat ramp, beach, dump station. (918) 341-3690. NRRS during 4/1-9/30. **GPS: 36.51083, -95.56111**

VERDIGRIS RIVER RECREATION AREA

From Oologah at jct with US 169, 3.1 mi E on SR 88, below the dam. All year; 14-day limit. 8 sites without hookups, $12 ($6 with federal senior pass). Picnic shelter. No day use fees.

PINE CREEK LAKE (TU) 15
GPS: 34.025, -95.0783

A 3,800-acre lake 8 mi N of Valliant off SR 98 in southeastern Oklahoma near the Texas state line. Campground checkout time 4. p.m. Lake Manager, Pine Creek Lake, Rt. 1, Box 400, Valliant, OK 74764-9615. (405) 933-4239.

LITTLE RIVER PARK

From Wright City, 6 mi N on SR 98; 8.5 mi W on SR 3, then SE, following signs; on W shore of lake. All year; 14-day limit. 25 sites without hookups, $12 ($6 with federal senior pass); 31 sites with wtr/ elec: $18 for 30-amp service, $23 with 50-amp service ($9 & $11.50 with federal senior pass). RV limit in excess of 65'; 4 pull-through sites. Group camping area with elec for up to 100 people and 25 vehicles, $65. At reserved sites, 2-night minimum stay required on weekends, 3 nights on holiday weekends. Nature trail, picnic shelter. Some campsites were renovated in 2010 & upgraded to 50-amp service; dirt sites replaced with concrete pads, tables & cookers replaced. Non-campers pay day use fees for dump station, boat ramp, beach. (580) 876-3720. NRRS during 4/1-9/30. Note: Park was closed part of 2010 due to flooding & renovations; call ahead for current status. **GPS: 34.16667, -95.125**

LOST RAPIDS PARK

From Wright City, 6 mi N on SR 98; 6 mi W on SR 3; then S following signs; on W shore of lake. All year; 14-day limit. 14 sites without hookups, $10 ($5 with federal senior pass); 15 sites with elec/wtr, $15

($7.50 with federal senior pass). RV limit in excess of 65'. Group camping area for up to 100 people & 25 vehicles, $65. At reserved sites, 2-night minimum stay required/weekends, 3 nights/holiday weekends. Picnic shelter. Non-campers pay day use fee for boat ramp, dump station. (580) 876-3720. NRRS during 4/1-9/30. Note: Park was closed part of 2010 due to flood damages; call ahead for current status. **GPS: 34.17639, -95.10833**

PINE CREEK COVE PARK

From Valliant, 8 mi N on Pine Creek Rd, following signs; on W shore of lake. All year; 14-day limit. 1 site without hookups, $12; 40 sites with elec/wtr: 30-amp sites $18, 50-amp sites $23 ($9 & $11.50 with federal senior pass). RV limit in excess of 65'. At reserved sites, 2-night minimum stay required on weekends, 3 nights on holiday weekends. Group camping area for up to 100 people & 25 vehicles, $65. At reserved sites, 2-night minimum stay required on weekends, 3 nights on holiday weekends. Picnic shelter. Non-campers pay day use fees for boat ramp, beach, dump station. During 2010, some campsites were renovated & upgraded to 50-amp service; dirt sites replaced with concrete ads, tables & cookers replaced. (580) 933-4214. NRRS during 4/1-9/30. Note: Park was closed part of 2010 due to flood damages & renovations; call ahead for current status. **GPS: 34.10694, -95.0875**

TURKEY CREEK PARK

From Little River Park at jct with SR 3, 0.5 mi W on SR 3; 0.5 mi N to Burwell; 0.5 mi W; 2 mi N on secondary road; 1.5 mi E on secondary rd, following signs. All year; 14-day limit. 24 sites without hookups, $10 ($5 with federal senior pass); 10 sites with elec, no wtr hookups, $15 ($7.50 with federal senior pass). RV limit in excess of 65'. Picnic shelter for up to 100 people & 25 vehicles, $40. At reserved sites, 2-night minimum stay required on weekends, 3 nights on holiday weekends. Non-campers pay day use fees for boat ramp, dump station. (580) 876-3720. NRRS during 4/1-9/30. Note: Park was closed part of 2010 due to flood damages; call ahead for current status. **GPS: 34.17639, -95.10833**

ROBERT S. KERR POOL ARKANSAS RIVER LOCK & DAM 15 (TU) 16

GPS: 35.3467, -94.7767

A 42,000-acre pool of the Arkansas River 8 mi S of Sallisaw on US 59 S of I-40 in E-central Oklahoma, 33 mi W of Ft. Smith, Arkansas. Day use facilities at the dam site include boat ramp, pickic area, beach. Project Engineer, Robert S. Kerr Project Office, HC 61, Box 238, Sallisaw, OK 74955-9945. (918) 775-4474/489-5541.

APPLEGATE COVE RECREATION AREA

From Sallisaw, 8 mi S on US 59, then 2 mi W, following signs. All year; 14-day limit. 27 sites with elec/wtr, $15 ($7.50 with federal senior pass). RV limit 50'. Picnic shelter for up to 50 people & 10 vehicles, $50. At reserved sites, 2-night minimum stay required on weekends, 3 nights on holiday weekends. Non-campers pay day use fee at boat ramp & dump station. NRRS during 4/28-9/28. **GPS: 35.34667, -94.81833**

COWLINGTON POINT RECREATION AREA

From Star, 2 mi E on county rd following signs. All year; 14-day limit. 6 sites without hookups, $10 ($5 with federal senior pass); 32 sites with elec/wtr, $15 ($7.50 with federal senior pass). RV limit 60 ft. Picnic shelter for up to 50 people & 10 vehicles, $50. At reserved sites, 2-night minimum stay required on weekends, 3 nights on holiday weekends. Non-campers pay day use fees for boat ramp, dump station. NRRS during 4/28-9/28. **GPS: 35.30333, -94.82833**

SHORT MOUNTAIN COVE RECREATION AREA

From Cowlington, 1 mi N on county rd following signs. All year; 14-day limit. 3 sites with no hookups, $10 ($5 with federal senior pass); 3 sites with wtr hookups, $11 ($5.50 with federal senior pass); 26 sites with elec/wtr, $15 ($7.50 with federal senior pass). RV limit 55 ft. Picnic shelter for up to 50 people & 10 vehicles, $50. At reserved sites, 2-night minimum stay required on weekends, 3 nights on holiday weekends. Nature trail. No day use fees. NRRS during 4/29-9/28. **GPS: 35.32, -94.78306**

SARDIS LAKE (TU) 17
GPS: 34.61, -95.34

A 14,360-acre lake 3 mi N of Clayton on SR 2/43 and S of Wilborton & US 270 in SE Oklahoma. Do not bring firewood to the campground to help prevent spreading the emeral ash borer insect. Lake Manager, Sardis Lake, HC 60, Box 175, Clayton, OK 74536-9727. (918) 569-4131.

POTATO HILLS CENTRAL RECREATION AREA

From jct with US 271, 3.3 mi N on SR 2. 4/1-10/31; 14-day limit. 80 sites with elec/wtr, $18 ($9 with federal senior pass). RV limit in excess of 65'. Two group camping areas with elec: GCA for up to 64 people & 20 vehicles, and GCB for up to 48 people 10 vehicles, both with picnic shelters, $150. At reserved sites, 2-night minimum stay required on weekends, 3 nights on holiday weekends. Firewood, nature trail. (918) 569-4146. NRRS. **GPS: 34.625, -95.325**

POTATO HILLS SOUTH RECREATION AREA

From jct with US 271, 2.5 mi N on SR 2. 4/1-10/31; 14-day limit. 18 sites without hookups, $10 ($5 with federal senior pass). RV limit in excess of 65'. Two picnic shelters for up to 100 people, $30. At reserved sites, 2-night minimum stay required on weekends, 3 nights on holiday weekends. Nature trail, change house. Non-campers pay day use fee for boat ramp, beach. (918) 569-4549. NRRS. **GPS: 34.625, -95.325**

SARDIS COVE RECREATION AREA

From jct with SR 2, 8.3 mi W on SR 43. 4/1-10/31; 14-day limit. 23 sites without hookups, $10 ($5 with federal senior pass); 22 sites with elec, no wtr hookups, $12 ($6 with federal senior pass. Non-campers pay day use fee for boat ramp, dump station. (918) 569-4637. **GPS: 37.0759, -80.4519**

SKIATOOK LAKE (TU) 18
GPS: 36.3517, -96.0917

The lake is mi W of Skiatook on SR 20 and NW of Tulsa. Campground checkout time 4 p.m. Marina concessions on the lake are Cross Timbers and Crystal Bay. Osage County manages Black Dog Park, a boat launch and fishing area. Visitor center. Lake Manager, Skiatook Lake, HC 67, Box 135, Skiatook, OK 74070-9107. (918) 396-3170.

BULL CREEK PENINSULA CAMPGROUND

From dam, 7.8 mi W on SR 20; 3.7 mi NW; access rd after second bridge crossing on the lake. All year; 14-day limit. 41 sites without hookups, $8 ($4 with federal senior pass). Non-campers pay day use fee at boat ramp. (918) 396-2444.

TALL CHIEF COVE CAMPGROUND

From dam, 1.7 mi S, then W on Lake Rd following signs. 5/1-10/31; 14-day limit. 10 overflow tent sites, $12 ($6 with federal senior pass); 55 sites with elec/wtr, $20; double sites $40 ($10 & $20 with federal senior pass). RV limit in excess of 65'. Picnic shelter for up to 200 people & 50 vehicles, $50. At reserved sites, 2-night minimum stay required on weekends, 3 nights on holiday weekends. Interpretive trail, amphitheater, handicap accessible swimming area, phone. Non-campers pay day use fee for boat ramp, beach, dump station. (918) 288-6320. NRRS. **GPS: 36.35056, -96.08657**

TWIN POINTS CAMPGROUND

From Skiatook, 7 mi W; N of SR 20 (signs). 4/1010/31; 14-day limit. 54 sites with elec/wtr, $20 ($10 with federal senior pass). RV limit in excess of 65'. At reserved sites, 2-night minimum stay required on weekends, 3 nights on holiday weekends. Non-campers pay day use fee for boat ramp, beach, dump station. NRRS. **GPS: 36.38417, -96.21778**

TENKILLER FERRY LAKE (TU) 19
GPS: 35.5933, -95.0367

A 12,900-acre lake 7 mi NE of Gore on SR 100, 22 mi SE of Muskogee. The lake frequently experiences low water levels. Corps-operated day use facilities: Blackgum Landing -- boat ramp; Dam Site -- boat ramp, picnicking, beach; Horseshoe Bend -- boat ramp; Overlook Park -- group shelter, playground, hiking trail. Facilities not operated by the Corps include: Burnt Cabin Marina & Resort; Cherokee Landing State Park; Sixshooter Resort & Marina; Caney Ridge Marina; Cookson Bend Resort & Marina; Elk Creek Landing Marina; Pettit Bay Marina; Piine Cove Marina; Snake Creek Marina; Strayhorn Landing Marina, and Tenkiller State Park. Visitor center. Tenkiller Project Office, Rt. 1, Box 259, Gore, OK 74435-9547. (918) 487-5252.

CARTERS LANDING RECREATION AREA

From Tahlequah, 4 mi SE on US 62; 6.6 mi S (left) on SR 82; 2 mi NE (left) on access road; on shore of upper IL River about 2.5 mi N of lake. All year; 14-day limit. 15 sites no hookups, $7 ($3.50 with federal senior pass); 10 sites with elec/wtr, $11 ($5.50 with federal senior pass). Reduced fees in winter. Picnic shelter $25 with $10 reservation fee. Non-campers pay day use fee at boat ramp. (918) 487-5252. **GPS: 35.79731, -94.90384**

CHICKEN CREEK RECREATION AREA

From Tahlequah, 4 mi SW on US 62; 16 mi S (left) on SR 82; 2 mi W (right) on access road; at E side of lake. All year; 14-day limit. 102 sites with elec, 36 with wtr hookups, $18 during 4/1-10/31 ($9 with federal senior pass), $16 during 11/1-3/31 ($8 with federal senior pass). No showers or flush toilets off-season. RV limit in excess of 65'. Two picnic shelters for up to 50 people & 30 vehicles, $25. At reserved sites, 2-night minimum stay required on weekends, 3 nights on holiday weekends. Non-campers pay day use fees for beach, dump station, boat ramp. NRRS during 4/1-9/30. **GPS: 35.68167, -994.96278**

COOKSON BEND RECREATION AREA

From Tahlequah, 4 mi SE on US 62; 13 mi S (left) on SR 82; 2 mi W (right) on access road. All year; 14-day limit. 65 sites without hookups, $10 during 4/1-10/31 ($5 with federal senior pass); $7 during 11/1-3/31 ($3.50 with federal senior pass). 45 sites with elec, no wtr hookups & 17 sites with wtr/elec, $18 during 4/1-10/31 ($9 with federal senior pass); $16 during 11/1-3/31 ($8 with federal senior pass); 7 sites have 50-amp elec; no showers or flush toilets off-season. RV limit in excess of 65'. Two picnic shelters for up to 50 people & 21 vehicles, $25. At reserved sites, 2-night minimum stay required on weekends, 3 nights on holiday weekends. Non-campers pay day use fee for boat ramp, beach, dump station. NRRS during 4/1-9/30. **GPS: 35.70667, -94.96**

ELK CREEK LANDING RECREATION AREA

From Tahlequah, 4 mi SE on US 62; 10 mi S (left) on SR 82; turn right after crossing Illinois River bridge. All year; 14-day limit. 21 sites without hookups, $10 during 4/1-10/31 ($5 with federal senior pass); $7 during 11/1-3/31. 18 sites with elec but no wtr hookups, $16 during 4/1-10/31 ($8 with federal senior pass); $13 during 11/1-3/31 ($6.50 with federal senior pass); no showers or flush toilets in off-season. RV limit in excess of 65'. Two picnic shelters for up to 50 people & 11 vehicles, $10. At reserved sites, 2-night minimum stay required on weekends, 3 nights on holiday weekends. Non-campers pay day use fees for boat ramp, beach, dump station. NRRS during 4/1-9/30. **GPS: 35.75139, -94.9025**

PETTIT BAY RECREATION AREA

From Tahlequah, 4 mi SE on US 62; 4.6 mi S (left) on SR 82; 2 mi S (right) on Indian Rd; 1 mi SE (left) on access rd. All year; 14-day limit. Pettit Bay has been operated as two parks with a marina between them; now it is a single park with 2 camping areas: Pettit I is on N side of the campground; it has non-reservable sites; Pettit II on the S and has reservable sites. 18 sites without hookups, $10 during 4/1-10/31 ($5 with federal senior pass); $7 during 11/1-3/31 ($3.50 with federal senior pass). 70 sites with elec, 7 with wtr hookups, $20 during 4/1-10/31 ($10 with federal senior pass); $16 during 11/1-3/31 ($8 with federal senior pass); no showers or flush toilets during off-season. Some sites have 50-amp elec. RV limit in excess of 65 ft. Three picnic shelters for up to 50 people & 11 vehicles, $10 to $25. At reserved sites, 2-night minimum stay required on weekends, 3 nights on holiday weekends. Non-campers pay day use fee for boat ramp, beach, dump station. NRRS during 4/1-9/30. Note: Pettit II area may be closed temporarily for renovation; check with lake office for current status. **GPS: 35.75361, -94.94778**

SIZEMORE LANDING RECREATION AREA

From Tahlequah, 4 mi SE on US 62; 5 mi S (left) on SR 82; 3.5 mi S (right)on Indian Rd; 1 mi left at sign on access road. All year; 14-day limit. 32 sites without hookups, $5 ($2.50 with federal senior pass. Picnic shelter, $10. RV limit 30'. Reduced fees in winter. No reservations. Non-campers pay day use fee for boat ramp.

SNAKE CREEK COVE RECREATION AREA

From Gore, 15 mi N on SR 100, then W (left) on access road. All year; 14-day limit. 3 sites without hookups, $10 during 4/1-10/31 ($5 with federal senior pass), $7 during 11/1-3/31 ($3.50 with federal senior pass). 104 sites with elec, 10 have no wtr hookups, $20 during 4/1-10/31 ($10 with federal senior pass); $16 during 11/1-3/31 ($8 with federal senior pass); some sites have 50-amp elec; 4 handicap sites. No showers or flush toilet off-season. RV limit in excess of 65 ft. Three picnic shelters for up to 50 people & 21 vehicles, $25. At reserved sites, 2-night minimum stay required on weekends, 3 nights on holiday weekends. Non-campers pay day use fee for boat ramp, dump station, beach. NRRS during 4/1-9/30. **GPS: 35.6475, -94.97222**

STRAYHORN LANDING RECREATION AREA

From Gore, 7 mi NE on SR 100; 1.5 mi N on SR 10A; 0.3 mi E (right) at sign on access road. All year; 14-day limit. 40 sites with elec, $20 during 4/1-10/31 ($10 with federal senior pass); $16 during 11/1-3/31 ($8 with federal senior pass); no flush toilets or showers in off-season. RV limit in excess of 65 ft. Three picnic shelters, $25. At reserved sites, 2-night minimum stay required on weekends, 3 nights on holiday weekends. NRRS during 4/1-9/30. **GPS: 35.61611, -95.05694**

WAURIKA LAKE (TU) 20
GPS: 34.235, -95.055

A 10,100-acre lake 6 mi NW of Waurika on SR 5, 25 mi NE of Wichita Falls, Texas. Visitor center. Lake Manager, Waurika Lake, P. O. Box 29, Waurika, OK 73573-0029. (580) 963-2111.

CHISHOLM TRAIL RECREATION AREA

From Hastings, 5.2 mi E on SR 5; merge onto gravel county rd, then 3 mi N on Advent Rd & 0.9 mi W. 5/1-9/30; 14-day limit. 95 sites with elec, 48 no wtr hookups, $14 base or $16 at premium sites ($7 & $8 with federal senior pass). RV limit 60 ft; 14 pull-through sites. Change house at beach, night-time exit provided, handicap accessible fishing area, nature trail. Non-campers pay day use fee for boat ramp, dump station. (580) 439-8040. NRRS. **GPS: 34.25917, -98.035**

KIOWA RECREATION AREA

From Hastings, 1.2 mi E on SR 5; 3 mi N on county rd. 3/1-10/31; 14-day limit. 178 sites with elec (79 no wtr hookups), $14 base, $18 at premium sites ($7 & $9 with federal senior pass). RV limit 60'; 47 pull-through sites. Two group camping areas for up to 64 people 3 vehicles with picnic shelter, $100. At group sites, 2-night minimum stay required on weekends, 3 nights on holiday weekends. (580) 963-9031. Change house at beach, nature trail, handicap accessible fishing area. Non-campers pay day use fee for boat ramp, dump station. NRRS. **GPS: 34.00, -98.08333**

MONEKA PARK

From Hastings, 3.7 mi E on SR 5; 0.8 mi N. 3/1-10/31; 14-day limit. 38 sites without hookups, $8 ($4 with federal senior pass). Nature trail. No day use fees.

WICHITA RIDGE RECREATION AREA

From Hastings, 1.2 mi E on SR 5; 3 mi N; 1 mi W; 2.1 mi N. All year; 14-day limit. 16 sites without hookups & 1 site with wtr, $8 ($4 with federal senior pass); 10 sites with elec, 2 with wtr hookups, $12 ($6 with federal senior pass). Nature trail, equestrian trail. New dump station. Picnic shelter, $20. Non-campers pay day use fee for boat ramp, dump station. No reservations. **GPS: 34.29287, -98.11282**

WEBBERS FALLS POOL ARKANSAS RIVER L&D 16 (TU) 21

GPS: 35.5533, -95.1683

A 10,900-acre lake 5 mi NW of Webbers Falls (30 mi southeast of Muskogee). Visitors may watch boats & barges go through locks from an observation platform. Project Manager, Rt. 2, Box 21, Gore, OK 74435-9404. (918) 489-5541.

BREWER BEND RECREATION AREA

From Webbers Falls, 2 mi W on US 64; 3 mi N & 2 mi NW (signs). All year; 14-day limit. 8 sites without hookups, $10 ($5 with federal senior pass); 34 sites with elec/wtr, $18 during 4/1-10/31 ($9 with federal senior pass); $15 during 11/1-3/31 ($7.50 with federal senior pass); no flush toilets or showers in off-season. Picnic shelter, $25. Amphitheater, change house. No day use fees NOTE: At last report, campground was closed due to storm damage; check current status before visiting. (918) 487-5252. **GPS: 35.592279, -95.186259**

SPANIARD CREEK CAMPGROUND

From Muskogee at jct with Muskogee Turnpike & SR 10, 3 mi S on SR 64, following signs. All year; 14-day limit. 1 site with elec, no wtr hookup, $14 ($7 with federal senior pass); 35 sites with wtr/elec, $18 during 4/1-10/31 ($9 with federal senior pass); $15 during 11/1-3/31 ($7.50 with federal senior pass). No day use fees. **GPS: 35.600874, -95.265398**

OREGON

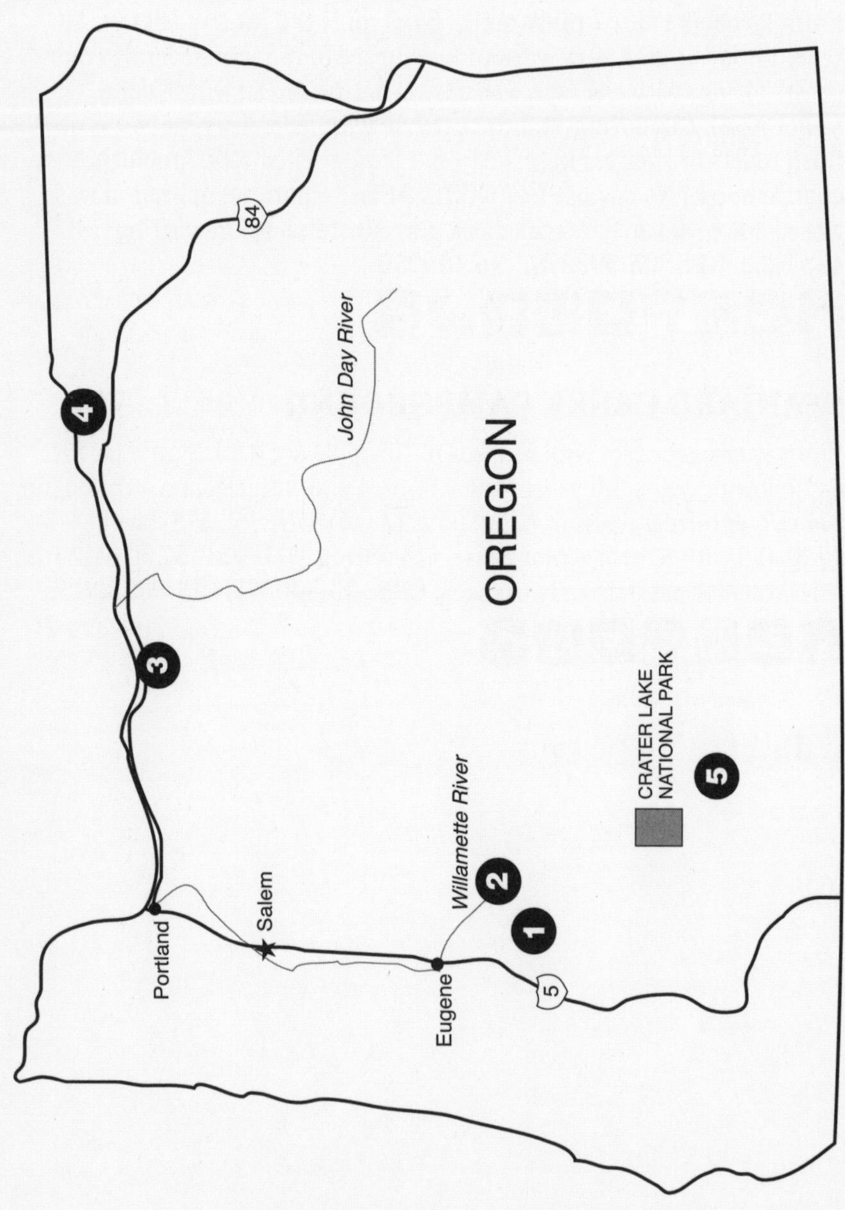
84
John Day River
OREGON
4
3
CRATER LAKE
NATIONAL PARK
5
Willamette River
2
1
Salem
Portland
Eugene
5

OREGON

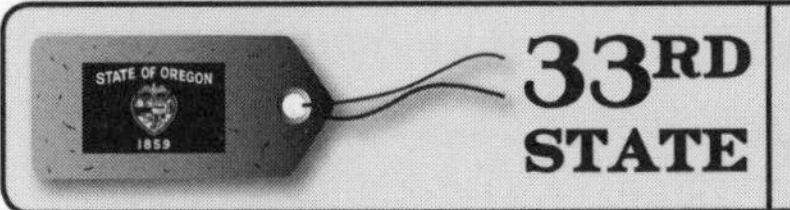

State Capital: **Salem**
Nickname: **Beaver State**
Statehood Year: **1859**

COTTAGE GROVE LAKE (PORT) 1
GPS: 43.80, -123.05

This 1,100-acre lake is 5 mi S of Cottage Grove off I-5 (exit 172) on London Rd, 20 mi S of Eugene. Visitor hours to 10 p.m. ORV & alcohol prohibited. Interpretive programs. For guided tours, call (541) 942-5631. Day use facilities: Lakeside Park -- boat ramp, picnicking, beach; Shortridge Park -- picnicking; Wilson Creek Park -- boat ramp, picnicking, beach. Project Manager, Cottage Grove Lake, 75819 Shortridge Hill Road, Cottage Grove, OR 97424.

PINE MEADOWS CAMPGROUND

From dam, 1 mi SW on Reservoir Rd, N side. 5/20-9/11; 14-day limit. 85 sites without hookups, $16 ($8 with federal senior pass). RV limit in excess of 65'; 26 pull-through sites. At reserved sites, 2-night minimum stay required on weekends, 3 nights on holiday weekends. Amphitheater. (541) 942-8657. NRRS. **GPS: 43.70028, -123.0575**

PRIMITIVE CAMPGROUND

Adjacent to Pine Meadows Campground. MD-LD; 14-day limit. 15 primitive sites with pit toilets, fire rings; no hookups or showers. $12 ($6 with federal senior pass). At reserves sites, 2-night minimum stay required on weekends, 3 nights on holiday weekends. NRRS.

DORENA LAKE (PORT) 2
GPS: 43.78, -122.9533

This 1,700-acre lake is 6 mi E of Cottage Grove off I-5, exit 174, on Row River Rd, 20 mi S of Eugene. Visitors to 10 p.m. ORV & alcohol prohibited.

Visitor center, interpretive programs, guided tours upon request. Day use facilities: Harms Park -- boat ramp, picnicking, hiking trail access; Bake-Stewart Park -- picnicking. Project Manager, Dorena Lake, 75819 Shortridge Hill Road, Cottage Grove, OR 97424. (541) 942-5631.

SCHWARZ CAMPGROUND

From below dam at jct with Row River Rd, 0.2 mi SE on Shoreline Dr, then E near outlet. 4/22-9/25; 14-day limit. 72 sites without hookups, $14 ($7 with federal senior pass); double sites $28. RV limit in excess of 65'; 3 pull-through sites. Six group camping areas without hookups for up to 100 people & 20 vehicles, $140. At reserves sites, 2-night minimum stay required on weekends, 3 nights on holiday weekends. (541) 942-1418. NRRS. **GPS: 43.78889, -122.96667**

LAKE UMATILLA
JOHN DAY LOCK & DAM (PORT) 3
GPS: 45.7167, -120.685

E of US 97, exit 109 off I-84 on the Columbia River. It is 216 mi upstream from the mouth of the Columbia River at Lake Celilo. Fish viewing window and self-guided tours. Corps-managed day use facilities include: Giles French Park -- boat ramp; Plymouth Park -- boat ramp, picnicking, beach; Railroad Island Park -- boat ramp; Rock Creek Park -- boat ramp, picnicking; Roosevelt Park -- boat ramp; Sundale Park -- boat ramp. Day use fees charged at boat ramps, dump stations. Facilities not managed by the Corps: Boardman Park -- nature trails, volleyball courts, tennis courts, hiking & biking trail, playground, concerts (Boardman Township); Irrigon Park & Marina -- boat ramp, picnicking, playground, beach; Unatilla National Wildlife Refuge -- boat ramp, hiking, biking, horseback riding. Visitor center. Resource Manager, Lake Umatilla, P. O. Box 564, The Dalles, OR 97058-9998. (541) 739-2713. See WA listings.

ALBERT PHILIPPI RECREATION AREA

On E side of the John Day River, 3.5 mi upstream from Lepage Park. Boat-in access only; anchor in river. All year; 14-day limit. Formerly free, now $3 day use fee, paid at Lepage Park. Undesignated primitive tent sites. Pit toilets.

GILES FRENCH RECREATION AREA

Below dam on Oregon side. All year; 14-day limit Free primitive camping. Pit toilets.

LE PAGE PARK

From John Day Dam, 9 mi E on I-84 to exit 114, then S; at confluence of John Day & Columbia Rivers. 4/1-11/27; 14-day limit. 20 walk-to tent sites, $14 base ($7 with federal senior pass), $16 at gazebo sites ($8 w/ federal senior pass). 22 RV/tent sites with elec, $20 base; $22 at riverfront sites ($10 & $11 with federal senior pass). Primitive overflow sites $12 ($6 w/federal senior pass). RV limit 55'; 8 pull-through sites. At reserved sites, 2-night minimum stay required on weekends, 3 nights on holiday weekends. Non-campers pay $5 day use fee for dump station, $3 for boat ramp. ORV prohibited. NRRS during 4/1-10/31. **GPS: 45.73, -120.65**

QUESNEL PARK

3 mi E of Lepage Park off I-84 exit 151. All year; 14-day limit. Primitive camping free. Pit toilets. Also known as Three Mi Park. Windsurfing.

LAKE WALLULA
MC NARY DAM (WW) 4
GPS: 45.9367, -119.2978

Lake Wallula is N of the junction of I-82 and US 730 and 1 mi N of Umatilla on I-82. Visitor center with interpretive displays, fish viewing rooms. Corps-operated facilities: Lewis and Clark Commemorative

Trail -- hiking/equestrian trail, picnicking, swimming; Locust Grove/ Martindale Park -- fishing, hiking, hunting; McNary Beach Park -- picnicking, group shelter, cold showers, swimming, hiking trails; McNary Wildlife Nature Area -- picnicking, hiking trails, nature trail, wildlife management trail, pond trail; Oregon Boat Launch -- boat ramp, docks, pit toilet; Pacific Salmon Visitor Center -- audiovisual program, lectures, interpretive displays; Spillway Park -- picnicking; Warehouse Beach -- picnicking, swimming; Washington Boat Launch -- boat launch; W Park -- picnicking, group shelters; Yakima Rver Delta Wildlife Nature Area -- hiking trails, bird watching. Resource Manager, Western Project, Monument Drive, Burbank, WA 99323. (541) 922-4388. See WA listings.

Facilities not operated by the Corps include: Chiawana Park & Road 54 Park -- picnicking, group shelters, hiking trails, playground, biking trail (City of Pasco Parks, WA); Columbia Park Marina -- camping area closed, swimming, hiking trails, playground, golf course, boat ramps (City of Kennewick Parks, WA); Hat Rock State Park -- picnicking, hiking trails, boat ramp, horseshoe pits, ponds; Howard Amon Park -- picnicking, group shelters, swimming, hiking trails, playground, tennis courts, sports fields, biking trail (City of Richland Parks, WA); Leslie R. Grove Park -- picnicking, group shelters, swimming, hiking trails, playground, biking trail, multi-purpose courts, sports fields (City of Richland Parks, WA); Madame Dorion Memorial Park -- primitive camping, dump station, picnicking (U.S. Fish & Wildlife Service); McNary Yacht Club -- marina, boat ramp; Pasco Boat Basin -- picnicking, boat ramp, playground (City of Pasco, WA); Peninsula Habitat Management Unit -- fishing, hiking, hunting (U.S. Fish & Wildlife Service, WA); Sacajawea State Park (WA) -- picnicking, horseshoe pits, sports fields, group shelters, swimming, interpretive center, playground, boat ramp; Two Rivers Park -- picnicking, hiking trail, swimming, playground, boat ramp (Benton County Parks, WA); Walla Walla Yacht Club -- boat ramp; Wye Park -- picnicking, shelters, playground (Richland Parks, WA).

SAND STATION RECREATION AREA

From Umatilla, 10.5 mi E on US 730. All year; 14-day limit. 20 free primitive sites (15 tent only). Pit toilets. **GPS: 45.5518, -119.0711**

LOST CREEK LAKE (PORT) 5
GPS: 44.27, -122.60

This 3,430-acre lake is 30 mi NE of Medford on SR 62 and the Rogue River. Powerhouse tours by appointment. Free electrical cook stoves at group picnic sites. Visitor center at McGregor Park. Cole M. Riven Fish Hatchery downstream from the dam. The lake has more than 20 developed parks, including campgrounds, picnic areas, trailheads, boat ramps and and group use areas. Visitor center with interpretive displays, interactive exhibits, interpretive boardwalk trail. Facilities not managed by the Corps include Stewart Park State Campground and Takelma Recreation Area with group picnicking & boat ramp. Park Manager, Rogue River Basin Projects, 100 Cole M. Rivers Drive, Trail, OR 97541-9607. (541) 878-2255.

FIRE GLEN CAMPGROUND

From jct with Takelma Dr, 3.6 mi NE on SR 62 across Peyton Bridge; 0.8 mi W on Lewis Rd, then SW. All year; 14-day limit. 4 primitive tent sites for up to 8 people. Hike-in or boat-in access only. Pit toilet.

FOUR CORNERS CAMPGROUND

From jct with SR 62, 1.4 mi N on Takelma Dr; 0.5 mi N on logging road, E side. All year; 14-day limit. Hike-in or boat-in access only. Free primitive tent camping for 4 tents & 8 people. Pit toilet.

PENNSYLVANIA

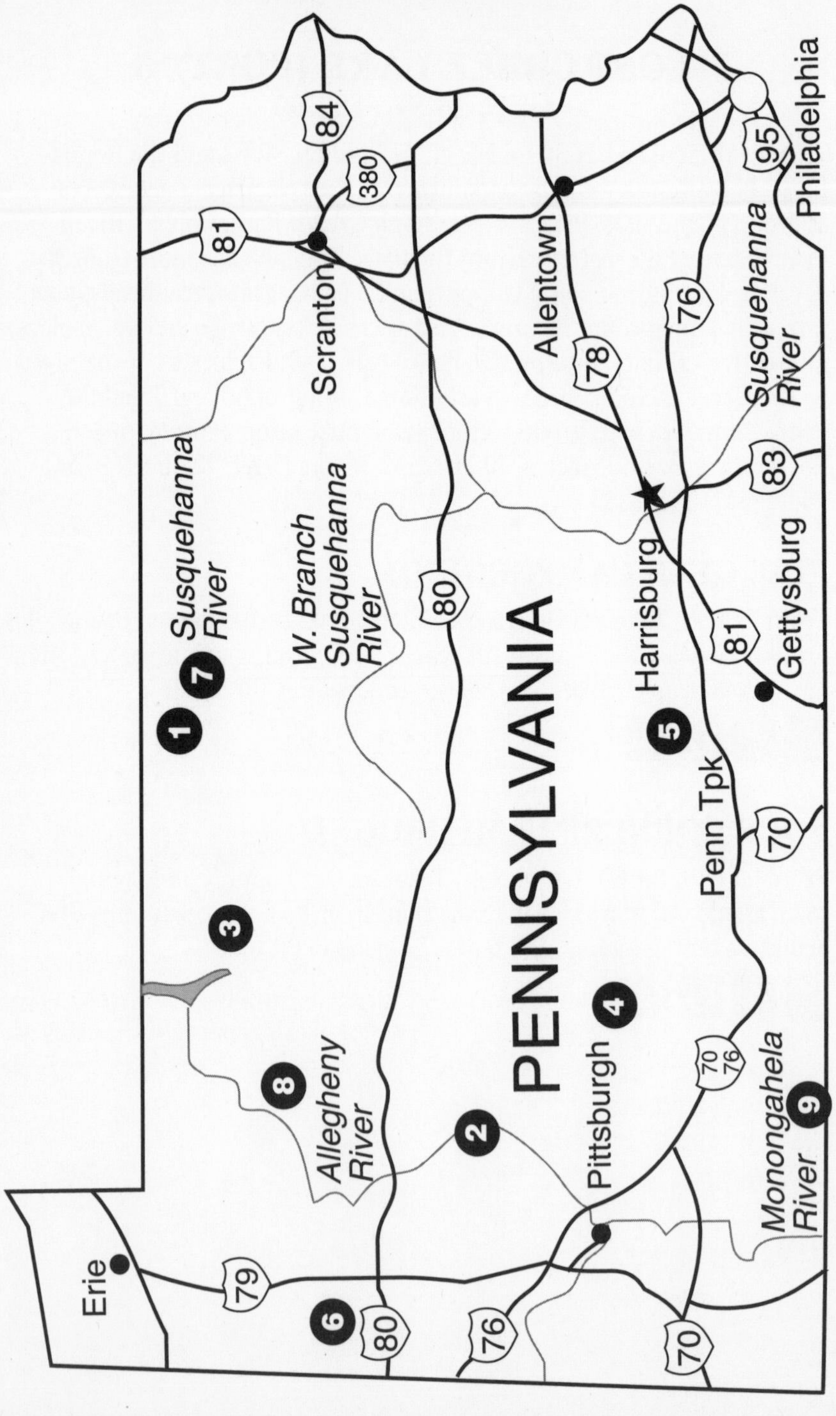

PENNSYLVANIA

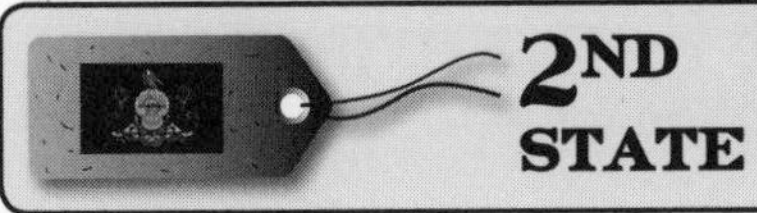

State Capital: **Harrisburg**
Nickname: **Keystone State**
Statehood Year: **1787**

Pittsburgh District - Alcoholic beverages are prohibited at all projects. A Rent-A-Tent (RAT) program includes 9'X12' cabin tent (sleeps 5-6), 10'X 12' dining fly, 36- quart cooler, sleeping pads, electric camp stove, camp light.

COWANESQUE LAKE (BL) 1
GPS: 41.9817, -77.1717

This 1,085-acre lake is 2.2 mi W of Lawrenceville on SR 49 and N of Williamsport. Campground checkout time 3 p.m. (a late fee applies). Visitors to 10 p.m. Corps-operated day use facilities: Lawrence Park -- picnicking, group shelter; N Tailrace Park -- group picnicking; S Shore Park -- boat ramp, picnicking, group shelter, playground, hiking trail. Operations Manager, Tioga-Hammond/Cowanesque Lakes, RR 1, Box 65, Tioga, PA 16946-9733. (570) 835-5281.

TOMPKINS CAMPGROUND

From Lawrenceville, 5 mi W on Bliss Rd, then S (W of the town of Nelson); on N shore of lake. 5/15-9/29; 14-day limit. 16 walk-to tent sites & 24 RV/tent sites without elec, $20 ($10 with federal senior pass); 34 sites with elec/wtr, $30 ($15 with federal senior pass); 52 sites with full hookups, $32 ($16 with federal senior pass). RV limit 55'. Group camping areas with 7 sites & 24 sites. At reserved sites, 2-night minimum stay required on weekends, 3 nights on holiday weekends. Amphitheater, fish cleaning station, camp store, handicap accessible swimming area, hiking trail, interpretive trail, phone. (570) 827-2109. NRRS.

CROOKED CREEK LAKE (PT) 2
GPS: 40.715, -79.51

This 350-acre lake is S of Kittanning and Ford City on E side of SR 66, 48 mi NE of Pittsburgh. Winter activities include an ice rink, sled area and cross country skiing. For daily lake information, call (724) 763-2764. Day use facilities: Beach Area -- picnicking, beach, hiking trail; Crooked Creek Park -- picnicking, group shelter, playground; Hancock Bend Park -- picnicking, group shelter, playground; Outflow Area -- picnicking, hiking trail. Visitor center with interpretive programs. Resource Mgr, Crooked Creek Lake, Rd. 3, Box 323A, Ford City, PA 16226-8815. (724) 763-2764.

CROOKED CREEK CAMPGROUND

From Ford City, 5 mi S on SR 66; 0.1 mi E on SR 2019 to park manager's office. 5/14-LD; 14-day limit. 46 sites no hookups, $10 ($5 with federal senior pass). Group camping area (MD-LD). Interpretive programs. Non-campers pay $4 day use fee for boat ramp, beach. No reservations.

CROOKED CREEK PRIMITIVE GROUP AREA

From Ford City, 5 mi S on SR 66; E on SR 2019 to park manager's office; call or visit for information. 5/14-LD. Group camping area, $35-$45. Picnic shelter. Non-campers pay $4 day use fee for boat ramp, beach.

EAST BRANCH CLARION RIVER (PT) 3
GPS: 41.5583, -78.5967

1,160-acre lake is 36 mi N of De Bois off US 219 and is 105 mi SE of Erie, E of Allegheny National Forest. Winter activities include ice fishing. Daily lake information, (814) 965-4762. Visitor center. Facilities not managed by the Corps include Elk State Park, Bendigo State Park, Clear Creek State Park and Elk State Forest. Resource Manager, 631 E Branch Dam Road, Wilcox, PA 15870-9709. (814) 965-5851.

EAST BRANCH RECREATION AREA

From Wilcox at jct with US 219, 5 mi SE on Glen Hazel Rd; exit E (left) past resource mgr. office to campground. About 4/15-10/15; 14-day limit. 16 sites no hookups, $15 ($7.50 with federal senior pass); 16 sites with elec, $20 ($10 with federal senior pass. Picnic shelter. (814) 965-2065.

LOYALHANNA LAKE (PT) 4
GPS: 40.2367, -79.4517

This 400-acre lake is S of Saltsburg and W of SR 981, 32 mi E of Pittsburgh. For daily lake information, call (724) 639-3785. Dam picnic area features group shelters, picnicking, playground and trails. Resource Manager, Loyalhanna Lake, 440 Loyalhanna Dam Road, Saltsburg, PA 15681-9302. (724) 639-9013.

BUSH RECREATION AREA

From Saltsburg, S on SR 981 past the dam, then 1 mi S on Bush Rd. 5/15-9/15; 14-day limit. 39 primitive sites, $16 ($8 with federal senior pass); 10 sites with elec/wtr, $22 ($11 with federal senior pass. Interpretive programs, picnic shelter ($40), coin-operated showers.

KISKI GROUP CAMPING AREA

From Bush Rec. Area, 0.3 mi N on Bush Road. 5/5-10/15; 14-day limit. Primitive group camping area for organized groups only. Call office.

RAYSTOWN LAKE (BL) 5
GPS: 40.43333, -78.04

8,300-acre lake is just SW of Huntingdon, E of Johnstown, N of PA Turnpike and E of US 220. Facilities for handicapped include special fishing at Aitch and Shy Beaver Recreational Areas. Other day use facilities: Aitch Rec. Area -- boat ramp, picnicking, group shelter; Corbins

Island -- boat ramp, picnicking, group shelter; James Creek -- boat ramp; Snyders Run -- boat ramp; Tatman Run -- boat ramp, picnicking, group shelter, playground, beach; Weaver Falls -- boat ramp, picnicking, group shelter, playground. Branch Camp is leased by the Corps to a private manager. Checkout time 4 p.m. Resource Manager, Raystown Lake, Rd. 1, Box 222, Hesston, PA 16647. (814) 658-3405. Raystown.

NANCY'S CAMP

From Marklesburg, 1.5 mi SW on SR 26, then 1 mi SE & N to trail. Access by boat-in or hike-in only; between marker 15 & 16 on W shore. All year; 14-day limit. 50 lakefront tent sites, $10 ($5 with federal senior pass). Campers have access to showers at Seven Points change house near marker 9. Pit toilets, fire rings. Self-registration at honor vault. Most campers boat in from launch at James Creek.

SEVEN POINTS CAMPGROUND

From McConnelstown, 1.2 mi SW on SR 26; 2 mi SE past Hesston & S of admin. building. 4/1-10/31; 14-day limit. 2 tent sites, $21 ($10.50 with federal senior pass); 5 sites with 30-amp elec/wtr & 8 sites at group camping area when not in use, $23 ($11.50 with federal senior pass); 145 sites with 50-amp elec/wtr, $25 ($12.50 with federal senior pass). RV limit in excess of 65'. Fee at picnic shelter. Group camping area, $80 for youth groups, $100 adults plus $6 for each RV in excess of 10. At reserved sites, 2-night minimum stay required/weekends, 3 nights/holiday weekends. Visitor center, interpretive trail, marina, phone, amphitheater, boat & kayak rentals, boat rentals. NRRS during MD-LD.
GPS: 40.38306, -78.07833

SUSQUEHANNOCK CAMPGROUND

From Seven Points campground, 1 mi NE past the administration building, then SE. MD-LD; 14-day limit. 24 tent sites & 36 RV/tent sites, $12 base; $15 at premium waterfront sites. RV limit in excess of 65';

many sites quite small. At reserved sites, 2-night minimum stay required on weekends, 3 nights on holiday weekends. Pit toilets, hiking & biking trails. (814) 658-6806. NRRS. **GPS: 40.3875, -78.05**

SHENANGO RIVER LAKE (PT) 6
GPS: 41.265, -80.4633

This 3,560-acre lake is 2 mi N of Hermitage and US 62 off SRs 18 and 518; it is 6 mi N of I-80, 21 mi NE of Youngstown, Ohio. Non-campers pay day use fees for dump stations & boat ramps. Campground checkout time 4 p.m. Alcohol prohibited. Visitors to 10 p.m. 250-acre area for ORV. Day use facilities: Chestnut Run -- group picnicking; Clark Recreation Area -- picnicking, group shelter; Golden Run Wildlife Area -- boat ramp; Hartford Rd Access -- boat ramp; Mahaney Outflow Recreation Area -- group shelter, playground; Mahaney Recreation Area -- boat ramp, group shelter, picnicking, playground, interpretive trail; Parkers Landing -- boat ramp. For daily lake information call (724) 962-4384. Resource Manager, Shenango River Lake, 2442 Kelly Road, Hermitage, PA 16150-9703. (724) 962-7746.

SHENANGO RECREATION AREA

From Hermitage at jct with US 62, 4.6 mi N on SR 18; 0.8 mi W on W Lake Rd, then S. MD-LD; 14-day limit. 5 rent-a-tent tent sites with elec, \$30 & \$35 (\$15 & \$17.50 with federal senior pass). 215 sites without elec, \$17 base, \$30 at premium locations (\$8.50 & \$15 with federal senior pass). 107 sites with elec, \$20 & \$22 (\$10 & \$11 with federal senior pass). RV limit in excess of 65'; 4 pull-through sites. Picnic shelter, \$40. Interpretive programs, firewood for a fee, amphitheater, interpretive trails, horseshoe pits. At reserved sites, 2-night minimum stay required on weekends, 3 nights on holiday weekends. (724) 646-1115/1118. NRRS. **GPS: 41.28889, -80.43833**

TIOGA HAMMOND LAKES (BL) 7
GPS: 41.9017, -77.145

680-acre Hammond Lake is a "twin" lake with Tioga Lake; they are 5 mi S of Tioga on SR 287 in N-central Pennsylvania, 72 mi W of Binghamton, New York. Display gardens. Campground checkout time 3 p.m. (late fee applies). Lambs Creek Park day use facilities -- boat ramp, group shelter, hiking/hiking trail. Operations Manager, Tioga-Hammond/Cowanesque Lakes, RR 1, Box 65, Tioga, PA 16946-9733. (570) 835-5278.

IVES RUN CAMPGROUND

From Tioga, 5 mi S on SR 287; exit E, following signs; on E shore of Hammond Lake. About 4/15-12/11; 14-day limit. During peak season through 10/30, 56 sites without hookups, $20 ($10 with federal senior pass); during 11/1-12/11, 32 of the sites are $10 with self-register at honor vault ($5 with federal senior pass). 131 sites with elec, $28 & $32 during peak season ($14 & $16 with federal senior pass). RV limit in excess of 65'; 5 pull-through sites. Picnic shelters with elec, $40-$80. At reserved sites, 2-night minimum stay required on weekends, 3 nights on holiday weekends. Fish cleaning station, amphitheater, handicap accessible swimming area. NRRS. **GPS: 41.880835, -77.20**

TIONESTA LAKE (PT) 8
GPS: 41.47, -79.4467

A 480-acre lake SW of Tionesta on SR 36, 60 mi SE of Erie near the southwestern corner of the Allegheny National Forest. Visitor center, interpretive programs. Resource Manager, 1 Tionesta Lake, Tionesta, PA 16353. (814) 755-3512.

LACKEY FLATS CAMPGROUND

By boat-in only. All year; 14-day limit. 17 free primitive tent sites. Pit toilets.

GLASNER RUN CAMPGROUND

By boat-in only. All year; 14-day limit. 10 free primitive sites.

KELLETTVILLE CAMPGROUND

From Kellettville at jct with SR 666, SW across bridge on FR 127. About 4/15-12/15; 14-day limit. 20 sites no hookups, $10 during 4/15-10/10 ($5 with federal senior pass); free during 10/11-12/15. Pit toilets, drkg wtr.

OUTFLOW RECREATION AREA

From Tionesta, 0.5 mi S on SR 36. All year; 14-day limit. 39 sites without hookups, $8 during 4/15-5/20 ($4 with federal senior pass); $12 during 5/21-10/31 ($6 with federal senior pass); free rest of year. Picnic shelter, fishing access for handicapped.

TIONESTA RECREATION AREA

From Tionesta, 0.5 mi S on SR 36 (signs); below the dam. 5/23-10/11; 14-day limit. 78 sites with full hookups, $28 ($14 with federal senior pass). 2 handicap sites held reserved for campers with disabilities. RV limit in excess of 65'. Group camping area for organized youth, scout or church groups with prior approval. NRRS during 5/23-9/4. **GPS: 41.48472, -79.44861**

YOUGHIOGHENY RIVER LAKE (PT) 9
GPS: 39.7983, -79.3683

This 2,840-acre lake is S of Confluence off SR 281 and N of US 40 in southwestern Pennsylvania, spanning the Mason-Dixon Line between Pennsylvania and Maryland. Trout stockings April-September. For lake/ recreation information, call (814) 395-3166. Non-campers pay $3 day use fees at boat ramps, $1 per person at beaches. Interpretive programs. Resource Manager, Youghiogheny River Lake, R.D. 497 Flanigan Road, Confluence, PA 15424-1932. (814) 395-3242. See Maryland listings.

MILL RUN CAMPGROUND

From I-68 exit 4 at Friendsville, 5 mi N on SR 53; S of Mill Run Reservoir just W of SR 381. All year; 14-day limit. Sites without hookups, $13 during 5/1-9/8, self-register ($6.50 with federal senior pass). Free rest of year for self-contained RVs. **GPS: 39.7161, -79.384**

OUTFLOW CAMPGROUND

From Confluence, 0.7 mi SW on SR 281. All year; 14-day limit. Sites without hookups, $13 with self-registration during 4/10-5/15 and during 9/8-10/6 ($6.50 with federal senior pass). During peak season of 5/15-9/8, 10 tent sites & 15 RV/tent sites without hookups are $18 ($9 with federal senior pass); 36 sites with elec, $22 ($11 with federal senior pass). During 10/7-4/9, camping free for self-contained RVs. RV limit 60 ft. Picnic shelter, amphitheater, bike rentals, firewood, bike trail, phone, fishing pier. Two group camping areas: 1A with wtr/elec hookups for up to 40 people, and 2A for up to 150 people. NRRS (MD-LD). **GPS: 39.805, -79.36694**

TUB RUN CAMPGROUND

From Confluence, 7 mi SW on SR 281; 1.5 mi S on Tub Run Rd. About 5/15-9/5; 14-day limit. 12 walk-to tent sites, $18 ($9 with federal senior pass); 59 RV/tent sites without hookups, $18 base, $19 at premium locations ($9 & $9.50 with federal senior pass); 30 sites with elec, $22 ($11 with federal senior pass). RV limit 55'. NRRS.
GPS: 39.77083, -79.40194

SOUTH CAROLINA

SOUTH CAROLINA

State Capital: **Columbia**
Nickname: **Palmetto State**
Statehood Year: **1788**

8TH STATE

HARTWELL LAKE (SV) 1
GPS: 34.35489, -82.912041

A 56,000-acre surface area lake with 962 miles of shoreline located 5 miles N of Hartwell, Georgia, on US 29 SW of Greenville on the Georgia-South Carolina state line. Guided tours of dam and power plant available. Alcohol prohibited in campgrounds. Golf carts, off-road vehicles, motorized scooters, etc., also are prohibited. The Corps manages nine campgrounds with a total of 524 campsites. Project Manager, Hartwell Lake and Powerplant, P. O. Box 278, Hartwell, GA 30643-0278. (706) 856-0300/(888) 893-0678. See Georgia listings.

CONEROSS CAMPGROUND

From Townville, 1.5 mi N on SR 24; E on Coneross Creek Rd, following signs. 5/1-9/30; 14-day limit. 106 sites, 94 with wtr & 50-amp elec; 36 pull-through, 1 handicap. Sites without elec, $14; sites with wtr/elec $20; premium sites $22; double site, $46 ($7, $10, $11 & $23 with federal senior pass. RV limit in excess of 65'. NRRS. **GPS: 34.59111, -82-89722**

CRESENT GROUP CAMPGROUND

From Anderson, 14 mi S on US 29. 5/1-10/31. Two group camping areas: Loop A for up to 100 people and 30 vehicles with 10 sites, $120. Loop B for up to 100 people and 66 vehicles with 22 sites having wtr & 50-amp elec, $120; from 101 to 150 people, $160; from 151 to 200 people, $200; from 201 to 300 people, $260. Loop B features a picnic shelter for up to 100 people. RV limit 38'. NRRS. **GPS: 34.38111, -82.81639**

OCONEE POINT CAMPGROUND

From Townville, 1.5 mi N on SR 24; 2.5 mi E on Coneross Creek Rd; 3 mi S on Friendship Rd, following signs. 5/1-10/31; 14-day limit. 60 sites with 50-amp elec/wtr (16 pull-through), $22 ($11 with federal senior pass); double sites $46. Also 15 overflow sites without hookups, $12 ($6 with federal senior pass). RV limit 25' at 3 sites, larger for other sites. NRRS. **GPS: 34.6017, -82.8708**

SPRINGFIELD CAMPGROUND

From Anderson, 4.5 mi W on SR 24; 4 mi S on SR 187, follow signs on Providence Church Rd. 4/1-10/31; 14-day limit. 79 sites (75 waterfront, 28 pull-through) with wtr/50-amp elec, $22 ($11 with federal senior pass) (double sites $46). RV limit 40'. Courtesy dock. NRRS.
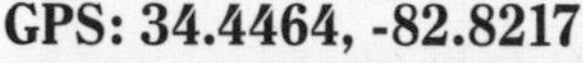
GPS: 34.4464, -82.8217

TWIN LAKES CAMPGROUND

From Clemson, 5.5 mi SE on US 76; 3 mi SW on CR 56, following signs. 4/1-11/30 (some sites open all year); 14-day limit. 102 sites (89 waterfront) with wtr/50-amp elec. 30-amp elec/wtr, $18; 50-amp elec, $20; double sites $46 ($9, $10 & $23 with federal senior pass). Non-reservable picnic shelter; 2 reservable shelters in day use area. RV limit 60'. NRRS. **GPS: 34.6281, -82.8656**

J. STROM THURMOND (SV) 2
GPS: 33.50, -81.96

A 70,000-acre surface area lake with 1,200 miles of shoreline located adjacent to the W side of Clarks Hill, SW of Greenville on US 221 and the Georgia state line. It is the largest Corps of Engineers lake east of the Mississippi River. The Corps operates 13 campgrounds with 554 sites, five major day use areas and numerous other recreational facilities. Exhibits at visitor center. Checkout time 2 p.m. Alcohol prohibited in campgrounds. $3 charged for extra vehicles. For current lake conditions, call 1 (800) 333-3478, ext. 1147. Resource Mgr., J. Strom Thurmond Lake, Rt. 1, Box 12, Clarks Hill, SC 29821-9701. (864) 333-1100/(800) 533-3478. See GA listings.

HAWE CREEK CAMPGROUND

From McCormick at jct with US 221, 0.5 mi SW US 378 past jct with SR 439, 4 mi S on Chamberlains Ferry Rd. 4/1-9/30; 14-day limit. 28 sites with wtr/elec, $20 ($10 with federal senior pass); 24 sites with 50-amp service, $22 ($11 with federal senior pass. RV limit 45 ft; 6 pull-through sites. At reserved sites, 2-night minimum stay required on weekends, 3 nights on holiday weekends. (864) 443-5441. NRRS. **GPS: 33.8361, -82.3386**

LEROYS FERRY CAMPGROUND

From Willington, 4 mi SW, following signs. All year; 14-day limit. $6. 10 primitive sites. Pit toilets, campfire grill areas. No reservations.
GPS: 33.921143, -82.489746

MODOC CAMPGROUND

From Modoc, 1 mi S on US 221, then E following signs. 4/1-11/30; 14-day limit. 70 sites, 69 with wtr/elec, 29 pull-through. $16 for 30-amp elec, $22 at premium sites with 50-amp elec ($8 & $11 with federal senior pass). Double sites, $42. RV limit 45'. At reserved sites, 2-night minimum stay required on weekends, 3 nights on holiday weekends. Recently renovated campground's sites were re-numbered. Picnic shelter. (864) 333-2272. NRRS. **GPS: 33.71917, -82.22417**

MOUNT CARMEL CAMPGROUND

From Mount Carmel, 4.3 mi SW, following signs. 4/1-9/6; 14-day limit. 44 sites, 39 with wtr/50-amp elec $18, 5 tent sites $16, premium location sites $22 ($9, $8 & $11 with federal senior pass. RV limit 40'; 12 pull-through sites. At reserved sites, 2-night minimum stay required on weekends, 3 nights on holiday weekends. Picnic shelter, fish cleaning station. (864) 391-2711. NRRS. **GPS: 33.9583, -82.5394**

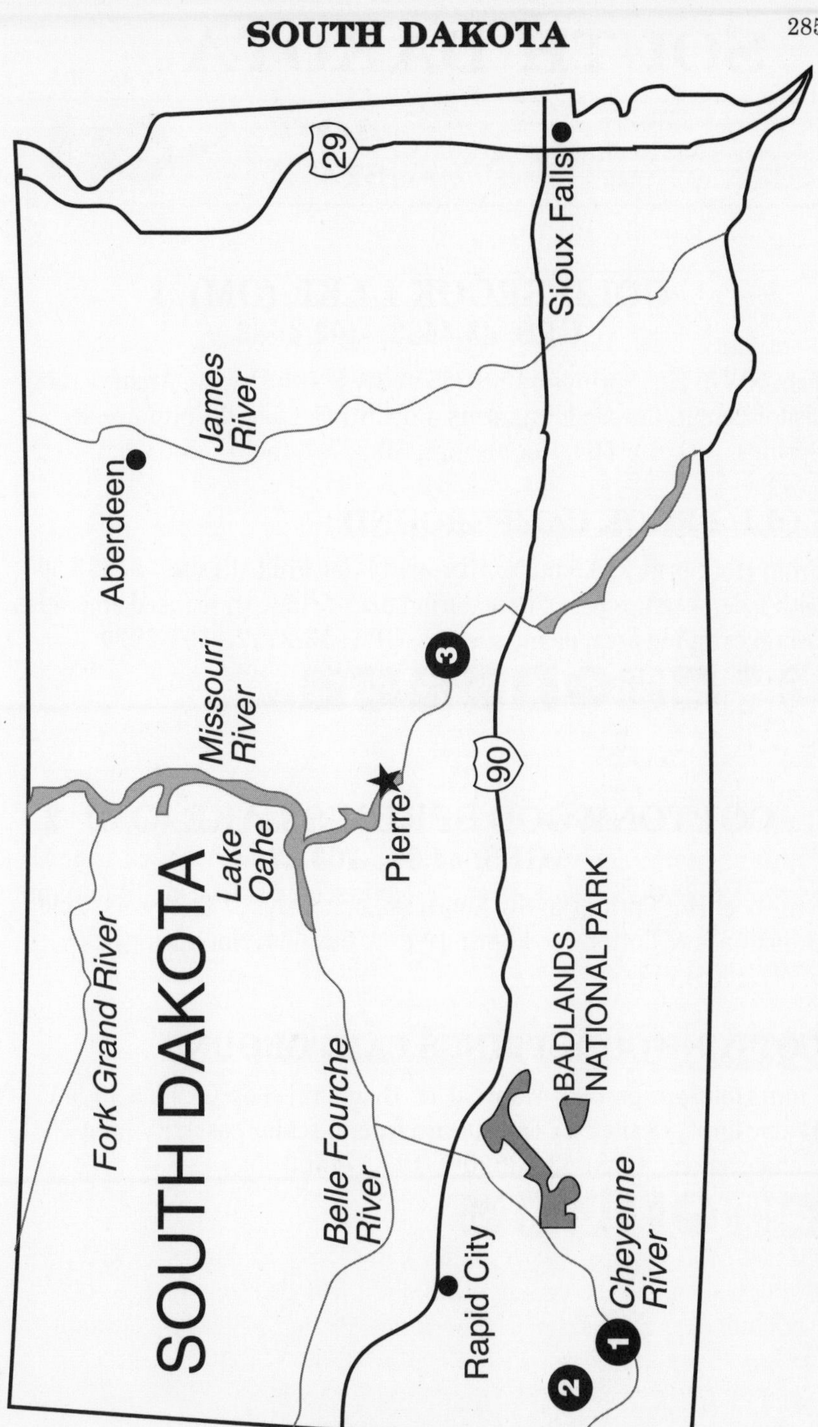
SOUTH DAKOTA
29
Sioux Falls
James River
Aberdeen
Missouri River
90
Lake Oahe
Pierre
Fork Grand River
BADLANDS NATIONAL PARK
Belle Fourche River
Rapid City
Cheyenne River
1
2
3

SOUTH DAKOTA

State Capital: **Pierre**
Nickname: **Mt. Rushmore State**
Statehood Year: **1889**

40TH STATE

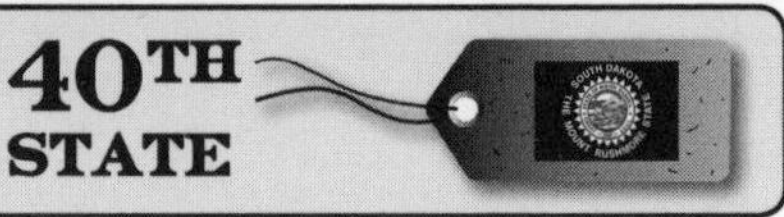

COLD BROOK LAKE (OM) 1
GPS: 43.4533, -103.4883

1 mi NW of Hot Springs off US 385 in SW South Dakota. Archery range, visitor center. Corps of Engineers, Cold Brook Lake & Cottonwood Springs, P. O. Box 664, Hot Springs, SD 57747. (605) 745-5476.

COLD BROOK CAMPGROUND

From Hot Springs, 0.5 mi N. All year; 14-day limit. 13 sites, $7 ($3.50 with federal senior pass). Free during 9/15-5/15 with reduced amenities. Group camping area, picnic shelters. **GPS: 43.2712, -103.2920**

COTTONWOOD SPRINGS LAKE (OM) 2
GPS: 44.84, -103.27

5 mi W of Hot Springs in SW South Dakota. Corps of Engineers, Cold Brook Lake & Cottonwood Springs, P. O. Box 664, Hot Springs, SD 57747. (605) 745-5476.

COTTONWOOD SPRINGS CAMPGROUND

From Hot Springs, 5 mi W on SR 18, then 2 mi N on CR 17. 5/15-9/15; 14-day limit. 18 sites, $7 ($3.50 with federal senior pass). RV limit 30 ft. Picnic shelters. **GPS: 43.439209, -103.574463**

LAKE SHARPE (OM) 3
GPS: 44.0383, -99.4467

2 miles SW of Fort Thompson & 60 miles SE of Pierre. Powerhouse tours daily during summer and during off-season by appointment. Visitor center with exhibits and artifact displays. Day use activities: Good Soldier Park -- boat ramp, picnic shelter, playground; Right Tailrace -- boat ramp, picnic shelter, playground; Spillway Dike -- boat ramp, picnic shelter; Spillway Overlook -- picnicking. Lake Manager, Lake Sharpe, HC 69, Box 74, Chamberlain, SD 57325-9407. (605) 245-2255.

OLD FORT THOMPSON CAMPGROUND

Below dam on E side of the spillway. All year; 14-day limit. Free. 13 primitive sites. Picnic shelter, showers, pit toilets. Dump station half mi.

NORTH SHORE CAMPGROUND

From dam at jct with SR 47, NW past the project office. All year; 14-day limit. 24 primitive sites, free. 2 handicap sites. Fish cleaning station, picnic shelter, pit toilets. Dump station 1 mi.

LEFT TAILRACE CAMPGROUND

Below dam on S side of spillway. May-Sept; 14-day limit. 81 sites with elec (35 pull-through), 2 handicap sites, $16. Picnic shelter, fish cleaning station, amphitheater, horseshoe pits. RV limit 35'. Dump station half mi.
GPS: 44.041016, -99.440186

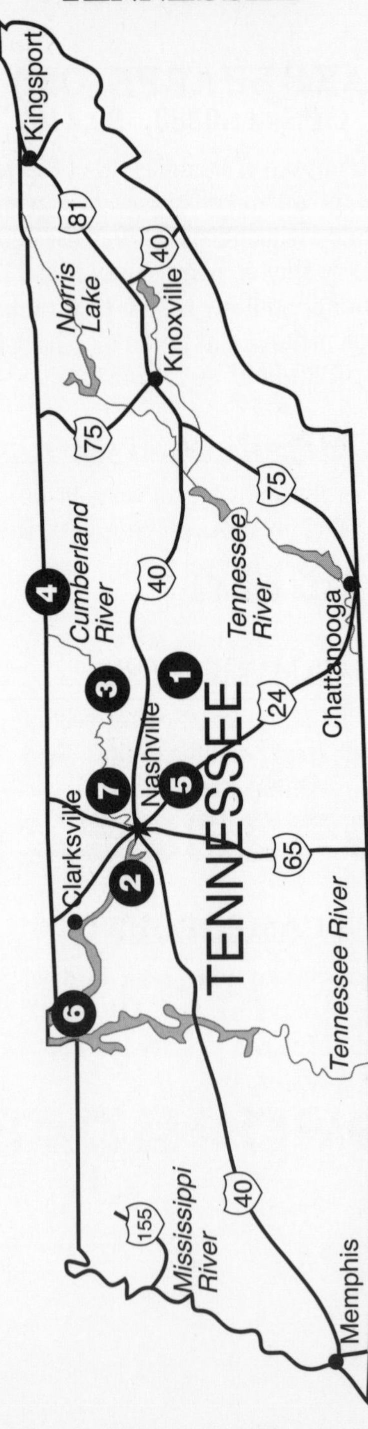
Kingsport
81
40
Norris Lake
Knoxville
75
75
Cumberland River
40
Tennessee River
Chattanooga
4
3
1
24
TENNESSEE
Nashville
7
5
Clarksville
2
65
Tennessee River
6
40
155
Mississippi River
Memphis

TENNESSEE

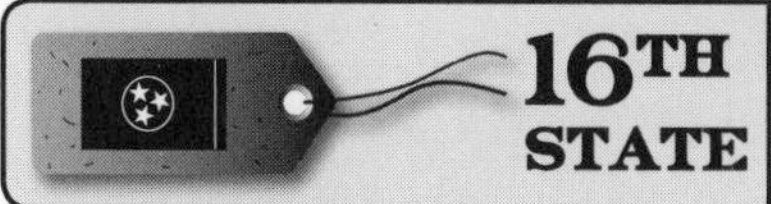

State Capital: **Nashville**
Nickname: **Volunteer State**
Statehood Year: **1796**

Nashville District - Fees may be higher on weekends. A day time visitor fee may be charged.

CENTER HILL LAKE (NV) 1
GPS: 36.1017, -85.82

An 18,220-acre surface area lake located south of I-40 on SR 96, NW of Smithville and 64 miles E of Nashville. Wildlife exhibit. Alcohol prohibited. Campground checkout time 3 p.m. Free primitive boat-in tent camping available at five locations on the lake; a camping permit is required. Resource Manager, Center Hill Lake, 158 Resource Lane, Lancaster, TN 38569-9410. (931) 858-3125/(615) 548-4521.

FLOATING MILL CAMPGROUND

From I-40 exit 273, 5 mi S on Floating Mill Rd; right at store following signs. 4/13-10/30; 14-day limit. 112 sites (44 with elec, 13 with 50-amp elec, 9 without elec, 39 tent sites with elec, 6 non-elec tent sites). Basic tent sites $14 ($7 with federal senior pass); premium elec/wtr tent sites $18 & $20 ($9 & $10 with federal senior pass); non-elec RV sites $16 ($8 with federal senior pass); elec RV sites $20 ($10 with federal senior pass); premium sites with 50-amp elec/wtr, $24. Picnic shelter $50. Amphitheater, fish cleaning station. RV limit 60'. At reserved sites, 2-night minimum stay required on weekends, 3 nights on holiday weekends. Recent improvements include new elec/wtr hookups, renovating 9 campsites, enlarging 4 sites and adding 50-amp service, improving 5 lakefront sites and adding wtr/elec service. (931) 858-4845. NRRS. **GPS: 36.04489, -85.76347**

LONG BRANCH CAMPGROUND

From I-40 exit 268, 5 mi W on SR 96; 2 mi W on Center Hill Dam Rd; 1 mi N on SR 141, on right (signs). 4/1-10/30; 14-day limit. 60 sites, 57 with elec, 3 with 50-amp elec, 3 handicap sites. Elec/wtr, $20; premium locations $24. ($24). Picnic shelter for up to 125 people, $50. Fish cleaning station. RV limit in excess of 65'. At reserved sites, 2-night minimum stay required on weekends, 3 nights on holiday weekends. (615) 548-8002. NRRS. **GPS: 36.09903, -85.83176**

RAGLAND BOTTOM CAMPGROUND

From Smithville, 8 mi NE on US 70, across lake bridge, left on Ragland Bottom Rd (signs). 4/20-10/15; 14-day limit. 57 sites (30 with 50-amp elec, 10 for tent). Basic tent sites $14 ($7 with federal senior pass); premium tent sites wtr/elec and RV sites with wtr/elec, $20 ($10 with federal senior pass); sites with full hookups and 50-amp elec, $22 ($11 with federal senior pass); premium sites with 50-amp elec/wtr, $24 ($12 with federal senior pass). Picnic shelter up to 125 people, $50. RV limit in excess of 65'. At reserved sites, 2-night minimum stay on weekends, 3 nights on holiday weekends. (931) 761-3616. NRRS.
GPS: 35.9758, -85.7228

CHEATHAM LAKE (NV) 2
GPS: 36.2303, -87.2228

A 7,450-acre lake 12 miles NW of Ashland City off SR 12, NW of Nashville. Resource Manager, Cheatham Lake, 1798 Cheatham Dam Road, Ashland City, TN 37015-9805. (615) 254-3734/792-5697.

HARPETH RIVER BRIDGE CAMPGROUND

From Ashland City, 6 mi W on SR 49 to Harpeth River Bridge. 4/30-10/15; 14-day limit. 15 sites elec/wtr, $12 ($6 with federal senior pass). Courtesy float. (615) 792-4195. No reservations. Campground closed in late 2010 due to river flooding; call for current status. **GPS: 36.28418, -87.118164**

LOCK A CAMPGROUND

From Ashland City, 8 mi W on SR 12 to Cheap Hill; 4 mi SW (left) on Cheatham Dam Rd. 4/1-10/30; 14-day limit. 45 sites with wtr/50-amp elec (7 for tents only), 2 handicap sites. Tent sites & RV sites with wtr/elec, $19 ($9.50 with federal senior pass); premium RV sites $23 ($11.50 with federal senior pass). Fish cleaning station, horseshoe pits, picnic shelter, handicap accessible fishing area, nature trail, courtesy floats. At reserved sites, 2-night minimum stay required on weekends, 3 nights on holiday weekends. (615) 792-3715. NRRS (4/1-9/7). **GPS: 36.31583, -87.18694**

CORDELL HULL LAKE (NV) 3
GPS: 36.29, -85.9417

An 11,960-acre lake 2.5 miles NE of Carthage off SR 263 and 49 miles E of Nashville. Wildlife exhibit at visitor center. Golf carts, off-road vehicles, electic schooters, etc., are prohibited. Visitor fee of $4 per car is assessed. Campgrounds may charge $1 per day extra on weekends and holiday weekends. Resource Manager, Cordell Hull Lake, 71 Corps Lane, Carthage, TN 37030-9710. (615) 735-1034.

DEFEATED CREEK CAMPGROUND

From Carthage, 4 mi W on SR 25; N on US 80; E on SR 85, then S following signs. 3/18-11/11; 14-day limit. 155 sites with elec/wtr (63 full hookups, 35 pull-throughs). Elec/wtr sites $15-18 ($7.50-$9 with federal senior pass); premium locations higher. Full hookups $26 ($13 with federal senior pass). A $1 per night additional fee may be charged on weekends and holidays. Picnic shelters $50-100. RV limit in excess of 65'. At reserved sites, 2-night minimum stay required on weekends, 3 nights on holiday weekends. (615) 774-3141. NRRS. **GPS: 36.29972, -85.90889**

SALT LICK CREEK CAMPGROUND

From Carthage, 4 mi W on SR 27; N on US 80; E on SR 85; right on Smith Bend Rd, following signs. 4/22-10/14; 14-day limit.150 sites with wtr/elec (31 full hookups), 15 pull-through. $15 at sites with wtr/elec ($7.50 with federal senior pass); premium sites higher. Premium sites with full hookups, $26 ($13 with federal senior pass). A $1 per night additional fee may be changed on weekends and holidays. RV limit in excess of 65'. Picnic shelter for up to 100 people & 1 vehicle, $50. At reserved sites, 2-night minimum stay required on weekends, 3 nights on holiday weekends. (931) 678-4718. NRRS. **GPS: 36.32278, -85.80861**

DALE HOLLOW LAKE (NV) 4
GPS: 36.5367, -85.4486

This 27,700-acre lake is 4 miles E of Celina and NE of Nashville on both sides of the Kentucky/Tennessee state lines. National fish hatchery just below dam. Visitor center with interpretive programs, historic and cultural site. Alcohol prohibited. Free primitive camping available at 24 locations around the lake; camping permits required Resource Manager, Dale Hollow Lake, 5050 Dale Hollow Dam Road, Celina, TN 38551-9708. (931) 243-3136.

DALE HOLLOW DAM CAMPGROUND

From Celina, 2 mi NW on SR 32; 1.5 mi NE (right) on SR 53 Dale Hollow Rd, signs), then S below spillway. 4/1-10/31; 14-day limit. 79 sites. 1 sites without hookups, $17 ($8.50 with federal senior pass); 16 sites paved with 50-amp elec/wtr, $24 ($12 with federal senior pass); 62 unpaved with wtr/elec, $17 base, $20 at premium locations ($8.50 & $10 with federal senior pass). RV limit 60 ft; 16 pull-through sites, 2 handicap sites. At reserved sites, 2-night minimum stay required on weekends, 3 nights on holiday weekends. Picnic shelter for up to 50 people, $50; 151-200 people, $200; 201-250 people, $250. Amphitheater, fish cleaning station, handicap-assessible fishing area. Dale Hollow National Fish Hatchery. (931) 243-3554. NRRS. **GPS: 36.53778, -85.4575**

LILLYDALE RECREATION AREA

From Hwy. 111, 13.3 mi N on SR 294 (Willow Grove Rd). 4/22-9/6; 14-day limit. 114 sites, 1 paved with 50-amp elec/wtr, $20 ($10 with federal senior pass); 79 unpaved with elec/wtr, $20 base, premium locations $24 ($10 & $12 with federal senior pass); 5 unpaved without hookups, $15 ($7.50 with federal senior pass); 4 tent sites with elec/wtr, $20 ($10 with federal senior pass); 10 tent sites without elec/wtr and 15 primitive walk-in island tent sites, $10 ($5 with federal senior pass). RV limit 40'; 3 pull-through sites. Picnic shelter for up to 100 people, $40. At reserved sites, 2-night minimum stay required on weekends, 3 nights on holiday weekends. Courtesy float. (931) 823-4155. NRRS. **GPS: 36.6044, -85.2997**

OBEY RIVER CAMPGROUND

From Livingston, 15 mi NE on SR 111 (signs); W before lake bridge. 4/15-10/17; 14-day limit. 132 sites, 9 premium paved RV sites with wtr/elec, $24 ($12 with federal senior pass); 63 unpaved with elec/wtr, $18 ($9 with federal senior pass); 30 unpaved without hookups, $12 & $15 ($6 & $7.50 with federal senior pass); 4 sites with wtr hookups, $20 ($10 with federal senior pass); 1 tent site with wtr/elec $24 ($12 with federal senior pass); 24 tent sites without hookups, $12 ($6 with federal senior pass). Premium tent sites with wtr/elec & premium RV sites without hookups, $20 ($10 with federal senior pass). Standard RV sites with 50-amp elec/wtr, $20 ($10 with federal senior pass). Premium sites with 50-amp elec/wtr, $24 ($12 with federal senior pass. RV limit 55'. At reserved sites, 2-night minimum stay required on weekends, 3 nights on holiday weekends. Two picnic shelters for up to 150 people, $40. (931) 864-6388. NRRS. **GPS: 36.53083, -85.16944**

WILLOW GROVE CAMPGROUND

From Oakley, 0.7 mi NE on SR 2260, then 10 mi N & W on SR 294. 5/20-9/6; 14-day limit. 83 sites, 62 with wtr/50-amp elec, $17 & $20, and premium sites $24 ($8.50, $10 & $12 with federal senior pass); 21 basic tent sites, $12 base, premium locations $15 ($6 & $7.50 with federal senior pass); 1 handicap site with wtr/50-amp elec. RV limit 45'. At reserved sites, 2-night minimum stay required on weekends, 3 nights on holiday weekends. Picnic shelter for up to 50 people, $50; 51-100 people, $100; 101-150 people, $150; 151-200 people, $200. Amphitheater. Scuba diving. (931) 823-4285. NRRS. **GPS: 36.5894, -85.34528**

J. PERCY PRIEST LAKE (NV) 5
GPS: 36.1583, -86.6133

This 14,200-acre lake is 10 miles E of Nashville off I-40. Alcohol and off-road vehicles prohibited. Visitor center with exhibits. Campground checkout time 2 p.m. A visitor fee may be charged at the campgrounds. Resource Manager, J. Percy Priest Lake, 3737 Bell Road, Nashville, TN 37214-2660. (615) 889-1975.

ANDERSON ROAD CAMPGROUND

From Nashville, 5 mi E on I-40 to exit 219; 5 mi S on Ferry Pike (becoming Bell Rd); 1 mi E on Smith Spring Rd; 1 mi N on Anderson Rd. 5/15-LD; 14-day limit. 37 sites without hookups (15 pull-through), $12 base, premium sites $14 ($6 & $7 with federal senior pass). RV limit in excess of 65'; 15 pull-through sites. At reserved sites, 2-night minimum stay required on weekends, 3 nights on holiday weekends. 2 picnic shelters with handicap facilities for up to 160 people and 60 vehicles available 4/1-10/29 ($40 reservation fee plus $4 per vehicle day-use fee). Non-campers pay day use fees for boat ramp, picnicking, dump station, beach. (615) 361-1980. NRRS. **GPS: 36.10611, -86.60389**

POOLE KNOBS CAMPGROUND

From Lavergne, SE on US 41, then 2 mi N on Fergus Rd, 4 mi NE on Jones Mill Rd. 5/1-9/30; 14-day limit. 87 sites. 6 basic tent sites, $14 base, $16 at premium locations ($7 & $8 with federal senior pass); 55 RV sites with wtr/50-amp elec, $18 base, $24 at premium locations ($9 & $12 with federal senior pass); 1 tent site with elec/wtr, $18 ($9 with federal senior pass); 23 RV/tent sites without elec, $14 base, $16 at premium locations

($7 & $8 with federal senior pass). RV limit in excess of 65'; 56 pull-through sites. Group camping area for up to 40 people & 12 vehicles, $50. At reserved sites, 2-night minimum stay required on weekends, 3 nights on holiday weekends. (615) 459-6948. NRRS. **GPS: 36.0508, -86.5103**

SEVEN POINTS CAMPGROUND

From I-40 exit 221B, S (right) on Old Hickory Blvd (sign), then E (left) on Bell Rd; 1 mi S (right) on New Hope Rd; 1 mi E (left) on Stewarts Ferry Pike (signs). 4/1-10/30; 14-day limit. 60 sites with wtr/elec, $20 base. $24 at premium locations ($10 & $24 with federal senior pass). RV limit in excess of 65 ft; 4 pull-through sites, 6 handicap sites. At reserved sites, 2-night minimum stay required on weekends, 3 nights on holiday weekends. 2 picnic shelters $40-$120. (615) 889-5198. NRRS. **GPS: 36.1331, -86.5703**

LAKE BARKLEY (NV) 6
GPS: 37.0217, -88.22

This 57,920-acre lake is S of junction I-24 and US 62 and E of Paducah, Kentucky. Visitor center with various exhibits. Resource Manager, Lake Barkley, Box 218, Highway 62, Grand River, KY 42045-0218. (502) 362-4236. See Kentucky listings.

BUMPUS MILLS CAMPGROUND

From Clarksville, 20 mi W on US 79; 10 mi NW SR 120 through Bumpus Mills; W on Tobaccoport Road (sign); 1 mi of gravel rd (continue straight at "Y" and sign, down hill). 5/7-9/6; 14-day limit. 15 sites with wtr/elec (2 pull-through), $18 base, $20 at premium locations ($9 & $10 with federal senior pass). RV limit 65'; 2 pull-through sites. At reserved sites, 2-night minimum stay on weekends, 3 nights on holiday weekends. (931) 232-8831. NRRS. **GPS: 36.6197, -87.8831**

OLD HICKORY LAKE (NV) 7
GPS: 36.295, -86.6117

This 22,500-acre lake is 2 miles W of Hendersonville, S of US 31E and 10 miles NE of Nashville. Visitor center displays, exhibits and video and interpretive programs. Visitors may by charged day use fee at the campgrounds. Resource Manager, Old Hickory Lake, No. 5 Power Plant Road, Hendersonville, TN 37075-3465. (615) 822-4846/847-2395.

CAGES BEND CAMPGROUND

From Hendersonville, 5.5 mi NE on SR 31E; SE on Benders Ferry Rd (signs). 4/1-10/31; 14-day limit. 43 sites with wtr/elec, \$20 base, \$24 at premium locations (\$10 & \$12 with federal senior pass). RV limit in excess of 65 ft; 1 pull-through site, 2 handicap sites. At reserved sites, 2-night minimum stay required on weekends, 3 nights on holiday weekends. (615) 824-4989. NRRS. **GPS: 36.30389, -86.51528**

CEDAR CREEK CAMPGROUND

From jct with CR 109, 6 mi W on US 70, then N. 4/1-10/31; 14-day limit. 59 sites wtr/elec, \$20 base, \$24 at premium locations (\$10 & \$12 with federal senior pass). RV limit in excess of 65'. At reserved sites, 2-night minimum stay required/weekends, 3 nights/holiday weekends. Picnic shelter up to 50 people, \$35. (615) 754-4947. NRRS.
GPS: 36.27861, -86.50861

TEXAS

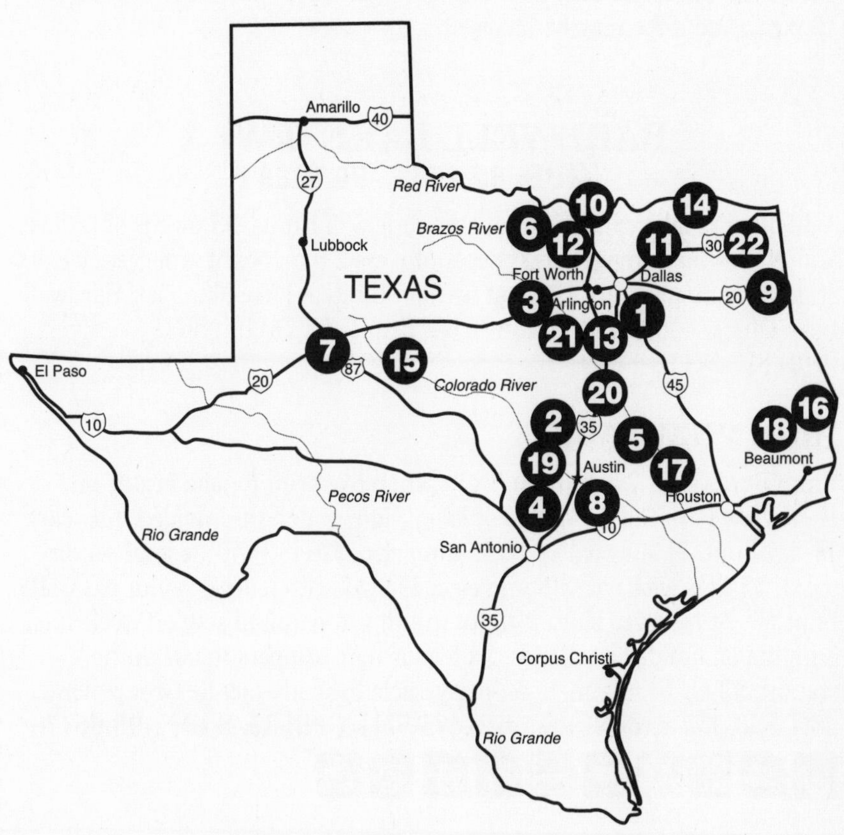
Amarillo
40
27
Red River
Brazos River
Lubbock
TEXAS
Fort Worth
Dallas
Arlington
30
20
El Paso
20
87
Colorado River
45
10
35
Austin
Beaumont
Houston
Pecos River
Rio Grande
San Antonio
10
35
Corpus Christi
Rio Grande
1
2
3
4
5
6
7
8
9
10
11
12
13
14
15
16
17
18
19
20
21
22

TEXAS

State Capital: **Austin**
Nickname: **Lone Star State**
Statehood Year: **1845**

28TH STATE

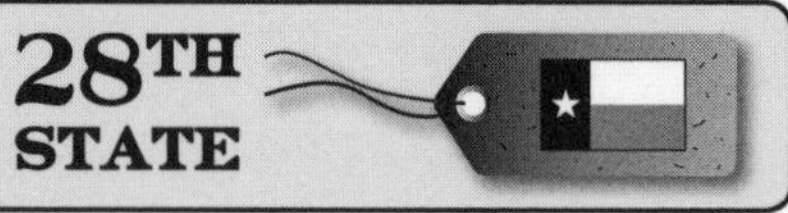

Fort Worth District - For non campers there is a fee charged for the use of the dump station, boat launching and for showers. Visitor's to 10 p.m., and a fee may be charged.

BARDWELL LAKE (FW) 1
GPS: 32.2667, -96.6333

A 3,500-acre lake with 25 mi of shoreline S of Ennis, 35 mi SE of Dallas and W of I-45. Campground checkout time 2 p.m. Night emergency exits at gated campgrounds. Ground fires prohibited. Lake Manager, Bardwell Lake Office, 4000 Observation Drive, Ennis, TX 75119-9563. (972) 875-5711.

HIGH VIEW PARK

From Bardwell, 1.7 mi NE on SR 34, then SW prior to lake bridge on High View Park Rd; on W side of lake. Night-time exit provided. All year; 14-day limit. 11 sites with wtr/50-amp elec, $16 ($8 with federal senior pass); 28 sites with wtr/30-amp elec, $14 ($7 with federal senior pass). RV limit 65'. At reserved sites, 2-night minimum required stay on weekends, 3 nights on holiday weekends. $4 fee for non-campers to use dump station; $3 for boat launch; $4 per vehicle to swim, picnic. Group picnic area, $50. 155 acres NRRS. (972) 875-5711. **GPS: 32.27139, -96.66778**

MOTT PARK

From Bardwell, 1 mi NE on SR 34, then SE (left) 1.6 mi on FM 985. southeast. Group camping area for up to 100 people & 31 vehicles, $80. Night exit provided. 4/1-9/30; 14-day limit. 33 sites with wtr/elec, $16 ($8 with federal senior pass); 7 sites without hookups, $14 ($7 with federal senior pass). RV limit 65'; 14 pull-through sites. Picnic shelter for up to 100 people & 31 vehicles, $80. Non-campers pay day use fees:

boat launch, $3; swimming $4 per vehicle, dump station $4. At reserved sites, 2-night minimum stay required on weekends, 3 nights on holiday weekends. 270 acres. NRRS. **GPS: 32.25444, -96.66694**

WAXAHACHIE CREEK PARK

From Bardwell, 1.2 mi NE on SR 24, then 1.6 mi NW (left) on FM 985. All year; 14-day limit. Group camping area $110. 69 sites with wtr/30-amp elec (including 4 horse sites), $16 base, premium sites $18($8 & $9 with federal senior pass); 7 sites without hookups, $14 ($7 with federal senior pass). RV limit 65'; 14 pull-through sites. Picnic shelter for up to 200 people & 100 vehicles, $120. At reserved sites, 2-night minimum stay required on weekends, 3 nights on holiday weekends. Boat rentals nearby. Nature trail, equestrian trail. Non-campers pay day use fees: $3 boat ramp, $3 equestrian trail, $4 dump station. Night exit provided. NRRS. **GPS: 32.2931, -96.6939**

BELTON LAKE (FW) 2
GPS: 31.1, 97.4833

This 12,300-acre lake is 5 mi NW of Belton on FM 2271; adjacent to Fort Hood Army Base and N of Austin. Campground checkout time 1 p.m. Restored historic bridge; nature area with hiking trail; wildlife viewing areas; visitor center; interpretive programs. Non-campers pay $4 vehicle day use fee for picnicking, beaches, dump station; $3 for boat ramps. Resource Manager, Little River Project Office, 3110 FM 2271, Belton, TX 76513-6522. (254) 939-2461.

CEDAR RIDGE PARK

From jct with SR 317 N of Belton, 2 mi NW on SR 36; 1 mi SW on Cedar Ridge Park Rd. Park access codes provided to campers for late entry. All year; 14-day limit. 72 sites with wtr/electric, 1 double site ($36), 8 screened shelters ($30). Tent sites $16 ($8 with federal senior pass); RV sites with wtr/50-amp elec, $20 ($10 with federal senior pass); RV/

tent sites with wtr/30-amp elec, $18 ($9 with federal senior pass). RV limit in excess of 65'; 2 pull-through sites, 49 handicap sites. For Turkey Roost group camping area, see listing below. At reserved sites, 2-night minimum stay requied on weekends, 3 nights on holiday weekends. 2 picnic shelters: Coveside, for up to 80 people & 40 vehicles; Sunset, for up to 100 people & 40 vehicles, both $40-$70. Handicap accessible swimming area & playground. Center for camper parties & meetings. Free wireless Internet at activity bldg. NRRS. **GPS: 31.16722, -97.44722**

IRON BRIDGE PARK

From jct of FM 2909 & SR 317, 9 mi W on SR 36, then N on Iron Bridge Rd. 5 sites, free. Open all year; 14-day limit. No drkg wtr. Isolated. Picnic area. **GPS: 31.284126, -97.479306**

LIVE OAK RIDGE PARK

From jct with SR 317, 1.7 mi NW on FM 2305, on right. All year; 14-day limit. 48 sites with wtr/elec, covered tbls, grills; 14 handicap sites. $18 for 30-amp elec, $20 for 50-amp ($9 & $10 with federal senior pass). RV limit in excess of 65'. At reserved sites, 2-night minimum stay required on weekends, 3 nights on holiday weekends. Amphitheater, center for parties & meetings, free wireless Internet at activity bldg. NRRS. **GPS: 31.11639, -97.47389**

OWL CREEK PARK

From jct with SR 317, 6.5 mi NW on SR 36, across lake bridge, then 1 mi W at "Y" and S. 10 free sites. No drkg wtr. Picnicking. All year; 14-day limit.

TURKEY ROOST GROUP CAMPGROUND

At Cedar Ridge Park. Horseshoe pits, picnic shelter, group camping only. Must be by reservation made in person at the Little River Project Office. Contact the office for maximum number of recreational vehicles and tents permitted. 6 sites, 2 double sites with 50am elec. Friday-Sunday nights, $175; Monday-Thursday nights $100. Open all year. NRRS.

WESTCLIFF PARK

From jct with SR 317 N of Belton, 3.7 mi NW FM 439 (Lake Rd); 0.2 mi NW on Sparta Rd, then NE on Westcliff Park Rd. All year; 14-day limit. 31 sites with covered tbls, grills, lantern poles, 27 with wtr/elec, 4 basic tent only sites. Basic tent sites $10 ($5 with federal senior pass); sites with wtr/elec $16 ($8 with federal senior pass). RV limit 65'; 20 pull-through sites, 4 handicap sites with elec, 8 handicap sites with wtr/elec. At reserved sites, 2-night minimum stay required on weekends, 3 nights on holiday weekends. Picnic shelter, handicap accessible swimming area. NRRS. **GPS: 31.12167, -97.51917**

WHITE FLINT PARK

From jct with SR 317, 5.5 mi NW on SR 36, across bridge, N side. Access codes provided to registered campers for late night entry. All year; 14-day limit. 13 sites with 50-amp elec/wtr with covered tbls, grills, $20 ($10 with federal senior pass. 6 handicap sites, 12 screened sites ($30). RV limit 60'. At reserved sites, 2-night minimum stay required on weekends. NRRS. **GPS: 31.23111, -97.47222**

WINKLER PARK

From jct with SR 317, 5.5 mi NW on SR 36; exit right (NE) 2 mi past White Flint Park. All year; 14-day limit. 14 semi-primitive sites with wtr hookups, $10 ($5 with federal senior pass). RV limit 35'. Register, pay fees at nearby White Flint Park. **GPS: 31.046143, -97.511963**

BENBROOK LAKE (FW) 3
GPS: 32.65, -97.45

3,770-acre lake 12 mi SW of Forth Worth on S side of Benbrook. Campground checkout time 2 p.m. Non-campers pay day use fees of $3 for boat ramps, $2 showers, $4 dump stations Resource Mgr., Benbrook Lake, P. O. Box 26619, Ft. Worth, TX 76126-0619. (817) 292-2400.

HOLIDAY CAMPGROUND

From Benbrook & I-20 exit 429A, 5.7 mi SW on US 377; 1.7 mi E on FM 1187 (Park Rod). 43 sites with 30-amp elec/wtr, $20 ($10 with federal senior pass); 31 sites with 30-50 amp elec/wtr, $20 ($10 with federal senior pass); 5 sites with enclosed screen shelters & 30-50 amp elec/wtr, $30 ($15 with federal senior pass); 26 sites without hookups; 1 equestrian site without elec, $10; 18 basic tent sites, $10 ($5 with federal senior pass); 7 walk-in tent sites, $10 ($5 with federal senior pass). RV sites have covered tbls, cookers. RV limit in excess of 65'; 40 pull-through sites. At reserved sites, 2-night minimum stay required on weekends, 3 nights on holiday weekends. Accessible fishing pier, horse trail access, phones. Fees for non-campers: $3 per vehicle for boat launch, swimming beach, picnicking; $2 for showers, $4 for dump station. Horse rentals nearby. NRRS. **GPS: 32.61833, -97.4975**

MUSTANG PARK - BEAR CREEK CAMPGROUND

From Benbrook & I-20 exit 429A, 6.4 mi SW on US 377; 1.4 mi SE on FM 1187; 1.7 mi N CR 1042. All year; 14-day limit. 40 sites with wtr/elec (6 with 50-amp service, 2 with sewers, $22 ($11 with federal senior pass); 30-amp sites $20 ($10 with federal senior pass). Sites have covered tbls, cookers. Group camping at 6 sites with wtr/elec, $100. Picnic shelter for up to 50 people & 11 vehicles. Night-time exit provided. RV limit in excess of 65'; 10 pull-through sites. Fees for non-campers: $3 per vehicle for boat launch, swimming beach, picnicking; $2 for showers, $4 for dump station. At reserved sites, 2-night minimum stay required on weekends, 3 nights on holiday weekends. NRRS. **GPS: 32.59972, -97.5**

MUSTANG POINT CAMPGROUND

Adjacent to Bear Creek Campground at Mustang Park. No designated sites, primitive area; 9 areas have covered tbls, but open shoreline camping for tents & RVs. 4/1-9/30; 14-day limit $10 ($5 with federal senior pass). Campers can use showers at other campgrounds for $2.

ROCKY CREEK CAMPGROUND

From Benbrook, S on US 377; 7 mi SE on FM 1187; 3.6 mi N on CR 1089; at jct with CR 1150, exit S to park. All year; 14-day limit. 11 sites with covered tbls, nearby wtr. $10 ($5 with federal senior pass). Open picnicking. **GPS: 32.602539, -97.457275**

WESTCREEK CIRCLE - BEAR CREEK CAMPGROUND

From Benbrook & I20 exit 429A, 6. mi SW on US 377; 1 mi SE on FM 1187; SE 1 mi to Ben Day-Murrin Rd (CR 1025), then E 1 mi to the park. Limited-development camping at Bear Creek shoreline. Free primitive camping, including equestrian camping (future equestrian facilities planned). 1 pit toilet, no drkg wtr. Trailhead to 14 mi of hiking & equestrian trails. Fee for use of showers, dump station, boat launch, beach at Bear Creek Campground.

CANYON LAKE (FW) 4
GPS: 29.8667, -98.2

8,230-acre lake with 80 mi of shoreline, located NE of San Antonio and 16 mi NW of New Braunfels off FM 306. Campground checkout time 2 p.m. Non-campers pay $4 day use fee for dump station, picnicking, beaches; $3 for boat ramp. Resource Manager, Canyon Lake, 601 COE Road, Canyon Lake, TX 78133-4129. (830) 964-3341.

CANYON PARK

From Canyon City, 3.2 mi NW on FM 306, then SW (right) on Canyon Park Rd; on NW shore of Canyon Lake. 4/1-9/30; 14-day limit. 150 primitive sites, $8 Mon-Thurs, $10 weekend nights ($4 & $5 with federal senior pass). Pit toilets. Picnic shelters $35 Mon-Thurs,$75 on weekends. Boat rentals nearby. **GPS: 29.896484, -98.234375**

CRANES MILLS PARK

From Startzville, 2.8 mi N. All year; 14-day limit. 46 primitive sites with tbls & cookers. $8 Mo-Thurs, $10 weekend nights ($4 & $5 with federal senior pass). Some sites open 10/1-2/28. Boat rentals nearby. No night-time entry or exit. Campground was closed in 2010 for renovations; status for 2011 uncertain. **GPS: 29.889648, -98.291992**

NORTH PARK

From Canyon City, 1.2 mi NW on FM 306, then 1 mi SE, near dam. Open 7 a.m. to 10 p.m., generally 3/1-10/30 (but sites were closed by 10/1 in 2010). 19 primitive sites. Mon-Thursday, sites are $8; Fri-Sun, $12 ($4 & $6 with federal senior pass). Divers welcome. **GPS: 29.874268, -98.205566**

POTTER'S CREEK PARK

From Canyon City, 6.2 mi NW on FM 306; 2 mi S on Potters's Creek Rd. All year; 14-day limit. Park open 7am-10pm. Five camping loops containing 114 RV/tent sites with wtr/elec hookups, covered tbls, fire rings, standng grills, $18 ($9 with federal senior pass); double sites $36, triple sites $54. 1 loop containing 10 tent only sites with covered tbls, fire rings, standing grills, elec/wtr hookups, $14 ($7 with federal senior pass). 7 screened shelters, $34. 50 handicap sites. Picnic shelter $50 Mon-Thurs, $100 Fri-Sun. RV limit 60'. Fishing pier, campfire programs, courtesy dock, interpretive programs, recycle station. NRRS 4/1-9/30. No day use. **GPS: 29.90472, -98.27306**

GRANGER LAKE (FW) 5

GPS: 30.7033, -97.3167

This 4,400-acre lake is 30 mi NE of Austin off SR 95 and 6.5 mi E of Granger on FM 971, then 1 mi S on local road. Non-campers pay day use fees of $4 for boat ramps, beaches, picnicking, hiking, horseback riding, fishing, dump stations. Resource Manager, Granger Lake, 3100 Granger Dam Road, Granger, TX 76530-5067. (512) 859-2668.

FOX BOTTOM CAMPING

Hike in from W Trailhead on CR 496 on the Comanche Bluff Hiking Trail, which starts at the park and ends at Taylor park; or boat-in from Taylor Park (paying boat ramp fee for number of days prior to departure); or 0.5 mi downstream from Box 7 primitive boat launch via jon boat or canoe. All year; 14-day limit. 8 free primitive sites, each with tent pad, lantern hanger, fire pit; no drkg wtr available; 2 central tbls & fire pit; compost toilet; group fire ring. Advance phone registration required (512-859-2668).

TAYLOR CAMPGROUND

From Circleville at jct with Highway 95, 9 mi NE on FM 1331, then NW. 3/1-9/30; 14-day limit. 48 sites with wtr/elec, $18 (4 double sites, $22); $9 & $11 with federal senior pass. RV limit 50'. At reserved sites, 2-night minimum stay required on weekends, 3 nights on holiday weekends. Comanche Bluff Hiking Trail starts at the park. Non-campers pay $4 day use fees for boat ramp, beach, picnicking, hiking, horseback riding, fishing, dump station. NRRS. **GPS: 30.66667, -97.36667**

WILLIS CREEK CAMPGROUND

From Granger at jct with Hwy 95, 0.8 mi E on FM 971; 4 mi SE on CR 348; NE on CR 346. All year; 14-day limit. 27 sites with wtr/elec, $18 ($9 with federal senior pass); 4 full hookup sites, $22 ($11 with federal senior pass); 5 primitive horse and horse trailer sites near 7-mi trailhead (for trail information call 512- 859-2668), $10 ($5 with federal senior pass);

1 group camping area with elec/wtr, $50. RV limit 50'. Picnic shelter for up to 50 people & 20 vehicles, $50. At reserved sites, 2-night minimum stay required on weekends, 3 nights on holiday weekends. Non-campers pay $4 day use fees for boat ramp, beach, picnicking, hiking, horseback riding, fishing, dump station. NRRS. **GPS: 30.69583, -97.40139**

WILSON H. FOX CAMPGROUND

From Taylor Park, 1 mi NE on FM 1331, then NW; adjacent to S side of dam. All year; 14-day limit. 58 sites with wtr/electric, including 5 group day use & camping sites ($34). Sites with 30-amp elec/wtr, $18 ($9 with federal senior pass); 50-amp elec/wtr, $22 ($11 with federal senior pass); double sites $30 ($15 with federal senior pass). 1 handicap site. RV limit 50'. Screened picnic shelter $50. Fish cleaning station. At reserved sites, 2-night minimum stay required on weekends, 3 nights on holiday weekends. Non-campers pay $4 day use fees for boat ramp, beach, picnicking, hiking, horseback riding, fishing, dump station. NRRS. **GPS: 30.70083, -97.34167**

GRAPEVINE LAKE (FW) 6
GPS: 32.9667, -97.05

This 7,380-acre lake is just northwest of Grapevine (Dallas-Fort Worth Airport) off SR 26, 23 mi NE of Fort Worth. Golf course below the dam. Alcoholic beverages prohibited. ORV area and an equestrian trail are provided. Former Corps campgrounds Silver Lake (now Vineyards Campground) and Twin Cove have been leased to commercial interests. Camping provided only at Murrell Park, and it is open only for primitive tent camping. Non-campers pay day use fee at boat ramp Resource Manager, Grapevine Lake, 110 Fairway Drive, Grapevine, TX 76051-3495. (817) 481-4541.

MURRELL PARK

From Grapevine at jct with SR 121, 4.5 mi N on FM 2499; 0.2 mi W (sign) on FM 3040; 0.4 mi W on McKamey Creek Rd, then S on Simmons Rd. All year; 14-day limit. Group camping area (some free for use by boy scouts, church groups, etc.). 22 primitive tent sites. $10 ($5 with federal senior pass). Pit toilets. **GPS: 32.9975, -97.08917**

HORDS CREEK LAKE (FW) 7
GPS: 31.85, -99.5667

This 510-acre lake is 8.7 mi W of Coleman and 55 mi S of Abilene. Resource Manager, Hords Creek Lake, HCR 75, Box 33, Coleman, TX 76834-9320. (915) 625-2322. Note: Due to low water levels, boat ramps except for one at Friendship Park were closed in 2010. Status unknown for 2011. Open fires in pits or uncovered grill areas prohibited.

FLAT ROCK I & II PARK

From Coleman, 8.7 mi W on Hwy 153; S across dam, then W to park (signs); on N side of lake. 5/1-9/30; 14-day limit. 39 sites with 30-amp elec/wtr, $16 ($8 with federal senior pass), $20 at premium locations ($10 with federal senior pass); 4 sites with 30-amp elec/wtr/sewer $22 ($11 with federal senior pass); 3 sites with screened shelters, $22-26; 10 sites with 50-amp elec/wtr, $20 ($10 with federal senior pass); 50-amp elec at premium locations, $22 ($11 with federal senior pass). 2 double sites with wtr/elec, $32 ($16 with federal senior pass); 1 double sites with full hookups, $44 ($22 with federal senior pass). RV limit in excess of 65'; 10 pull-through sites. Two group areas with shelters, $100-$130. Fish cleaning station. At reserved sites, 2-night minimum stay required on weekends, 3 nights holiday weekends. NRRS. **GPS: 31.82611, -99.56583**

LAKESIDE I & II PARK

From Coleman, 8 mi W on Hwy 153 past Friendship Park, then S, following signs. All year; 14-day limit. 44 sites with 30-amp elec/wtr, $16 ($8 with federal senior pass), $20 at premium locations ($10 with federal senior pass); 16 sites with 30-amp elec/wtr/sewer $22 ($11 with federal senior pass); 3 sites with screened shelters, $22-$26; 8 sites with 50-amp elec/wtr, $20 ($10 with federal senior pass); 50-amp elec at premium locations, $22 ($11 with federal senior pass); 5 double sites with full hookups, $44 ($22 with federal senior pass). 5 Five group camping areas with shelter -- one for up to 80 people and 12 RVs, $100; a second for up to 80 people and 8 RVs, $120; a third for up to 80 pelple and 12 RVs, $150, a fourth for up to 80 people and 12 RVs, is $130, and the fifth for up to 200 people and 28 RVs, $260. Fish cleaning station, horseshoe pits, handicap accessible fishing area. RV limit in excess of 65'; 9 pull-through sites. At reserved sites, 2-night minimum stay required on weekends, 3 nights on holiday weekends. NRRS. **GPS: 31.84667, -99.57944**

LAKE GEORGETOWN (FW) 8
GPS: 30.675, -97.725

This 1,310-acre lake is 25 mi N of Austin off I-35 and 2 mi W of Georgetown on FM 2338. Fee at developed campgrounds for extra vehicles. Campground checkout time 2 p.m. Non-campers pay day use fee of $4 for picnicking, boat ramps, dump stations. Resource Manager, Lake Georgetown, 500 Cedar Breaks Road, Georgetown, TX 78268-4901. (512) 930-5253.

CEDAR BREAKS CAMPGROUND

From I-35, 3.5 mi W on FM 2338; 2 mi S on Cedar Breaks Rd, following signs. Late night emergency exit provided. All year; 14-day limit. 59 sites with wtr/elec, covered tbl, $24 ($12 with federal senior pass). RV limit 55'. 2 picnic shelters for up to 25 people, $25. At reserved sites, 2-night minimum stay required on weekends, 3 nights on holiday weekends. Note: Campground was closed indefinitely beginning in 2010 due to extensive electrical upgrade work; only boat ramp and day use areas open. NRRS. **GPS: 30.68167, -97.78633**

CEDAR HOLLOW CAMP

Access either by boat or hike in on the Good Water Hiking Trail; between mileposts 4 & 5. Primitive area, free. Tbl, fire ring, lantern stand, pit toilet, no drkg wtr. Open all year; 14-day limit.

JIM HOGG CAMPGROUND

From lake's project office, 2.5 mi NW on FM 2338, then 2 mi S on Jim Hogg Rd. Night exit provided. All year; 14-day limit. 148 sites with wtr/elec, $18 (10 double sites, $26); sites $9 & 13 with federal senior pass. 5 screened shelters with 4 beds, bunk type, $30. RV limit 55'. At reserved sites, 2-night minimum stay on weekends, 3 nights on holiday weekends. Phone. Note: Campground was closed indefinitely beginning in 2010 due to extensive electrical upgrade work; only boat ramp and day use areas open. (512) 819-9046). NRRS. **GPS: 30.68167, -97.73306**

RUSSELL PARK

From lake's project office, 3 mi NW on FM Rd 2338 (past exit to Jim Hogg Park); 0.7 mi W on FM 3405; 1 mi W on Rt 262. All year; 14-day limit (but park was closed for the season on 10/1/2010). 16 basic sites without hookups, $12 ($6 with federal senior pass); 2 screened shelters without elec, $24 ($12 with federal senior pass); three group camping areas for up to 50 people, $75. **GPS: 30.6775, -97.75917**

SAWYER CAMP

Access by boat or hike in on the Good Water Hiking Trail; between mileposts 6 & 7. Primitive tent area, free. Tbls, fire rings, lantern stands, pit toilet, no drkg wtr. Open all year; 14-day limit.

TEJAS CAMPGROUND

NW of lake's project office. From jct with SR 2338, 5.5 mi W on FM 3405, then SE on CR 258. All year; 14-day limit. $6. 12 primitive tent only sites, 3 walk-in/boat-in sites. Fire rings, tbls, drkg wtr, pit toilets. Group camping for up to 25 people, $15. Register at Russell Park gatehouse.
GPS: 30.687886, -97.816941

WALNUT SPRINGS CAMP

Access by water or hike in on the Good Water Hiking Trail; between mileposts 15 & 16. Free primitive tent area. Tbls, fire rings, lantern stands, pit toilet, no drkg wtr. Open all year; 14-day limit.

LAKE O' THE PINES (FW) 9
GPS: 32.765, -94.967

This 19,780-acre lake is 9 mi W of Jefferson and 25 mi NW of Marshall. Campground checkout time 2 p.m. Fee campgrounds have emergency night-time exits. Operation of ORV, golf carts and motorized scooters prohibited in parks unless properly licensed in the state. Activities include watching wintering bald eagles. Non-campers pay day use fees: $3 for boat ramps, $4 for dump stations, picnicking, beaches. Visitor center Resource Manager, Lake O' The Pines, 2669 FM 726, Jefferson, TX 75657. (903) 665-2336.

ALLEY CREEK CAMPGROUND

From Jefferson, 4 mi NW on SR 49; 12 mi W on FM 729, past jct with FM 726, then S following signs. 3/1-9/30; 14-day limit. 49 RV sites with elec/wtr, $22 ($11 with federal senior pass), double RV sites $38 ($19 with federal senior pass); 30 tent sites, $12 base ($6 with federal senior pass), $14 at premium locations ($7 with federal senior pass); 11 RV sites with tent pads, $18-$20 ($9-10 with federal senior pass; group camping area for 12 RVs, $150. RV limit in excess of 65'. At reserved sites, 2-night minimum stay required on weekends, 3 nights on holiday weekends. (903) 755-2637. NRRS. **GPS: 32.79944, -94.59194**

BRUSHY CREEK CAMPGROUND

From Jefferson, 4 mi NW on SR 49; 3.5 mi W on FM 729; 4.8 mi S on FM 726 past dam, on right (sign). 3/1-11/30; 14-day limit. 79 sites (13 pull-through). 25 basic tent sites, $10 base, $14 at premium locations ($5-7 with federal senior pass); 12 tent sites with wtr/elec, $16 ($8 with federal senior pass). 15 RV sites with wtr/elec, $24 ($26 at premium sites); with federal senior pass, $12 & $13. 15 standard RV sites with wtr/elec, $24 ($12 with federal senior pass); premium sites $26 ($13 with senior pass). Double RV sites with wtr/elec, $36. RV limit in excess of 65'. At reserved sites, 2-night minimum stay required on weekends, 3 nights on holiday weekends. (903) 777-3491. NRRS. **GPS: 32.74278, -94.53583**

BUCKHORN CREEK CAMPGROUND

From Jefferson, 4 mi NW on SR 49; 3.5 mi W on FM 729; 2.4 mi S on FM 726, on right (sign) before the dam. 3/1-9/30; 14-day limit. 77 sites, 39 with wtr/elec (13 pull-through), 38 basic tent only sites, 2 double sites with 50-amp elec/wtr. Tent sites $14 ($7 with federal senior pass). RV sites with elec/wtr, $20-$22 ($10-11 with federal senior pass; double sites $36-38. RV limit in excess of 65'. At reserved sites, 2-night minimum stay required on weekends, 3 nights on holiday weekends. (903) 665-8261. NRRS. **GPS: 32.75528, -94.49444**

CEDAR SPRINGS CAMPGROUND

From Jefferson, NW on SR 49, W on FM 729, S on SR 155 (sign), across lake on left. 28 sites. Free. All year; 14-day limit. Pit toilets, drkg wtr.

HURRICANE CREEK CAMPGROUND

From Jefferson, NW on SR 49; 2.5 mi W on FM 729 past FM 726, then S following signs. All year; 14-day limit 23 sites. Free. Pit toilets, drkg wtr.

JOHNSON CREEK CAMPGROUND

From Jefferson, 4 mi NW on SR 49; 8.5 mi W on FM 729, on left. All year; 14-day limit. 12 basic tent sites (5 walk-to), $14 ($7 with federal senior pass), 10 tent sites with elec, $16 ($8 with federal senior pass). RV sites with elec/wtr, $20-$22 ($10-$11 with federal senior pass); premium RV sites, $24 & $26 ($12 & $13 with federal senior pass). Group camping area with 12 elec sites, $150. Picnic shelter for up to 200 people and 1 vehicle, $75. Amphitheater available. RV limit in excess of 65'. At reserved sites, 2-night minimum stay on weekends, 3 nights on holiday weekends. Fish cleaning station. (903) 755-2435. NRRS. **GPS: 32.78667, -94.55056**

LAKE TEXOMA (TU) 10
GPS: 33.8333, -96.5667

This 89,000-acre lake is 5 mi NW of Denison on SR 91 and 88 mi N of Dallas/Ft. Worth on the Oklahoma state line. ORV prohibited. The Corps operates 10 campgrounds with more than 600 campsites. Lake Manager, Texoma Lake, 351 Corps Road, Denison, TX 75020. (903) 465-4490. See Oklahoma listings.

DAM SITE CAMPGROUND

From Denison, 5 mi N on SR 91; on S side of the dam. All year; 14-day limit. 30 sites. 9 sites without elec, $15 ($7.50 with federal senior pass); 21 sites with wtr/elec, $20 ($12 with federal senior pass). During 11/1-3/31, some sites open with fees $12 ($6 with federal senior pass) and reduced facilities (elec & 1 frost-free wtr faucet available). RV limit in excess of 65'. **GPS: 33.726181, -96.543327**

JUNIPER POINT CAMPGROUND

From Madill, 17 mi S on SR 99, across lake bridge, then E. All year; 14-day limit. 70 sites, 44 RV sites with wtr/elec, $20 & $22 ($10 & $11 with federal senior pass; 26 basic tent sites, $15 ($7.50 with federal senior pass). RV limit 50'. During 10/1-3/31, E Juniper area is closed, but W Juniper open; elec/wtr sites $20 in Oct; elec with 1 frost-free faucet $12 11/1-3/31 (those fees $10 & $6 with federal senior pass). Picnic shelter for up to 100 people & 20 vehicles, $50. (903) 523-4022. NRRS (4/1-9/30). Note: New 50-amp elec sites added for 2011. **GPS: 33.85972, -96.83194**

PRESTON BEND RECREATION AREA

From Pottsboro, 9 mi N on SR 120, on right. 4/1-10/31. 38 sites. 26 RV sites with wtr/elec, $20 ($10 with federal senior pass); 12 basic tent sites, $15 ($7.50 with federal senior pass). RV limit in excess of 65'. Picnic shelter. (903) 786-8408. NRRS 4/1-9/30. **GPS: 33.87833, -96.64722**

LAVON LAKE (FW) 11
GPS: 33.0333, -96.4833

A 21,400-acre lake 30 mi NE of Dallas and 3 mi E of Wylie off SR 78. Alcohol prohibited. Besides the campgrounds below, the Corp also leases Collin Park to Collin Park Marina; it has 45 sites and fees ranging from $15-$25. Non-campers pay day use fees: $3 at boat ramps, $4 for dump stations, beach, picnicking. Resource Manager, Lavon Lake, 3375 Skyview Drive, Wylie, TX 75098-0429. (972) 442-3014/3141.

CLEAR LAKE PARK

From Princeton, 9 mi S on FM 982 (changes into CR 735). 4/1-9/30; 14-day limit. 23 sites with wtr/elec, $18 ($9 with federal senior pass). 1 handicap site. RV limit in excess of 65'. At reserved sites, 2-night minimum stay required on weekends, 3 nights on holiday weekends. Picnic shelter for up to 200 people & 1 vehicle, $100; it is equipped with 12 tbls, 1 large cooker, 3 small cookers, fire ring, elec/wtr, restrooms, open area for sports or games. Handicap accessible fishing area; 18 picnic sites. NRRS. **GPS: 33.05528, -96.48194**

EAST FORK PARK

From Wylie, E on SR 98; N on FM 389; right at fork to camp. All year; 14-day limit. 50 sites with elec/wtr, $18 ($9 with federal senior pass); 11 equestrian sites with 30 & 50-amp elec/wtr, $18 ($9 with federal senior pass); 12 tent sites with wtr, $10 ($5 with federal senior pass). Group camping area with picnic shelter for up to 175 people and 6 sites with wtr/elec, $130. RV limit 55'. At reserved sites, 2-night minimum stay required on weekends, 3 nights on holiday weekends. NRRS. **GPS: 33.03889, -96.51028**

LAKELAND PARK

From Princeton, 6.8 mi E on US 380; 4.1 mi S on SR 78, access W. 4/1-9/30; 14-day limit. 32 primitive tent only sites, $8 ($4 with federal senior pass). Picnic shelter $100. **GPS: 33.103549, -96.442971**

LAVONIA PARK

From Wylie, 7.5 mi E on SR 78; N & W on CR 486 (Lake Rd); on E side of dam. All year; 14-day limit. 34 sites with wtr/elec, $18 ($9 with federal senior pass); 15 tent only sites, $10 ($5 with federal senior pass). RV limit 60'. At reserved sites, 2-night minimum stay on weekends, 3 nights on holiday weekends. NRRS. **GPS: 33.03778, -96.44556**

LITTLE AVALON CAMPGROUND

Located at the dam on the W side. All year; 14-day limit. Group camping area with 13 tent only sites, $30. Tbls with canopies, cookers, toilets **GPS: 33.034555, -96.490812**

LEWISVILLE LAKE (FW) 12
GPS: 33.0667, -97.0167

A 28,980-acre lake just N of and adjacent to Lewisville (E of Mill St and I-35E) and NW of Dallas. ORV prohibited. Campground checkout time 2 p.m. Observation drive-through of fee parks is not permitted on weekends from Easter through Labor Day weekend. Hickory Creek Campground no longer part of the National Recreation Reservation

Service (NRRS). The Corps has leased camping areas to other entities and companies. They include Lewisville Lake Environmental Learning Center ($10 for primitive camping, plus $5 per person day use fee); Smithville's Lake Park, $16 for wtr/elec sites ($8 for seniors), $18 premium site ($9 seniors); Pilot Knoll Park at Highland Village; Willow Grove Park, Lake Dallas ($11 primitive sites, $20 wtr/elec); Hidden Cove Park, The Colony. Resource Manager, Lewisville Lake, 1801 N Mill Street, Lewisville, TX 75067-1821. (469) 645-9100.

HICKORY CREEK CAMPGROUND

From Lewisville, 4 mi N on I-35E, across lake bridge, then exit 457B (from the N, use exit 458) toward Lake Dallas; take overpass W over I-35E; 0.2 mi W on Turbeville Rd; 0.5 mi S on Pt. Vista Rd, on right. All year; 14-day limit. 131 sites (10 pull-through, 33 handicap). 10 primitive walk-to tent sites, $10 ($5 with federal senior pass); 30-amp elec/wtr sites $16 ($8 with federal senior pass); 50-amp elec/wtr sites $18 ($9 with federal senior pass). Group camping area with 20 sites & up to 80 people. Amphitheater. Night-time exit available. RV limit 65'. At reserved sites, 2-night minimum stay required on weekends, 3 nights on holiday weekends. Non-campers pay $3 day use fee for boat ramp. (940) 497-2902. NRRS. **GPS: 33.10389, -97.04333**

NAVARRO MILLS LAKE (FW) 13
GPS: 31.95, -96.7

This 5,070-acre lake is 71 mi S of Dallas and 11 mi SW of Corsicana off SR 31. Campground checkout time 1 p.m. ORV prohibited. Resource Manager, Navarro Mills Lake, 1175 Farm to Market Road 677, Purdon, TX 76679. (254) 578-1058/1431.

LIBERTY HILL CAMPGROUND

From Dawson at jct with SR 31, 4 mi NW on FM 709, on right; on S shore of lake. All year; 14-day limit. 100 sites, 92 with wtr/electric (6 full hookups, 3 double sites, 24 pull-through); 2 sites without elec; 1 basic tent site, 5 overnight screened shelters with elec. During 11/1-2/28, basic tent sites and RV sites without elec $12 ($6 with federal senior pass); RV sites with elec/wtr $14 ($7 with federal senior pass) & double sites $28 ($14 with federal senior pass); screened overnight shelters with elec $22. During peak season of 3/1-10/31, basic tent sites & RV sites without elec $16 ($8 with federal senior pass); RV sites with elec/wtr $18 ($9 with federal senior pass) & double sites $36 ($18 with senior pass); screened overnight shelters $26. RV limit in excess of 65'. At reserved sites, 2-night minimum stay required on weekends, 3 nights on holiday weekends. Picnic shelter for up to 125 people & 70 vehicles, $80. Handicap accessible fishing area. Dump station $4, boat launch $3, swimming $1 per person for non-campers. NRRS. **GPS: 31.96667, -96.6831**

OAK CAMPGROUND

From Dawson, 4.3 mi NE on SR 31, 1.5 mi N on FM 667, on left; on NE shore of lake. 48 RV sites with wtr/electric (6 full hookups, 1 pull-through site). During 3/1-10/31, sites $14 ($7 with federal senior pass) & $18 for full hookups ($9 with federal senior pass). During peak season of 3/1-10/31, sites $18 ($9 with federal senior pass) & $22 for full hookups ($11 with federal senior pass). RV limit in excess of 65'. At reserved sites, 2-night minimum stay on weekends, 3 nights on holiday weekends. Picnic shelter for up to 125 people & 70 vehicles, $80. Fishing pier, handicap accessible fishing area. Dump station $4, boat launch $3 for non-campers. NRRS. **GPS: 31.9667, -96.6833**

PECAN POINT CAMPGROUND

From Dawson, 3.5 mi NE on SR 31; 3.2 mi N on FM 667; SW on FM 744; SE on FM 1578 to park on N shore of lake. 4/1-9/30; 14-day limit. 35 sites, 5 with 50-amp elec/wtr (11 pull-through), $12 ($6 with federal senior pass); 30 sites without hookups, $10 ($5 with federal senior pass). RV limit in excess of 65'. Dump station $4 for non-campers. NRRS. **GPS: 31.96667, -96.68333**

WOLF CREEK CAMPGROUND

From jct with FM 639, 2.2 mi SW on FM 744; 2 mi SE on FM 1578; on N shore of lake. 4/1-9/30; 14-day limit. 73 sites, 50 with wtr/elec (12 pull-through), 2 double sites, 22 without hookups. Sites without elec & sites with wtr hookups, $14 ($7 with federal senior pass); sites with wtr/elec, $16 ($8 with federal senior pass; double sites without elec, $24 ($12 with federal senior pass). RV limit in excess of 65'. At reserved sites, 2-night minimum stay on weekends, 3 nights on holiday weekends. Picnic shelter for up to 125 people & 70 vehicles, $80. Handicap accessible fishing area. Dump station $4, boat launch $3 for non-campers. NRRS.
GPS: 31.9667, -96.68333

PAT MAYSE LAKE (TU) 14
GPS: 33.8533, -95.5483

A 5,990-acre lake 1 mi S of Chicota off FM 197 and 12 mi N of Paris in northeastern Texas; 100 mi W of Texarkana. ORV prohibited. Gated campgrounds provide emergency late night exits. Lake Manager, Pat Mayse Lake, P. O. Box 129, Powderly, TX 75473-0129. (903) 732-3020.

LAMAR POINT CAMPGROUND

From jct with FM 1499, N on FM 1500. All year; 14-day limit. 9 primitive sites. $8 ($4 with federal senior pass). Pit toilets, no drkg wtr. Day use fees for beach, boat ramp.

PAT MAYSE EAST CAMPGROUND

From Chicota, 0.8 mi W on FM 197; S on county rd. All year; 14-day limit. 26 sites with wtr/elec, $15 ($7.50 with federal senior pass). Day use fees for boat ramp, beach, dump station. **GPS: 33.843506, -95.587158**

PAT MAYSE WEST CAMPGROUND

From Chicota, 2.3 mi W on FM 197, then S on county road. All year; 14-day limit. 83 sites with wtr/elec, $18 ($9 with federal senior pass); 5 sites with wtr, $12 ($6 with federal senior pass); 1 pull-through site, 7 handicap sites. RV limit in excess of 65'. At reserved sites, 2-night minimum stay required on weekends, 3 nights on holidays. Day use fees for boat ramp, dump station. (903) 732-4955. NRRS 4/1-9/30.
GPS: 33.84778, -95.60694

SANDERS COVE CAMPGROUND

From Chicota, 3.2 mi E on FM 906, then S on entrance rd. All year; 14-day limit. 89 sites. 85 sites with wtr/elec, $18 & $22 ($9 & $11 with federal senior pass); 4 sites without hookups, $12 ($6 with federal senior pass). 9 handicap sites. Group camping area $75; picnic shelter $25. Night-time exit provided. RV limit in excess of 65'. At reserved sites, 2-night minimum stay required on weekends, 3 nights on holidays. Day use fees for boat ramp, dump station, beach. (903) 732-4956. NRRS 4/1-9/30. **GPS: 33.84083, -95.53417**

PROCTOR LAKE (FW) 15
GPS: 31.9667, -98.5

This 4,610-acre lake is 8 mi NE of Comanche off US 67 on FM 1476 and 97 mi SW of Ft. Worth. Gated campgrounds provide emergency late night exits. Extra vehicle fee may be charged for each vehicle over two. Resource Manager, Proctor Lake, 2180 Farm to Market Road 2861, Comanche, TX 76442-7248. ((254) 879)2424.

COOPERAS CREEK PARK

From Proctor at jct with FM 1476, 5.5 mi S through Hasse on US 377; 2.5 mi N on FM 2861. All year; 14-day limit. 66 sites with wtr/elec (2 with 50amp service, 7 full hookups, 4 double sites, 4 pull-through sites. Sites with 30-amp elec/wtr, $16 ($8 with federal senior pass); sites 50-

amp elec/wtr, $20 ($10 with federal senior pass); sites with full hookups, $22 ($11 with federal senior pass); double sites $32 ($16 with federal senior pass. Two group camping areas for up to 100 people and 26 vehicles, $100 & $130. RV limit in excess of 65'. At reserved sites, 2-night minimum stay required on weekends, 3 nights stay on holiday weekends. E side of park closes about 9/15. Open all year. (254) 879-2498. NRRS 3/1-9/30. **GPS: 31.996667, -95.50417**

PROMONTORY CAMPGROUND

From Comanche at jct with US 377, 12 mi N SR 16; 5 mi E on FM 2318; on NW side of lake. 4/1-9/30; 14-day limit. 30 sites without hookups, $8 ($4 with federal senior pass); 52 sites with elec/wtr $16, double sites $32, premium site with 50-amp elec/wtr $20 ($8, $16 & $10 with federal senior pass); 1 quad site with 50-amp/wtr $50 (no senior discount); 4 overnight screened shelters $22; 1 screened shelter with RV site, $38. Three group camping areas for up to 100 people and 26 vehicles with picnic shelter, $90, $100, $130. RV limit in excess of 65'; 4 pull-through sites. At reserved sites, 2-night minimum stay on weekends, 3 nights on holiday weekends. (254) 893-7545. (254) 893-7545. NRRS. **GPS: 31.98, -98.49**

SOWELL CREEK PARK

From Proctor at jct with US 377, 2 mi W on FM 1476; S before dam on recreation road. All year; 14-day limit. 60 sites with elec/wtr, $16 base ($8 with federal senior pass), $20 for 50-amp elec ($10 with federal senior pass), $26 full hookups ($13 with federal senior pass), double sites $32 ($16 with senior pass), 30-amp quad sites $50 (no senior passes accepted). 2 group camping areas for up to 100 people & 26 vehicles with picnic shelters, $90 with wtr hookups & $190 with elec/wtr. RV limit in excess of 65'. At reserved sites, 2-night minimum stay required on weekends, 3 nights on holiday weekends. (254) 879-2322. NRRS 3/1-9/30. **GPS: 31.99, -98.46**

SAM RAYBURN LAKE (FW) 16
GPS: 31.1067, -94.1072

This 114,500-acre lake is 15 mi N of Jasper on US 96 in E-central Texas. It is 89 mi N of Beaumont and 30 mi W of the Louisiana state line. Equestrian trail. Campground checkout time 2 p.m. $3 extra vehicle fee may be charged; each campsite allowed 2 vehicles plus the camping unit. Boat launch fee $3, dump station & swimming beach $4 per vehicle for non-campers. Resource Manager, Sam Rayburn Reservoir, Rt. 3, Box 486, Jasper, TX 75951-9598. (409) 384-5716.

EBENEZER PARK

From Jasper, 12 mi N on US 96, 8 mi W on Recreation Rd 255 across dam, then N; on S shore of lake. All year; 14-day limit. Equestrian sites open all year; other sites open 3/1-LD; 14-day limit.10 equestrian sites, all with wtr, 7 with 30-amp elec, 3 with 50-amp elec (3 new sites being developed using donations); each site includes RV space, hitching posts, tbl, fire ring; each site must have 1-4 horses. Corral provided. Equestrian sites $16 for 30-amp elec, $20 for 50-amp elec. 2 basic tent sites $12. 7 basic RV sites without hookups, $9-$12 ($4.50-$6 with federal senior pass). RV limit 50'. Ebenezer the only Rayburn campground allowing equestrian camping. Nearest boat ramp at Twin Dikes Park (4 mi). NRRS. **GPS: 31.07028, -94.12472**

HANKS CREEK PARK

From Huntington, 12 mi SE on FM 3801; 2 mi NE on FM 2801, following signs; on NW shore of lake. All year; 14-day limit. 43 sites with 30-amp elec/wtr, 6 sites with 50-amp elec/wtr. 30-amp sites $18 ($9 with federal senior pass), 50-amp sites $20 ($10 with federal senior pass). Group camping area with elec, $100. 8 new screened shelters with RV sites, $30. Picnic shelter $30. RV limit 60'. At reserved sites, 2-night minimum stay required on weekends, 3 nights on holiday weekends. Entry gates closed at 9pm; late arrivals are turned away; registered campers must make late entry arrangements before leaving campground. NRRS. **GPS: 31.2719, -94.4031**

MILL CREEK PARK

From Brookeland, 2 mi W on Loop 149; 1 mi W on Spur 165. All year; 14-day limit. 110 sites with wtr/elec. 59 sites with 30-amp elec, $16 ($18 at premium locations); 51 sites with 50-amp elec $18 ($20 at premium locations). Picnic shelter for up to 50 people and 30 vehicles, $50. Horseshoe pits, public phone. RV limit in excess of 65'. At reserved sites, 2-night minimum stay required on weekends, 3 nights on holiday weekends. NRRS. **GPS: 31.1514, -94.0064**

RAYBURN PARK

From Pineland at jct of US 96; 10 mi N on FM 83; 11 mi S on FM 705; 1 mi W on FM 3127; on N shore of lake. (NOTE: FM 83 bridge at Ayish Bayou closed until about May 2011; use alternate Rt., following US 96 to Hwy 103 W, then pick up FM 705S, crossing FM 83). All year; 14-day limit. 21 sites without hookups, $11 ($5.50 with federal senior pass); 16 RV back-in sites with 30-amp elec/wtr, $18 ($9 with federal senior pass); 8 pull-through sites with 50-amp elec/wtr, $20 ($10 with federal senior pass). (About 20 more sites closed temporarily due to budget constraints). Free designated picnic sites. RV limit in excess of 65'. At reserved sites, 2-night minimum stay required on weekends, 3 nights on holiday weekends. NRRS. **GPS: 31.10667, -94.10722**

SAN AUGUSTINE PARK

From Pineland at jct with US 96; 6 mi W on FM 83; 4 mi S on FM 1751. All year; 14-day limit. 6 tent sites with elec $16 ($8 with federal senior pass); 94 RV sites with 30-amp elec/wtr $16, $20 at premium locations ($8 & $10 with federal senior pass). Picnic shelter for up to 50 people and 26 vehicles, $50. Fish cleaning station, horseshoe pits, interpretive trail, public phone. Non-campers pay $4 per vehicle for dump station, swimming beach. RV limit in excess of 65'. At reserved sites, 2-night minimum stay required on weekends, 3 nights on holidays. NRRS. **GPS: 31.19917, -94.07889**

TWIN DIKES PARK

From Jasper, 13 mi N on US 96; 5 mi W on FM 255, then; on S shore of lake. 3/1-LD weekend; 14-day limit. 3 tent sites & 21 RV sites no hookups, $12 ($6 with federal senior pass); 6 sites with 30-amp elec/wtr, $16 ($8 with federal senior pass); 6 sites with 30-amp elec/wtr/sewer, $20 ($10 with federal senior pass); 4 sites with 50-amp elec/wtr, $18 ($9 with federal senior pass); 3 sites with screened shelters & full hookups, $30. Picnic shelter for up to 30 people and 16 vehicles, $30. RV limit 60'. At reserved sites, 2-night minimum stay/weekends, 3 nights/holiday weekends. Dump station $4 for non-campers. NRRS. **GPS: 31.0725, -94.05944**

SOMERVILLE LAKE (FW) 17
GPS: 30.3333, -96.5333

An 11,460-acre lake with 85 mi of shoreline, located 1 mi W of Somerville on SR 36 on Thornberry Ave and 84 mi E of Austin. Three camping areas are leased by the Corps to other operators. They include Big Creek Park and Marina, Overbrook Park and Marina and Welch Park, operated by the City of Somerville. Visitor center, wildlife viewing. Resource Manager, Somerville Lake, P. O. Box 549, Somerville, TX 77879-0549. (409) 596-1622-1622.

ROCKY CREEK CAMPGROUND

From Somerville, W on SR6; 4.5 mi W on FM 1948. All year; 14-day limit. 46 primitive sites $12 ($6 with federal senior pass). 75 RV sites without elec $18 during 3/1-9/30 & $16 during 10/1-2/28 ($9 & $8 with federal senior pass). 40 sites with 30-amp elec/wtr, $20 during 3/1-9/30 & $18 during 10/1-2/28 ($10 & $9 with federal senior pass). 34 sites with 30-amp & 50-amp elec/wtr, $22 during 3/1-9/30 & $18 during 10/1-2/28 ($11 & $9 with federal senior pass). RV limit in excess of 65'. 2-night minimum stay on weekends, 3 nights on holiday weekends. Nature trail. Picnic shelter for up to 100 people & 20 vehicles, $100 off-season & $125 during 3/1-9/30. Sites available on a first-come, first-served basis (no reservations) until construction begins of extensive improvements; then the park will be closed. **GPS: 30.29861, -96.56806**

YEGUA CREEK CAMPGROUND

From Somerville, SE on SR 36; 2 mi W on FM 1948; right into park. All year; 14-day limit. 35 sites without hookups (including 5 tent sites), $16 during 3/1-9/30 & $14 during 10/1-2/28 ($8 & $7 with federal senior pass); at premium locations, fees are $18 during 3/1-9/30 & $16 during 10/1-2/28 ($9 & $8 with federal senior pass). 47 sites with 30-amp elec/wtr $20 during 3/1-9/30 & $18 during 10/1-2/28 ($10 & $9 with federal senior pass). RV limit in excess of 65'. At reserved sites, 2-night minimum stay required on weekends, 3 nights on holiday weekends. NRRS. **GPS: 30.30278, -96.54472**

B. A. STEINHAGEN LAKE (FW) 18
GPS: 30.7833, -94.1667

This 13,700-acre lake is 15 mi SW of Jasper off FM 1746 in E-central Texas, 75 mi N of Beaumont. ORV prohibited. Gated campgrounds may charge an extra vehicle fee. Non-campers pay day use fees: $3 for boat ramp, $2 for showers, $4 dump station. Resource Manager, Town Bluff Dam & B. A. Steinhagen Lake, 890 Farm to Market Road Road 92, Woodville, TX 75979-9631. (409) 429-3491.

CAMPERS COVE CAMPGROUND

From Woodville, 12.1 mi SE on US 190; 2.5 mi SE on FM 92, then N 2.4 mi on CR 4130. 4/1-9/30; 14-day limit. 25 sites. Free. Campground closed to camping while it is being renovated. **GPS: 30.822646, -94.201959**

MAGNOLIA RIDGE CAMPGROUND

From Woodville, 11 mi E on US 190; 1.5 mi NW on FM 92, then NE on park entrance rd. All year; 14-day limit. 32 sites with 30-amp elec/wtr, $16 ($8 with federal senior pass). 8 sites without hookups, $10 ($5 with federal senior pass). 1 site with screened shelter, elec/wtr $25. Picnic shelter for up to 200 people & 30 vehicles, $45. Children's fishing pond, convenience store, handicap accessible fishing area. RV limit in excess of 65'. At reserved sites, 2-night minimum stay required on weekends, 3 nights on holidays. (409) 283-5493. NRRS. Note: At press time, the campground was under a burning ban, with open fires and uncovered barbecue pits prohibited. **GPS: 30.86667, -94.2375**

SANDY CREEK CAMPGROUND

From Woodville, 14.1 mi NE on US 190 across lake; 1.4 mi S on FM 777; 2.5 mi SW on CR 155, gravel (signs); on SE shore of lake. All year; 14-day limit. 34 sites with 30-amp elec/wtr, $16 ($8 with federal senior pass). 35 sites with 50-amp wtr/elec, $18 ($9 with federal senior pass). 6 sites without hookups, $10 ($5 with federal senior pass). 2 sites with screened shelters & 30-amp elec/wtr, $25 ($12.50 with federal senior pass). Group picnic shelter with elec, $45. Boat rentals nearby. RV limit in excess of 65'. At reserved sites, 2-night minimum stay on weekends, 3 nights on holidays. Dump station, swimming beach $4 per vehicle for non-campers; showers $2 per person non-campers. (409) 384-6166. NRRS. **GPS: 30.80833, -94.15833**

STILLHOUSE HOLLOW LAKE (FW) 19
GPS: 31.0333, -97.5333

A 6,430-acre lake 5 mi SW of Belton on FM 1670, S of Fort Hood and 80 mi N of Austin. Campground checkout time 2 p.m. Visitor center, interpretive programs. Chalk Ride Falls Environmental Learning Center below the dam includes hiking trail along Lampasas River, a spring-fed creek with waterfall and several wildlife viewing points. Non-campers pay $4 day use fees for dump stations, picnicking, beaches; $3 for boat ramps. Resource Manager, Stillhouse Hollow Lake, 3740 Farm to Market Road 1670, Belton, TX 7651. (254) 939-2461.

DANA PEAK CAMPGROUND

From jct with US 190, 0.3 mi S on Simmons Rd; 5 mi W on FM 2410; 5 mi S on Comanche Gap Rd. All year; 14-day limit. 8 primitive tent sites, $10 ($5 with federal senior pass; 5 tent sites with elec/wtr, $16 ($8 with federal senior pass). 20 RV/tent sites with elec $20 ($10 with federal senior pass). 2 double sites with elec/wtr $36. Group shelters $40-70. RV limit in excess of 65'. At reserved sites, 2-night minimum stay required on weekends, 3 nights on holiday weekends. NRRS. **GPS: 31.02889, -97.61306**

UNION GROVE CAMPGROUND

From junction I-35, 0.8 mi W on FM 1670;5.3 mi W FM 2484. All year; 14-day limit. 7 tent sites with elec, $16 ($8 with federal senior pass). 30 RV/tent sites with elec, $20 ($10 with senior pass); 2 double sites $36. 3 screened overnight shelters, $30. RV limit in excess of 65'. At reserved sites, 2-night minimum stay required on weekends, 3 nights on holiday weekends. NRRS. **GPS: 31.00833, -97.62111**

WACO LAKE (FW) 20
GPS: 31.6, -97.2167

This 8,900-acre lake is on the NW side of Waco off FM 1637. ORV prohibited, Wildlife viewing area, fossil pit, Gated campgrounds may charge an extra vehicle fee. Day use facilities include Bosque Park, for fishing below the dam; Lacy Point Access, boat ramp and hiking/biking/bridle trails; Twin Bridges Park, swimming beaches, picnicking, boat ramp, group shelter; Flat Rock Park, boat ramp, bird watching, fishing; Airport Beach Park, swimming beach, picnicking, boat ramp, group shelter; Koehne Park, boat ramp, picnicking. Non-campers pay day use fees of $4 for beaches, boat ramps, picnicking, dump stations. Resource Manager, Waco Lake, Rt. 10, Box 173-G, Waco, TX 76708-9602. (254) 756-5359.

AIRPORT PARK

From I-35 exit 339, W on Industrial; at 2nd light, right on Stienback Bend Dr; right at 4-way stop sign; 2 mi E on Skeet Leson Rd (just behind the regional airport); on N shore of lake. All year; 14-day limit. 19 basic tent sites, $12 ($6 with federal senior pass). 39 RV sites with elec/wtr, $20 ($10 with federal senior pass); 21 sites with full hookups

$24 ($12 with federal senior pass). Group camping area with shelter & elec, $275. Newly remodeled overnight group shelter with 8 sites (6 with full hookups, 2 with elec/wtr), 6-foot barbecue grill, 12-foot serving bar, accommodations for 80 guests, parking for 35 vehicles, $275. Floating restaurant at the nearby marina. Courtesy dock. RV limit in excess of 65'. At reserved sites, 2-night minimum stay required on weekends, 3 nights on holiday weekends. NRRS. **GPS: 31.59722, -97.23694**

MIDWAY PARK

From Waco & I-35 exit 330, 5 mi W on SR 6; exit on Fish Pond Rd and circle under SR 6, then stay on access road; on E shore of S Bosque River. All year; 14-day limit. 5 primitive tent sites $12 ($6 with federal senior pass). 22 sites with 30-amp elec/wtr, $20 ($10 with federal senior pass). 4 double sites with elec ($36). 11 sites with full hookups, $24 ($12 with federal senior pass). RV limit in excess of 65'. At reserved sites, 2-night minimum stay required on weekends, 3 nights on holidays. Multi-use play area for children. NRRS. **GPS: 31.5, -97.20833**

REYNOLDS CREEK PARK

From Waco I-35 exit 330, 7 mi W on SR 6 across lake; 1 mi NE on Speegleville Rd, pass 4-way stop sign; approximately 1 mi on right; on W shore of lake. All year; 14-day limit. 6 primitive tent sites $12 ($6 with federal senior pass). 51 RV/tent sites with wtr/elec, $20 ($10 with federal senior pass); sites with full hookups, $24 ($12 with federal senior pass); some sites with 50-amp elec. Picnic shelter with elec, $20. At reserved sites, 2-night minimum stay required on weekends, 3 nights on holidays. Interpretive programs, public phone, amphitheater, picnic shelter. Formerly known as Speegleville I Park. NRRS. **GPS: 31.54972, -97.25**

SPEEGLEVILLE PARK

From Waco I-35, 6 mi N on SR 6; after crossing lake on Twin Bridges, exit left on access rd, past Twin Bridges Park about 0.25 mi; continue on

Overflow Rd to park entrance; on W shore of lake. All year; 14-day limit. Primitive sites $16 ($8 with federal senior pass). 9 sites with elec, $16 ($8 with federal senior pass). 21 sites with wtr/elec, $20 ($10 with federal senior pass). 2 screened picnic shelters, $30. At reserved sites, 2-night minimum stay required on weekends, 3 nights on holiday weekends. NRRS. **GPS: 31.60333, -97.23361**

WHITNEY LAKE (FW) 21
GPS: 31.85, -97.3667

This 23,560-acre lake is 5.5 mi SW of Whitney on SR 22 and 79 mi S of Fort Worth. Dam tours available. Checkout time 2 p.m. ORV prohibited. The Corps leases Ham Creek Park to a private marina. Hopewell Trail is a 12.5-mi equestrian and multi-use trail through wildlife areas. Equestrian camping available at Plowman Creek Park. Day use facilities are at Lofers Bend, 2 swimming beaches, boat ramp, picnic facilities with BBQ grills, 2 sand volleyball courts; at McCown Valley, 7 picnic sites, 6 beach shelters, picnic sites, swimming beach, 2 sand volleyball courts. Whitney Lake's Corps campgrounds require non-campers to pay day use fees for boat ramps, dump stations, beaches. Resource Manager, Whitney Lake, 285 County Road 3602, Clifton, TX 76634. (254) 694-3189.

CEDAR CREEK PARK

From Whitney, 5.5 mi NW on FM 933; 2.2 mi SW & SE on FM 2604; on E side of lake. 20 free basic sites with wtr nearby, fire rings, 1 toilet, group pavilion for up to 100 people. All year; 14-day limit.
GPS: 31.990085, -97.373333

CEDRON CREEK PARK

From Whitney, 2.4 mi NW on FM 933; 6 mi SW on FM 1713 across Katy Bridge on left, signs; on W side of lake. All; 14-day limit. 57 sites with 30-amp wtr/elec, $14-18 during 10/1-3/31 ($7-9 with federal senior pass); $16-20 during peak period of 4/1-9/30 ($8-10 with federal senior pass). However, in 2010, camping facilities were closed 9/30-4/1.

Group camping area with 8 wtr/elec sites, $140. Horseshoe pits, picnic shelter RV limit 45'. At reserved sites 2-night minimum stay on required weekends, 3 nights on holiday weekends. Shower houses renovated in 2010. NRRS. **GPS: 31.96444, -97.41417**

KIMBALL BEND PARK

From Blum at jct with FM 933, 6 mi SW on SR 174, across bridge, then NW; on N end of lake. All year; 14-day limit. 35 free sites. 1 toilet. **GPS: 32.123449, -97.497529**

LOFERS BEND E PARK

From Whitney, 5.7 mi S on SR 22, the W, following signs. All year; 14-day limit. 6 sites with wtr, no elec, $10 during 10/1-3/31 ($5 with federal senior pass); $12 during peak period of 4/1-9/30 ($6 with federal senior pass). 60 sites with wtr/elec, $14 during 10/1-3/31 ($7 with federal senior pass); $16 during peak period of 4/1-9/30 ($8 with federal senior pass). Group camping area for up to 75 people & 10 vehicles, $105. RV limit 45'. At reserved sites, 2-night minimum stay required on weekends, 3 nights on holidays. NRRS. **GPS: 31.88528, -97.36111**

LOFERS BEND W PARK

Adjacent to Loafer's Bend E; on main stem of Brazos River. 4/1-9/30; 14-day limit. 21 sites with wtr, no elec, $12 ($6 with federal senior pass). 37 sites with 30-amp elec/wtr, $18 ($9 with federal senior pass). 5 sites with 50-amp elec/wtr, $20 ($10 with federal senior pass). 5 pull-through sites. Group camping area for up to 75 people, $80. Group picnic shelter, $50. RV limit 45'. At reserved sites, 2-night minimum stay required on weekends, 3 nights on holiday weekends. NRRS. **GPS: 31.88528, -97.36111**

MCCOWN VALLEY PARK

From Whitney, 2.4 mi NW on FM 933; 4 mi SW on FM 1713; on E side of lake. All year; 14-day limit. 31 sites with 30-amp elec/wtr, $16 during peak season of 4/1-9/30 ($8 with federal senior pass), $14 rest of year ($7 with federal senior pass). 14 sites with 50-amp wtr/elec, $20 during peak season of 4/1-9/30 ($10 with federal senior pass), $18 rest of year ($9 with federal senior pass). 7 sites with wtr hookups (no elec), $12 during peak season of 4/1-9/30 ($6 with federal senior pass), $10 rest of year ($5 with federal senior pass). Cabins with 30-amp RV hookups, $30; cabins without hookups, $24. 39 equestrian sites with elec, $18 off-season, $20 during peak season. Picnic shelter for up to 150 people, $45. Horseshoe pits, equestrian trails. RV limit 50'. At reserved sites, 2-night minimum stay required on weekends, 3 nights on holiday weekends. NRRS.
GPS: 31.95, -97.38306

PLOWMAN CREEK PARK

From jct with SR 174, 2.5 mi SE on FM 56; 1 mi S of Kopper on W side of lake. All year; 14-day limit. 22 sites with 30-amp elec/wtr, $16 during peak period of 4/1-9/30 ($8 with federal senior pass); $14 rest of year ($7 with federal senior pass). 12 sites with wtr (no elec), $12 during 4/1-9/30 ($6 with federal senior pass), $10 rest of year ($5 with federal senior pass). 10 equestrian sites with elec, $16 during peak season, $14 off-season ($8 & $7 with federal senior pass); primitive camping in equestrian area, $10 ($5 with senior pass). RV limit 45'. At reserved sites, 2-night minimum stay required on weekends, 3 nights on holiday weekends. NRRS. **GPS: 32.07, -97.49333**

RIVERSIDE PARK

Downstream from Whitney Dam on SR 22, both sides of river. All year; 14-day limit. Free. 5 primitive sites. Tbls, pit toilet, fishing platform on W side; 1 toilet on E side. **GPS: 31.868045, -97.367785**

SOLDIER BLUFF PARK

PARK On W side of the dam, S of outlet. All year; 14-day limit. Free. 14 primitive sites. 1 pit toilet, picnic shelter ($30), tbls.
GPS: 31.862041, -97.372373

STEELE CREEK CAMPGROUND

From jct with FM 927, 1 mi SE on FM 56, then NE gravel rd. All year; 14-day limit. Free. 21 sites with tbls, ground cookers, central wtr, 2 pit toilets. **GPS: 32.005741, -97.451559**

WALLING BEND

From jct with SR 22, 2 mi NW on FM 56; NE on FM 2841. All year; 14-day limit. Free. 6 primitive sites. Tbls, pit toilet, picnic shelter.
GPS: 31.897557, -100.739791

WRIGHT PATMAN LAKE (FW) 22
GPS: 33.305, -94.16

This 33,750-acre lake is 9 mi SW of Texarkana and the junction of US 82 off US 59. Visitor center, wildlife viewing area. Campground checkout time 2 p.m. Besides camping facilities, the Corps operates four day-use areas at the lake: N Shore Park, with picnicking, swimming beach, sand volleyball, basketball court, showers, boat ramp; Oak Park, with picnicking, RV dump station, swing set, volleyball court; Spillway Park, with picnicking, and Malden Lake Day Use Area, with picnicking, boat ramp; Elliott Bluff, picnicking, boat launch. Free boat ramps at Hwy 59 Park, Jackson Creek, Herron Creek, Overcup, Thomas Lake. Non-camper pay $4 for dump station, $1-$2 for showers, $3 for boat launch at Malden Lake, Elliott Bluff. Eight free primitive camping areas are scattered around the lake; most have no facilities, but a few have fire rings; for locations, get maps from the lake office. Leased facilities include Atlanta

State Park, Cass Coounty Park, Berry Farm, Kelly Creek Marina, Big Creek Landing & Campground, Sulphur Point Concession Area, and Highway 59 Park. Project Manager, Wright Patman Lake, P. O. Box 1817, Texarkana, TX 75504-1817. (903) 838-8781.

CLEAR SPRINGS PARK

From Texarkana, 9 mi S on US 59; 0.5 mi W on SR 2148; 2 mi W on park road. All year; 14-day limit. 15 primitive tent sites, $10 ($5 with federal senior pass). 75 sites with 30-amp elec/wtr $18 ($9 with federal senior pass); 1 site has deck, $20. 11 sites with 50-amp elec/wtr, $20 ($10 with federal senior pass); 1 site with 50-amp elec & deck, $24. Group camping area with 12 elec/wtr sites & shelter, $80 plus $16 per site. Picnic shelter, $60. Horseshoe pits. RV limit in excess of 65 ft. At reserved sites, 2-night minimum stay required on weekends, 3 nights on holiday weekends. NRRS. **GPS: 33.35833, -94.49444**

JACKSON CREEK PARK

From Douglassville at jct with SR 8, 4.1 mi E on SR 77; 1.5 mi N on FM 2791, then 3 mi N. All year; 14-day limit. Free. 10 primitive sites. RV limit 25'. Pit toilet, fire rings. **GPS: 33.221191, -94.301758**

MALDEN LAKE PARK

From Maud at jct with US 67, 8.4 mi S on SR 8; before bridge, on left. All year; 14-day limit. 29 sites with 30-amp elec/wtr, $18 ($9 with federal senior pass); 10 sites with 50-amp elec/wtr, $20 ($10 with federal senior pass); double sites $36. Coded gate locks provided for late entry by registered campers. RV limit 55'. At reserved sites, 2-night minimum stay required on weekends, 3 nights on holiday weekends. NRRS. **GPS: 33.35833, -94.18639**

PINEY POINT PARK

From Texarkana, 12 mi S on US 59;, lst right past Sulphur River bridge, following signs. 3/1-11/30; 14-day limit. 42 sites with 30-amp elec/wtr, $16 ($8 with federal senior pass). 6 sites with 50-amp elec/wtr, $18 ($9 with federal senior pass); sites with 50-amp elec/wtr & deck, $20 ($10 with federal senior pass). 41 primitive tent sites, $10 ($5 with federal senior pass). Picnic shelter for up to 75 people & 31 vehicles, $50. Coded gate entrance provided for registered campers. RV limit 55'. At reserved sites, 2-night minimum stay on weekends, 3 nights on holiday weekends. NRRS. **GPS: 33.29861, -94.16806**

ROCKY POINT PARK

Just S of Piney Point campground, S of dam. All year; 14-day limit. 100 sites with 30-amp elec/wtr, $16 ($8 with federal senior pass). 10 sites with full hookups, $18 ($9 with federal senior pass). 5 sites with 50-amp elec/wtr/sewer, $22 ($11 with federal senior pass). 3 sites with 50-amp elec/wtr, $18 ($9 with federal senior pass). Picnic shelter for up to 60 people & 31 vehicles, $50. Fish cleaning station, amphitheater. RV limit in excess of 65'. 2-night minimum stay on weekends, 3 nights on holiday weekends. NRRS. **GPS: 33.28694, -94.16583**

THOMAS LAKE PARK

From I-35E near Eagan, S on Pilot Knob Rd; enter park just past jct with Wilderness Run Rd near fire station. All year; 14-day limit. Free primitive camping; no facilities except tbls, no toilet, no drkg wtr.

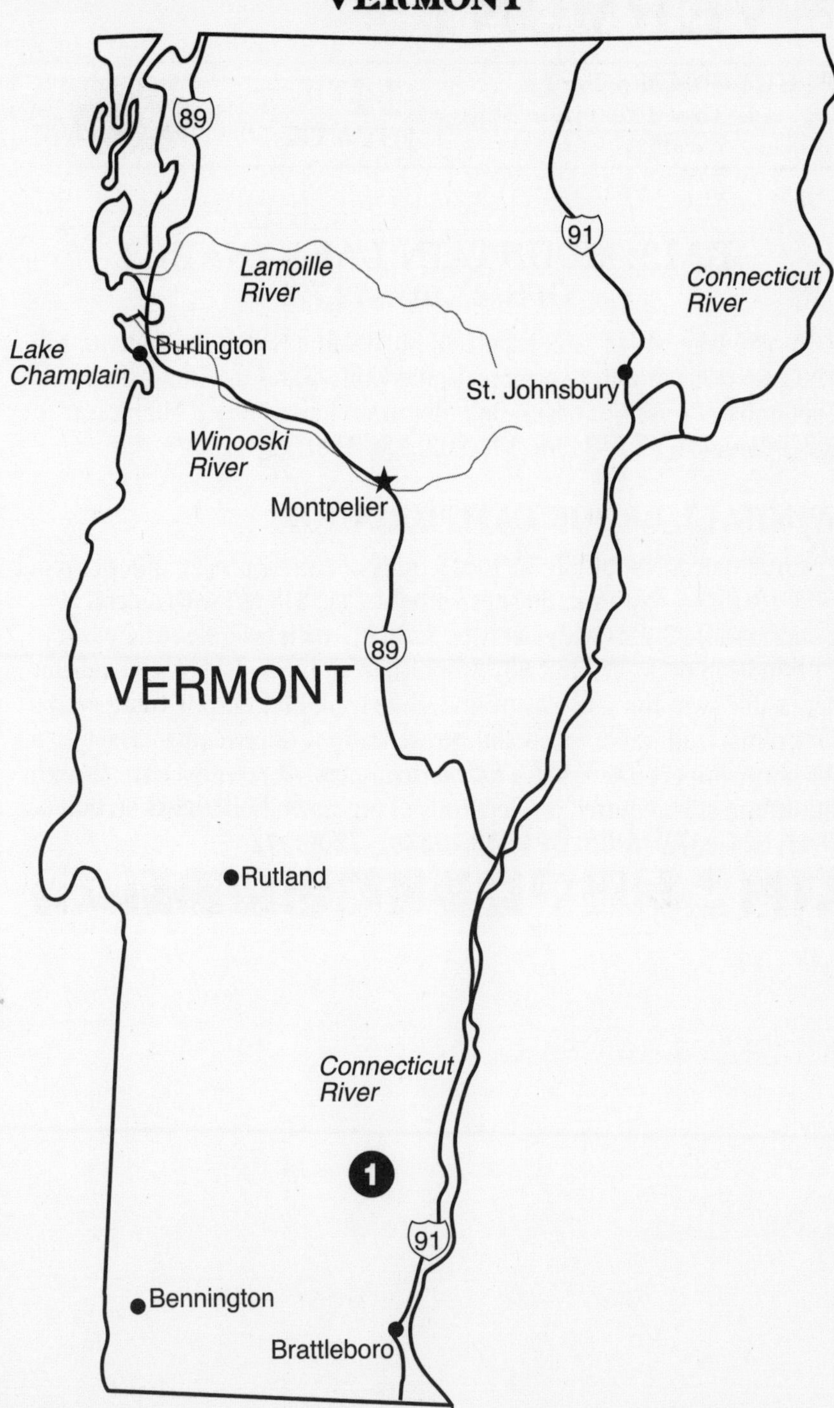
89
Lamoille
River
91
Connecticut
River
Lake
Champlain
Burlington
St. Johnsbury
Winooski
River
Montpelier
89
VERMONT
Rutland
Connecticut
River
1
91
Bennington
Brattleboro

VERMONT

State Capital: **Montpelier**
Nickname: **Green Mountain State**
Statehood Year: **1791**

14TH STATE

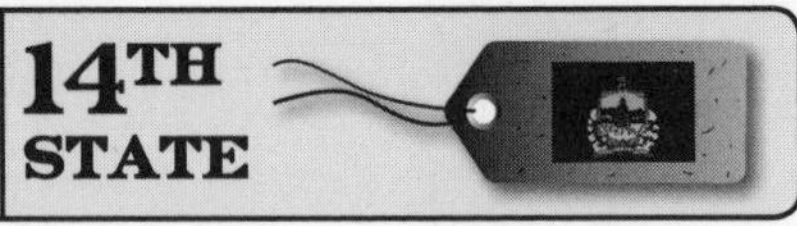

BALL MOUNTAIN LAKE (NAE) 1
GPS: 43.105, -72.775

A 75-acre lake NW of Jamaica off SR 30/100 and NW of Brattleboro. The lake releases water for recreational white-water use in April and September. Project Manager, Ball Mountain Lake, 88 Ball Mountain Road, Jamaica, VT 05343-9713. (802) 874-4881.

WINHALL BROOK CAMPGROUND

From Jamaica, NW off SR 30/100; 5 mi N of dam & project offices. About 5/15-10/15; 14-day limit. 88 sites without elec, $18 ($9 with federal senior pass); 23 sites with elec/wtr, $22 ($11 with federal senior pass). 21 handicap sites. RV limit 60'. Amphitheater, horseshoe pits. Handicap accessible swimming & playground. Bike trail, hiking trail, interpretive programs, trail walks, video/slide presentations. Firewood($). Day use fee for non-campers. Day use fee for non-campers. At reserved sites, 2-night minimum stay required on weekends, 3 nights on holiday weekends. (802) 824-4570. NRRS. **GPS: 43.16333, -72.80972**

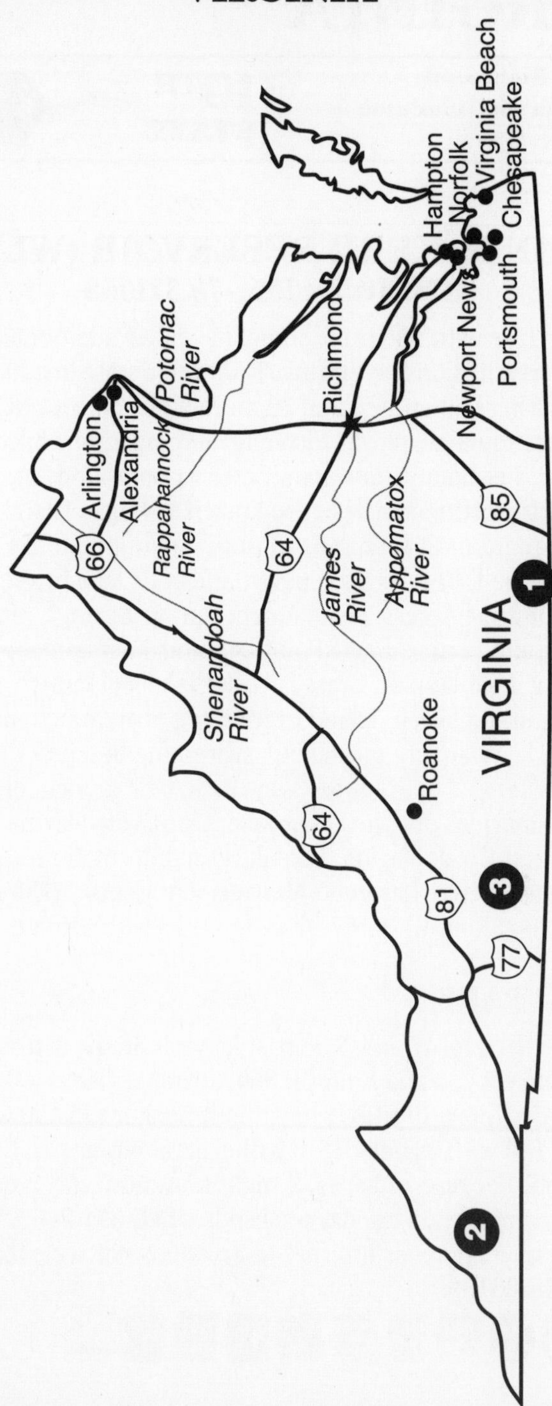

VIRGINIA
Arlington
Alexandria
Potomac River
Rappahannock River
Richmond
Hampton
Norfolk
Virginia Beach
Chesapeake
Portsmouth
Newport News
Shenandoah River
James River
Appomatox River
Roanoke
66
64
64
85
81
77
1
2
3

VIRGINIA

State Capital: **Richmond**
Nickname: **The Old Dominion**
Statehood Year: **1788**

10TH STATE

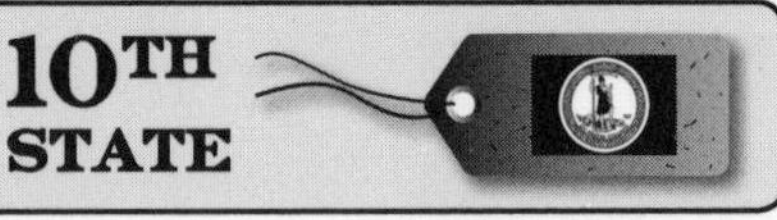

JOHN H. KERR RESERVOIR (WL) 1
GPS: 36.594702, -78.311058

A 50,000-acre lake with 900 mi of shoreline and an additional 50,000 acres of property, it is on the Virginia/N Carolina state line near Boydton, 20 mi W of Spring Hill on I-85 and 20 mi N of Henderson, NC on I-85. No powerhouse tours currently. Alcoholic beverages, dirt bikes and ORV are prohibited. Checkout time 4 p.m. Gated campgrounds may charge a $4 fee for extra visitor vehicles. Also known as Buggs Island Lake. Interpretive programs at Joseph S.J. Tanner Environmental Education Center. Nature trail. Besides its campgrounds, the lake has several day use areas: Bluestone Access, boat launch; Buffalo Springs, picnicking, pit toilets, drinking water; Eagle Point Landing, boat launch; Eastland Creek Landing, boat launch, Grassy Creek Park, boat launch, picnicking, pit toilet, swimming beach; Island Creek Park, boat launch, pit toilet; Palmer Point, boat launch, picnicking, swimming beach ($4 day use fee) and picnic shelter ($25); Staunton View Park, boat launch, picnicking. Three private marinas operate at the lake: Clarksville Marina, Satterwite Marina and Steel Creek Marina. For lake level information, call (434) 738-6371. John H. Kerr Reservoir Management Center, 1930 Mays Chapel Road, Boydton, VA 23917-9725. (434) 738-6143/6144.

BUFFALO PARK

From Clarksville, 8 mi W on US 58 past jct with SR 49, across bridge, then 3 mi N on CR 732 and E on CR 869; at end of Carter's Point Rd. 5/1-9/30; 14-day limit. 19 sites, $15 without hookups ($7.50 with federal senior pass), $20 with wtr/elec ($10 with federal senior pass). RV limit in excess of 65'. For reserved sites, 2-night minimum stay required on weekends, 3 nights on holiday weekends. (434) 374-2063. Walk-in reservations only; phone or Internet reservations not accepted. **GPS: 36.66194, -78.63139.**

IVY HILL PARK

From Townsville, NC, N on SR 39 to Virginia state line, then N on CR 825. 5/1-9/30; 14-day limit 25 primitive sites. $10 ($5 with national senior pass). RV limit 32'. Non-campers pay $4 day use fee for boat launch, picnicking, swimming beach, dump station. Picnic shelter $25. (434) 252-0903.

LONGWOOD PARK

From Clarksville at jct of US 58/15, 5 mi S on US 15; on the W side. All year; 14-day limit. 32 sites without hookups, $5 during 11/1-3/31 ($2.50 with federal senior pass); $18 rest of year ($9 with federal senior pass); double sites $36 ($18 for seniors). 34 sites with elec/wtr, $24 during 4/1-10/31 ($12 with federal senior pass). Picnic shelter $25. Non-campers pay $4 day use fee for boat launch, picnicking, swimming, dump station. RV limit in excess of 65'. At reserved sites, 2-night minimum stay required on weekends, 3 nights on holiday weekends. (434) 374-2711. NRRS. **GPS: 36.57722, -78.55139**

NORTH BEND CAMPGROUND

From Boydton, 5 mi E on US 58; 6 mi S on SR 4 (Buggs Island Rd). All year; 14-day limit. 150 sites no hookups, $5 during 11/-3/31 ($2.50 with federal senior pass); $18 during 4/1-10/31 ($9 with federal senior pass). 94 sites with wtr/elec, $24 during 4/1-10/31 ($12 with federal senior pass). Non-campers pay $4 fee for boat launch, picnicking, fishing pier, beach, dump. 3 group camping areas. Amphitheater. RV limit in excess of 65'. At reserved sites, 2-night minimum stay required on weekends, 3 nights on holiday weekends. NRRS. **GPS: 36.58833, -78.32483**

RUDDS CREEK RECREATION AREA

From Boydton, 3 mi W on US 58; on S side of road before lake bridge; on Roanoke River. 24 sites without hookups $5 during 11/1-3/31 ($2.50 with federal senior pass); $18 during 4/1-10/31, ($9 with federal senior pass),

$36 at double sites. 75 sites with elec/wtr, $24 during 4/1-10/31 ($12 with federal senior pass), $48 double sites ($24 with federal senior pass). Picnic shelter, $25. Amphitheater, public phone. RV limit in excess of 65'. At reserved sites, 2-night minimum stay required/weekends, 3 nights/ holiday weekends. (434) 738-6827. NRRS. **GPS: 36.65528, -78.44028**

JOHN W. FLANNAGAN LAKE (HU) 2
GPS: 37.240021, -82.378006

A 1,145-acre lake with almost 40 mi of shoreline, it is near the KY state line NW of Haysi on SR 63 and NW of Bristol. No camping reservations accepted. Boat launches are at the spillway launch area, Junction Area (fees) and Cranesnest Area. Resource Manager, John W. Flannagan Dam & Reservoir, Rt. 1, Box 268, Haysi, VA 24256-9736. (276) 835-9544.

CRANESNEST #1 & #2 CAMPGROUND

From Clintwood, 2 mi SE on SR 83, then N. MD-LD; 14-day limit. 24 sites. $10-12 ($5-$6 with federal senior pass). Picnic shelter, amphitheater. **GPS: 36.974, -82.4724**

CRANESNEST #3 CAMPGROUND

CAMPGROUND From Cranesnest #1 & #2, 1 mi NE. 11 sites. MD-LD; 14-day limit. Sites without elec, $10 ($5 with federal senior pass); sites with elec, $12 ($6 with federal senior pass).

LOWER TWIN CAMPGROUND

From SR 739, 3 mi W on SR 611; exit SE on SR 683. MD-LD; 14-day limit. 33 sites, 15 elec, $12 ($6 with federal senior pass); sites no elec, $10 ($5 with federal senior pass. Amphitheater. **GPS: 37.231934, -82.340332.**

POUND RIVER CAMPGROUND

From Clintwood, 0.2 mi W on SR 83; 2 mi N on SR 631; 1.2 mi E on SR 754. MD-LD; 14-day limit. 27 sites, some pull through sites. Sites with elec $14 ($7 with federal senior pass); sites without elec, $10 ($5 with federal senior pass). **GPS: 37.23389, -82,34327**

PHILPOTT LAKE (WL) 3
GPS: 36.7833, -80.0283

A 2,880-acre lake with 100 mi of shoreline, Philpott is NW of Martinsburg off US 220, SR 57 and Philpott Dam Rd. Visitor center, visitors to 10 p.m. Campground checkout time 4 p.m. Alcoholic beverages prohibited. $4 may be charged for extra/visitor vehicles. Free loan of fishing rod and tackle provided at the visitor center and parks. Visitor center. Day use parks include Bowens Creek, boat ramp, courtesy dock, swimming, picnicking, flush toilets ($4 day use fee); Runnet Bag Park, boat ramp (no fee); Ryans Branch, boat ramp (no fee); Turkey Island, picnicking (no fee); Twin Bridges, boat ramp, courtesy dock, picnicking, pit toilet (no fee). Project Manager, Philpott Lake, 1058 Philpott Dam Road, Basset, VA 24055-8618. (276) 629-2703/7385.

DEER ISLAND CAMPGROUND

Access by boat only. S of Salthouse Branch Park on Deer Island, 2 mi N of dam. All year; 14-day limit. 21 primitive tent sites, $18 during 4/1-10/30 ($9 with federal senior pass); $5 rest of year ($2.50 with federal senior pass). Get camping permits at Salt Branch or Bowens Creek, or off-season at Goose Point entrance and Ramp 1 honor vaults.

GOOSE POINT PARK

From Martinsville, N on US 220, 11 mi N on SR 57; access on CR 822 (winding access roads). All year; 14-day limit. 10 sites without hookups, $10 during 11/1-3/31 ($5 with federal senior pass); $18 during peak period of 4/1-10/30 ($9 with federal senior pass). 53 sites with elec/wtr,

$22, available only during 4/1-10/30 ($11 with federal senior pass). Off-season, 9 sites open with elec, no wtr, for $10 ($5 with federal senior pass). No showers or flush toilets in off-season; portable toilets provided. $4 day use fee for non-campers using boat ramp, swimming area, playground, dump. Amphitheater, picnic shelter. RV limit 60'. At reserved sites, 2-night minimum stay required on weekends. (276) 629-1847. NRRS. **GPS: 36.80389, -80.05722**

HORSESHOE POINT CAMPGROUND

From Martinsville, N on US 220; 6.2 mi W on CR 605 through Henry; 2.3 mi SW on CR 903; 1 mi W on CR 934. 5/1-9/30; 14-day limit. 34 sites without hookups, $18 ($9 with federal senior pass); 15 sites with wtr/elec & waterfront sites, $22 ($11 with federal senior pass). $4 per vehicle day use fee for non-campers using boat ramp, courtesy dock, picnic area, swimming area, playground, dump station. RV limit 40'. Picnic shelter. At reserved sites, 2-night minimum stay required on weekends. (276) 365-7385. NRRS. **GPS: 36.83306, 80.06333**

JAMISON MILL CAMPGROUND

From Henry at jct with CR 606, 5 mi NW on CR 605; 2 mi S on CR 778. 4/1-10/31; 14-day limit. 5 sites with wtr/elec, $21 ($10.50 with federal senior pass); 6 sites & 4-site overflow areas without hookups, $18 ($9 with federal senior pass); some pull-through sites. No reservations accepted; no day use fees. **GPS: 36.84954, -80.07395**

PHILPOTT PARK

From Bassett at jct with Hwy 220, 6 mi W on SR 57; right on Philpott Dam Rd for 1 mi; near dam, S side. 4/1-10/30. Group camping area, by permit only, $100. Picnic shelter $75. Hiking trails, exhibit museum. Non-campers, $3 for boat ramp; no other day use fees.
GPS: 36.77611, -80.03694

SALTHOUSE BRANCH CAMPGROUND

From Henry, 3 mi W on CR 605; 1.4 mi SW on CR 798, then S on CR 603. 4/1-10/31; 14-day limit. 14 RV/tent sites without hookups, 21 boat-in tent sites & 32 basic tent sites, $18 ($9 with federal senior pass). 44 sites with elec/wtr, $22 ($11 with federal senior pass); 17 pull-through sites. Amphitheater. Picnic shelter for up to 100 people, $75. RV limit 50'. Interpretive trail, hiking trail. At reserved sites, 2-night minimum stay required on weekends. (276) 365-7005. NRRS. **GPS: 36.81361, -80.04**

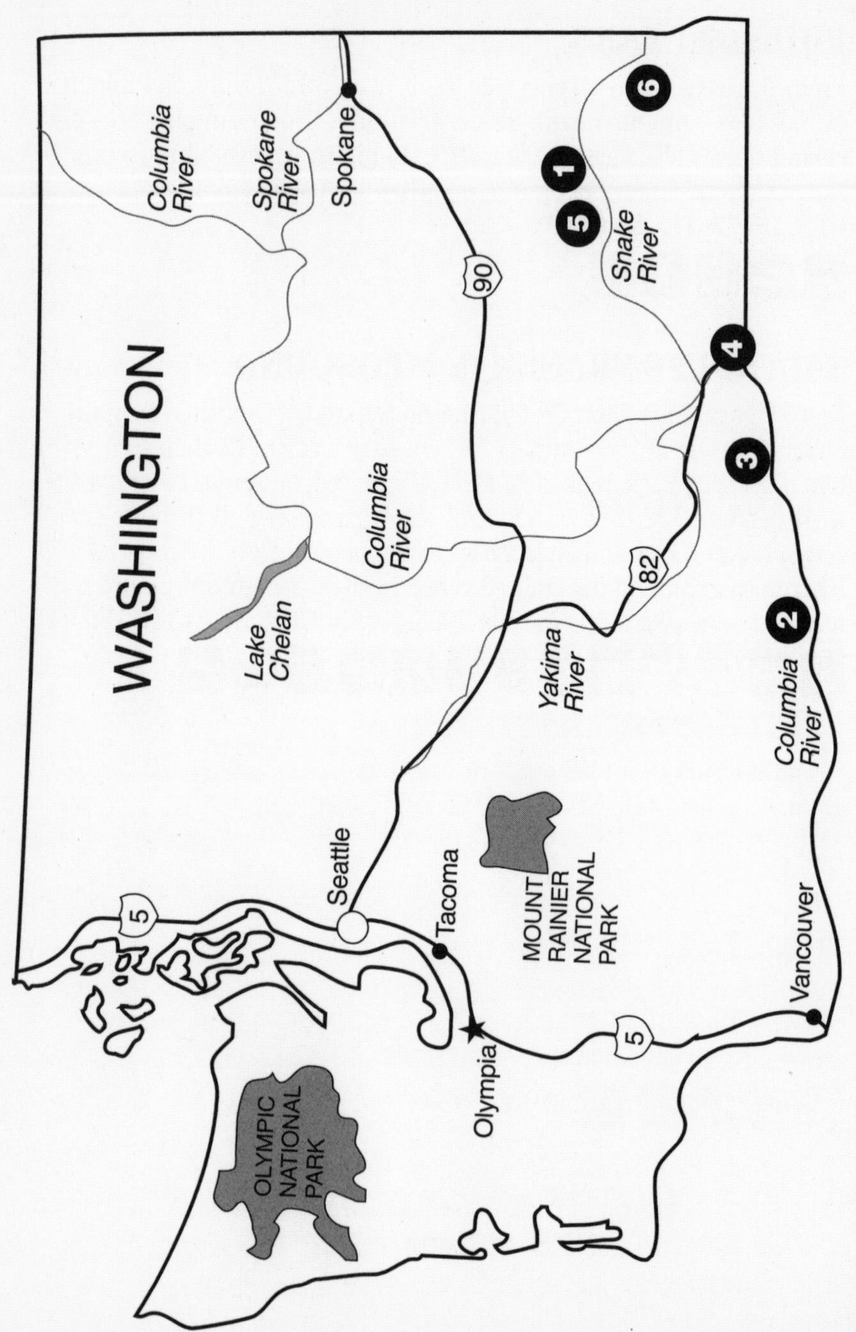
WASHINGTON
Columbia River
Spokane River
Spokane
90
Snake River
6
1
5
4
3
2
Columbia River
82
Lake Chelan
Yakima River
Columbia River
Seattle
Tacoma
MOUNT RAINIER NATIONAL PARK
Vancouver
5
5
Olympia
OLYMPIC NATIONAL PARK

WASHINGTON

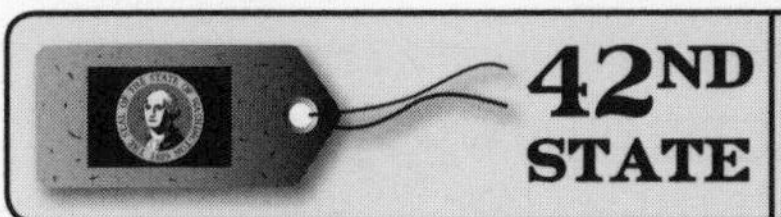

42ND STATE

State Capital: **Olympia**
Nickname: **Evergreen State**
Statehood Year: **1889**

LAKE BRYAN (WW) 1
GPS: 45.58329,-114.697266

From Starbuck, 9 mi NE on Little Goose Dam Rd along the Snake River. Semi-primitive camping. No open fires permitted from 6/10-10/10 (charcoal and gas grills permitted). Visitor center. Park Manager, Clarkston Natural Resource Office, 100 Fair Street, Clarkston, WA 99403-1943. (509) 751-0240/0250.

ILLIA LANDING

From Lower Granite Dam, 3 mi W on Almota Ferry Rd. All year; 14-day limit. Free primitive camping area. **GPS: 46.7018, -117.471**

LITTLE GOOSE LANDING

From Starbuck, 9 mi NE on Little Goose Dam Rd; 1 mi E of Little Goose Dam. All year; 14-day limit. Free primitive camping area.

WILLOW LANDING

From Central Ferry State Park, 1 mi S on Hwy 127; 4 mi E on Deadman Rd; 5 mi N on Hasting Hill Rd. All year; 14-day limit. Free primitive camping area. **GPS: 46.6827, -117.7494**

LAKE SACAJAWEA (WW) 2
GPS: 46.2489, -118.8794

9,200-acre reservoir at full pool. Located 5.5 mi E of Burbank, 2.4 mi N on Monument Drive. Campground checkout time 12 p.m. Visitor center features interpretive displays and a fish viewing room open daily

April through October. Alcoholic beverages prohibited by state law. No tours of the powerhouse/navigation lock due to security measures. Road over dam and powerhouse closed. Visitor center open 9-5 during 4/1-10/31. Day use facilities include: Big Flat Park, boat ramp; Ice Harbor Dam, picnicking, pit toilets, phone, boat ramp; Levey Park, swimming, picnicking, flush toilets, drinking water, playgrounds, volleyball court, group shelter; Resource Manager, Ice Harbor Project, 1215 E Ainsworth, Pasco, WA 99301. (509) 547-2048/543-6060.

CHARBONNEAU PARK

From Burbank, 8.3 mi E on SR 124; 1.5 mi N on Sun Harbor Dr; left on Charbonneau Rd. 4/1-10/31; 14-day limit. 37 RV/tent sites with 50-amp elec/wtr, $22 ($11 with federal senior pass); 14 of the sites on shoreline at $24 ($12 with federal senior pass). 15 sites with full hookups, $28 ($14 with federal senior pass); 15 primitive overflow sites without elec, wtr or fire pits, $11 ($5.50 with federal senior pass). Sun shelters, volleyball court. Picnic shelter $90; overlook group shelter $110. Marine dump station. RV limit 60'. At reserved sites, 2-night minimum stay required on weekends, 3 nights on holiday weekends. (509) 547-9252. NRRS. **GPS: 46.25556, -118.84472**

FISHHOOK PARK

From Burbank, 18 mi E on SR 124; 4 mi N on Fishhook Park Rd. 5/24-9/12; 14-day limit. 41 RV/tent sites with 50-amp elec/wtr, $22 ($11 with federal senior pass); 10 of the sites on shoreline at $24 ($12 with federal senior pass). 1 primitive shoreline site without hookup, $16 ($8 with federal senior pass). 20 walk-to tent sites, $16 ($8 with federal senior pass); 2 of these sites have sun shelters, $24 ($12 with senior pass). Boat camping $8. Picnic shelter with elec, $75. RV limit 45'. At reserved sites, 2-night minimum stay required on weekends, 3 nights on holiday weekends. NRRS. **GPS: 46.315, -118.76611**

LAKE EMMA PARK

From From Kahlotus at jct with Pasco/Kahlotus Rd, 3 mi W on Murphy Rd, then 1 mi S on Page Rd; on N shore of Snake River. All year; 14-day limit. Free primitive camping at undesignated sites; no facilities.

MATTHEWS PARK

From 26 mi E of Burbank, 8.6 mi N on SR 124 to Clyde; left 15.2 mi on Lower Monument Rd; left 1 mi before the dam, then 1 mi E; on S shore of Snake River. All year; 14-day limit. Free primitive camping at undesignated sites. Pit toilets, boat ramp, dock, no drkg wtr.

WALKER PARK

From 26 mi E of Burbank, 8.6 mi N on SR 124 to Clyde; turn left, then 4 mi NW on Lower Monument Rd; 9.2 mi W on Wooden Rd; on S shore of Snake River. All year; 14-day limit. Free primitive camping at undesignated sites. No facilities.

WINDUST CAMPGROUND

From Kahlotus, 4 mi SW on Pasco/Kahlotus Rd; 5.2 mi SE on Burr Canyon Rd; on N shore of Snake River. Facilities open 5/24-9/30; primitive camping without facilities rest of year; no wtr, portable toilets off-season; 14-day limit. Free. 24 grass sites, no hookups. Covered sun shelters, picnic shelter available. 24 primitive sites, plus boat camping. RV limit 40'. **GPS: 46.53306, -118.58333.**

LAKE UMATILLA (PORT) 3
JOHN DAY LOCK & DAM
GPS: 47.100045, -120.9375

Located on the Columbia River off SR 14 near Rufus, Oregon, 25 mi E of The Dalles, Oregon. Corps parks now under lease include Crow Butte, operated by the Port of Benton County. Resource Manager, Lake Umatilla, P. O. Box 564, The Dalles, OR 97058-9998. (503) 296-1181. See Oregon listings.

CLIFFS

Located near the dam on the N of United States Route 97, Washington side. Free camping area.

PLYMOUTH CAMPGROUND

From McNary Dam on SR 14, 1.2 mi W below the dam on the N side. 4/1-10/31; 14-day limit. Sites with wtr/elec, $22 ($11 with federal senior pass). Full hookups, $24 ($12 with federal senior pass); 29 pull-through sites. Overflow tent camping available on weekends and holidays, $14 ($7 with federal senior pass). Dump & boat launch fees for non-campers. RV limit 40'. At reserved sites, 2-night minimum stay required on weekends, 3 nights on holiday weekends. (509) 783-1270. NRRS.
GPS: 45.9317, -119.3483.

ROCK CREEK PARK

From Lyle, 36 mi E on Hwy 14; left on Rock Creek Rd 1.5 mi, then left into park. All year; 14-day limit. Free primitive undesignated sites. Tbls, pit toilets, campfire rings, boat launch. No drkg wtr.
GPS: 45.7640038, -122.3242595

ROOSEVELT PARK

On W side of Roosevelt via SR 14, follow signs; on Columbia River. All year; 14-day limit. Free primitive undesignated sites; park RVs on asphalt near lawns. Pit toilets all year; flush toilets during 4/1-9/30. Swimming beach, boat ramp, picnic sites, drkg wtr. Windsurfing, fishing.

SUNDALE PARK

From I-82 exit 131, 61 mi W on SR 14 to milepost 128; left at sign. All year; 14-day limit. Free primitive undesignated sites. No facilities, no drkg wtr. Boat ramp, fishing.

LAKE WALLULA (WW) 4

GPS: 45.9367, -119.2978

A 38,800-acre surface area lake with 242 mi of shoreline N of junction I-82/US 730, 1 mi N of Umatilla. Interpretive displays and fish viewing rooms at visitor center. Alcohol prohibited by state law. Several day-use parks are available. They include: Columbia Park, closed until further notice by City of Kennewick; Chiawana Park and Road 54 Park (leased to city of Pasco), picnicking, hiking trails, playground, biking trail; Hover Park (leased to Benton County Parks); Locust Grove/Martindale, fishing, hiking, hunting; Madame Dorion Memorial Park (leased to U.S. Fish & Wildlife), primitive camping, dump station, picnicking; Pasco Boat Basin (leased to City of Pasco), picnicking, playground, boat ramp); Wye Park (leased to City of Richland), picnicking, playground, fishing, boat ramp; Yakima River Delta Wildlife Nature Area, hiking trails, bird watching, fishing. Park Manager, Western Project, 2339 Ice Harbor Drive, Burbank, WA 99323. (541) 922-2268/4388. See Oregon listings.

HOOD CAMPGROUND

From Pasco, 3 mi S on US 12/395 to jct with SR 124 E of Burbank; continue 65 yds to park. 4/1-9/30; 14-day limit. 46 RV/tent sites with elec/wtr, $22 ($11 with federal senior pass); 21 shoreline sites with elec/wtr, $24 ($12 with federal senior pass); 20 overflow sites without hookups, $11 ($5.50 with federal senior pass). 2 sites have 50-amp elec. Horseshoe pits, basketball court, phone, amphitheater. Picnic shelter $110. RV limit 65'. At reserved sites, 2-night minimum stay required on weekends, 3 nights on holiday weekends. 509-547-7781. NRRS.
GPS: 46.2122, -119.0136

LAKE WEST (WW) 5

GPS: 46.5779, -118.5374

Located off US 260 S of Kahlotus on the Snake River. Four free primitive camping areas. Fish viewing rooms at Little Goose and Lower Granite Dams. Visitor center. No open fires 6/10-10/10. Resource Manager, 5520 Devil's Canyon Rd, Kahlotus, WA 99335. (509) 282-3219.

AYER BOAT BASIN

From Burbank, 26 mi E on SR 124; 24 mi N through Clyde & Pleasant View to Ayers. All year; 14-day limit. Free primitive camping at undesignated sites. Covered shelters, pit toilets. RV limit 40 ft. **GPS: 46.3505, -118.2219.**

DEVILS BENCH

From Kahlotus, 6 mi S on SR 263. All year; 14-day limit. Free primitive camping at undesignated sites. Pit toilets.

RIPARIA CAMPGROUND

From Little Goose Dam, 3 mi W on N Shore Rd. All year; 14-day limit. Free primitive camping at undesignated sites. Pit toilets. RV limit 40'.

TEXAS RAPIDS CAMPGROUND

From Starbuck, 6 mi NE on Little Goose Rd; 2 mi W of Little Goose Dam. All year; 14-day limit. Free primitive camping at undesignated sites. Pit toilets (flush toilets in summer), fire pits, grills, drkg wtr, boat ramp, tbls, covered shelters. **GPS: 46.334559, -118.060124.**

LOWER GRANITE LAKE (WW) 6

GPS: 46.6006, -117.4283

From Lewiston, Idaho/Clarkston, WA, 19 mi W on US 12; 2 mi N on Ledgerwood Spur Rd, 16 mi N on Kirby Mayview Rd, 12 mi E on Casey Creek Rd. No open fires during 6/10-10/10 (charcoal & gas grills permitted). Interpretive programs, visit center, Clearwater & Snake River National Recreation Trail. Fish viewing rooms at Little Goose and Lower Granite Dams. Lower Granite Dam also has visitor center that features movies, interactive displays, guided tours. Day use areas include: Chief Looking Glass Park (leased to City of Asotin), picnicking, flush toilets, cold showers, playground, swimming area, tennis court, basketball court; Clearwater Park (leased to City of Lewiston), picnicking, flush toilets, softball, fishing pond, portable toilets, burling pond; Greenbelt Ramp, phone, swimming area, flush toilets, hiking & biking trails, fishing pier, boat ramp; Lewiston Levee Parkway, picnicking, grills, flush toilets, interpretive center, biking, hiking, wildlife viewing, playground; N Lewiston Ramp (leased to Nez Perce County), hiking trails, camping, picnicking, boat ramp; Southway Ramp (leased to Nez Perce County), hiking trails, handicap fishing, boating, pit toilet, boat ramp; Swallows Park, picnicking, covered shelters, tot lot playground, fire pits, flush toilets, swimming area, hiking & biking trails, phone, playground, volleyball court. Park Manager, Clarkston Natural Resource Office, 100 Fair Street, Clarkston, WA 99403-1943. (509) 751-0240/0250.

BLYTON LANDING

From Lewiston, Idaho, 20 mi W on CR 9000 (N Shore Snake River Rd). All year; 14-day limit. Free primitive camping at undesignated sites. Fire pits, pit toilets.

NISQUALLY JOHN LANDING

From Lewiston, Idaho, 15 mi W on CR 9000 (N Shore Snake River Rd). Free Primitive camping at undesignated sites. Fire pits, pit toilets.

OFFIELD LANDING

1 mi E of Lower Granite Dam on Lower Granite Lake, Snake River milepost 108, S shore. All year; 14-day limit. Free primitive RV/tent camping at undesignated sites. Fire pits, grills, pit toilets. **GPS: 46.3908, -117.2504**

WAWAWAI LANDING

From Lewiston, Idaho, 28 mi W on CR 9000 (N Shore Snake River Rd) or 19 mi SW of Pullman on Wawawai Rd. All year; 14-day limit Free primitive camping at undesignated sites. Pit toilets, fire pits. **GPS: 46.3747, -117.2252**

WEST VIRGINIA

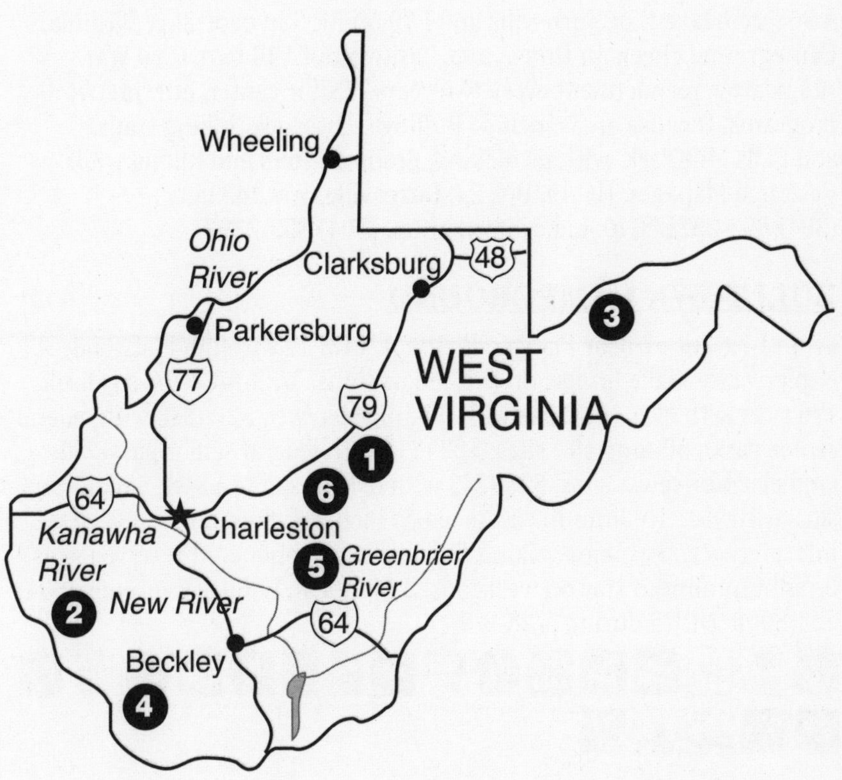

WEST VIRGINIA

State Capital: **Charleston**
Nickname: **Mountain State**
Statehood Year: **1863**

35TH STATE

BURNSVILLE LAKE (HU) 1
GPS: 38.34, -80.6183

A 968-acre lake E of Burnsville and I-79 on SR 5 in central W Virginia. Campground checkout time 5 p.m., visitors until 10 p.m. Civil War site nearby; reenactment every two years. Visitor center, interpretive programs. Day use areas include Bulltown Overlook, hiking trails, and Falls Mill Park, with picnicking, group shelters and hiking trails. Resource Manager, HC 10, Box 24, Burnsville, WV 26335. (304) 853-2371/8170. Lake information, (304) 853-2398.

BULLTOWN CAMPGROUND

From I-79 exit 67 near Flatwoods, 10 mi N US 19 through Flatwoods & Napier, across lake bridge, on left; follow signs. 4/23-9/28; 14-day limit. 196 sites with elec/wtr. Sites with 30-amp elec/wtr, $20 ($10 with federal senior pass); 50-amp elec sites, $22 ($11 with federal senior pass); 50-amp elec/wtr/sewer sites, $26 ($13 with federal senior pass). 5 handicap sites with elec. RV limit in excess of 65'. Picnic shelter, horseshoe pits, interpretive trail, hiking, biking & bridle trails, phone. At reserved sites, 2-night minimum stay on weekends, 3 nights on holiday weekends.(304) 452-8006. NRRS during 5/28-9/6.

RIFFLE RUN CAMPGROUND

From Burnsville at I-79 exit 79, 3 mi E on SR 5. 4/23-9/7; 14-day limit. Sites with elec $12 during 4/23-6/14 ($6 with federal senior pass), $20 during during 5/28-9/7 ($10 with federal senior pass); $26 full hookups during peak season ($13 with federal senior pass). Primitive sites $12. Picnic shelter. (304) 853-2583. No reservations. **GPS: 38.5029, -80.3655**

EAST LYNN LAKE (HU) 2
GPS: 38.145, -82.385

A 1,005-acre lake 12 mi S of Wayne on Twelvepole Creek off SR 37 in southwestern W Virginia. Visitor center Resource Manager, E Lynn Lake, E Lynn, WV 25512. Lake information, (304) 849-2355.

E FORK CAMPGROUND

10 mi E of the dam on SR 37. About 5/10-10/18; 14-day limit. 166 sites with elec, $18 ($9 with federal senior pass), $20 at premium locations ($10 with federal senior pass. Horseshoe pits, nature trail, amphitheater. RV limit in excess of 65'. At reserved sites, 2-night minimum stay required on weekends, 3 nights on holidays. (304) 849-5000. NRRS. **GPS: 38.09972, -82.31778**

JENNINGS RANDOLPH LAKE (BL) 3
GPS: 39.4803, -79.0717

A 952-acre 5 mi N of Elk Garden, E of Morgantown and W of Kyser in northeastern W Virginia. An excellent trout fishing river nearby. Campground checkout time is noon. Day use areas include Howell Run Boat Launch ($3 at boat ramp, $25 picnic shelter); Maryland Boat Launch; Maryland Overlook, picnicking, hiking trails; W Virginia Overlook, picnicking, playground, beach. Resource Manager, Jennings Randolph lake, P. O. Box 247, Elk Garden, WV 26717. (301) 359-3861/ (304) 355-2346.

ROBERT W. CRAIG CAMPGROUND

From Elk Garden, 5 mi NE on SR 46; exit N at sign. 5/1-10/11; 14-day limit. 12 sites without hookups, $18 ($9 with federal senior pass); 70 sites with elec, $22 ($11 with federal senior pass). Picnic shelter, horseshoe pits, amphitheater, interpretive trail, phone, hiking trail. RV limit 55'. At reserved sites, 2-night stay required on weekends, 3 nights on holiday weekends. NRRS. **GPS: 39.44556, -79.1275**

R. D. BAILEY LAKE (HU) 4
GPS: 37.6069, -81.7781

A 630-acre lake near Justice, 4 mi E of Gilbert on US 52 and SR 97. ORV prohibited. Visitor center offers picnicking, picnic shelter with grill, hiking trail. Other day use areas include: Big Branch, picnicking, shelter with grills, playground, horseshoe pits, basketball court; Dam Overlook, picnicking, picnic shelter, playground, Downstream Area, boat ramp, picnicking, hiking trails; Guyandotte Point, picnicking, playground, shelters $45-$50. Resource Manager, R. D. Bailey Lake, P. O. Drawer 70, Justice, WV 24851-0070. (304) 664-3220/3229.

GUYANDOTTE CAMPGROUND

From the dam, 1.1 mi to US 52, then 2.2 mi S; 5.8 mi S on SR 97. Camping is in 4 areas along 6 mi of the "Guyandotte River. MD-LD; 14-day limit. 163 sites with elec, $14 ($7 with federal senior pass); sites without hookups, $12 ($6 with federal senior pass). Free primitive camping area open only during archery hunting season. **GPS: 37.59082, -81.719238**

SUMMERSVILLE LAKE (HU) 5
GPS: 38.22, -80.89

A 2,790-acre lake located S of Summersville off US 19, 69 mi E of Charleston and W of Mt. Nebo on SR 129 in S-central W Virginia. Visitors to 10 p.m. for a fee. Picnic shelters, Civil War site nearby, whitewater rafting below dam, visitor center. Checkout time 5 p.m. Trout stocked below dam in spring and fall. Day use facilities: Damsite Park, group picnic shelter, playground; Roadside Park, group picnicking; Salmon Run Park, boat ramp, picnicking, hiking trails; Long Point Park, boat ramp, hiking trail. Facilities leased by the Corps include Summersville Marina, with boat launch & campground. 3 group picnic shelters at Damsite Park, $45. Resource Manager, Summersville Lake, Route 2, Box 470, Summersville, WV 26651-9802. (304) 872-3412/5809.

BATTLE RUN CAMPGROUND

From S of Summersville at jct with US 19; 3.4 mi W on SR 129 across dam, then N (right) at sign. 5/1-Columbus Day; 14-day limit. 7 walk-in tent sites, $16 ($8 with federal senior pass); 110 sites with 30-amp elec, $24 ($12 with federal senior pass). Horseshoe pits, handicap accessible swimming pier, submerged ramp for wheelchairs, handicap accessible fishing area. RV limit in excess of 65'. At reserved sites, 2-night minimum stay required on weekends, 3 nights on holiday weekends. Pets & ORV prohibited. Group picnic shelter $45. (304) 872-3459. NRRS (MD-LD). **GPS: 38.22167, -80.90972**

SUTTON LAKE (HU) 6
GPS: 38.6617, -80.6933

A 1,440-acre lake located 1 mi E of Sutton off US 19, NE of Charleston in central W Virginia. Visitor Center, interpretive program. Day use facilities: Downstream Park, picnicking, group shelter, playground; S Abutment Park, boat ramp, group shelter, beach, hiking trail. Lake information, (304) 765-2816. Resource Manager, Sutton Lake, P. O. Box 426, Sutton, WV 26601. (304) 765-2816.

BEE RUN CAMPGROUND

From near Sutton on I-79, at exit 67, 1 mi E on SR 4; 1.2 mi E on SR 15; turn right. About 4/1-12/6; 14-day limit. 12 primitive pull through sites, $8 ($4 with federal senior pass) RV limit 20'. No shoreline camping. **GPS: 38.666992, -80.678467**

BAKER'S RUN - MILL CREEK CAMPGROUND

From exit 62 of I-79, 2 mi to Sutton; 4 mi S on old US 19 (CR 19/40); 12 mi E on CR 17. 4/23-10/19; 14-day limit. 79 sites, some pull-through. Sites without hookups, $16 ($8 with federal senior pass); sites with elec,

$22 ($11 with federal senior pass. RV limit 58'. Horseshoe pits, volleyball, biking trails. (304) 765-5631. **GPS: 38.63501, -80.547951**

GERALD R. FREEMAN

From near Sutton I-79, at exit 67, 1 mi S on SR 4; 12 mi E on SR 15. 4/23-11/30; 14-day limit. 81 sites without hookups, $16 ($8 with federal senior pass); sites with elec, $18 ($9 with federal senior pass), $22 at premium locations ($11 with federal senior pass). Horseshoe pits, hikng trail, ball courts, phone. ORV prohibited. At reserved sites, 2-night minimum stay required on weekends, 3 nights on holiday weekends. (304) 765-7756. NRRS during MD-LD. **GPS: 38.68, -80.54694**

Superior
WISCONSIN
St. Croix
River
Flambeau
River
Wisconsin
River
51
1
Eau Claire
Green Bay
43
94
Lake
Winnebago
90
41
Mississippi
River
Milwaukee
94
3
Madison
43
90
2

WISCONSIN

State Capital: **Madison**
Nickname: **Badger State**
Statehood Year: **1848**

30TH STATE

WISCONSIN 1848

EAU GALLE LAKE (SP) 1
GPS: 44.8583, -92.24

An 150-acre lake 45 mi SE of St. Paul off I-94; exit 24 S; 2 mi S on CR B; 2 mi N on CR N; 2 mi S on CR NN; 0.5 mi N of Spring Valley, 40 mi W of Eau Galle. Electric motors only are permitted on the lake. Lake surrounded by two day use areas, a beach, two boat ramps, one campground and several mi of hiking and equestrian trails. Day use facilities: at Main Day Use Park, accessible restrooms, boat launch, hiking trail, horseshoe pits, interpretive trail, playground, swimming beach, phone, volleyball court, group picnic shelter with elec $40; at Lousy Creek Access, boat ramp, bridle trail; at Northwest Area, group picnic shelter, bridle trails. Park Manager, Eau Galle Lake, P. O. Box 190, Spring Valley, WI 54767-0190. (715) 778-5562.

HIGHLAND RIDGE CAMPGROUND

From I-95 exit 24, 2 mi S on CR B; 2 mi E on CR N; 2 mi S on CR NN. 4/1-10/22; 14-day limit. 7 walk-to tent sites, $16 ($8 with federal senior pass); 10 equestrian sites without hookups, $14 ($7 with federal senior pass); 3 RV/tent sites without hookups, $18 ($9 with federal senior pass); 35 sites with elec, $20 ($10 with federal senior pass. Horseshoe pits, picnic shelter, group camping area, firewood, ice machines. Free movies or interpretive programs on weekends. Hiking trail, interpretive trail. Electric motors only on the lake. Fee for showers. RV limit 65'. At reserved sites, 2-night minimum stay required on weekends, 3 nights on holiday weekends. (715) 778-5562. NRRS during 4/29-9/31. **GPS: 44.86722, -92.24417**

MISSISSIPPI RIVER PUA (RI) 2

For information, contact Park Ranger, L&D #11, Dubuque, IA 52001, (563) 582-0881. See Illinois, Iowa & Missouri listings.

GRANT RIVER RECREATION AREA

From Dubuque, IA, E across river, then N on US 61; 2 mi W on SR 133, following signs (2 mi S of Potosi). 4/1-10/24; 14-day limit. 10 tent sites, $10 ($5 with federal senior pass); 63 sites with 30-amp elec, $16 ($8 with federal senior pass); premium sites with 50-amp elec, $18 ($9 with federal senior pass). No wtr hookups. RV limit 55'. Picnic shelter ($25), amphitheater. At reserved sites, 2-night minimum stay on weekends, 3 nights on holiday weekends. (608) 763-2140, 1-800-645-0248. NRRS. **GPS: 42.6594, -90.7097**

POOL 9 MISSISSIPPI RIVER (SP) 3

Located 30 mi S of La Crosse off SR 35 on CR B1. Resource Manager, Blackhawk Park, E 590 County Road B1, DeSoto, WI 54624. (608) 648-3314.

BLACKHAWK CAMPGROUND

From DeSoto, 3 mi N on SR 35, then SW on CR B1. 4/1-10/30; 14-day limit. 100 sites without hookups, $18 ($9 with federal senior pass); 73 sites with elec, $24 ($12 with federal senior pass). Picnic shelters, $40. Interpretive programs, fish cleaning station, horseshoe pits. Handicap accessible fishing area. ORV & other unlicensed motorized vehicles prohibited. Free movies on weekends. Checkout time 2 p.m. Fee for showers. RV limit 65'. At reserved sites, 2- night minimum stay required on weekends, 3 nights on holiday weekends. (608) 648-3314. NRRS (6/1-10/31). **GPS: 43.4608, -91.2231**

Seattle
Olympia
Washington
Montana
North Dakota
Salem
Helena
Oregon
Idaho
Boise
Wyoming
Pierre
Cheyenne
Nebraska
Sacramento
Carson City
Nevada
Salt Lake City
San Francisco
Utah
Denver
Colorado
California
Las Vegas
Los Angeles
Santa Fe
Arizona
Phoenix
New Mexico
Texas

Maine
Augusta
Montpelier
Vt.
N.H.
Concord
Albany
Mass.
Boston
Providence
R.I.
Hartford
Conn.
New York
Wisconsin
Michigan
Madison
Lansing
Detroit
Chicago
Iowa
Des Moines
Pennsylvania
Philadelphia
Harrisburg
New York
Trenton
New Jersey
Dover
Delaware
Md.
Annapolis
Washington, D.C.
Ohio
Columbus
Indiana
Indianapolis
Illinois
Springfield
West Virginia
Charleston
Richmond
Virginia
St. Louis
Jefferson City
Missouri
Frankfort
Kentucky
Raleigh
North Carolina
Nashville
Tennessee
Memphis
Arkansas
Little Rock
Columbia
South Carolina
Atlanta
Georgia
Mississippi
Jackson
Alabama
Montgomery
Louisiana
Baton Rouge
New Orleans
Tallahassee
Florida
Miami

ABBREVIATIONS

AQ .... Albuquerque District
BL .... Baltimore District
CR .... County Route
E .... East
Fr .... From
FW .... Fort Worth District
HU .... Huntington District
JX .... Jacksonville District
JCT .... Junction
KC .... Kansas City District
LD .... Labor Day
LR .... Little Rock District
MB .... Mobile District
MD .... Memorial Day
N .... North
NE .... New England District
NRRS .... National Recreation Reservation Service
NV .... Nashville District
OM .... Omaha District
ORV .... Off-Road Vehicle(s)
POR .... Portland District
PRIM .... Primitive
PT .... Pittsburgh District
PT's .... Pull Throughs (preceded by a number)
Resv .... Reservation
RV .... Recreational Vehicle
SAC .... Sacramento District
SEA .... Seattle District
SF .... San Francisco District
SL .... St. Louis District
SP .... St. Paul District
SPT .... Some Pull Throughs
SR .... State Route
S .... South
SV .... Savannah District
TU .... Tulsa District
TO .... Tents Only
US .... United States Route
VK .... Vicksburg District
W .... West
WL .... Wilmington District
WW .... Walla Walla District